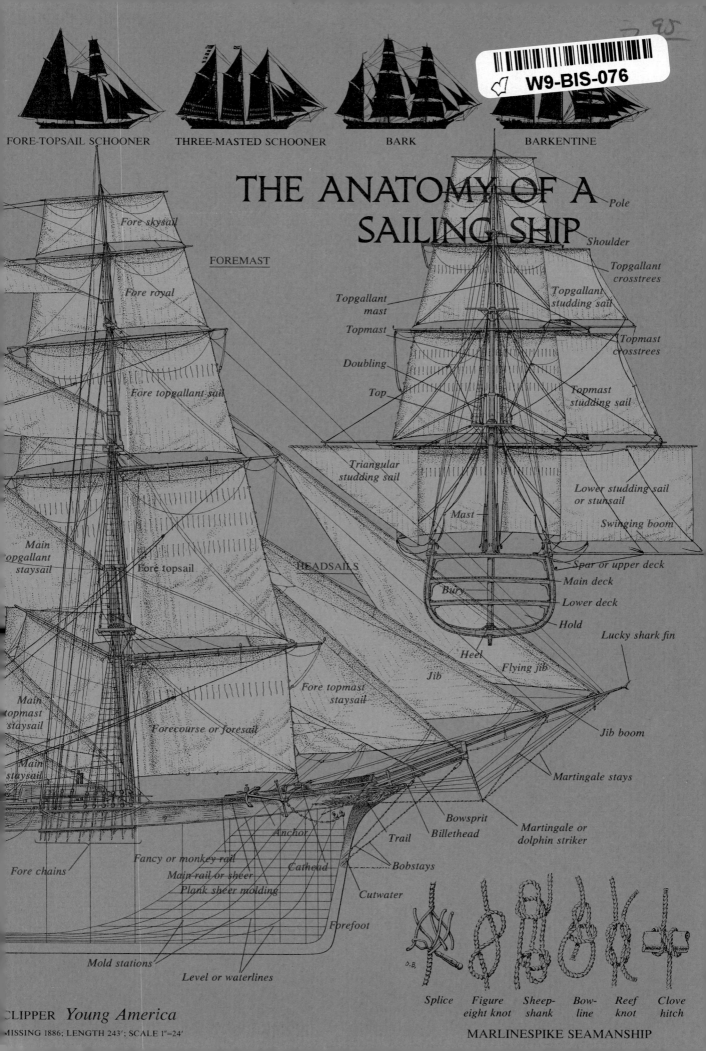

FORE-TOPSAIL SCHOONER   THREE-MASTED SCHOONER   BARK   BARKENTINE

THE ANATOMY OF A SAILING SHIP

FOREMAST

Fore skysail

Fore royal

Fore topgallant sail

Main topgallant staysail

Fore topsail

HEADSAILS

Main topmast staysail

Fore topmast staysail

Main staysail

Forecourse or foresail

Fore chains

Fancy or monkey rail

Main rail or sheer

Plank sheer molding

Anchor

Cathead

Trail

Bowsprit
Billethead

Bobstays

Cutwater

Forefoot

Mold stations

Level or waterlines

Pole

Shoulder

Topgallant crosstrees

Topgallant studding sail

Topgallant mast

Topmast

Topmast crosstrees

Doubling

Topmast studding sail

Top

Topmast studding sail

Triangular studding sail

Lower studding sail or stunsail

Swinging boom

Mast

Spar or upper deck

Main deck

Bury

Lower deck

Hold

Lucky shark fin

Heel

Flying jib

Jib

Jib boom

Martingale stays

Martingale or dolphin striker

CLIPPER *Young America*

MISSING 1886; LENGTH 243'; SCALE 1"=24'

Splice   Figure eight knot   Sheep-shank   Bow-line   Reef knot   Clove hitch

MARLINESPIKE SEAMANSHIP

MEN, SHIPS, and the SEA

SEASCAPE: BROWN BROTHERS. DRAWING: HADLEY'S OCTANT, USED BY 18TH CENTURY MARINERS

MEN
SHIPS
and the
SEA

By CAPT. ALAN VILLIERS

and other adventurers on the sea

A VOLUME IN THE STORY OF MAN LIBRARY

PREPARED BY NATIONAL GEOGRAPHIC BOOK SERVICE

MERLE SEVERY, *Chief*

FOREWORD BY MELVILLE BELL GROSVENOR

President and Editor, National Geographic Society

NATIONAL GEOGRAPHIC SOCIETY

WASHINGTON, D. C.

ANGRY SEAS POUND ABOARD THE CAPE HORNER "PARMA" AS THE PORT WATCH MANS THE BRACES. ALAN VILLIERS, 1932

442 illustrations
260 in full color
27 maps

Foreword

THE STOUT KETCH took the seas bravely, a bone in her teeth, as we headed down the historic sea road between England and France. The sound of seas hissing aft, the wind song in the rigging summoned memories of great events these waters had seen.

Julius Caesar crossed here with his Roman legions; William the Conqueror with his Norman knights. The Spanish Armada swept proudly up the Channel to be met by Drake and his sea dogs. The Pilgrims sailed from here to the New World; Captain Cook to meet destiny in the Pacific. And the greatest fleet the world has ever known bridged this narrow sea on D-day in World War II.

Beside me on the tossing deck stood Alan Villiers, who had sailed these waters before, many times, in many ships. For years I had shared his adventures in *National Geographic* and his fascinating sea books, in his memorable lectures before members of our Society, and swapping yarns on visits to each other's homes. But now for the first time I stood a watch with him, savoring the wonder of a ship's way in the sea.

With me was my eight-year-old son Edwin. Not ten minutes aboard, he had scampered up the ratlines to the masthead 60 feet above the deck to survey his new home afloat. Eyes wide and tongue full of questions he joined the crew to set and furl sail, watched the skipper take sights with his sextant, and learned from the bos'n to splice, whip, and tie sailors' knots.

What a marvelous thing a sailing ship is as she bowls gracefully along, curved sails pulling like winged horses. No wonder the questions poured from Eddie like raindrops in a squall. How had man found the way to harness so fickle a power as the wind? How had he learned to balance the sails, to design rigging, part of it to give strength, part to control the spars and sails? To fashion a rudder that would turn a ship? To find his way across trackless oceans?

How did man come to develop the steamships and motorships that paraded by us on this busy sea highway—coasters and deep-water freighters, tankers and trawlers, and great passenger liners that looked at night like floating cities ablaze with lights?

As Captain Villiers and I answered Eddie's questions, I shared my son's sense of wonder and discovery. The fascination of the sea and ships has been part of my life since I was six months old, when my parents took me on my first cruise afloat. The tang of salt spray, the cry of gulls wheeling in the air, the scent of balsam along Nova Scotia's coast run through my earliest memories. It was aboard my father's yawl *Elsie,* knifing through the blue waters of the Bras d' Or Lakes, that I learned to skipper.

At the U. S. Naval Academy at Annapolis I absorbed the significance of the sea. How different history might have been if the outnumbered Athenian galleys had not stemmed the Persian tide at Salamis; if the French fleet had not cut off reinforcements to Cornwallis at Yorktown; if Nelson had not denied Napoleon the sea route to conquest at Trafalgar.

As a midshipman on the battleship *Connecticut* I shared the rugged life of men at sea. Forty days I served in the black gang in the bowels of that fine old ship in tropic waters. I shoveled coal into raging fireboxes, broke up clinkers with a slice bar. The heat was ferocious there in the fireroom; 16 midshipmen passed out on one watch. But most were soon back at their boilers, like the stout lads they were.

Later I came to know the thrill of racing a Star on Chesapeake Bay, sails taut, spray flying, nerves straining to bring *Escape* in first. I found serenity cruising West Indies waters to San Salvador in the wake of Columbus, and to Tortuga, pirate's lair off Hispaniola.

COLUMBUS! How he and other great sailors had changed the world with their voyages of discovery. Magellan, Cabot, Hudson, all were pioneers in commerce and civilization. Da Gama's trailblazing voyage to India is said to have reaped 6,000 percent profit. It also ushered in a new era. The new trade route around Africa made a backwater of the Mediterranean and cast Venice into eclipse. Portugal, Spain, England, Holland rose—the Atlantic Age began.

So much has happened, so much has depended on the sea. I long wished for a well-illustrated book that did justice to the sweep and surge of man's story there; that traced and explained the development of his ships, and showed how they have helped shape the course of civilization. Such a book could be written only by one who knows ships intimately, who has lived the sea and writes of it with all the might and flavor of the sea itself.

Such a man is Alan Villiers. In commissioning him as chief author of *Men, Ships, and the Sea*, the Society chose the greatest sea writer of our time. He has sailed since boyhood—in windjammers, in World War II landing craft, in Arab dhows, in the Nuclear Ship *Savannah*. He brings to this book unique knowledge and a sailor's gift for spinning a yarn.

It was a happy day when my father first brought Alan Villiers to the worldwide audience of the National Geographic Society. Aboard a steamship in the Atlantic, Gilbert Grosvenor had photographed a splendid vision out of the past—the full-rigged *Grace Harwar* under a cloud of canvas. Learning that Alan Villiers, a young seaman and writer, had sailed in her around Cape Horn, my father asked him to relive this voyage in *National Geographic*.

Since then, members have eagerly followed his salt-sprayed adventures in many parts of the world. Now they will be enthralled with his account of man's long and turbulent romance with a capricious and often cruel mistress.

Joining him in this book, French explorer Jacques-Yves Cousteau dives to an ancient Greek wine ship wrecked 2,100 years ago. *National Geographic*'s own Luis Marden carries us back to Tahiti and *Bounty* days. Irving and Electa Johnson take us aboard *Yankee* for a 40,000-mile voyage round the world. Famed yachtsman Carleton Mitchell is our skipper in an ocean race and our guide to the pleasures of small boating.

With pride and pleasure I worked beside editor Merle Severy and watched the frame of this book take shape like a graceful ship under his knowing hands. His love of the sea goes deep; he sailed the oceans in the merchant marine. His researches for these pages took him to maritime exhibits, museums, galleries, libraries, and private collections in more than 20 countries.

From 100,000 pictures—color photographs, paintings, woodcuts, stone carvings, tapestries, medieval miniatures, portraits—he and designer Howard E. Paine selected more than 400 of the most exciting and significant. The arrangement of these pictorial treasures shows Mr. Paine's artistry on every page. Staff men Edwards Park and John J. Putman helped steer the text on a true and purposeful course.

We commissioned Hervey Garrett Smith and other artists to re-create great ships and historic battles. The Society's cartographers fashioned special maps. Scores of diagrams and drawings were prepared.

Museum directors, librarians, researchers, scholars in many parts of the world contributed their fund of knowledge. Howard I. Chapelle, Curator of Transportation of the U. S. National Museum and a noted maritime authority, was a reliable lighthouse to guide us past the shoals of technical controversy.

Let us cast off lines, hoist sail, and set course for the adventure of *Men, Ships, and the Sea*.

Melville Bell Grosvenor

CHAPTERS BY

JACQUES-YVES COUSTEAU
JAMES DUGAN, ANDERS FRANZÉN
IRVING *and* ELECTA JOHNSON
LUIS MARDEN, CARLETON MITCHELL
JOHN E. SCHULTZ, PHILLIP M. SWATEK

STAFF FOR THIS BOOK

MELVILLE BELL GROSVENOR
Editor-in-chief

MERLE SEVERY
Editor

EDWARDS PARK
Associate editor

THOMAS Y. CANBY, JOHN J. PUTMAN
Editor-writers

ROSS BENNETT, MARY SWAIN HOOVER
Editorial assistants

ANNE DIRKES KOBOR
Picture research

HOWARD E. PAINE
Design

CHARLES C. UHL
Production

JOAN M. PIPER, JUDITH PETTRY PROPPS
ELIZABETH R. QUINN
Assistants

WILLIAM W. SMITH, JOE M. BARLETT
Engravings and printing

CONTRIBUTORS

DOROTHY M. CORSON (*Index*)
GILBERT H. EMERSON (*Maps*)
OSWALD BRETT, ANDREW POGGENPOHL
JOSEPH BAYLOR ROBERTS
W. EDWARD ROSCHER, JOHN SCOFIELD
HERVEY GARRETT SMITH, *and others*

Set on Linofilm Times Roman by National
Geographic's Phototypographic Division
Herman J. A. C. Arens, Director
Robert C. Ellis, Jr., Manager
Printed and bound by
R. R. Donnelley and Sons Co., Chicago
First printing: 150,000 copies
Second printing 1963: 150,000 copies

CAPTAIN VILLIERS *has followed the way of the
sea 44 adventurous years. As a boy in Australia
he'd look at the picture of a square-rigger by
his bed and dream of serving in such ships.
Alan Villiers made his dreams come true.
Shipping out at 15, he has sailed the seven seas
in windjammers and many other ships, including
his own full-rigged* Joseph Conrad. *Author of
25 books, he now lives in England, where he is
Chairman of the Society for Nautical Research,
a Trustee of the National Maritime Museum, and
Governor of the Cutty Sark Preservation Society.
He holds the British Distinguished Service Cross
for landings in Normandy, Sicily, and Burma as
Commander in the Royal Naval Volunteer Reserve,
and is a Commander of the Portuguese Order of
St. James of the Sword. Here Captain Villiers
plots his course to America aboard* Mayflower II.

Contents

MAN LEARNS TO SAIL

C RAB-CLAW SAIL set against blue
Pacific sky, a *tepukei* bears its
Melanesian passengers on a trading voyage in the Santa Cruz Islands.
Weird yet wondrous creation of tree
trunks, sticks, palm fronds and fiber,
this ageless craft still plays its part
in one of man's greatest adventures—
journeying upon the sea.

Water covers more than two-thirds
of the earth; man had to find his way
across it. And so, down through the
ages, man with his ingenuity and his
courage fashioned the ship—free,
charged with the strength and grace
and poetry of the singing sea. And
where once dugout and raft, galley and

galleon, tall clipper and
beamy paddle-wheeler
tracked the sea, now
giant freighters, tank-
ers, and liners steam
in endless movement
around the world, bear-
ing man's cargoes, his
hopes, himself. But as he created the
ship, the ship has shaped his course.
Harbinger of civilization, agent of discovery and migration, it became the
mightiest mobile creation the world
has ever known.

How did the ship evolve? How did
man use it? That is our story.

TEPUKEI PHOTOGRAPHED FROM THE BRIGANTINE "YANKEE" BY JUDY HUGGINS SUMNER; ANCIENT ROMAN COIN, COLLECTION OF MENDEL PETERSON

CHAPTER ONE

Man's first brave ventures on the water

In reedy streams and coral-fringed lagoons early man poked his timid toe. With ingenuity he fashioned dugouts and coracles, bulrush boats and skin canoes, balsa rafts and outriggers. Captain Villiers portrays the craft that carried man in ever widening circles over the once untraveled sea.

LOGS FLOAT. Bark floats. Inflated hides float. Early man noted these things and used them. He could grasp a log and propel himself with a cupped hand and kicking feet. He could blow up a hide, cling to its neck, and travel with the running stream.

He learned to lash a few logs or bundles of reeds together with lengths of vine or twisted hide. He had then a raft. In time he began to hollow the logs, shape the bark, and sit inside. He made wickerwork baskets, caulked them with bitumen or mud. He learned to stretch animal skins upon a solid frame and set himself afloat.

He poled himself along or traveled at the current's whim. He learned to make crude paddles and used these. He developed a thole pin as a fulcrum for his paddle. The paddle became an oar, and he could row.

He saw the upturned edges of drifting leaves catch the wind and drive upon the water. He raised leafy boughs for the same effect and contrived sails from matted reeds. In his crude boats he ventured upon calm coastal waters, fished and hunted in rivers and estuaries, from quiet beaches facing the summer seas.

Slowly he learned to use skins, mats, and woven cloth for his sails, to twist cordage from fibers, to steer with an oar. A thousand years rolled by between developments. He built bigger rafts, larger canoes; put crude shelters upon platforms over twin or single hulls. He held up his sails with stumpy bipod or tripod masts, set them on booms, and controlled them with thongs or twisted grass. He learned to sail both before and *into* the wind.

Crab-claw sails, triangular sails, square sails — he developed them all according to the best use of the materials at hand and the strength of the local winds.

Why did man do all this? He is a mobile creature. He has always had to move from place to place to seek food, to flee invaders, to find new land, to trade — or simply to wander, to see what lies so tantalizingly over the horizon. Rivers offered paths through jungles, mountains, wastelands; seas linked islands. Man *had* to sail.

I have always been fascinated by primitive man's response to this challenge. Early rec-

AUSTRALIAN ABORIGINE *rides out of the past on a mangrove raft, one of man's earliest forms of water transport. Lacking sail, paddle, and pole, he can propel himself with arms or feet. Early rafts were lashed with vines or thongs; pegs hold these logs together.*

CAMDEN SOUND, WESTERN AUSTRALIA; WILLIAM JACKSON

GIVE A MAN SOMETHING THAT FLOATS *and he will make a boat. On the Sutlej River in the Himalayas, pig or cow skins are inflated and lashed together to form rafts. Ancient Nineveh's wall carvings show similar scenes on the Tigris. A hull of bundled bulrushes and a sail of reeds still serve the Lake Titicaca fisherman, 12,506 feet high in the Andes. Bamboo makes the raft in Fiji and the gum-caulked basket being poled in Indochina. Greenland Eskimos stretch hides over wood or bone frames to fashion watertight kayaks.*

ords are nonexistent. Man made history long before he could record it; he could sail before he could write. Yet, remarkably, there is scarcely a phase in the development of ships that has quite disappeared. The most primitive craft survive in the world's backwaters, still serving their purpose.

Xenophon, writing of the manner in which Cyrus' fighting men crossed the Euphrates 2,400 years ago, says they used inflated skins. "They filled with light hay the skins from their tents, and drew them together and stitched them so that the water could not come in." In parts of Asia the traveler yet crosses streams on the backs of inflated animal hides.

Julius Caesar noted the use of the skin-covered, wickerwork boat in Britain 50 years before the birth of Christ. In Wales and Ireland similar coracles are still used by river fishermen. The reed-bundle canoe is seen today on the upper Nile, and on Lake Titicaca high in the Andes. The dugout still serves as local transport in many parts of the world.

WANDERING THE SEVEN SEAS I've come upon many such primitive craft, homey reminders of the seaman's ageless past. I've watched the clumsy, oxhide *pelotas* of the Amazon, the sewn-plank surf boats of Galle in the south of Ceylon, the crude *ballams* far up the Brahmaputra in Pakistan. When I could, I have sailed in these boats. To me the sea story is a vivid and living thing. In what other field could one so readily turn back the pages of history, really live in the days of the otherwise long-gone past?

On the far Euphrates I've watched pot-shaped *gufas* drifting with the current like a fleet of outsized waterlilies. The people here had no supply of good boat timber. They wove

14

CANOES CARRIED *bold voyagers to distant Pacific island homes centuries before Columbus braved the Atlantic. Light draft got them through coral reefs; stability came from a float attached to a boom, as on the Yap outrigger above, or a second hull connected by a platform. Large double canoes, 120 feet long, could hold 300 men. New Georgia war canoe (left) is built of stitched planks; cowrie "eyes" on prow help it find its way.*

Islanders navigated by the stars, bird flights, and a stick chart like that studied by two Marshallese. Tiny shells represent islands, bent withes show direction of swells caused by prevailing winds. Waves, deflected by the islands, sometimes produce a confused sea, helping the primitive navigator sense his position.

reeds into a round hull, bound it with cross-ribs, and caulked the whole with pitch. In a small gufa a man stood in the "bow" and paddled and steered with uncanny skill. Larger ones can carry a horse or bags of grain, and once served as lighters at Baghdad.

How old is the gufa? A relief from the Palace of Sennacherib at Nineveh, carved about 700 B.C., shows four bearded Assyrians rowing one with great dignity.

Not far from a tanker berth in the Persian Gulf I saw fishermen going about their business in reed-bundle boats. I wondered: Was the infant Moses discovered on the Nile in some such simple craft, fashioned from bulrushes that line rivers in that part of the world?

I have marveled too at how Eskimos in their barren, ice-covered lands from Greenland and North America to Siberia were able to create boats so wonderfully suited to their needs. To live, they must fish and hunt seals in stormy, frigid waters. They build a slender frame of driftwood or bone, then cover it with sealskin. Slipping into the snug manhole, the Eskimo laces the skin deck tightly about his waist. No water can enter; man and kayak are as one. Threatened by a wave, the Eskimo rolls upside down, takes it on the kayak's rounded bottom. Levering with his double-bladed paddle, he rights his craft. Snug clothing keeps all but hands and face dry.

The Eskimo's skin-covered umiak—the "woman's boat"—is never decked over. It can carry up to 50 people, is used to move entire families with their belongings.

Off the Brazilian coast I sailed in a *jangada*, a raft of balsa trunks. The Indians there had long ago learned that five or so logs of this buoyant wood, pinned together with hardwood rods and equipped with a triangular sail, would serve them well for fishing. The logs are arranged so that the slimmer ends form a somewhat pointed and upturned bow. A kind of centerboard can be lowered to resist drift.

When Pizarro and his Spanish conquistadores sailed down the coast of Ecuador they were surprised to see Indians carrying on coastal trade in *balsas* like these. Thor Heyerdahl demonstrated their seaworthiness when he and his companions drifted 3,700 nautical miles from Peru to the Polynesian island of Raroia in the *Kon-Tiki*.

I sailed once with Trobriand islanders off New Guinea. Since times unrecorded they have felled the trees of their islands, hollowed the trunks, and fitted on outriggers for stability. Their primitive tools were adequate for this. These fine sailors still make the daring open-sea voyages that link their home with other coral isles. A platform atop the slender hull provides space for cargo and passengers.

WHO INVENTED the first boat? I don't know. No one knows. Perhaps there was a "first edition" someplace, sometime. But I think it's more likely that different men in different places discovered how to build a boat in their own way. It could have occurred to both the North American Indian and to his counterpart in Siberia that birchbark on a frame would make a satisfactory canoe. The Sioux, a nomad of the plains, fashioned his round bullboat of buffalo hide stretched over withes; the nomad of Tibet made his coracle of yak- or sheepskin.

Only the outrigger canoe seems sharply con-

17

fined to one part of the world — the Pacific and Indian Oceans. The outrigger is possibly the ancestor of the double canoe, the vessel that carried the Polynesians and their Asiatic forebears in great migrations from southeast Asia across the Pacific to Tahiti, Hawaii, New Zealand, and hundreds of other islands.

They probably left overcrowded Indonesia many centuries before the Christian Era. They began to set their prows toward the rising sun; for untold years they spread and settled island after island in the east-central Pacific, now called Polynesia. Some of their voyages must have been nightmares — sailing in an open boat, unable to carry sufficient food or water, lacking compass or sextant, unsure of what lay ahead.

Those old double canoes of Oceania were beautiful things. How Captain Cook must have stared at the trim canoe of the King of Hawaii with its graceful crab-claw sail arched above,

a dozen paddlers dipping at each side, feather-robed nobles crowding the platform between the hulls.

But handsome and worthy as these double canoes were, they were not ships. They could not carry a regular and economical commerce over the seas. Neither could a buffalo-hide coracle, a bundle of reeds, or a balsa.

Man could not build ships until he invented tools to shape planks, and learned to build up those planks on a keel. Perhaps the ship grew from a dugout. Primitive builders added planks to keep out waves; eventually the dugout base became a keel. Maybe the skin boat is the ship's ancestor. It has a frame; all you need do is substitute planking for the animal hide. Some of the earliest planked ships, including the seagoing dhow, were indeed sewn together with fiber rope, and then caulked.

Given tools and knowledge, man could build ships and set his course for civilization.

SEMINOLE SHAPES A DUGOUT *from a fallen Florida cypress. He molds bottom with an ax, forms prow, then scoops out center with an adz. His ancestors used sharp stones and fire. Buoyant, thin-shelled dugouts like the one shooting rapids in Brazil evolved early. Ancient builders, raising the sides with planks to keep out water, helped create the ship.*

BAS RELIEF IN VATICAN MUSEUM; ALINARI. EGYPTIAN SHIP PORTRAYED ON HATSHEPSUT'S TEMPLE, DEIR EL BAHRI; HULTON PICTURE LIBRARY

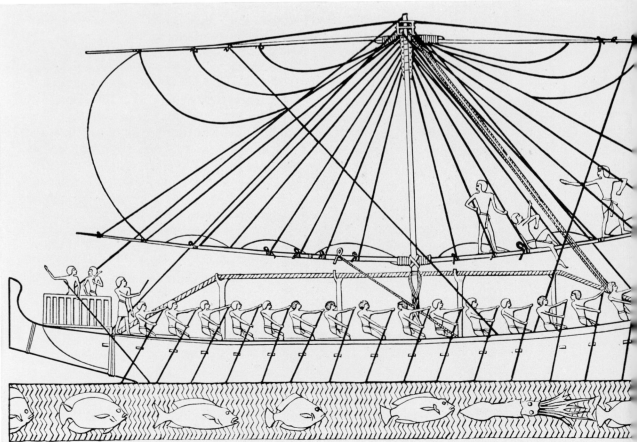

CHAPTER TWO

On the Nile and the Mediterranean

Here Western civilization was born, and here were spawned the first ships — merchantmen to meet the needs of growing trade, war galleys for conquest. A great sea becomes a Roman lake.

T HE EARLIEST KNOWN RECORDS of ships come from Egypt. It was a great, civilized nation, and the Nile a perfect highway for waterborne commerce. Ships were the "trucks" that rode upon it. Their crews sailed south before the almost constant north wind and paddled, rowed, and drifted north again with the stream. Primitive Egyptians ventured on it in bundles of papyrus reeds lashed together in the shape of boats. And almost 5,000 years ago Pharaohs were building barges big enough to haul blocks of granite downriver from Aswan for their pyramids.

Egyptians also made coastal voyages. Their carvings tell of expeditions to the "Land of Punt," probably Somaliland. The sculptured ships of Queen Hatshepsut (left) still sail upon the stones of the temple of Deir el Bahri, near Thebes, after 3,500 years.

An inscription there describes "the loading of the ships very heavily with marvels of the country of Punt; all goodly fragrant woods of God's Land, heaps of myrrh-resin, with fresh myrrh trees, with ebony and pure ivory, with green gold of Emu, with cinnamon wood, khesyt wood, with ihmut-incense, sonter-incense, eye-cosmetic, with apes, monkeys, dogs, and with skins of the southern panther, with natives and their children. . . ."

If this seems a big freight, remember the Queen sent five ships, about 70 feet long with 18-foot beam. They had to be shallow-draft to sail the reef-choked inshore channels of the Red Sea, to beach and handle cargoes. Their overhanging ends made it easy

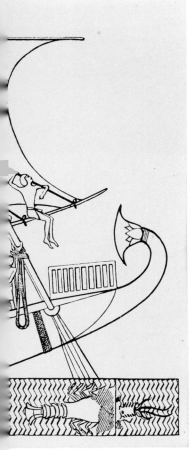

ROMAN GALLEYS *helped build an empire. Ships like that above fought Battle of Actium, 31* B.C., *where Octavian defeated Antony and Cleopatra. Tower held archers, stone throwers. Below: Vessels of Egypt's Queen Hatshepsut voyage to Punt.*

21

to get on and off. I've seen the same long, high bow on a 70-foot fishing canoe on the Brahmaputra in Pakistan. To go ashore, the boatman swung his bow over the riverbank and jumped.

Egyptian ships carried one big sail. Early vessels had a bipod mast; later the sail was set on a single pole between a long slim yard at its head and a boom of the same length at its foot. Wood was scarce in Egypt, and ships were weakly built without keel or ribs. Herodotus says their longest planks were about three feet, and he likens the boatbuilders to bricklayers.

To strengthen their vessels Egyptians rigged a truss—a heavy rope which ran aft over a series of forked poles from a sling around the raised bow to another sling around the stern. It was set by a simple tourniquet.

The first real seafarers of the Mediterranean were the Minoans of Crete. An Egyptian tomb painting shows strange sailors in kilts and sandals. Perhaps these "People of the Isles in the midst of the Sea" are Minoans. They traded pottery as far west as Sicily, and Thucydides says their legendary king Minos conquered

Black Sea

ROMANS

Mediterranean Sea

GREEKS

CRETE   RHODES

PHOENICIANS

PILLARS OF HERCULES

EGYPTIANS

The Nile

Red Sea

THE MEDITERRANEAN *nurtured nations of mariners. First to build seagoing ships were Egyptians. Here a vessel of the third millennium* B.C. *moves up the Nile under a single sail, while steersmen man their oars and one sailor sounds with a pole. A rope truss strengthens the keelless hull made of short, pinned planks. Bipod mast distributes pressure. A nearby ship slips downriver with mast lowered, oarsmen pulling. Tomb relief (below) shows boatbuilders wielding chisel and adz.*

HERVEY GARRETT SMITH; RIGHT: RELIEF ON TOMB
OF TI, SAQQARA, LEHNERT AND LANDROCK, CAIRO

and colonized the isles of the Aegean. But we know almost nothing of their ships.

Wider-ranging sailors were the swarthy Phoenicians. They had timber to build sturdy ships, and from Tyre and Sidon they voyaged to Greece, Italy, North Africa, Spain, even to far-off Britain, rich in tin. They founded Carthage, Gadir (Cádiz), and other colonies.

A Carthaginian named Hanno pushed west through the Pillars of Hercules (the Strait of Gibraltar) and down the coast of Africa, perhaps as far as Guinea. He and his men found a great river "infested with crocodiles and hippopotami," and "gorillas" who appeared to them as "women with hairy bodies." They captured three, took the skins back to Carthage.

A century earlier, about 600 B.C., Phoenicians made an even greater voyage; they circumnavigated Africa from east to west. It took three years. Herodotus tells why: "When autumn came, they went ashore, wherever they might happen to be, and having sown a tract of land with corn, waited until the grain was fit to cut. Having reaped it, they again set sail."

Some scholars doubt this voyage. As a sailing ship seaman, I don't. These crews could have sailed down East Africa with the favoring monsoon, around the Cape of Good Hope, then up the west coast with the trade winds.

The Phoenicians were tight-lipped with their nautical knowledge. But the Bible, in the 27th chapter of Ezekiel, throws some light on their ships: "They have taken cedars from Lebanon to make masts for thee. Of the oaks of Bashan have they made thine oars.... Fine linen with broidered work from Egypt was that which thou spreadest forth to be thy sail."

THE GREEKS remembered their sailor-heroes better—Jason and his Argonauts seeking the Golden Fleece, Agamemnon leading the sea assault on Troy, Odysseus

SWEEPING PAST GIBRALTAR *on crests of Atlantic seas, Phoenicians aim their horse-headed prows*

wandering back after the wars. These are legendary tales, but fact must be behind them.

Homer tells us how Odysseus built a boat: "Twenty trees in all he felled, and then trimmed them with the axe of bronze, and deftly smoothed them, and over them made straight the line. Meanwhile Calypso, the fair goddess, brought him augers, so he bored each piece and jointed them together, and then made all fast with trenails and dowels. . . . And thereat he wrought, and set up the deckings, fitting them to the close-set uprights, and finished them off with long gunwales, and therein he set a mast, and a yard-arm fitted thereto, and moreover he made him a rudder to guide the craft. . . . And he made fast therein braces and halyards and sheets, and at last he pushed the raft with levers down to the fair salt sea."

Later the Greeks wrought splendid fighting galleys, propelled by one, two, or three banks of oars. They must have made a brave sight, rowing among the Greek islands, oar blades flashing wet in the golden sunshine, spray curling white along the powerful ram, large sail swelling in the soft, warm breeze.

The Greeks founded Massalia (Marseille), settled in Sicily, Italy, North Africa, and along the Black Sea. Their ships carried grain from Egypt and the Crimea, wine from Asia Minor, purple-dyed fabrics from Tyre, glassware from

25

for home after circumnavigating Africa about 600 B.C. The feat was not duplicated for 21 centuries.

Sidon, pottery from Greek cities. As commerce flourished, two of the Seven Wonders of the World rose over busy harbors — the Pharos (lighthouse) at Alexandria and the Colossus of Rhodes. Brisk, fair-dealing Rhodians codified the first known sea law and suppressed pirates. But neither they nor other Mediterranean peoples could resist newcomer Rome.

The Romans were landlubbers, farmers and soldiers. But their life-and-death struggle with Carthage taught them to build and to fight in

26

war galleys. By Christ's time, the Mediterranean was *mare nostrum* — "our sea." All summer it was speckled with Roman sails.

Galleys wouldn't do for this commerce; they lacked cargo space and their crews ate too much. So stubby "round ships" using sail alone hauled grain from Egypt to Rome's multitudes; they reached nearly 200 feet in length. We know quite a bit about these round ships, for the Romans, like the Greeks and Egyptians before them, left proud records in stone.

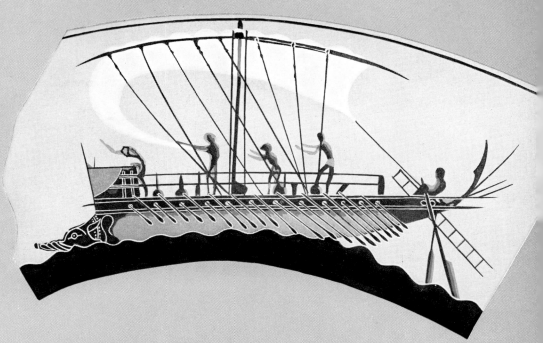

From pyramid and pottery we learn of ancient ships

ANCIENT MARINERS *left few written records, so knowledge of their ships comes from other sources. Tomb of Egyptian King Khufu at Giza preserved a funerary ship buried 4,500 years (top left). Probably dismantled to fit the crypt, it was 152 feet long, had two cabins, was joined by dowels and copper staples. Reassembled, it is now housed beside Khufu's Great Pyramid. Model from King Tutankhamun's tomb was expected to expand, whisk him along the celestial Nile. Instead it gives visitors to the Cairo Museum a peek at vessels of 33 centuries ago. Carving on a sarcophagus from Sidon pictures a Roman round ship; painting on a Greek cup from Tuscany shows seafaring in sixth century* B.C. *Girl diver below glides over amphorae from ship that sank off Turkey about* A.D. 100. *Turkish waters also yielded a Bronze Age wreck some 3,200 years old.*

DOUBLE BANKS *of oars speed a bireme past a Roman round ship. The galley's outboard platform makes room for a second level of rowers; catwalks allow marines to move freely. Sail is furled and human machines, keeping time to a flutist's tune, pull against a head wind. For combat, the mast would be lowered.*

Legend credits King Minos of Crete with the first navy. The ram—the "big gun" of antiquity— was probably developed by the Greeks sometime before 800 B.C. Battleships of their day, galleys lacked space. Crews went ashore at night to cook and sleep.

BEAMY MERCHANTMAN *steers for the open sea. Sail at bow, called an artemon, helps to keep the ship before the wind. Twin topsails add power. Brails, the vertical lines on mainsail and artemon, are used to shorten sail. Shrouds of tough cordage set on deadeyes brace the pine mast. Hulls stretching as much as 180 feet, with 45-foot beams, stowed up to 1,200 tons of grain. In such a vessel St. Paul was shipwrecked on Malta.*

HERVEY GARRETT SMITH

29

XERXES' FLEET *hugged the coast to support his army, sparred with Greek ships off Artemisium, then sailed on to disaster.*

CHAPTER THREE

Athenians beat Xerxes at Salamis

Ancient Greece was fighting to survive after King Xerxes won at Thermopylae and sacked Athens. Only a fleet remained to face the Persians. Captain Villiers takes up the yarn.

THE BATTLE OF SALAMIS was fought in a narrow channel off the mainland of Greece some 2,400 years ago. It taught for all time the importance of sea warfare.

A great army of invading Persians under famous King Xerxes had rampaged over the eastern Mediterranean. Nearly two million strong and ably led, they conquered wherever they struck. Athens fell and the Greeks were beaten almost to their knees.

The Athenians and their allies still had a fleet, three or four hundred well-manned ships. Xerxes had more than a thousand, commandeered from Phoenicia, Egypt, and Asia Minor.

The Greek war galleys were long, fast ships. They were 125 feet or so from stem to stern with 18-foot beam and three- or four-foot draft. They usually had 170 oars arranged in three tiers—62 in the upper bank and 54 in each lower bank. With the full power of their oarsmen they could cut through flat water at seven knots, and get up to ten for brief bursts. Yet they remained wonderfully maneuverable.

A trained crew could spin a galley on its axis and go ahead or astern with equal facility. Captains could keep whole squadrons in perfect station, in circles, squares, or spearheads—with rams outward, all but impregnable.

The Greeks knew how to attack with those powerful bronze-sheathed rams, placed awash at strengthened bows. They would rush the enemy and suddenly, close-to, bring their oars inboard along one side and with a quick, spinning thrust smash off the foeman's oars. Then, quick as lightning, while he lay helpless as a fish without fins, they would swing around again and speed in to deliver fatal ram-head blows. It was like a modern fighter firing a rocket burst into the defenseless side of a transport airplane.

The Greek fleet was based on the island of Salamis, and Xerxes had to attack it there. He was wary. Land warfare he understood, but the sea was different. To go into the mile-wide narrows between Salamis and the mainland was dangerous; triremes took up a lot of room with their three wide banks of oars. The Persians must advance on a narrow front and could bring only a limited part of their force to bear at any one time. Xerxes' ships would be vulnerable.

Themistocles, the Athenian admiral, appreciated the advantages of Salamis: the restricted approach presented ideal conditions for a fleet inferior in size, secure from flank attack, to fight off a superior. Outnumbered four to one? Then this was the place to fight! But how to lure Xerxes' ships into the bottleneck?

Themistocles—skillful, cunning, courageous —arranged by stratagem for a servant to carry word to the Persian fleet that the Greeks were demoralized and were planning to slip out of the channel and scatter, each to save his own skin. They were quarreling among themselves and would offer little opposition. If Xerxes moved swiftly he could destroy the enemy fleet at one blow.

Xerxes took joy in these tidings, dispatched squadrons under cover of night to seal off escape from Salamis, and ordered the main body of his fleet to make a surprise attack through the channel at dawn. He hoped to catch many of the Greek ships still on the beaches.

The great King, eager to witness the spectacle, established himself ashore on the hill Aegaleos, overlooking Salamis. Here he sat on his golden throne, bejeweled, dressed in shining robes. His scribes made ready to record the action on tablets, that no detail of the impending victory be lost.

ON COMES the Persian fleet "like a stream, filling the straits from shore to shore." The Persians sight some Greek ships; they must be in flight! The vast fleet sweeps forward, dark ships upon the blue morning sea, beating the water white with the foam of thousands of oars.

Suddenly a cheer rings out from Salamis, loud and defiant. A trumpet blasts the call to war. With orderly, intense activity, the Greek fleet moves out and forms up across the bay.

Still Themistocles plays the fox. To draw the Persians into the narrows of Salamis, he orders his ships to backwater, as if in fear of the oncoming fleet.

The invaders jam-pack the narrow sea, galleys jostling for room, oars brushing close to oars. From the Persians comes a great roar! Xerxes licks his lips at the prospect of overwhelming victory.

But now the morning breeze springs up, as Themistocles knew it would; it brings up a ground swell among the Persian fleet, as Themistocles knew it would. Their ships pitch and roll. Oars flail. Lancers, javelin throwers, and archers are caught off-balance. Heaving platforms are not for land warriors.

Now it is the Greeks who "smite the sounding sea with the even stroke of foaming oars." (So sings the Greek poet Aeschylus, himself a veteran of Salamis.) In calm waters the Greek galleys advance, an orderly crescent of menacing rams, racing across the bay. Every Greek trierarch commanding his trireme that sunlit September morning, every Greek freeman at those long oars is fired with one idea: to crush the invader.

Too late the Persians realize they have been misled about the Greeks' low morale. From behind, the press of their ships out in the open water forces the Xerxian spearhead farther into the narrows.

Now the Greeks fall upon the Persians without mercy!

"Ship dashed against ship its brazen prow." The rolling Persian triremes present vulnerable

BIREME *with heroic archers adorns a water jar of 500 B.C. Giant eye gazes out over beak.*

FROM HIS THRONE, *Xerxes sees the ordered crescent of Greek galleys surge forward in the calm waters off Salamis to crush the wave-tossed Persian fleet streaming in from the sea. The Greeks chose Salamis as the place to "defend against the Barbarian" at the urging of Themistocles, records this marble tablet.*

broadsides. Greek after Greek falls on them, smashing them, rolling them over, brushing away their floundering oars. Ram, ram, ram!

Still the long lines of ships come on, inexorably, to their doom, unaware of their fate until it is upon them. Vanguard ships try to turn. They cannot. They are boxed in. Desperately, the oarsmen flail at the water with their great oars reversed. Backwater all! No use, for the swell, lifting now one oar bank and dipping the other, makes control impossible.

> *. . . and the hulls of ships*
> *Floated capsized, nor could the sea be seen,*
> *Filled as it was with wrecks and carcasses:*
> *And all the shores and rocks were full of*
>   *corpses*
> *And every ship was wildly rowed in flight. . . .*

Xerxes on his throne screams with impotent rage. Captains, their triremes lost, their crews drowned, struggle ashore to apologize.

"Off with their heads!" shouts the King.

Persian losses are enormous: more than 200 ships, 20,000 men. A detachment of troops, landed to exploit the victory, is cut off and annihilated at Greek leisure. Only one small squadron, handled with skill and presence of mind, escapes without loss. It is the five-ship group of the admiral-queen Artemisia of Caria in Asia Minor. Hotly pressed by the Greeks, she attacks a Persian ship. The Greeks think her an ally and veer off. She flees.

"My men have turned into women, my women into men," says Xerxes grimly. The Queen's wiliness is his only satisfaction.

Soon after Salamis, he pulls out of Greece, out of the Mediterranean. His defeat means the glories of ancient Greece have their chance to flower, for the infinite benefit of mankind.

32

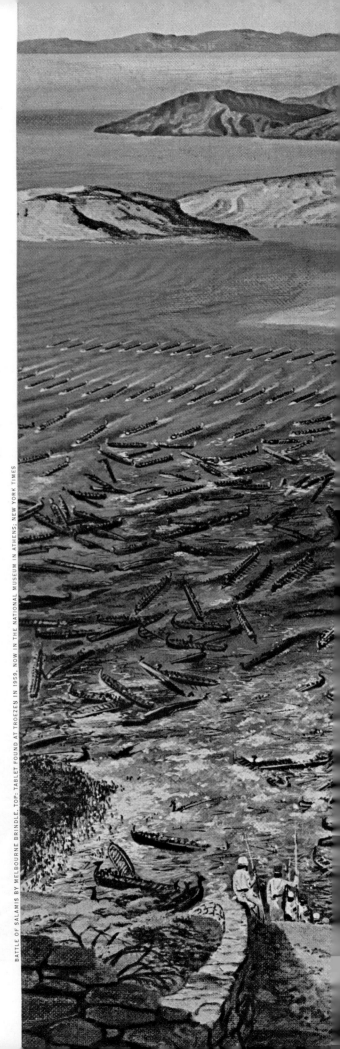

CHAPTER FOUR

Diving to a Greek ship wrecked 2,100 years ago

A century and a half before Christ a wine-laden merchantman sank off southern France. Capt. Jacques-Yves Cousteau, leader of the National Geographic Society–*Calypso* Oceanographic Expeditions and co-inventor of the Aqua-Lung, tells how he found the ship and brought up her cargo.

MY OLD COMRADE Frédéric Dumas learned of the wreck from a free-lance Aqua-Lung diver in Marseille who had gone down too deep and too long. An attack of the bends had paralyzed his legs and he would never dive again. From his hospital bed the crippled diver told Dumas a secret: he had found an incredible colony of lobsters along the submarine walls of Grand Congloué, a great rock crouching in the Mediterranean 10 miles off Marseille.

"You can tell where the lobsters are when you see the old pots," said the diver.

The pots intrigued Dumas. They might be amphorae—jars in which the ancients carried wine and oil.

Sunken cargo could mean a sunken vessel. So when Dumas and I were off Grand Congloué in our research ship *Calypso* in Au-

ALBERT FALCO

gust, 1952, we donned Aqua-Lungs and took a look. Dumas found nothing.

I slanted down past lovely coral shelves and grottoes, reaching 200 feet without seeing an amphora. I began to ascend. Sixty feet up I saw the "pots." Amphora necks stood out from a huge mound of mud. Dishes were strewn about. I had time only to grasp three wine cups and a corroded bronze boathook.

Prof. Fernand Benoît, Director of Antiquities of Provence and head of Marseille's Archeological Museum, saw a hand come out of the sea with the cups. "Campanian!" he shouted, recognizing a type of pottery dating from the 2d century B.C.

That night as we sat at *Calypso*'s mess table we lifted the cups, carefully nested with twin handles at right angles to each

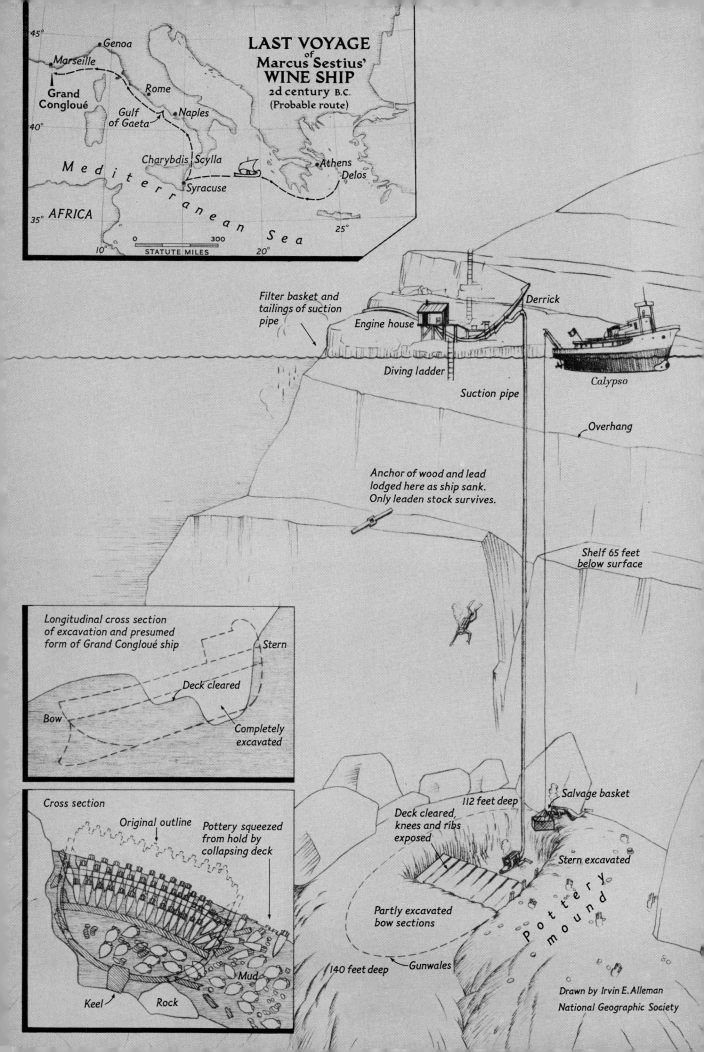

LAST VOYAGE of Marcus Sestius' WINE SHIP
2d century B.C.
(Probable route)

Genoa
Marseille
Grand Congloué
Rome
Gulf of Gaeta
Naples
Charybdis · Scylla
Syracuse
Athens
Delos
AFRICA
Mediterranean Sea

45°
40°
35°
10°
20°
25°

0   300
STATUTE MILES

Filter basket and tailings of suction pipe

Engine house

Derrick

Diving ladder

Suction pipe

Calypso

Overhang

Anchor of wood and lead lodged here as ship sank. Only leaden stock survives.

Shelf 65 feet below surface

Longitudinal cross section of excavation and presumed form of Grand Congloué ship

Stern
Deck cleared
Bow
Completely excavated

Cross section

Original outline

Pottery squeezed from hold by collapsing deck

112 feet deep

Salvage basket

Deck cleared, knees and ribs exposed

Stern excavated

Partly excavated bow sections

Pottery mound

Mud

Keel   Rock

140 feet deep   Gunwales

Drawn by Irvin E. Alleman
National Geographic Society

CARGO UNLOADED—21 CENTURIES LATE! *Like upside-down stevedores, Cousteau's divers pried neatly stacked amphorae from the buried vessel. These terra-cotta jars, once holding wine from the Greek islands, from Syracuse, and from the hills near Rome, rose to* Calypso's *deck in a cargo net.*

In foam-rubber suits divers finned to their job 140 feet down. Temperature there remains a chilly 52° F. whether the winter mistral whips the Mediterranean or summer sun warms its surface. Men worked fast, then rose at the recall signal—the watery echo of a shot. If they stayed longer than 17 minutes they had to decompress in stages. Three dives a day were enough. The last left a touch of depth drunkenness.

Underwater television sped the job by giving shipboard archeologists a firsthand view of their sea-bottom dig. A built-in speaker enabled the experts to instruct the divers. The steel-encased camera submerges (above) as the author, with raised hand, signals to the winch, "Lower away!"

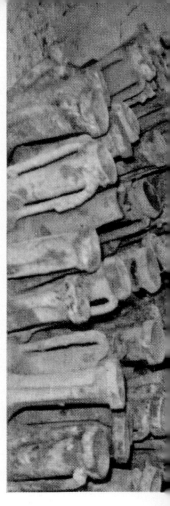

TREASURES FROM THE DEEP *include cups, candy dishes, a jug, and a perfume flask. Ferdinand Lallemand records them aboard* Calypso. *His son Rémy (below) holds a bronze nail 200 times his age. Bowl and cone may have counterweighted the ship's steering oars.*

COUSTEAU *sorts the*

other, and ceremoniously separated them. We were taking apart things an expert had stacked 21 centuries ago for stowage aboard a Greek ship now buried beneath that mound of mud.

THE DAYS AND MONTHS following our discovery were frantic. Heavy buoys held *Calypso* just off Grand Congloué. A house that slept eight rose on the bleak island. From an 85-foot boom dangled a suction pipe.

Fifteen topnotch divers plunged like porpoises, working quickly in the diffused gray radiance 140 feet down. We loosened amphorae and dishes with our hands, pried them out of the cementlike mud with crowbars, and used the pipe like a vacuum cleaner. It browsed on shells, sand, and shards. Sometimes it would choke on an amphora neck and the operator had to turn off the sucking air. Then the pipe would cough apologetically, belch, and spit its impedimenta on the sea floor.

Ferdinand Lallemand, who logged our finds, pored over baskets of amphorae winched onto

38

amphorae in a Marseille museum. Tall Italian jars held 5¼ gallons; plumper Greek type held 6½.

Calypso's deck or watched for smaller prizes fetched up by the suction pump. It poured out an ornamented Megarian bowl fragment, bronze hooks and knives, and a finger ring.

Occasionally the divers used the "bazooka," as they called the suction pipe, to torment Lallemand. When he mentioned the possibility of finding ancient coins, they fed modern 5-franc pieces into the pipe to give him a deceptive thrill. Once they sent up a small octopus which arrived alive and indignant at his feet.

We uncovered thousands of pieces of Campanian ware—by far the largest lode ever found. More than 40 standardized types of dishes, bowls, and pots were identified. This led to a discovery. All the dishes have slight circular indentations which could not have been made by a potter's hand. We concluded that the ancients had shaped them in wooden frames—a remarkable evidence of mass production a century and a half before Christ.

Early in the digging we raised an amphora still sealed. Uncorking it, we took out about a quart of dregs. Lallemand and I poured glasses and downed the "nectar." He managed to spit his out on deck, but I swallowed mine. I tasted all the mustiness and age there is in this world. A poor vintage century, that wine.

The play of ages had opened all but a few amphorae, and in excavating them we found that most held an octopus. The ship had been "octopied" for two millenniums!

We brought up fragments of the ship herself, and they showed the skill of shipwrights who worked in oak and Aleppo pine. The rotten wood shrank in air. We reached the keel, and its size indicated our ship was large.

The ill-fated argosy must have been nearly 100 feet long with a cargo capacity of more than 120 tons. Far too big to row, she probably carried a single mast and a sail of coarse linen. The ancients had armored her hull with ¹⁄₁₆-inch lead sheathing, tons of it. Copper nails fastened it on. Thousands came up in the suction pipe. We also found iron fittings and bronze nails, some 15 inches long.

JEAN AUNIAC AND (BELOW) HAROLD E. EDGERTON

CLUES IN MOSAIC *point to Marcus Sestius, possible owner of the argosy, as builder of this ancient villa at Delos. Floor design (left) has twin S's and an E-shaped trident. This repeats his motif on amphora (above): the abbreviation "SES" and a trident.*

Excavating the cargo and learning the order of its stowage told us the ship's itinerary, throwing light on the blank pages of early Greek commerce.

The argosy left the merchant port of the sacred Greek isle of Delos, birthplace of Apollo, laden with Aegean wine, stored in fat-bellied amphorae, and some pottery. Because she was to take on her principal cargo in western ports of call, these were stowed aft under the main deck.

Westward she sailed, through the friendly Greek islands. The next one was always in sight to comfort the navigator. Then she took the plunge across the Ionian Sea, open water that might mean 20 days without sight of land, or four if the ship was blessed by Poseidon, god of the sea. Raising Sicily, she could coast the rest of the way.

The great ship probably stopped first at Syracuse, where she took on more wine and pottery, then passed the Strait of Messina between Sicily and Italy, avoiding the rock of Scylla and the whirlpool of Charybdis.

She put into a port northwest of modern Naples and took on a huge lading of black-varnished export dinnerware. This was stowed below with the wine and other pottery.

The Greeks in Massalia (Marseille) would pay excellent prices for the dinnerware and would bid high for the wine. You could trade an amphora of wine for a slave, for viticulture was only beginning in France.

Stevedores loaded the main deck with three tiers of slender Roman amphorae, each jar containing several gallons of Latium wine. Doubtless the shipper wanted a big profit. But by now the argosy was riding dangerously low in the water.

She set out into the Tyrrhenian and Ligurian seas and reached the savage coastal waters off Marseille. She may have struck Grand Congloué, or the crew may have sailed her there to save themselves as she swamped beneath their feet. All hands may have been drunk from having broken into the wine cargo — several of the salvaged amphorae have holes drilled in the necks. In any event, down went the ship, sinking slowly in an upright position and alighting on a sloping shelf of rock.

The sea adopted her. Worms attacked the wood. Then came sponges, ascidians, and sea urchins, which settled on the deck, the hull, the cargo of amphorae. Gradually the wreck was covered by sand pulverized from the lime-stone walls, by silt scoured from the rock, by fossil mud made up of the skeletons of trillions of small marine animals.

The mud falling, falling, falling, while Christ was briefly alive, through the short flourish of Imperial Rome to the age of Constantine, then the Middle Ages, covered the wreck and preserved it against the destruction these natural processes had started.

In modern times it became a tumulus, the big bump that we excavated on the sea bottom.

I HAVE VENTURED to give the probable time of the sinking. I can also name the probable owner, even though there were no human remains in the wreck and no documents. The startling facts came from scholars.

From his study of our amphorae and dishes, Professor Benoît determined that the ship most likely sailed in the second century B.C. The amphorae taken on near Naples were stamped with "SES" in Roman letters, followed sometimes by an anchor symbol, sometimes by a trident. SES probably stood for the shipper's name, since Romans were great abbreviators.

Ransacking classical genealogies and annals, Benoît came up with references to a prominent and powerful Roman clan named Sestius. Apparently the family prospered in the shipping business and set up some of its members in the important trading center of Delos. Records of Delos mention a Marcus Sestius living there in the second century B.C.

We sailed Calypso to Delos to retrace the argosy's voyage. We found the sacred city in ruins, sacked by ancient invaders, bypassed by trade routes. An expert led us past broken columns and statuary to the merchants' quarters. We divers walked sadly among the ruins.

Then came a yell of triumph. In the mosaic floor of a large villa we discovered a trident symbol almost identical to the ones on the sunken amphorae. The trident's tines exactly resembled a Roman E. Between them were two S-shaped brackets. By rearranging this possible cipher we had SES!

Our guide remarked that the villa had never been finished. We wondered whether Sestius had gone broke when the big ship sank.

We realize, of course, that there is no real proof that this was our shipper's house. We live in a skeptical age of science. Some of us, however, will always secretly believe that this was the villa of Marcus Sestius, owner of the argosy that sank at Grand Congloué.

LOWELL THOMAS, JR.

ARAB SAILORS, *sidestepping jam-packed passengers, hoist the yard on an Oman* jalboot.

SPORTING ALL SAILS, Bayan *feels for a morning breeze. The author found that her lateen rig moved her handily, either close-hauled or running before the wind.*

ALAN VILLIERS

CHAPTER FIVE

The Arab dhow

Little changed by the centuries, these rakish hand-hewn vessels still ply the Indian Ocean as regularly as the monsoons that drive them. Scarcely a Westerner has joined the crew and sailed aboard one, save Alan Villiers.

PARIAH DOGS barked themselves hoarse and Arab sailors and stevedores eyed me with interest as I walked along the harbor of Maala one October morning not so many years ago. I had come to Aden to sail back into the past, to ship out with the Arabs in their ancient dhows.

Friends had arranged for me to sail first in a small Red Sea dhow with graceful lines and a single big cotton sail. But when I found the *nakhoda* (captain), he shouted to all and sundry that his ship had no comforts for such a softy as I—not even a cabin.

"Look here," I said, "don't you worry about me. I'm a sailor." A sailor? A foreigner in a white suit? Laughter swept the wharf. At last I persuaded him and signed aboard.

The first thing I discovered was that the Arabs know none of their vessels as "dhows." They are classed by their hull forms: *sambuks, booms, baggalas.* All their rigs are much the same. My ship, a swift double-ender named *Sheikh Mansur*, was a *zaruq* of about 50 tons and 45 feet on the waterline. Her mainmast was a twisted tree, and the lateen yard appeared to be two branches of the same tree tied together. Her crew had lashed up extra "bulwarks"—mats woven from old date fronds —to keep spray out of the cargo in her open hold. A boy bailed the bilge with a bucket

43

BAREFOOT SINDBADS TUG ON CORDAGE *of coconut husk fiber as they rig down a mast. Medieval*

made from the skin of a long-dead goat. Ugh! That bilge water! Even the hull, smeared with fish oil to preserve the teak, stank.

That evening, with wind and tide in our favor, we slipped from the harbor. The nakhoda took the tiller; the crew weighed the grapnel anchor by hand, then sheeted home the lateen sail. Ahead lay the Strait of Bab al Mandab, southern entrance to the Red Sea.

We sailed only by day and in calm water inside coastal reefs. The men offered up five prayers daily. They slept. They steered. Sometimes they looked after the sail. This was the

sum total of their lives, yet they were a merry crowd for all that. Their attitude was that if Allah was kind *Sheikh Mansur* would arrive safely in port.

At night we anchored by a cay. Here a little brushwood or camel thorn was gathered — enough to get a small fire going in a clay-lined barrel. Any fish we managed to catch were broiled in the ashes.

Ahmed, our nakhoda, was a lean, bearded Yemenite of 35 years. He wore a short sarong, and in his gold-cloth waistcoat carried all the ship's papers. He knew the Red Sea by heart.

Arabs used this coir to stitch hulls. Bayan *is nail-joined; her long teak nose marks her as Kuwaiti.*

On hazy days he sent a man aloft to pick out landmarks. In shallow water he took soundings with his fishing line. He had no charts, took no bearings, and never fixed the ship's position accurately. At sunset he munched his unleavened bread and fish, and he bunked on the cargo with the rest of us. He was a good sailor and did his best for ship and crew.

During those six days from Maala to Jizan, up the Red Sea, the modern world just slipped away. We saw steamships distantly, but they belonged to another age—they seemed inhuman things going along unmanned.

AFTER THAT APPRENTICESHIP I wandered back to Aden, where I found the Kuwait fleet unloading the new season's crop of Iraqi dates from the valley of the Shatt al Arab. These big Kuwaiti booms, with their sleek and massive hulls of Malabar teak, towered above the lesser fry of the Red Sea trades. They were decked, had stout masts, wheels to steer by, great cabins below high poops, and all the usual fittings of real ships. I watched their longboats pulling ashore, each manned by a dozen chanting men clad in flowing gowns.

It was not easy to get passage on one of

these dhows. I had merchant and official friends, or there would have been little hope. At last I quieted the suspicion that I was some customs inspector and shipped aboard a 115-tonner. It took weeks even to find out her name, for Arabs don't like their ships to be identified too closely. Sometimes she was *Nejdi,* sometimes *Triumph of Righteousness,* but most often *Bayan.*

The boom was only four years old. Her mainmast was an 80-foot tree, and the lateen yard consisted of three Persian trees lashed together, the whole more than 130 feet long. She had three suits of good sails, and her gear was stout.

Our voyage was first along the coast of the Hadhramaut, thence to Somaliland, Mombasa, Zanzibar, and Tanganyika, and then homeward to the Persian Gulf. The nakhoda assigned me to be his navigating mate—a nominal job—and gave me six feet on the officers' bench in the stern on which to spread my sleeping carpet. But he gave me neither chronometer nor any charts. He had none.

I assigned to myself the tasks of learning all I could and of treating cuts and infections among the crew of 27. I had a good stock of medicines and they had nothing.

We set out on a December morning with a cargo of salt, grain, tinned *ghee* (semiliquid butter), and cased goods, bound for Mukalla and Ash Shihr on the coast of Arabia.

Our ship was under the temporary command of the mate Hamed bin Salim, for Nejdi the captain had gone ahead to Mukalla to collect passengers. Nakhodas often do this. Merchants as well as commanders, they have to buy and sell cargoes and look for fares.

For ten days an adverse wind slowed our progress, and we had to beat. The big boom was a weatherly ship, lying up four points from the wind. I became acquainted with the crew, kindly fellows. But with all life necessarily lived in full public view, they showed an embarrassing interest in everything I did. The food, though rough, was better than the zaruq's. We had aboard several Somali goats. Once a month one of these was killed, skinned, and thrown into the pot. Often we ate dried shark. I found it dreadful.

The ship's cook crouched and worked in a small shed on deck. Fresh water, taken from mosque wells and brought aboard in skins, sloshed in two wooden tanks into which all hands dipped at will. I would suffer in the months ahead—malaria, dysentery, even a bit of blindness, which was treated by bathing my eyes with human milk from a harem.

My stalwart shipmates were marvels of energy. The amount of singing, chanteying, yelling, grunting, clapping, dancing, and other noise they succeeded in creating would have exhausted most seamen. They were magnificent specimens. Many were deep-chested pearl divers from the Persian Gulf. We had a few freed slaves, huge muscular Negroes. All had been at sea since boyhood. All obeyed orders on the instant, so that *Bayan's* chores were done as efficiently as a liner's.

Paid on shares, the men took an interest in seeing that the vessel made a productive voyage. Each sailor was allowed to bring a chest of his own wares, as in ancient times when a merchant carried his goods and helped sail the ship. These chests, teakwood boxes from Bombay and Malabar, stood ranged around the elevated poop. In them were all manner of cheap manufactured goods bought at Aden for sale to Arab bazaar merchants, Somalis, Swahilis—anyone who would buy.

When there was no work afoot, the sailors loved to crowd up on the poop and examine the treasures in their chests, one man turning out his wares, his friends admiringly pawing them and guessing their price in Mogadishu, Salale, or Lamu. I could visualize Sindbad and his companions doing the same.

O N THE ELEVENTH NIGHT out of Aden we came into Mukalla, a striking place squeezed between mountains and the sea. We shipped 40 Bedouins bound for Somaliland and elsewhere in East Africa. Their women, poor creatures, were bundled into the "great cabin"—a frightful place below the poop, unlit and unventilated. Here 14 pathetic, docile bundles wrapped in black had to stay the next six weeks, with their babies and baggage. They had no comforts save a few datefrond mats.

From Mukalla we went to Ash Shihr, a walled city facing the Arabian Sea. Here 100 more passengers embarked! Some were seasoned travelers, having voyaged as far as Java, Mombasa, Ethiopia, and the Sudan. Others were unsophisticated Bedouins leaving their desert homes for the first time. Gaping at everyone, they never got used to shipboard life. A few became seasick. Their remedies—stuffing paper in nostrils and ears, or sniffing a cut

SPRAWLED IN THE SHADE *of Bayan's sail, mariners catch a daytime snooze. Captain's call will bring them running. Their nighttime bunks are the same: mattress of coir anchor cables, springs of mangrove poles. Cross-legged quartermaster puffs on a water pipe as he steers by compass and by eye. Smart brass binnacle and handsome wheel come from a Bombay junkyard. Short on materials, Arabs buy teak from India, nails anywhere. Shipwrights spurn blueprints, use curved tree trunks for ribs. Dhow is measured not in tons but in date packages it can stow.*

ALAN VILLIERS

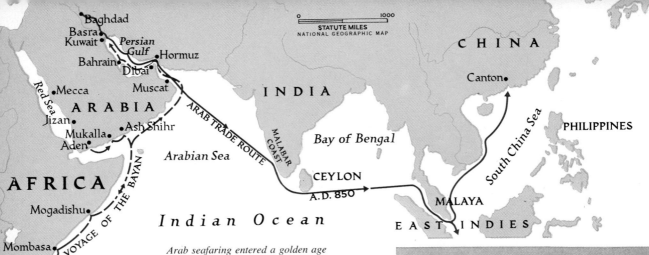

Arab seafaring entered a golden age in the ninth century when the Moslem world centered on Baghdad. Dhows from Basra and other Persian Gulf ports sailed to India, Ceylon, Malaya, the East Indies, even to China. Other vessels coasted Africa along the route Captain Villiers followed in the Bayan.

lemon—failed. There was many a rush to the rail. But they knew how to look after themselves. Each man cooked his evening meal on deck and selected a deck-plank bunk under the stars. An Arab can rest his bones on the space ordinarily occupied by a clothesline.

By night several of the senior passengers would gather by the officers' bench with Nejdi and Hamed, pass around the bubbly pipe, and yarn. In their view, I gathered, Allah had been too lenient with Europeans, whom they considered recent upstarts on the Indian Ocean.

They were a picturesque group, sitting in earnest haggle. I listened to their discourses and noticed that our nakhoda always had the last say. Aboard his boom he was king.

AUTHORITIES AT MOGADISHU, our first large port of call in East Africa, took a dim view of our human cargo. Any immigrant not previously resident in Somaliland must go elsewhere, they declared. From the Bedouins who had exhausted their provisions arose a wail of anguish. But they had to go on to Mombasa, where even the blind beggars were permitted to land. They paid their fare—$2.50 for an 1,800-mile passage.

The voyage to Mombasa was made with a steady wind, and we caught plenty of fish. We were always in sight of the coast, which the captain knew thoroughly. The ship sailed very well. One day, with a fresh monsoon and south-going stream, she made 280 miles. As to navigation, Nejdi said, all he had to do was run down with Africa on his right and then back again with Africa on his left. He knew

A SMALL SAMBUK GLIDES INTO DIBAI HARBOR, *her cargo perhaps a handful of pearls. The tattered sail suffices for the short runs to nearby pearling banks. To change tack, a dhow wears ship—swings its stern to the wind. Sailors haul the yard upright before the mast, pull the sheet around, and shove the foot of the yard to the opposite side. Arabs probably brought the lateen rig to the Mediterranean in the 7th and 8th centuries. On Portuguese ships it served the Age of Discovery.*

the ports by their landmarks. He always knew where he was. His maritime knowledge descended from a line of seafaring ancestors going back hundreds of years.

A day and a night out of Mombasa we put into Zanzibar. Here Nejdi sold the last of the cargo, distributed a few East African shillings to the sailors, and moved ashore.

We stayed at anchorage for weeks while the crew had fun. Maybe they knew our next stop was the dreadful Rufiji River. We were a month in the deltas of that muddy river loading mangrove poles for sale in an Arabia always short of timber. It rained every day. Every mosquito bite was a stab with a red-hot needle; every scratch festered.

The crew worked dreadfully hard cutting poles, and all hands thinned down. When we sailed with full cargo, the exhausted and emaciated sailors thanked Allah.

Back in Zanzibar we loaded coconuts, vermicelli, and big silver coins so prized by the Arabs. Then we hurried northward up the Indian Ocean and across the Arabian Sea to Muscat. In 24 days we were out of sight of land only one day. We sailed with another boom, close together, an idea from the days of piracy.

I'd read how the Arabs sailed south with the northeast monsoon, north with the southwest. But this time Nejdi didn't wait for any southwest monsoon; he feared it would bring bad weather. "We have to be home before that breaks," he told me.

We were. Our cargo was sold in Bahrain and *Bayan* was back in Kuwait by early June. She was rigged down, beached, propped up on stilts, and covered with matting to protect her from the Persian Gulf sun. Thus she would wait for a new date crop to ripen. Meanwhile the southwest monsoon blew itself out in the Indian Ocean hundreds of miles away.

Bayan's voyage took nine months, covered about 10,000 miles, and netted each sailor about $50. I learned something about the ancient lateen sail — a wonderful puller on the wind, a powerful driver before it.

I learned something about Arab sailors, too. When we struggled into port they did not rush off the ship. They sat down and made themselves a cup of coffee. Only later, with dignity and peace of mind, did they go ashore. I liked that.

LIKE GALLEY SLAVES OF OLD, *Persian Gulf pearlers haul on giant sweeps lashed to tholepins. Over the oyster beds (top) divers don noseclips and descend stone-weighted lines as deep as 90 feet. Down 60 seconds or so, they are pulled up clutching their harvests in rope baskets.*
A small boy (right) cools off with a swim; his high-pitched voice relays orders above men's deep-throated chants.

51

CHAPTER SIX

The Chinese junk

Marco Polo recited the wonders of this ship, first in the world with watertight compartments, balanced rudder, and battened sails. Honored for epic voyages of old, it is still going strong.

To ME, the big junk was the shapeliest and most interesting ship in all Singapore Roads that morning. A landsman, or even some sailors, might have thought she looked awkward with her high stern, tilting masts, and ragtag sails.

That's because the junk is so different from the ships we know. But so are Chinese art and architecture different. Independent in ideas and customs, with their civilization flourishing thousands of years ago, the Chinese went their own way, developed their own vessels owing nothing to Europe.

Marco Polo sailed on junks in the 13th century. I can imagine him listening wide-eyed to the singsong chant of the sailors at the windlass, being jostled by gowned merchants who fluttered about their teak chests and their dainty concubines.

There were no ships in Venice to match those great junks—they had crews of 200 to 300, four masts, and sturdy hulls strengthened by two or more layers of planks. Polo marveled that "each of them contains some 50 or 60 cabins, wherein the merchants abide greatly at their ease."

Reading these descriptions I could understand how junks made the wonderful voyages credited to them hundreds of years ago—throughout the

GLIDING ACROSS HONG KONG HARBOR, *a modern junk resembles the upper vessel carved on an 800-year-old Cambodian temple (right). Both show graceful sheer of hull and overhanging stern with rudder slung beneath. In the relief, sailors lower the anchor and trim sheets. Two passengers play chess. Below them, fishermen cast nets and riverboats dodge crocodiles.*

TEMPLE RELIEF AT ANGKOR THOM, W. ROBERT MOORE, NATIONAL GEOGRAPHIC STAFF. OPPOSITE: MELVILLE BELL GROSVENOR

China Seas, to Ceylon, India, Arabia, and the east coast of Africa, where Chinese coins are still dug up occasionally.

Moslem chroniclers report Chinese vessels on the Euphrates in the seventh century. Arab dhows long continued supreme in the Eastern trade, but in time Hormuz in Persia (map, page 48) became a turnaround port for junks as well.

The voyage there was long and tough, probably taking several seasons. The junks had to sail the length of the reef-littered South China Sea (even now not completely surveyed), swing past the pirate-infested Malay Peninsula, slip across the Bay of Bengal and the Arabian Sea to the mouth of the Persian Gulf. The sea-weary Chinese must have made an exotic picture mingling with turbaned Arabs and perhaps darkskinned Africans in flowing robes.

Chinese records speak of 20 days as the average sailing time between Hormuz and the mouths of the Indus, where Karachi stands today. This is not bad going. But then the junk is an able vessel, infinitely maneuverable, sweet in its underwater body no matter how clumsy it may appear above.

That day in Singapore I saw junks swing their way easily through the anchored shipping, spinning in their own lengths as Greek galleys used to do. They had no banks of oars to help them turn. It was the quick, skillful use of their odd-shaped sails at bow and stern that swung them around. The drive of their big, often dirty mainsails brought them bounding in, a wash of white water churning at their blunt bows, a clean wake trailing away past the balanced rudder astern.

BRIAN BRAKE, MAGNUM

PATCHED SAILS BELLYING, *junks from Hong Kong head for the China coast. Bamboo battens simplify reefing. When the halyard is slacked off, lower battens bunch together like slats in a Venetian blind. Each batten is controlled by its own sheet.*

The big junk I visited had sails of patched cotton, flimsy by Western standards. But those battens take up much of the strain, so that until a few years back the Chinese got along quite well with sails of fiber matting. The junk's mainmast was massive and solid. I learned that these great pine trunks are often seasoned by burial in damp earth. Strengthened by iron hoops, they last to a great age and are sometimes festooned with paper scrolls reading "general commanding 10,000 soldiers" and "may this mast scorn the tempest."

A colorful weather vane atop the mast indicates the junk's home district. Sometimes it is the image of a benign rooster. More popular is the fish, a symbol of vigilance because it never closes its eyes. Mirrors adorn these devices to frighten off evil spirits. Streamers of red, blue, and yellow ripple behind.

THE ORIGIN of the junk is lost in the dim past. One ancient scribe wrote that the emperor Fu Hsi, described as the off-spring of a nymph and a rainbow, taught the Chinese to build boats. That was around 4,800 years ago. But for long centuries, we may be sure, the Chinese had only small, flat-bottomed rivercraft, descendants of the raft.

Today's sampan is just such a boat—a skiff shaped like a wedge, sitting on the water like a high-heeled shoe—without a keel, shallow, broadening toward the stern where the gunwales curve upward like a couple of big horns.

Blow up the sampan's lines, add a long cabin built out over the stern, a balanced rudder and a well to house it, masts with battened sails, and you have the junk.

Having developed so satisfactory a vessel for fishing, fighting, and coastal trading, it was only a matter of time before the Chinese sailed farther afield. An expedition is recorded in 219 B.C. to the "Isles of the Blest," apparently Japan. And there is an old tradition—doubted by most scholars—of a junk's being

That balanced rudder is one of the improvements embodied in junks centuries before being "discovered" in Europe. The Chinese simply moved the stock back from the rudder's leading edge, which made it easier to turn. On many junks the rudder is slung from a windlass so that it can be hauled up for shallow water or lowered for stability, like the blade of a centerboard. Captains prefer a long tiller—handy and quick-acting—to a wheel.

The Chinese have a saying about their distinctive battened sail that I like. They claim it resembles a human ear and is "always listening for the wind." Yachtsmen using battens find the phrase apt. Junk sailors lace the bamboo slats to their sails to hold them out stiff and flat. This lets them sail closer to the wind and catch every breath of a breeze.

driven eastward by a storm to a mysterious land called Fu-Sang, possibly California.

During the golden age of the great sea-wandering junks, the 12th to the 15th centuries, there is no reason why they couldn't have sailed around Africa and "discovered" Europe, instead of waiting for Europeans to come the other way. In 1848, just to show it could be done, a junk was sailed from China to England by way of the Cape of Good Hope. She had no particular difficulty on the passage.

THE CHINESE respect for the old, their reverence for the past is reflected in the Code of Malacca, a sea law Marco Polo found them sailing under. It stated: "The captain becomes king when he is at sea. Even if he is young, he must be considered an old man as long as he is head of the vessel."

Old and worthy of respect, the bluff and solid junk stayed on, changing very little. And when the Western powers came knocking at China's door, it couldn't turn them back. Great

war junks, beautifully finished and magnificent in their scarlet and gold decorations, sailed out armed with brass guns, matchlocks, stink-pots, and crude floating mines to battle steam-driven, iron-hulled warships.

In the action at Woosung in 1842 the British ship *Nemesis* was challenged, strangely enough, by several junks propelled by two paddle wheels on each side. After an exchange of volleys, they paddled away at some three knots. *Nemesis* gave chase and boarded. The British officers were amazed to discover that the paddle wheels were turned by men strain-ing at a capstan.

Yet the Chinese might have had the last laugh. *Nemesis* was one of the first Western ships with watertight compartments. Benjamin Franklin had suggested the idea in 1787, point-ing out that a hull divided by watertight bulk-heads would "not be so subject as others to founder and sink at sea." He admitted his plan was "after the Chinese manner."

The Chinese, you see, were already building watertight bulkheads into their great ocean-going junks when Europeans were still coast-ing in cockleshells.

HEAVE AWAY! *Nine pairs of hands, even a few feet, turn a junk's windlass to haul in a fishing trawl (below). Bushels of the silvery catch are tossed aboard with dip nets (left). Then crew members sort the fish, icing the choice species and salting down others.*

On China's teeming waters John Scofield visits the people of the sampan

IN HONG KONG, where 2,400 people may jam together in an acre of two-story tenements, even the harbor is crowded. Thousands of Chinese families spill out onto the waters of this tiny British crown colony, creating floating communities with stores, schools, even "city halls"—big blue houseboats that can be rented for weddings and celebrations. Lavish floating restaurants provide a touch of splendor and a livelihood for swarms of water taxis that shuttle diners to and from shore.

One rainy morning I hired a water taxi—a 13-foot craft propelled by a long oar—to take me out into the bewildering crush of sampans and junks moored within the curving arms of a typhoon shelter (right). Here, relatively safe from the storms that sometimes smash hundreds of boats in unprotected anchorages, live the *Tanka,* the water folk.

At a boatyard nestled amid a forest of masts I watched shipwrights building a sampan. Beside them were piled boards of teak and *cha ma* —a light-colored, mahoganylike wood. Construction, they told me, had started on a day selected by a soothsayer; no Tanka would buy a boat whose keel had been laid on an unlucky day. Launching would require the burning of candles and incense sticks and the lighting of firecrackers. The craft would last 15 to 20 years if its owners took care of it.

Passing a jaunty yacht built along the lines of a junk, my aquatic taxi threaded deeper into the maze of vessels. I found myself lulled by the shuffle of the woman's feet—two steps forward, two steps back—as she monotonously swung the long sculling oar. I was jolted awake as we hit another blue-canopied sampan.

A fortunate collision. I exchanged smiles with the woman in the other boat. Behind her a child's head appeared for a moment. Here was one of the thousands of sampans on which whole families live.

Friendly, 26-year-old Chou Un Lui invited me aboard her tiny craft, where she kept house for a family of six. Four children clustered around her as she tended a charcoal fire beneath a clay brazier. She showed me the meal: rice garnished with three tiny, jewel-like fish that retained their bright pink and yellow stripes even when cooked. Behind her a joss stick burned fragrantly at a little red shrine dedicated to Tien Hau, the sea goddess.

Some of the old women among the water people boast that they have spent their entire lives afloat. I asked Chou Un Lui how often she went ashore.

"Perhaps twice a week," she said. Her expression told me that this was at least once too often. "But I can buy rice and vegetables a little cheaper there than from the hawkers who sell food from their boats."

Her husband works aboard a "walla walla" —a harbor launch—and brings home 36 cents a day. "It is only half what we need to live on," she said without bitterness. "I earn the rest operating the sampan as a water taxi."

Her eldest child, a boy of about ten, grinned impishly at me. I asked if he went to school, and a hint of sadness crossed her face.

"How can we afford it? Even in the mission school"—she pointed toward a squat houseboat—"tuition for each child would cost five days of my husband's pay each month."

Inside the school I talked with missionary Grace White of Seattle, who had spent six years among the water people of Hong Kong, many of them refugees from their Communist homeland. This floating suburb has three schools and two clinics, she told me. Shops circulate among the moored craft, and a boatman delivers two five-gallon cans of fresh water for a penny.

People of the sampan traditionally keep to themselves, guarding their conservative ways. But slowly life is changing for the Tanka. Some now learn to read, Miss White told me. Not that they want to, but they plan to install engines in their fishing boats, and to get a license they must be able to read.

58

THOUSANDS LIVE AFLOAT *in crammed cities like Hong Kong. Woman (left) drives a sampan taxi.*

CHAPTER SEVEN

Vikings and longships, scourge of northern seas

Not for the sheltered Mediterranean was the swift Norse ship built, but for rocky fjords and stormy seas. With it the Vikings struck Europe's coasts, seized half of England, thrust deep into Russia, and drove westward to America. Captain Villiers sings the saga of their brazen exploits.

FROM THE FURY OF THE NORTHMEN, good Lord deliver us!" Time and again that prayer rose from the despairing people of western Europe as square-sailed, high-prowed longships came rushing at the beaches or sweeping up the rivers.

For two centuries the chronicles of France and England are filled with mourning at the devastation spread by Viking marauders. Described as flinging babies from spear to spear for sport, they razed monasteries, ripped defenseless villages apart. Near the close of the ninth century, wherever these sea raiders struck, there was no road "which was not littered with dead, including priests, women, and children... it seemed that all Christian people would perish."

Who were these wild men of rugged stature and barbaric ways? Whence did they come?

They were Scandinavians. *Vik* in old Norse means "fjord"; *ing* means "son of"—a Viking was a son of the fjords. His home was a harsh land of high mountains and deep inlets where the readiest means of transport was by water. It was a largely unproductive land, offering little to its ambitious warrior sons. So it was natural they should turn to the sea.

Young chieftains coming of age were assigned longships so they could prove their fitness to lead; overpopulation provided the followers. What better way to make one's fortune than to raid England's farmlands across the North Sea, or sack a port on the continent?

Sea roving like this demanded the swiftest and sturdiest of ships. Savage storms swept the North Sea and battered Norway's rockbound coasts. If caught away from a haven, ships had to stay at sea to survive; they could seldom be beached.

And swift and sturdy ships the sea rovers had, for the Vikings were the best naval architects of their day. Thanks to those chieftains whose ships were buried with them, we know a good deal about their craft. Two especially fine vessels have been dug from grave mounds at the Gokstad and Oseberg farms in Norway. Both date from the ninth century and are preserved in Oslo's Viking Ship Hall.

Far earlier is the famed Nydam boat, dug out of a bog in Jutland and now in a museum in

RIDING THE STORM, *Viking raiders speed toward glory and booty. Helmsman keeps the undecked craft stern-to, lest she broach. Shields are slung outboard ready for attack. In such a ship sailed fierce Sweyn Forkbeard, son of Harald Bluetooth.*

HERVEY GARRETT SMITH

HERVEY GARRETT SMITH

Schleswig, Germany. Dating from the early fourth century, it is 76 feet long with an 11-foot beam. Oddly enough it apparently had been scuttled, for holes were slashed in it, and bundles of loot lay nearby. You can almost see the burly raiders, hotly pursued, tossing the plunder overboard, then sinking their ship. They preferred to die by their own hand rather than give their enemies the satisfaction of capturing and killing them.

ALL THREE VESSELS are long, shallow double-enders. Unlike the carvel-built Mediterranean and Indian Ocean vessels, whose planks are fitted edge to edge over a frame with caulking in between, Norse ships were clinker-built of overlapped planks. This allowed more caulking to be tucked into the joints and made hulls tighter. Shipwrights adzed the planks out of logs, leaving a cleat at intervals. Then light ribs were inserted and lashed to the cleats with withes.

SHIPS FROM THE VIKING AGE *sailed into modern times from Norway's blue clay. The Oseberg ship (above), dug from a royal burial mound in 1904, had a pine mast and 15 pairs of oars. Probably a pleasure craft for sailing the fjords, she measures 70 feet. The sturdier, seagoing Gokstad ship, excavated in 1880 and restored (right), extends only 76, though scholars say longships reached 100 feet and more. Supple as a serpent, she shows the sweeping bow that cleaved heavy seas.*

Figureheads, carved like the Oseberg animal-head post at left, were removed near shore so as not to frighten friendly land spirits.

A Viking ship had only a single bank of oars, for its sail was used more than the sail in a Mediterranean galley. It was strongly sewn and often beautifully decorated by Viking women. The yard, though swung athwartships in the manner of square-rigged vessels, could be braced quickly to the fore-and-aft line.

Such ships could sail close to the wind, but their shallow draft and lack of a deep keel might cause them to make considerable leeway. They were steered with a deep oar fastened to the starboard quarter. With a 40-inch tiller one man could turn the blade easily in the roughest seas.

An awning in the forepart of the ship sheltered the fighting men on the longer passages. The sailors slept in leather sleeping bags and kept their weapons handy beneath the thwarts from which they rowed. They took along bronze cooking pots, but prepared their meals ashore whenever possible because of the danger from fires aboard.

At the time of the Chicago World's Fair of 1893, a replica of the Gokstad ship was built in Norway and sailed across the North Atlantic. She was constructed, rigged, manned, and handled just as her long-buried predecessor might have been on such a voyage, except that the replica sailed a harder way. No calls at Iceland, no rest at any Greenland haven for her.

Under Capt. Magnus Andersen she sailed from near Bergen to St. John's, Newfoundland. She had no escort. She was never towed or rowed. She took 27 days and despite bad weather behaved excellently. She could do 10, sometimes 11 knots. The big sail proved not only efficient but tractable.

Captain Andersen reported the wooden ship remarkably tight, even in storms. As in the original, construction was not rigid. In a big sea the whole hull worked. The gunwale would twist half a foot out of line, and frequently the crew saw the bottom rise nearly an inch, like the chest of a breathing whale. But the plank-

GOKSTAD SHIP AND OSEBERG CARVING (FAR LEFT) IN OSLO'S VIKING SHIP HALL; NORWEGIAN INFORMATION SERVICE. LEFT: UNIVERSITETETS OLDSAKSAMLING, OSLO.

ing let in no sea. The ship's elasticity was part of her strength.

I was looking at her the other day, preserved in Chicago's Lincoln Park. I looked and I marveled. She seemed so frail a vessel to bring across the North Atlantic. What seamen those old Vikings must have been!

They probably knew little about finding their position or following a precise course. But they knew the sun and stars, the tides and ocean currents. Above all, they knew their

ships and how they performed in various winds. They observed the migratory flights of birds and like them ventured forth in the spring. At the autumnal equinox they brought their ships home and put them ashore under winter covers.

Vikings gave their ships loving care and called them "Snake of the Sea," "Raven of the Wind," "Lion of the Waves," and other poetic names. Even their sails bore names like "Cloak of the Wind" and "Mastheaded Tapestry." No temple meant more to an ancient Greek

Northmen swept out of Scandinavia in the ninth century to attack Nantes (843), Lisbon and Cádiz (844), Hamburg and Paris (845), London (c.850), and Pisa (860). They settled Dublin in Ireland, Novgorod and Kiev in Russia. From Iceland, reached in 874, they ranged to Greenland, North America, and finally Spitsbergen.

WILLIAM THE CONQUEROR, *Duke of Normandy, invaded England in ships like those of his Viking forebears. Some 700 transports sailed the English Channel on a September night in 1066 and landed unopposed next morning. Stepping ashore, William stumbled and fell, the story goes. Clutching the soil, he cried, "I have taken England with both my hands."*

The Bayeux Tapestry records the conquest. This 231-foot pageant in linen was probably embroidered in the 11th century. It shows William's flagship Mora *(left) bearing a masthead signal lantern topped with a cross blessed by the Pope. Below, the Norman army embarks and crosses the Channel; horses leap ashore at Pevensey while mariners unstep a mast; knights ride off to Hastings and victory.*

than the longship to the Viking. It signified manhood, adventure, self-respect, the very hope of eternity. In it the Viking sought to achieve his goals: perpetuation of his memory by a heroic feat, and the piling up of plunder. The more wealth he took to the next world, the greater his happiness there.

The *Havamal*, a poem based on the wisdom of Odin, god of war, offered advice: "A man who wishes to despoil others of their lives and goods must be up betimes. A loafing wolf never gets fat, a sleeping man never wins a battle."

Physical courage was the highest virtue and death in battle the passport to paradise. Valkyries, maidens sent by Odin, selected warriors to be slain for Valhalla. There in the glittering, shield-roofed palace they would feast and sport in daily combat until Doomsday. Little wonder the Vikings were fearless!

"What do you think now of death?" asked Thorkel Leira, putting captured countrymen to the ax after a sea battle.

COMBIER, COURTESY MUNICIPALITÉ DE BAYEUX

"What happened to my father must happen to me," one replied. "He died. So must I."

Another asked that he be beheaded from the front, so all could observe that he did not flinch nor even close his eyes.

Nor did he.

The Danish king Sweyn Forkbeard was typical of Viking leaders. He exulted in the sea life. He could handle the largest ship as a skillful rider might handle a spirited horse. He liked to run along the oars outboard while they flashed through the water. He liked to juggle three javelins, flinging them to the masthead. Half mad with battle intoxication, the *berserkr* Sweyn would stand in the prow, roaring a war song to his crew, infecting them with his fearlessness, driving them berserk also.

THESE WERE THE MEN who ravaged every coast of Europe and braved the trackless sea. As in ancient times, raiding and trading and settling often went hand in hand. Northmen invaded Ireland and settled Dublin. They sailed up the Seine to beyond the walls of Paris; settled Normandy (which derives its name from the Northmen); pushed up the Elbe and burned Hamburg; struck London, Nantes, Lisbon, Cádiz; penetrated the Mediterranean and pillaged Pisa.

They colonized the Orkney, Shetland, and Faeroe Islands; settled Iceland and Greenland; doubled the North Cape to the White Sea; discovered Spitsbergen.

More intent on trading than raiding, Swedish Vikings called Varangians swept out of the Baltic through the Russian rivers and opened routes of commerce to the Black and Caspian seas. Rurik the Varangian is said to have founded at Novgorod in 862 what later became the Russian empire. Others settled Kiev; some got as far as Constantinople, where they served as exotic, fair-haired bodyguards to the Byzantine emperor. In the Dardanelles, a Norse saga says, Sigurd the King waited many days "for a side wind that his sails might be set fore-and-aft," the better to show off their colorings in purple and gold.

Later, a Norman named Roger Guiscard wrested Sicily from the Saracens and set up a kingdom—this at a time when the western Mediterranean was a Moslem lake and only descendants of the Vikings stood up to the Saracen ships there.

Meanwhile, seamanship and chance had carried the Vikings to North America. Bjarni Herjulfson, who went off course sailing from Iceland to Greenland in 986, may have sighted the continent.

Leif Ericson bought Bjarni's boat and sailed from Greenland, searching fogbound waters for the coast Bjarni had reported. He found a wild, rocky shore and landed at "Wineland" or "Vinland the Good," where an abundance of grapes grew. Then he returned home.

Other groups voyaged to Wineland, one led by Thorfinn Karlsefni, who took some 160 men and stayed several years. While there his wife bore him a son, Snorri, first child of European parentage born in America. Constantly harassed by the *skraelings* (Indians), Thorfinn finally gave up and went back to Iceland.

So sing the sagas, and sagas though hard to follow are not imaginary. To a seaman the voyages to America are easy to accept. They follow naturally the runs to Iceland and Greenland. In those high latitudes there is plenty of easterly wind, and from Greenland to Labrador is no great distance. One week at sea could well have fetched a landfall. Off Labrador the pioneers could catch a south-setting current to help them down the eastern seaboard at least as far as Cape Cod.

These voyages represent the ultimate in Viking daring and exploration. But the Northmen made other contributions even more important. Where they settled they developed a tradition for government based on a respect for the law and a rough kind of democracy. In England the Danes of East Anglia were a model for their Saxon neighbors. Normandy became the best-run part of France.

A Norman descendant of the Viking Rollo, William the Conqueror, taught England the importance of sea power when he invaded in 1066—a lesson the English would never forget. And the wondrous longships left a priceless legacy to the vessels that would follow their wakes through the cold northern waters.

DRAGON SHIP BREATHES FIRE *as Shetland islanders put it to the torch. This winter festival echoes a funeral rite of their Viking forebears. Hand atop pole commemorates valor of a fabled sea raider. Racing another ship, he hacked off his left hand and hurled it ashore to win first right to plunder.*

CHAPTER EIGHT

Medieval mariners and the ships they built

As trade grew in northern Europe so did the vessels to carry it. Single-masters evolved into slow but sturdy three-masters with castles at bow and stern. Fat with cargoes, they bobbed from port to port, even carrying a few miserable passengers. The compass and a maritime code make their debut.

GEOFFREY CHAUCER, poet, customs official, and envoy of the king, steps aboard the little vessel lying in the Thames and prepares for the worst. He has voyaged before and holds no illusions about shipboard travel in the Lord's Year 1378.

Pulling his hooded cloak about him until only his straight nose and forked beard can be seen, he settles himself on the sterncastle and watches the crew set to work.

The master commands his shipmen in all haste to line up about the mast, relates a contemporary chronicle. "Ho! Hoist now!" they cry. A boy or two climb up and lie overthwart the yard. "Yo ho! Tally there!" the shipmen bellow, and pull with all their might.

Haul the bowline! Now veer the sheet!
Yo ho! Furl 'em! Haul in the brails!
Oh, see how well our good ship sails!

Passengers lie with their bowls beside them and cry for hot wine to restore their calm. Then comes the ship's owner like a lord. "A sack of straw there," he shouts. For some have only their cloaks to bed on.

The sterncastle might be clean and airy, but the passenger deck is something else. They sleep packed close together. Below sloshes the foul bilge water: "A man might just as well be dead as smell thereof the stink."

Seasickness is as common as sympathy is rare. "Rush to the rail. Hope not for a charitable hand to hold thy head, for all near split themselves with laughter," lamented a bishop.

The medieval mariner ran no Cunard Line, certainly, but the important thing was that commerce had been growing and coastal shipping was on a regular and peaceful basis. The shipman of Chaucer's *Canterbury Tales*, with his sea-tanned face and gale-blown beard, had every chance to know

> *. . . alle the havens, as they were,*
> *From Gotland to the cape of Finistere,*
> *And every creke in Bretagne and in Spaine.*

All summer long the English Channel, the Bay of Biscay, and the Baltic were flecked with the white sails of ships. Tubby little single-masters waddled forth from ports like Dover, Bordeaux, Antwerp, Visby, Bremen. Up from the Mediterranean came fleets of great galleys on their annual trading voyages.

A chronicler gives us a glimpse of some of their cargoes: "The Pisans, Genoese, and Venetians supply England with the Eastern gems, as sapphires, emeralds, and carbuncles. From Asia was brought the rich silks and purples; from Africa the cinnamon and balm; from Spain the kingdom was enriched with gold; with silver from Germany; from Flanders

CASTLES AND FIGHTING TOP *adorn a 13th century round ship flying the golden lions of England. Bowsprit, stouter rigging, and roomier, decked hull for cargo mark progress over her Viking predecessor. Masthead banner heralds the lord warden of the Cinque Ports, towns in Sussex and Kent that supplied ships to the king in return for privileges. Seal of Dover, enlarged in background, authenticates the model.*

69

came the rich materials for the garments of the people, while plentiful streams of wine flowed from their own province of Gascoigny...."

Commerce in the Mediterranean lay in the hands of aggressive Italian city-states, but in northern Europe the Hanseatic League dominated. Led by German commercial cities like Lübeck, Hamburg, and Cologne, the League grew so strong that it negotiated treaties of state, waged war (twice defeating Denmark), and even governed Stockholm for a time as a sort of early-day United Nations.

It established trading compounds in cities as far apart as Novgorod, Bergen, and Bruges. Chaucer knew the stout burghers of its London colony, the Steelyard. They led monastic lives dedicated to trade.

The League's ships, called cogs and hulks, sailed from port to port loading English wool, Flemish cloth, Russian fur, Swedish iron, Biscay salt. But their most important commodity was the humble herring.

Caught in the Baltic Sea off the coast of southern Sweden, salted and packed in spruce barrels, the herring was a staple of meat-poor Europe. When the great shoals vanished from the Baltic in the 16th century, perhaps because of a decline in its salinity, the power of the Hanseatic League waned.

The League was a tightfisted monopoly, yet it made its contributions. It demonstrated the benefits of a well-regulated commerce, and its demands for more and more cargo space spurred improvements in ship design.

CHANGE HAD COME SLOWLY; those old sea dogs were a conservative lot. The early merchant vessel of northern Europe had been simply a plump cousin of the Viking ship, minus the oars. It was double-ended, had the same single mast and sail, the same steering oar on the quarter.

In time the wooden fighting castles tacked on fore and aft became permanent parts of the ship. The officers had their cabins in the sterncastle; from its elevated deck they could view the entire ship. Builders began to shape the stern to accommodate the rudder there. Now even a landsman could tell bow from stern.

As ships grew bigger, there had to be more masts, more sails. A giant single sail was too heavy and awkward to handle. "Yo ho, hoist!" was the only power. So, as the Chinese had done countless years before, the Europeans added masts at bow and stern. They also built a spar out from the bow to carry a spritsail like the old Roman artemon. Hulls were made deeper, the better to grip the sea; sturdier, to take increased sails and cargo. Planking, no longer overlapped as in the light Viking ships, became a smooth skin over a heavy frame.

The result was a slow, clumsy-looking, but basically sound sailing ship—the "Model T" version of the great windjammers.

The medieval mariner took other great strides. He formulated codes of the sea. To settle maritime disputes and fix responsibility in mishaps, the Laws of Oléron (named for a French island) were widely adopted. A pilot who lost a ship through carelessness or ignorance had to give financial satisfaction or lose his head. Ships had to mark their anchors with buoys to prevent fouled moorings. When a shift in the wind gave a weather-bound shipmaster an opportunity to sail, he had to assemble his crew and ask, "Gentlemen, what think ye of this wind?" If they thought it an ill wind the ship was not to sail.

Mariners began to use the compass. No one knows who invented it, but we do know that at first it was just a magnetized needle stuck into a cork that floated in a bowl of water.

The pilot used a little abracadabra when he magnetized the needle. With the grizzled sailors gathered around, he would remove his lodestone from its little cask and hold it close to the edge of the bowl. As the floating needle swung toward the stone, he would move the stone around the bowl—faster and faster until the needle was spinning. Then he would jerk the stone away. The needle would slowly come to rest pointing north-south. The sailors would shake their heads in amazement. All agreed this was the best way to magnetize a needle.

With the compass the mariner divided his horizon into 32 directions or "rhumbs of the wind." He drew rhumb lines on his charts (page 78), and the helmsman followed them rigidly when out of sight of land. Beside him stood the patient pilot: "Nor do they ever turn their eyes away. One always gazes at the compass and chants a sweet song which shows that all goes well...." If they wandered off course through compass error it was too bad—they had no way to check their position.

The medieval mariner made considerable progress in man's struggle to use the sea. But the greatest change was to come in himself. Not much longer would he be content to sail only the well-beaten paths.

SWORDS CLANG, ARROWS WHISTLE *as French and English fleets clash during the Hundred Years' War. Round ships doubled for trading and fighting. Grapneled together, they formed battlefields for charging men-at-arms. Topmen hurled spears. If a knight in armor fell overboard, he sank like an iron stove. Here at Sluis in Flanders in 1340, England's Edward III took or sank 166 ships, inflicted 25,000 casualties, opened way to invade France.*

FLEMISH MERCHANTMAN *(left) sprouts light fore- and mizzenmasts that developed during the 15th century. Soon these will grow and shift more amidships. The rudder has moved to the stern.*

SHIPWRECKED MARINERS *build a vessel. Sawyers cut a log to brace the timbers; a lad drives trenails into the stern frame while a crouching adz man shapes the keelson. Planks at water's edge will cover the ribs; pitch bubbling in caldron will seal the seams. Shipwrights worked by eye, following traditional models, or copying lines of sweet-sailing vessels they had known.*

HANSEATIC TRADER, *sturdy as the Gothic buildings of Visby, takes a tow into the prosperous Gotland port. Fenders strengthen her hull; channels hold shrouds outboard; early topsail crowns her mainmast.*

ENGRAVING BY THEODORE DE BRY, 1594, LIBRARY OF CONGRESS

72

ADMIRAL J. HÄGG, COURTESY ANGFARTYGSAKTIEBOLAGET, GOTLAND

Development of the anchor and rudder

THE *early mariner anchored his craft with a stone. He simply tied a line to it and tossed it overboard. But stones slide, so he added arms to bite bottom and hold fast.*

By the time of Christ the traditional shape had evolved. A wooden and an iron anchor dug up with Emperor Caligula's barges in Italy have stocks set at 90° angles from arms. They brace anchor, keep dug-in arm from twisting out.

Arrowhead-shaped palms of Nelson's day gave firmer grip. Hinged palms of the stockless anchor burrow in as cable drags it along.

Steering evolved in a similar manner. Egyptians used two oars, turned with tillers. Angle of blades determined ship's course. Vikings used a single oar on starboard (steerboard) side. But rolling of ship might lift oar from water.

A stern rudder, hinged on center line and presenting greater surface, gripped better, turned ship faster. When added decks buried the helmsman, the whipstaff enabled him to swing tiller by remote control. Block and tackle rig smoothed the action and multiplied his power. Still it took lots of brawn to manhandle a windjammer's wheel in a gale. Motors now turn rudders.

73

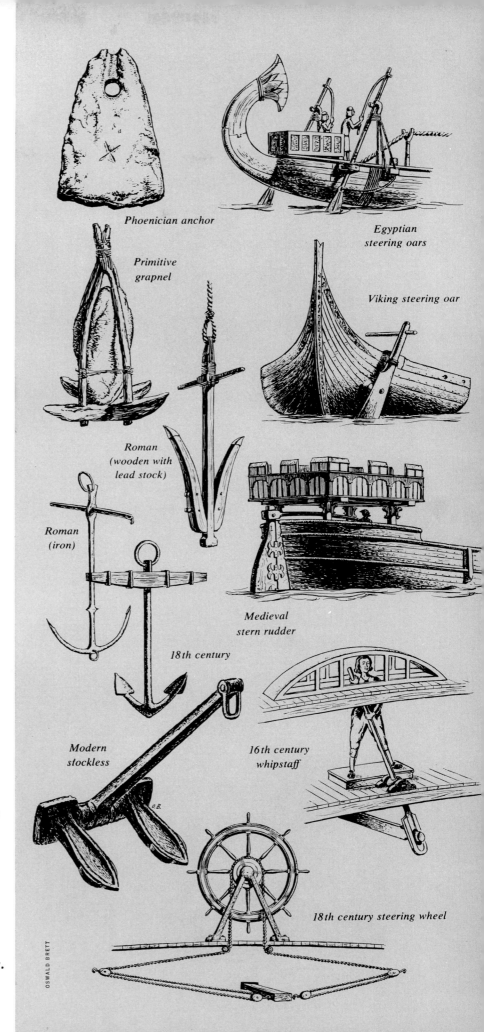

Phoenician anchor

Egyptian steering oars

Primitive grapnel

Viking steering oar

Roman (wooden with lead stock)

Roman (iron)

Medieval stern rudder

18th century

Modern stockless

16th century whipstaff

18th century steering wheel

OSWALD BRETT

HE DIS-
COVERS
NEW
WORLDS

PORTUGUESE GALLEONS, SCHOOL OF JOACHIM PATINIR, 1485-1524, NATIONAL MARITIME MUSEUM, GREENWICH, ENGLAND. ASTROLABE, 1603, USED BY FRENCH EXPLORER SAMUEL DE CHAMPLAIN, NEW YORK HISTORICAL SOCIETY

T HERE is no land unhabitable, nor Sea innavigable." Bold words these of Robert Thorne, an Englishman of the Renaissance. But why not? His age surged with commerce and learning. It saw Dias sail to the end of the Dark Continent, Da Gama push through forbidden seas to the Indies, Columbus discover what man had not dreamed of—a new continent!

Marco Polo and other overland travelers had kindled Europe's fascination  with the East. They told of precious stones and "all kinds of spicery," of "Idolaters who go all naked," and of Cathay's great walled cities and gorgeous palaces "all painted in gold."

The West yearned to tap these fabled riches. Yet the way was not known, ships were too weak, men too timid. To break down these barriers there would come a prince of Portugal who brooded and labored on a windswept promontory where Europe faces only the endless sea.

CHAPTER NINE

Henry the Navigator, prince of explorers

Though a king's son, he lived like a recluse, studying the stars and sea and training others in his knowledge. His captains probed dark regions, dispelled superstitious fear with geographic fact. Alan Villiers relates the deeds of the stay-at-home explorer who fathered the Age of Discovery.

ATLANTIC STORMS blow hard on somber Sagres Point. Seas crash into arching caverns and low caves and shatter in a smother of spray. Winds lash the rock. Plants seem to cower, never higher than a foot. When you stand as I have here at the southwest tip of Europe, the muffled growling of the sea's anger is endless in your ears.

Beyond this Portuguese promontory you see liners, tankers, and freighters pitching in a constant line, northbound and south. They are silent ships, heavy laden. At a certain distance from nearby Cape St. Vincent they turn, seemingly of their own volition, as if they had no crews—as if voyages to the ends of the earth had become so commonplace that ships may sail untended.

When you look seaward from this bleak point your thoughts turn as effortlessly as those great steel ships, back to the days of the 15th century when the wild Atlantic was a sea of mystery, and there were no real ocean-going ships, no daring mariners to venture far beyond sight of land. For at Sagres lived the man who changed all that, who first coaxed cautious Europe onto the broad highway of the sea. It

was here that the prince called Henry the Navigator lived and worked 500 years ago.

He was born in Pôrto, namesake of the nation and the wine, in 1394, fourth son of

HUGE COMPASS ROSE, *laid in stones, remains from the*

THOMAS NEBBIA, NATIONAL GEOGRAPHIC PHOTOGRAPHER

76

King John I and his English queen. At 21 he led Portugal's knights against the Moorish stronghold of Ceuta in nearby North Africa. Given the southern province of Portugal called the Algarve, Henry, still in his twenties, retired there to a simple retreat at Sagres.

Azurara, his chronicler, saw him "big and strong of limb, his hair . . . of a color naturally fair, but which by constant toil and exposure had become dark. His expression at first sight inspired fear in those who did not know him, and when wroth, though such times were rare, his countenance was harsh.

"Strength of heart and keenness of mind were in him to a very excellent degree, and beyond comparison, he was ambitious of achieving great and lofty deeds. . . . All his days were passed in the greatest toil . . . his palace was a school of hospitality for all the good and high-born of the realm, and still more for strangers."

Henry never married or took his regular place at court. He did not sail to strange places, discovered nothing, left few records beyond the stones of Sagres. Yet this brooding prince lit and sustained the flame of discovery, changing the thinking and the shape of the world.

Henry's world was small: a medieval Christian enclave huddled on that neck of Asia known as Europe, imprisoned by a Moslem empire that stretched from the Middle East to Gibraltar and by superstitions that shackled the mind. Ships were too frail to challenge the open oceans; men were afraid to try.

But Europe was awakening; the force known as the Renaissance was stirring. Horizons of the mind were retreating before a revival of classical learning and bold ventures in science and art. Horizons of the earth would be pushed back by Prince Henry's ships.

Another force was the hunger for spices. Europe's drab diet offered few vegetables, few fruits, little sugar, no tea, coffee, or chocolate. Fresh meat was scarce in winter; animals were butchered in the fall for lack of fodder. Pungent flavorings would enliven this fare and conceal meat's putridity. Spices also "cured" many ills, were extolled as aphrodisiacs, sought for balms, and incense, and perfumes.

But their cost was nearly prohibitive. Nutmeg or cloves, worth little in their native East Indies, traveled a tortuous and costly road to Europe. Malay and Hindu merchants shipped them to India. From there the Arab monopoly brought them to the Persian Gulf or Red Sea, then put them on camel caravans to Alexandria or Beirut. Stowed aboard Genoese and Venetian ships, they traveled to these city-

days when the Prince and his men plotted bold voyages at Sagres.   **HENRY:** *"a stern master to himself."*

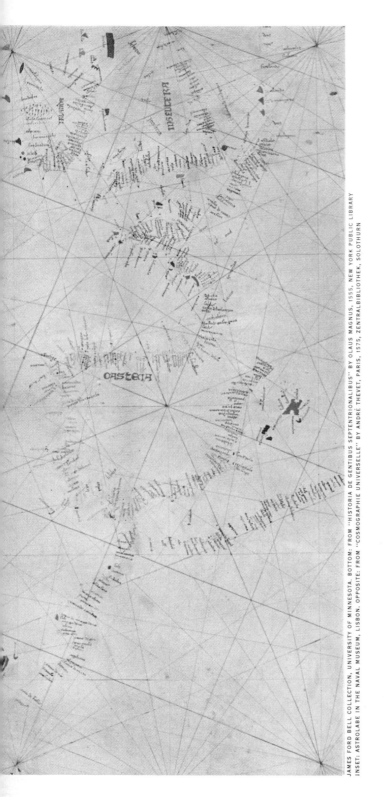

Mariners found a compass in the sky

N° one knows when the sailor quit crawling from headland to headland and braved open water with only the stars to guide him. Homer tells how Odysseus "spread his sail to catch the wind and . . . never closed his eyes in sleep, but kept them on the Pleiades, or watched the late-setting Boötes and the Great Bear." Taught by Phoenicians, Greeks sailed by the Lesser Bear, measuring star altitude against the rigging or by the width of the hand.

Astronomers helped. Hipparchus and Ptolemy cataloged stars and divided the globe into latitudes and longitudes. This knowledge was lost to the West in the Dark Ages but regained after A.D. 1000 from the Arabs.

In 1409 Ptolemy's Geography was translated into Latin. Soon Prince Henry's captains, swallowing their fear of sea monsters (below), charted the unknown with the astronomer's quadrant, a wedge-shaped device with a plumb line falling across a scale of degrees. Like the ancient astrolabe (inset) and later cross-staff, seen in the woodcut at right, it was sighted at sun or star, and the angle above the horizon read from it. Celestial tables gave the observer his north-south position or latitude.

Rolling decks made readings inaccurate; errors of a hundred miles were common. But these would be reduced with the coming of precise instruments—the octant and sextant.

HAVEN-FINDING CHARTS *showed medieval navigators the way along familiar coasts. From compilations of sailing directions the face of Europe and North Africa emerged. This portolan chart of 1424 gives compass courses along a gridiron of rhumb lines.*

states and from there were distributed to the markets of Europe. Each handler took a profit. Costs pyramided to a price that only the rich could afford. The Moslem belt around southern Europe shrouded this spice trade in mystery and guarded it with the sword.

ONLY ON THE SEA could Prince Henry outflank Islam and break the Arab stranglehold on Europe. But his purposes were manifold: not only to extend Portuguese trade and power but to increase geographical knowledge and spread Christianity. He hoped, too, to make contact with Prester John, legendary Christian king whose fabled realm lay somewhere to the east.

The Prince's plan was to push ships down the west coast of Africa and chart the unknown. In time his captains must reach the Indian Ocean, gateway to the empires of the Orient.

Others had dreamed of this. More than a century before the Prince was born, two Genoese ships had sailed through the Strait of Gibraltar and headed south, "that they might go by sea to the ports of India." That was the last ever heard of them. Seamen—conservative, fearful, accustomed to heavy losses even on short voyages—knew of these disasters. They respected the sea.

Prince Henry had to work a revolution. The first step was to improve navigation. Navigating by guess and by eye would not get ships far into the unknown.

Medieval Europeans knew only piloting—sailing within sight of land—and "dead" (deduced) reckoning. This is a way of determining a ship's position by noting compass course, speed, elapsed time, "drift" from wind, "set" from current. Masters achieved surprising accuracy by dead reckoning, but they avoided long voyages over open sea. Where they could not coast, they did not go.

Knowledge of coasts and ports and harbors, of landfalls, departures, distances, and courses was a personal matter, the stock in trade not of mates and masters but of individual pilots who had painfully attained it and preserved it in closely guarded manuscript books.

At Sagres the Prince assembled mathema-ticians, chart makers, astronomers, pilots, master mariners, students, and chroniclers of voyages. They came, made their contributions, and left: Portuguese, Spaniards, Jews, Arabs, Italians. At this first navigational school in Europe they helped Henry create better charts, improve such shipboard instruments as the compass, astrolabe, and quadrant, and compile more detailed astronomical tables.

Other men worked under Henry's supervision to improve the design of ships. The simple square-rigged vessels of the day—round-bellied cargo carriers often with just one big sail—would not do. Before a favorable wind they managed to get somewhere, sooner or later as the Lord willed. But they were of little use when continuously working to windward.

The Arabs had a good, fast design: the lithe dhow with its lateen sails. It was able and weatherly but also weak; ideal to sail before the gentle monsoon winds but no ship for the storm-tossed western sea. Why not combine the best of the two types of ships? This was done in the Portuguese caravel.

There is evidence that the Prince's coterie designed the caravel. It is certain that his yards at the port of Lagos, near Sagres, built them. Strong European hulls capable of stowing ample stores supported two or three masts with fore-and-aft lateen rig.

Larger caravels often had a big square sail and topsail on the foremast for driving before the wind. Two more masts carried the lateen sails, good off the wind or tacking against it. About 100 to 200 tons, comparatively cheap to rig and man, caravels gave Prince Henry's mariners more range, speed, and maneuverability than any seamen had previously enjoyed.

You may still see, as I have seen, fishing craft being built the time-honored way in Portugal: the great trees sawed into stout logs in medieval sawpits, the swinging adz skillfully used either as an ax or a plane, the shape of the ship growing strong and fast and beautiful from a pile of wood.

Prince Henry built them thus. And he had no problem about where to sail them. At his door lay a whole world of water. What waited

TUBBY FISHING CRAFT, *gear aboard, park on rollers in the street when storms lash the Nazaré beach. When weather clears they are launched through the pounding surf. For centuries tough fishermen from Portuguese towns like this have wrested a living from the open Atlantic. Among them Prince Henry recruited his crews.*

beyond that tumbling gray sea stretching westward from Sagres? Stories abounded of lost lands, mysterious islands. Legendary, perhaps, but consistently named on charts: St. Brendan's Isle, an ill-defined place called Brazil (no connection with the real Brazil, then undiscovered), a group of islands called Antillia.

From Lagos out into the Atlantic went the Prince's first explorers to see for themselves. In 1420 two of them brought back exciting news. A storm had driven them on to the Madeiras. Henry sent colonists and some Malmsey grapes from Crete. Soon lush vineyards draped the isles.

By 1432 his emboldened seafarers had reached the Azores, a thousand miles over the western sea. But beyond lay only an endless stretch of water harassed by great storms, with wind and current mainly from the west. The way to the Indies certainly did not lie there. No, the way would open after constant, searching voyages south along Africa. Prince Henry sent his ships that way—ship after ship.

It was slow going. Seamen were superstitious; the sea was unknown to them and its imagined dangers seemed very real. Medieval scholars had written with macabre relish of the horrors of the torrid zone. And now Henry was asking his sailors to venture into it.

THE BIG BARRIER was Cape Bojador, not a thousand miles from Sagres. Scarcely noticeable on a map (page 90), this angle of the Sahara, jutting seaward, marked the line where geographical knowledge stopped and mythical terrors took over. Past its turbulent shallows lay the tropical Sea of Darkness. Enter, and white men would turn black.

"Beyond this," wrote Azurara, "there is no race of men or place of inhabitants: nor is the land less sandy than the deserts of Libya, where there is no water, no tree, no green herb—and the sea so shallow that a whole league from land it is only a fathom deep, while the currents are so terrible that no ship, having once passed the Cape, will ever be able to return."

It took 19 years for Henry to get his first captain past Bojador.

"Go back, go back while we may!" was always their cry, until one braver than the rest sailed on. Such a one was Gil Eannes, conqueror of the myths.

Gil Eannes had to make two tries.

On his first he came in sight of the Cape, but his sailors refused to round it. They could see the water boiling on the other side, they declared, and indeed it was obvious from the masthead that some disturbance was causing a great swirling in the sea. Boiling waters, adverse currents—no place to go! Go back, put about and go back!

Gil Eannes was a courtier, not a pilot; a leader, not a seaman. Not knowing the answer to the sea's strange appearance, he went back.

Henry's disappointment can be imagined.

"But the sea *was* boiling," we hear the courtier insist. "I saw it myself."

"The sea was not boiling but racing at ebb tide over shoals," the Prince explains. "Have you not seen this along our own coasts?"

Indeed Gil Eannes had. And so in 1434 he

A PORTUGUESE FISHERMAN *is never far from his boat, even when relaxing ashore. He carries pipe tobacco and some cash in the tasseled end of his black* barrete, *ready for a voyage. Men like these, brine in their veins, sailed the sturdy caravels that probed the length of Africa 500 years ago.*

HIGH-PROWED BOAT *drives ashore with a heave of four-man oars. Hastily hitched oxen drag her up.*

sailed for the much-feared Cape once more, this time with a different crew, and when he saw the water boil, sailed on, skirting it. And indeed there were shoals there, just as the Prince had said.

Having found one myth baseless, why not sail on to conquer others? After a seven-year interruption during which the Prince fought the Moslems, another captain, Antão Gonçalves, was sent out.

Past the desert belt he sailed, and into the zone of Negroes. Back to Sagres he came with captives. The Portuguese baptized them, pampered them, absorbed many into the population, but the insidious slave trade had begun.

In the years 1444-6 the Prince licensed 30 voyages. Dinis Dias rounded Cape Verde, Alvaro Fernandez neared Sierra Leone. The discovery of the Cape Verde Islands naturally followed these comings and goings.

It must have profoundly discouraged the Prince to have his trusted discoverers come back from voyage after voyage to report that Africa still stretched away as far as the eye could see. The explorations were being ridiculed as expensive absurdities. But Henry carried on, pouring his revenues from the Algarve into these endless ventures — the money from the rich tuna fishing, from the olive and cork trees, the almonds and grain. His own wants were simple — a chapel, a lookout, a rough bed. The only luxuries at Sagres went to the endless stream of map makers and mariners who came to Prince Henry's school.

AS THE LITTLE CARAVELS inched down the great bulge of Africa, their crews found gold dust, ivory, and more slaves. Some captains took more interest in trade than in discovery. It was asking a lot of them to pass up rich profits, and as trading stations rose along the coast, many went no farther. Others, searching for gold up turbid rivers, fell before poisoned darts fired from ambush.

Patiently Henry quizzed the captains-turned-traders, the survivors of ambuscades, the natives who were brought to him, and the men who persevered in exploring. His instructions remained unchanged. "Go on — go south!"

By the time Henry the Navigator died in 1460 his caravels had reached Sierra Leone, still only a third of the way down Africa. But the momentum of his efforts drove his captains on. The real fruits of his labor came after him.

The Crown took over the task of discovery.

Now the caravels slipped out of Lisbon and down the Tagus River on their way to Africa. Round the bulge of the continent the dogged captains probed. The coast of Guinea ran eastward here, and they named its lands for the trade they offered: Grain Coast, Ivory Coast, Gold Coast, and Slave Coast. They erected a great stone castle on the Gold Coast.

"Perpendicularly under the equator," wrote a young Genoese visitor who was a little off in his reckoning, "is the castle of Mina of the most serene King of Portugal, which we have seen." The visitor was Christopher Columbus, sailing with the Portuguese in the early 1480's. We can imagine that he learned much about the men who were then its masters.

Still the coast ran eastward. Could this at last be the end of the continent? But after a thousand miles the discoverers found themselves brought up again by the bulking land, stretching interminably to the south.

Would it never end?

The seamen were finding the sailing more arduous. In the northern hemisphere, wind and current had been with them; getting back was the difficulty. Once in the southern hemisphere, conditions changed. Winds blew from the south and southeast — the famous trade winds — and the coastal current set 10 to 30 miles a day toward the north. It says a great deal for the weatherly qualities of the Portuguese caravels that they were able to continue.

By 1484 Diogo Cão had pushed nearly 6,000 miles south, setting up stone pillars called *padrões* at important points. He came within a thousand miles of the end of the continent and set the stage for Bartholomeu Dias.

Little is known about the gallant Dias, for Portugal cloaked her explorations in a "conspiracy of silence." Lisbon and Lagos swarmed with spies from nations interested in thwarting Portuguese discoverers or profiting from what they found. But we do know that Dias fitted out his two ships of discovery with special care, and that he added something other explorers would copy: a supply ship with extra provisions for the ever lengthening voyages.

Dias sailed in 1487 and touched at several points down the African coast. He passed the southernmost pillar erected by Diogo Cão. Then, the sketchy records tell us, a hard wind blew him off the land and sped him southward, driving him on and on for 13 days.

The huge seas abated and he sailed eastward, expecting to connect again with the coast.

MONUMENT OF THE DISCOVERIES, *a caravel manned by Henry and his captains, overlooks the Tagus at Lisbon. Flags honoring 500th anniversary of the Prince's death flutter in the north wind that blew the explorers seaward to immortality.*

None appeared, so he turned north. Finally mountains rose over the horizon.

Before mutinous crews turned him back, Dias planted a pillar and determined that the coast trended northeastward—that he had reached Africa's far side. Hugging shore on his return, he discovered the continent's tip. An elated Portugal named it the Cape of Good Hope, for surely the way to India lay open.

This is the standard story about Dias, but a 13-day gale is a mighty long storm anywhere (except perhaps off Iceland). And it blew him southward against the prevailing winds. Without these two unlikely circumstances Dias could not have rounded the Cape.

I don't believe in that 13-day gale, but I do believe in Dias. It's my guess that he *deliberately* stood seaward and then south. How did he know that this was the only way? He might have had an inspired hunch. Or prior knowledge. Prior knowledge from whom? I think it could have been in the lost records of that sea school at Sagres. The conspiracy of silence veiled many voyages in secrecy; perhaps earlier and unknown captains told Bartholomeu Dias of the Cape's winds and currents.

NO MATTER how it happened, Dias's doubling of the Cape of Good Hope was an epochal event, the triumph of Prince Henry's dreams. Now, as the Navigator had foreseen, Europe could sail its way free of its medieval bonds.

After the pioneering caravels emblazoned with the Cross of Christ would come the carracks and the galleons, the great *naus* of the passage to India, to sail on their stately voyages for the next two centuries. For in the very decade that Henry died was born the man who would finally achieve the first Portuguese foothold in the Indies. He paved the way for an empire that encompassed half the earth and fulfilled the vision of the recluse Prince.

His name was Vasco da Gama.

85

CHAPTER TEN

Vasco da Gama, pathfinder to the Indies

Portugal's caravels had rounded the tip of Africa, and the door to the East stood open. In 1497 a king's cavalier led four ships down the broad Tagus River. His orders: to proclaim the Christian faith and to wrest "kingdoms and new states with much riches . . . from the hands of the barbarians."

VASCO DA GAMA was in his usual place for this time of evening: on the quarterdeck of his flagship *São Gabriel*. Mustered before him were the sailors and the military, the convicts and the cooks, the *fidalgos*, priests, and pilots, all chanting the evening hymn before the image of the Virgin Mary. A particular solemnity came from the throats of these Portuguese mariners, for they were attempting the first voyage to India.

The chant, the sighing of the *nortada* (north wind) in the rigging, the gentle creak of the ship's timbers as she rolled with the easiest of motions—all these were sweet music in Da Gama's ears. Pennants and banners flew; the Cross of Christ stood out in brilliant red on the graceful sails; the evening sun picked out the scrollwork and gilded shields which decorated high castles fore and aft.

Trumpets and drums sounded, and the two consort ships ranged alongside to salute Da Gama and hear the course for the night shouted to them. Then they dropped back to join the supply ship, fourth member of the fleet.

He watched the lighting of the night lanthorn atop the high poop, saw the cooks douse their fires, listened with half an ear to the pilot of the watch singing his monotonous chant to the steersman as he kept his eye on course and compass card.

The seamen, in turn, measured the man on the quarterdeck—short, thickset, with eyes like black opals above a black spade beard. In God and Da Gama the men had faith.

On this first leg of the voyage, down Africa's bulge, the fleet was accompanied by Bartholomeu Dias, discoverer of the Cape of Good Hope. In a few days Dias's caravel would veer off for the Gold Coast. But now the veteran explorer was aboard to discuss the course around Africa.

Da Gama led the way below to his cabin and lit his one candle. (A candle for the master and one for the compass—no more were allowed on these wooden ships.) The two men talked about the nortada which had brought them past Madeira and the Canaries on the well-tried West African route; it could be

LISBON in the 1490's (right) boomed with trade. Cargoes thumped ashore from big three-masted naus *like those Dias designed for Vasco da Gama's Indian voyage. Small* fragatas *served as lighters. The modern version (above) is little changed. She romps past the 16th century Tower of Belém, whose turrets show Indian influence.*

FLAGSHIP *of Da Gama's fleet, the*
São Gabriel *in miniature, rides the*
waves in Lisbon's Naval Museum beside
a figurehead portraying the Admiral.
Sails of this nau bear the Cross of
Christ. Cross at rear surmounts a stone
column erected by Diogo Cão near the
mouth of the Congo River in 1482.

During the voyage to India, Da Gama
dismantled his supply ship; homeward
bound he had to abandon another vessel,
half wrecked by storm. The venture cost
two-thirds of his men. Most died of scurvy.

trusted to turn into the northeast trade wind
and carry the ships farther south. What then?
Coast down Africa, fighting adverse winds?

No. Da Gama would stand out into the Atlantic—southwestward, *away* from the coast,
then eastward to raise the Cape of Good
Hope. It meant some 3,500 miles of open sea,
more than anyone had ever crossed before!

Did he know that in swinging out boldly
he would find other steady winds to blow his
ships a thousand miles and more toward the
south? And that westerlies would then drive
them to the Cape?

Perhaps unrecorded voyages had solved the
riddle of Atlantic sailing. All we know is that
Da Gama took the mid-ocean route.

THE FLEET lumbered on, past the Cape
Verdes where Dias bade farewell, and
past the bulge of Africa where Da Gama
altered course and swung out into the untried
sea. He picked up the southeast trades. A week
sped by, two weeks, three. The ships bounded
along over the white-flecked sea with the wind
abeam. Good-weather clouds rode high in the
blue sky. The pilots were happy with their calculations, for constant wind made steering
easy, and the gentle heel of the decks allowed
accurate observations with the astrolabe.

But after the fleet changed course toward
Africa the good wind gave way to baffling
calms broken by sudden squalls. Often the
four ships lay still, sails slatting themselves
threadbare against masts and rigging. Sharks
lazed alongside, gobbling up garbage. Disease
spread. Food moldered. Water stank.

Da Gama had turned east too soon and entered the zone which later sailors were to call
the horse latitudes. But his wide swing came
astonishingly close to what became the classic
sailing route to the East (map, page 140).

After three long months the explorers broke
out banners, sounded trumpets, and sang sol-
emn chants: ahead rose the coast of Africa.
They fetched it a little north of the Cape.

Rounding the tip of the continent, the ships
encountered the powerful Agulhas current. It
held them back. And when the wind rose and
blew against it there was a terrible sea. The
ships tossed and rolled and all but turned over;
some sailors thought of mutiny.

But they struggled on up the east coast of
Africa, past lands of the Hottentots, past the
farthest point Dias had reached, northward to
the island of Mozambique within the Moslem

world. Here was a thriving trading center. The sailors gaped at dhows laden with cloves and pepper, gold and silver, pearls and precious stones. They saw their first coconuts, "fruit as large as a melon, of which the kernel is eaten," recorded the chronicler.

At first the Arabs, who controlled the trade at Mozambique, took the sun-darkened strangers for some different kind of Moslems. Da Gama did not undeceive them. But the Arabs scorned the cheap trinkets that the Portuguese offered and soon learned they were Christians. Clashes followed, and Da Gama sailed on.

At Mombasa, terraced houses reminded the homesick mariners of "some part of our kingdom." Da Gama thwarted Arab intrigues and led his ships on to Malindi. Here whitewashed homes gleamed against a backdrop of palms and fields. And here fortunes changed.

Malindi was at loggerheads with Mombasa; the king welcomed the Portuguese as allies. He and Da Gama ate each other's food without fear of poison. The crews took on supplies, caulked ship, and learned to make rope of coconut fiber. Best of all, the king sent Da Gama a pilot to lead him to the final goal—the rich Indian port of Calicut.

A GOOD BREEZE bellied the sails as the fleet cut straight across the Arabian Sea. Da Gama's officers came to respect their Arabian pilot, Ibn Majid, envying his instruments and charts. After 25 days and some 2,200 miles, the lookout sighted the Western Ghats, mountain landmark of Malabar. Two days later the ships anchored before Calicut. All hands were on deck to savor a great moment in history, this 20th day of May, 1498.

The long-sought city was not imposing. Low, thatched houses crowded narrow streets that wound down to the harborless sea. Insects swarmed, and snakes slithered underfoot.

But Calicut throbbed with trade. Waterfront warehouses bulged with spices from the Indies, fabrics from China, drugs from the interior to be carried in Arab bottoms across the Indian Ocean to the markets of the West. The streets teemed with Arabs, Hindus, and Chinese trading in the riches of Asia.

Mistaking Calicut's Hindus for Christians, Da Gama gave thanks to the Holy Virgin in a Hindu temple. We can imagine that paintings of "saints" with inch-long teeth and four or five arms disturbed his sense of orthodoxy! Next he paid his respects to the local ruler called the zamorin, a haughty tyrant dressed in rich silks, who chewed betel nuts from a golden bowl and spat the juice into a jeweled cup that a slave held at the ready.

At first the zamorin was friendly. But his advisers were the same Arab merchants who controlled Calicut's trade, and they resented the intruders. They belittled the piffling Portuguese presents to the ruler and whispered warnings in his ear. The potentate cooled. Da Gama's life was threatened.

He tarried three precarious months to load what spices he could, then set sail for home. Even Vasco da Gama dared not tackle a whole subcontinent with so small a fleet.

His return trip was wracked by storms and blighted by scurvy. But his arrival in 1499 was a triumph. King Manuel greeted him with ceremony and bestowed rewards, which Da Gama calmly accepted as his due.

Now that the way was known, Portugal acted swiftly. Within a year Pedro Alvares Cabral sailed for the East with 13 ships. Like Da Gama he swung wide around Africa—so wide he touched Brazil and claimed it for his king. He returned from India with incredible riches. But the church bells that greeted him also tolled in sorrow, for a storm had sunk four of his ships, one captained by the gallant Dias.

Fleets began sailing annually to India, and their cargoes made Lisbon the marketplace of Europe. Feeling the pinch in their shipping profits, Moslems—with Venetian backing—massed an armada to stop this trade that was sidestepping the old Mediterranean route. But off Diu, in India, a handful of Portuguese vessels scattered it to the winds.

Commerce led to conquest. In 1510 Affonso de Albuquerque seized Goa, north of Calicut, and made it the anchor of Portugal's overseas empire. He led a fleet to the Malay Peninsula and stormed Malacca, trading emporium for the East Indies. His captains, one of them named Ferdinand Magellan, explored eastward to the Moluccas.

Albuquerque's assaults on Moslem ports reduced the Indian Ocean to a Portuguese sea. By 1524 the little European kingdom of fewer than two million people dominated the vast trade of Asia.

In that year there came to Goa a new viceroy, an honest man but arrogant, a stocky man whose once-black beard was now a flowing white. Back to India came Dom Vasco da Gama, the man who had opened its door.

EUROPA

ITALIA

CORSICA

SARDINIA

SICILIA

Porto

Lisbona

Sagres

Seuta

MADEIRA

GRAN
CANARIA

DESERTO

CRETE

CIPRO

Tarsus

ASIA

In th

MARE MEDITERANEU

EGYPTO

LIBIA

These lands are inhabited
by men having faces like dogs.

Africa takes its name from one
of the descendants of Abraham
who was called Affer.

Cape Bojador

Cape Verde

Land of those
who eat human
flesh.

DESERTO

AFRICA

Here
the Nile
pours down
with great
impetus
and noise
and also
with great
dignity.

ABASSIA

Here stands a column
with a hand showing in
writing that beyond this
point one should not go.

DIAS 1487-8

OCEANUS
ATHLANTICUS

ETHYOPIA
AFRICA

The Abyssinians narrate
many things about this land,
bestial habits of the people,
dragons, and other things
which I cannot mention.

ETHYOPIA·OCCIDETAL

It may cause wonder to see in
Europe cities so small, while in
Asia cities appear so large...where
able to do so I made the places large
and where I had no room I made
them small. Let them who are not
pleased with what I did have
patience.
            Fra Mauro

DA GAMA, 1497-8

WORLD MAP OF 1459 *depicted Africa accurately as far as Prince Henry's caravels had explored, then*

of Tarsus
rn the
tle Paul

TIGRIS
PERSIA

FRATES

STINA

Babilonia. almost impossible that
human mind could build such a beautiful thing
and that human power could destroy it.

ESERTO

DESERTO
PERSIA

ARABIA

Aden

MARE ARABICUM

Inhabitants practice
necromancy selling to
sailors their knowledge
of prosperous winds.

Here the water ends.

ASIA

TEBET

EUROPA

ASIA

AFRICA

INDIA
PRIMA

Temple
of Abraham

SAYLAM

Mote de
Ada

Mount Ada... so high that it
cannot feel any wind, ...
on the summit... is the imprint
of the right foot of Adam...

. according to sailors
expert in navigating
this Indian Sea, there
are 12,600 islands.

MARE INDICUM

Ships going toward the south...
will be drawn by the currents
toward the darkness, wherein
...death will be sure.

Only a little distance
from the foreign
islands the darkness
begins to appear...

Adapted by National Geographic artists
W.N. Palmstrom & J.W. Lothers from the
MAPPEMONDE by FRA MAURO, 1459
©National Geographic Society, 1960

J. Lothers

THE ORIGINAL IS PRESERVED IN THE BIBLIOTECA NAZIONALE MARCIANA, VENICE

mixed fact and fancy. Routes of Dias and Da Gama are added. Inset shows complete "mappemonde."

HERVEY GARRETT SMITH

COMING TO ANCHOR *along the Malay coast, a big caravel with square-rigged foremast fires a salute to the Portuguese governor of Malacca. Exotic cargoes piled up in this 16th century trading center, crossroads of the Orient and one of many outposts of empire that were established in Da Gama's wake. Junks brought Chinese silks, dhows carried spices and ivory. Sampans off-loaded goods, their painted eyes keeping watch to help their scullers.*

Portuguese influence still marks some Arab dhows: their sterncastles continue the ornate style copied from Da Gama's ships. Only recently Captain Villiers watched Indians far up the Brahmaputra River build what they called a nau— *Portuguese for "ship."*

GOLD, GOD, AND GLORY *brought Columbus to Hispaniola in 1492. Natives, shown bearing tribute, in reality usually "fled with such speed that a father would not wait for his son."*

CHAPTER ELEVEN

Columbus: westward to a new world

This stubborn visionary pitched across an unknown sea, groping for the Indies, and collided with a savage continent. Though a mistake, says Alan Villiers, it was history's greatest voyage of discovery.

THE THICKSET LITTLE SHIP lumbered through blue waters, and a roll of protesting foam hissed and tumbled away from her clumsy bows. It was as if the sea were reluctant to let this ambling ark pass by. Yet day after sunlit day she drove westward before the northeast trades.

Christopher Columbus labeled her "a dull sailer and unfit for discovery." Those of his writings that survive never once mention her name, *Santa Maria*. Instead he calls her "the ship." She was perhaps 90 feet by 20, smaller than many a tug.

I once boarded a replica in the harbor at Barcelona. I would hate to sail it to America.

Columbus, pacing the small poop deck, was not thinking of the ship nor of her two companions, the caravels *Niña* and *Pinta*. His mind was on the Bible — a quotation from the apocryphal Second Book of Esdras: "Thou didst command the waters to be gathered together in the seventh part of the earth; six parts thou didst dry up and keep."

The words sustained him greatly. If this ocean were only a seventh part of the world (and to Columbus, what other ocean was there?), then he should be nearly across it. Soon he must arrive in the fabulous East, and Europe would have new access to the riches of Asia. He would be Admiral of the Ocean Sea, supreme governor of all those lands, a don of Spain. An eighth of all the profits from his discoveries would be his and his family's forever. Glittering prizes!

But already more than three weeks had passed since the little fleet left the Canary Islands. From there to Japan was 3,000 miles according to the chart of Toscanelli, the Florentine who shared Columbus's views. Toscanelli was half right. It was about 3,000 miles — but not to Japan; to a new world!

Columbus figured the distance to Asia as even less. Old sailors at Madeira had told him of land to the west where one of their number had been blown in a storm. (A very odd storm it must have been to blow a ship that far!)

Even at an average of only 100 miles a day, the ships should be getting close to the fringe islands of Asia by now, thought Columbus. *Santa Maria*'s sailors were muttering together, glancing at him with fearful looks. They were an average crew, some good hands, some mere riffraff released from jail by royal amnesty.

Superstition, a tradition of their hazardous calling, was all that they had in common. They dreaded such things as sailing on Friday, finding knives crossed on a table, spilling salt. When the weather was good they scrupulously avoided cutting fingernails, trimming hair, or whistling (unless done deliberately by a senior officer who saw a need for the wind it was sure to bring). They shuddered if their ship listed to starboard while in port: a very bad omen. And a newly joined seaman, hearing a sneeze at his left as he went aboard, would jump ship, for the voyage was doomed. While at sea, snarled running gear and torn sails were often thought the work of goblins.

Columbus's men saw sargassum weed lying on the sea so that acres of ocean looked like a summer field in Spain. They hauled up buckets of it, and it had no roots.

At first they smiled, thinking the weed grew on rocks as it did back home, and had drifted out to sea from land nearby. But the weed continued for many days. No sight of land. The sea must be getting shallow then. Danger was imminent — beware of shoals! And they sounded with a deep-sea lead. No bottom.

Their fears grew.

There were calms, and the men moaned that they could not get back to Spain without a good wind. Nature was against them! Then the wind returned and pushed the ship along. Columbus looked on it as the direct intervention of God. But the good wind, always easterly, set the sailors wailing that the vessels could never beat home against such constant winds. Food and water would give out, and they would perish in this bleak emptiness.

The leader tried to calm their fears. He always reported the distance traveled each day as less than his calculations actually showed. He hoped this small deceit would make the men feel that they were not really such a long way from home. Still the wind blew from the east and northeast, as it does today in these latitudes. Day after day the little ships stumbled on, rolling, creaking, slowly pitching, cordage chafing, canvas thinning. And the brooding figure of Columbus seemed to grow ever more fanatical as each day's westing took the crews farther and farther from Spain.

COLUMBUS was used to doubters. For seven years he had fought them for a chance to make this voyage. He had appealed to John II of Portugal, grandnephew of Henry the Navigator, and been turned aside by a commission of experts: "They all con-

ADMIRAL *of the Ocean Sea was the son of a Genoese weaver. No two portraits agree. This one, painted after his death, shows hands of an artist, not a seaman.*

Columbus followed the perfect route west, making use of winds and currents that still wash Portuguese fishing floats ashore at San Salvador (also called Watling Island), thought by many to be his first landfall.

sidered the words of Christovão Colom as vain, simply founded on imagination." He had spent six years at the court of Spain arguing that the East could be reached by sailing west, and had met the scorn and ridicule of scholars and learned men.

Who did this fumbling Genoese upstart think he was? They "agreed that what the Admiral said could not possibly be true." Some say that to refute him they even dredged up the old belief that the world was flat!

But Isabella of Castile, who shared the throne of Spain with Ferdinand of Aragon, saw something in this tall, redhaired adventurer that escaped the less discerning. Ferdinand and Isabella had much to thank God for in 1492. Christian forces had finally captured Granada, last stronghold of the Moors who had occupied Spain for nearly eight centuries. Perhaps the Queen saw in this mystic mariner a chance to achieve a great thing for reborn Spain and to make converts to Christianity across the sea. Columbus's plan, the Enterprise of the Indies, was finally granted backing by the Spanish Crown.

THE GROWLING OF THE CREW came close to open mutiny on October 10. They would continue no farther. They would throw this Genoese madman to the fishes and put about. Columbus told them to hang on for a few more days. A few days westward....

On October 11, weeds, driftwood, and a branch of thorn bearing new leaves drifted by. "At these signs, all breathed again," says the chronicle of the voyage as transcribed in the mid-16th century by Bartolomé de las Casas.

October 12, 2 A.M. Lookouts strain their eyes in the moonlight. Aboard the lead ship *Pinta,* Rodrigo de Triana spots a shape on the horizon. A cloud perhaps.... No, it is solid; it bulks big as only a landfall can seem to men wearied of the everlasting sea.

Land ho! Land ho at last!

"Pinta . . . found land and made the signals which the admiral had commanded. . . . They took in all sail, remaining with the mainsail, which is the great sail without bonnets, and kept jogging, waiting for day. . . ."

And so Columbus reached San Salvador, outermost of the Bahamas. In the morning he hung out all flags, donned his most splendid dress, and landed on the sandy beach with pomp and ceremony. Seamen who had plotted his murder now crowded around him. He had been right!

Timorous inhabitants, naked and unadorned, came out of the woods to gaze upon these men from heaven. No cities, no sign of civilization. Nobody had heard of the Great Khan for whom Columbus brought letters.

This island must lie far offshore. Somewhere beyond they would find Cathay.

So Columbus cruised the Bahamas, coasted Cuba and Hispaniola searching for Asia. He found wild cotton, strange plants and fruits, and a little—a very little—gold. But no spices, nor silks, nor pearls. No potentates—only unclothed natives who remained convinced that he had descended from the heavens with his ships and crews.

On Christmas Eve, *Santa Maria* drifted off Hispaniola in a dead calm. Columbus turned in, and "the sailor, who was steering the ship, decided to go to sleep, and he left the steering to a young ship's boy, a thing which the admiral had always strictly forbidden." The poor vessel grounded, quietly but fatally, on a reef. Her seams opened.

Columbus transferred most of her crew to a stockade ashore (where they later died). He boarded *Niña,* his favorite of the three, and set out for Spain in mid-January, 1493.

Just as this extraordinary man had sailed the ideal route westward with favoring trade winds, he now followed a good track home, passing north, then east with the variables and westerlies, as if the way were known.

The return to Spain was a glorious triumph. Ferdinand and Isabella welcomed Columbus as if he were a fellow monarch. Those who had scoffed at him now vied with each other to do him honor. He passed through Spain like a conquering hero, reaped all his promised honors, and within six months was leading a fleet of 17 ships and 1,500 men to follow up his discoveries and find the Asian mainland.

COLUMBUS made four voyages in all. He discovered more islands, founded the settlement of Isabela on Hispaniola, the first European outpost in the New World, and gave the natives a lasting name, "Indians," based on his fixed idea that they were in fact people of the Indies.

The Admiral proved a poor administrator. Ambitious underlings, eager to exploit what had already been found, thwarted him, undermined his authority, and complained of him to Spain. The Portuguese found the real route to the Orient and brought home fabulous cargoes. Columbus found himself disgraced but did not yield in his conviction that Asia lay just past the coast of Cuba, just beyond "Terra Firma" (his label for South America). On his last voyage he coasted the Isthmus of Panama, declaring he was "within ten days sail of the Ganges River."

And so he aged, relentlessly pursuing his Great Khan, his Cathay, his spices and gold. A few more miles, westward. . . .

But it was hopeless, of course. The Indies did indeed lie beyond—10,000 miles beyond a whole great continent and a tremendous ocean that Europeans did not know existed. Stripped of titles and honors, broken in health, Columbus came home from his last voyage in 1504. Within two years he died still convinced that he had found the way to Asia.

No one was sure just what he had found. But he put Spain into the business of discovery, formerly a Portuguese monopoly. Disputes arose between the countries. In 1494 a line of demarcation was drawn 370 leagues west of the Cape Verdes. Lands found west of it were Spain's, those east of it (and the line cut through Brazil) were Portugal's.

Columbus's star faded in the rush for gold and glory. His continents bear another's name. But nothing can take from him the triumph of that first 33-day run across an unknown ocean, the greatest voyage of discovery ever made.

LITTLE TOBAGO (IN DISTANCE), SANCTUARY FOR BIRDS OF PARADISE: CHARLES ALLMON, NATIONAL GEOGRAPHIC STAFF

14TH CENTURY MINIATURE FROM "THE BOOK OF MARVELS"; BIBLIOTHÈQUE NATIONALE, PARIS

COULD THIS BE CATHAY? *The puzzled Columbus explored many Caribbean harbors as lush as this one at Tobago, expecting always to find a rich Asian city (left) awaiting him around the next headland. He had read Marco Polo's accounts and carried a letter for "a Prince who is called Grand Can."*

Columbus's mistake sprang from medieval ignorance of geography. Maps of the day vastly underestimated the size of the earth, showing only one ocean, the Atlantic, between Europe and Asia. With no way to fix longitude, Columbus compounded the error by calculating a degree as 45 nautical miles instead of 60. He expected to find Japan about where the Antilles lie, and China sprawling over what is actually Mexico. Because he was so wrong, he found support for his voyage.

99

CHAPTER TWELVE

Magellan's fleet girdles the globe

Spain had yet to draw wealth from her new domain. Costly searchings had yielded no spiceries and little treasure. She pinned her hopes on Ferdinand Magellan, who sought a passage south around America to the riches of the Orient. His was a voyage of bitter hardship—and triumph.

BALBOA, astride a peak in Panama, had seen the "Great South Sea." Portuguese explorers in the Orient had sailed its western fringe. What lay between? European mapmakers couldn't agree except on one point: this ocean was narrow!

The thought bolstered Ferdinand Magellan as he outfitted his fleet in Seville. Spain had commissioned him, a Portuguese, to cross this unknown expanse after finding a way around America.

Magellan knew that South America tapered westward, just as Africa tapered eastward toward its cape. There must be a passage around one as well as the other, and he was prepared to sail to 70° S. to find it.

Once he had discovered this "outlet to the Moluccas," trade would inevitably follow, and the purse of Spain would grow as fat as that of her rival Portugal.

By September 20, 1519, the five small ships, *Trinidad, San Antonio, Concepción, Victoria,* and *Santiago,* were provisioned and ready to sail from Sanlúcar. Magellan and his captains inspected for stowaway wives, fired cannon in farewell, and set out on one of the boldest voyages in the annals of the sea.

The fleet drove easily down the North Atlantic, heading for Brazil. Pilots lost the North Star and picked up the Southern Cross. Antonio Pigafetta, a Venetian, watched and took notes for the journal that provides the major source book for the voyage.

After nearly three months the ships anchored where Rio de Janeiro stands. The crews feasted on fowl, tapir, sweet potatoes, and pineapples, and traded with good-natured Indians.

But Brazil lay in the half of the world that papal decree had assigned to Portugal.

MAGELLAN'S TRACK *shows on this polar projection of 1703. California appears as an island!*

Fearing attack, Magellan led his ships southward, ever searching for the strait that would take them into the Great South Sea.

At the vast estuary of the Río de la Plata he thought he had it. A height of land evoked the cry "Montevideo!" (I see a mountain), and so christened a future city there. But the great body of water was only a river, and the ships pushed south. Cold swept up from the Antarctic, and the men shivered.

Frostbite was crippling the crews when Magellan found a protected bay to winter in. Men caught strange "geese" and "sea wolves"—penguins and seals—and cured their meat. Gigantic natives appeared, and Pigafetta noted that they ate rats without skinning them. Ma-

101

gellan called them *Patagones* (Big Feet) and the name stuck to these Argentine Indians and their region, Patagonia.

The leader outwitted would-be mutineers, executed three, and marooned two. But when he sent *Santiago* to reconnoiter southward a squall smashed her on the beach. Her crew survived and joined the fleet of four as it ventured on in the springtime of October, 1520. Soon a lookout sighted "an opening like unto a bay." It was the strait.

Magellan conferred with his officers. All were game to continue but the pilot of *San Antonio,* the largest ship. He turned back, while the leader swore, "Even if we have to eat the leather wrappings on the masts and yards, I will go on."

Cautiously the three remaining vessels wound between the strait's bleak shores, fighting racing currents and 40-foot tides. Indian fires twinkled on the south shore, and Magellan named the land Tierra del Fuego, Land of Fire.

It took a month to feel their way through the stormy strait that would immortalize Magellan's name. Then, firing salvos that startled the seabirds, the three ships rode jubilantly into the Great South Sea. It was sunny and calm after the terrors of the strait. The explorer renamed it Pacific.

THEIR SPIRITS BUOYED, the weary men drove up the coast of what is now Chile and headed west into the emptiness. Eagerly Magellan awaited a lookout's cry that the Moluccas, the Spice Islands of the East Indies, were in view. But the weeks dragged on.

The smoked penguins spoiled. Biscuits turned to a powder crawling with worms. Drinking water was yellow and alive, and the men held their noses to get it down. Scurvy set in. Weakened men sought shade from the sun.

Two months out they found the tiny atoll now called Puka Puka, Dog Island, of the Tuamotu group. The crews caught fish and seabirds and trapped rainwater in sails. But there were no fruits or vegetables, and scurvy still covered the men's bodies with sores. When they chewed, teeth fell from swollen gums and black blood oozed. To move aching joints brought a shriek of pain.

As the ships plowed on, hunger and disease increased until only a handful of sailors could work the gear. A gale would have destroyed them. Magellan ground up maggots for whatever nutrition they offered. Rats fetched half

a year's pay. And in fulfillment of their leader's words, men dragged the ships' leather astern to soften it, then pulverized and boiled it into a sort of broth. By March 5, 1521, the fleet was almost helpless, the crews absolutely out of food.

At dawn next morning a lookout saw a mountain. He wet his lips, tried to cry out, and croaked pitifully. Finally he shrieked, "Praise God! Praise God! Land! Land! Land! Land!" and burst into tears. It was Guam.

Islanders swarmed out in their swift praus and promptly stole a skiff from under *Trinidad*'s stern. Climbing aboard the ships like monkeys, they took everything not nailed down. A haughty chief knocked down two decrepit seamen. The Spaniards struggled to their crossbows and one buried an arrow in the chief's chest. He pulled out the crimson shaft and looked at it curiously as he fell.

After firing broadsides, Magellan's men landed, dispersed the villagers, and recovered the skiff. Then they gorged on "long figs," which were bananas, drank the refreshing milk of coconuts, chewed toothsome sugar cane. They called the archipelago the Ladrones, meaning Thieves, to this day a name for the Mariana Islands.

Another week brought the explorers to a "high island" — Samar, in the Philippines. Magellan had sailed that far east for Portugal. Now he had reached the same meridian sailing westward for Spain. He had circumnavigated the globe! And behind him lay some 9,000 miles of the "narrow" Pacific Ocean!

The fleet threaded the forested islands off Leyte, passed through Surigao Strait, and anchored at the tiny isle of Limasawa. Islanders hovered about in boats but would not approach. A Malayan slave that Magellan had acquired in the service of Portugal hailed them in his native tongue. They replied. Now Magellan knew that he had reached the Orient.

The Spaniards put gifts on a plank and floated it toward the shy islanders. After two days of such arm-length diplomacy their king himself came aboard. Magellan gave him a robe and a scarlet cap, and the two made a pledge of brotherhood, each pricking himself and tasting the blood of the other.

Pigafetta and Magellan's slave went ashore as the king's guests. Sitting in state, they dined on "a dish of pig's flesh . . . and at each mouthful we drank a cup of wine." In his journal Pigafetta noted apologetically, "I ate flesh on

Good Friday, not being able to do otherwise."

On they sailed to the populous island of Cebu where Magellan induced the king to swear fealty to the crown of Spain. In this moment of triumph the explorer wept with joy, embracing the king and pledging eternal peace between Spain and Cebu.

He turned missionary and converted the king, and a rush of baptisms followed until the fleet's tired priest could scarcely raise his arms in blessing. To this day the people of the Philippines are Asia's only Christian nation.

Other chiefs embraced the Cross, but one on the nearby island of Mactan refused. Magellan decided to coerce him—against the advice of his fellow officers. With about 50 followers he landed in the shallows off Mactan. A howling horde met them with a shower of "arrows, javelins, spears hardened in fire, stones, and even mud." Armor protected the Europeans—except for their legs. The warriors aimed low.

After an inconclusive battle most of the Europeans bolted to the boats offshore. Only a handful stayed with their leader.

The natives closed in. Magellan and his guard fought them off in the water, inching their way toward the boats. Magellan stabbed an assailant with his lance and saw it wrenched from his grasp as the man fell. He reached for

QUESTING SHIPS *of Juan Rodríguez Cabrillo coasted California two decades after Magellan showed the way to the Pacific. In two more decades the Manila galleons, laden with silks and spices, began annual runs to Acapulco, Mexico, that continued 250 years.*

his sword but could not draw it because of a javelin wound in his arm. Seeing his plight, the warriors centered their attack on him. One drove a spear with full force into Magellan's legs. He fell face forward in the water.

In an instant the mob threw themselves on him, hacking at him with their weapons. Pigafetta, who had fought beside him until the end, sorrowfully recorded the death of "our mirror, light, comfort, and true guide."

THE SLAYING OF MAGELLAN wrecked the prestige of the Europeans. A large party of Spaniards was lured ashore and slaughtered. Those who had remained aboard, including Pigafetta, cut the anchor cables and fled.

The survivors still had enough pluck to explore for spices. Abandoning the leaky *Concepción,* they traded at Borneo and found cloves in abundance at Tidore in the long-sought Moluccas. As the first loads came

aboard the crews fired a salute, "as they were the chief object of our voyage." When the supply of barter articles gave out, men traded their coats and shirts for yet more cloves.

By late December, 1521, both vessels were overladen with spices. Then *Trinidad* fell prey to the Portuguese. Only *Victoria* remained, commanded by Juan Sebastián del Cano. He had been one of the mutinous officers early in the voyage. Now, by a quirk of fate, he must hold this last ship together and somehow get it home. Only 47 men remained out of the 275 who had left Spain.

The worm-eaten ship and her emaciated crew fought storms and adverse currents as they crossed the Indian Ocean and coasted Africa. Keeping far south of the Cape of Good Hope, *Victoria* finally limped around it and set course to the northward in the Atlantic.

Scurvy and starvation set in again. Not until June did the ship struggle across the equator,

TIERRA DEL FUEGO,
named by Magellan, is a
land of ice rather than fire.
This Chilean frigate passes
Romanche Glacier whose runoff
colors the bleak sea.

Juan Sebastián del Cano
(below) brought Victoria, *lone*
survivor of the fleet, back to
Spain after the three-year
voyage. He died attempting
a second Pacific crossing.
Resting on a rudder, he now
surveys Guetaria, his
hometown in the Basque
country of Spain.

and by that time there was a funeral every day.

The last thing Del Cano wanted was to stop at the Cape Verde Islands and run into the Portuguese. Bitter necessity forced him to. He warned his men to say they had come from America, but the secret leaked out that they had been trading in the Portuguese sphere of influence. Every sailor ashore was seized and Del Cano had to weigh anchor to save his ship. He had hardly enough hands aboard to man it.

They discussed a strange thing. By their records, they had arrived at the Cape Verdes on July 9. But ashore it had been July 10! In girdling the earth from east to west, with the sun, they had gained 24 hours.

On September 8, 1522, *Victoria* bore 18 wretched survivors into Seville. Magellan's fame rang through Europe. For though the great feat dashed Spain's hopes of rich trade routes, it opened the eyes of questing men to the true dimensions of their home planet.

JOHN CABOT *takes leave of robed Henry VII and sets out from Bristol to discover lands "o*

HENRY VII OF ENGLAND preferred the countinghouse to the battlefield. He was building a merchant marine on the trade in herring and wine and wool. Eyeing the East whence came "all the golde, spices, aromatikes, and pretiose stones," he puzzled over the route his ships might take.

Spain and Portugal maintained a jealous monopoly over southern sea-lanes to the Indies. What other way was left?

John Cabot, "citizen of Venice" now residing in England, offered a solution. Why not sail west by a northern route? Henry agreed. In 1497, Cabot boarded the bark *Mathewe* and put to sea with the blessings of the "Huckster King" and the backing of merchants of Bristol.

Like Columbus, whom he preceded to the mainland, Cabot thought America was Asia.

He ran down the coast, found neither gold nor spices, but discovered wealth in the sea: codfish off Cape Breton Island and Newfoundland. Tightfisted Henry gave him £10 for his pains.

Portugal's Gaspar Corte Real followed Cabot's track to this "new found land," then vanished. In 1509, Sebastian Cabot, John's son, began looking for a way around it. Thus started the quest for a Northwest Passage, that will-o'-the-wisp that would lure mariners the next four centuries.

Sebastian drove his two ships north "until even in the month of July he found great icebergs." He swung west, entered Hudson Strait, perhaps gazed on Hudson Bay. Ice frightened his men, and they forced him to put about.

Other nations took up the search. Estevan Gomez for Spain and Giovanni da Verrazano

106

CHAPTER THIRTEEN

The search for a Northwest Passage around America

Surely a way to Cathay lay "to the northe" in a passage "most probable, its execution easie." With great hearts and incurable optimism generations of brave mariners set out into the baffling mists in tiny ships stalked by death.

the heathen and infidels."

for France probed rivers and bays. Jacques Cartier sailed up the St. Lawrence to the rapids that he named for China—Lachine.

"The voyage to Cathaio by the East is doubtlesse verie easie and short," declared Flemish map maker Mercator, secure in a warm study and with no intention of leaving it. Sir Hugh Willoughby carried English hopes north around Norway, but froze to death in Lapland with all his company. Willem Barents of Holland put Spitsbergen, Novaya Zemlya, the Barents Sea on the map; then the Arctic claimed his life.

ON ARCTIC and Antarctic voyages I have met the white, silent enemy—cold. It weakens the body, assails the mind, numbs the workings of a sailing ship. Frozen gear will not travel through the blocks. Sails

freeze and must be handled with bare hands, for gloved fingers cannot claw canvas. It takes men of iron constitution and supreme confidence to face the frigid seas. Men like Martin Frobisher, one of Queen Elizabeth's sea dogs.

In 1576, when England's interest in the Northwest Passage had revived, he threaded among Greenland's icebergs, fought through a tempest that knocked the *Gabriel* on her beam ends, crossed to Baffin Island, and started up the bay that now bears Frobisher's name. The natives' sallow skin, "much like to the ... Tartar nation," helped convince him that he had Asia on his right, America on his left. Then five of his men disappeared in his only small boat, and Frobisher was forced to return.

A decade later John Davis, skilled pilot and inventor of the backstaff (a forerunner of the sextant), pushed up the west coast of Greenland. At 72° 12′ N. he found "no ice towards the north, but a great sea.... The passage is most probable, the execution easie." Davis, who thought America an island, underestimated the problem. But he was on the right track. When Roald Amundsen finally navigated the Northwest Passage three centuries later, he used this entrance—Davis Strait.

War with Spain interrupted England's quest until 1602 when George Weymouth, sailing for the newly chartered East India Company, stumbled into Hudson Strait. Ice sheathed his ship, and his entire crew, including the chaplain, mutinied. They "bare up the helme" and limped home through storm-tossed seas.

Then came the stubbornest passage-seeker of all, Henry Hudson, whose name lives on in the bay, the strait, and the river. He had tried to reach Cathay over the top of the world, a route that airliners fly today. Ice forced him to Spitsbergen. He tried the northeast route. Again ice blocked him. Sailing for the Dutch, he tried the Hudson River.

In 1610 he wrestled Weymouth's old ship *Discovery* into Hudson Strait, dodging icebergs, hazarding the furious turbulence at the strait's entrance. "Some of our men this day fell sicke," wrote a crew member. "I will not say it was for feare, although I saw small signe of other griefe."

Ice beset the little ship. Men muttered of returning home. Hudson pressed on and the land fell away, revealing an immense open sea. "Confidently proud that he had won the passage," Hudson sailed south.

Of course it was only Hudson Bay. *Discovery* wandered through a labyrinth of islands while nerves grew taut. Then ice locked the ship fast near the southern shore of James Bay. Men sickened through the winter. Supplies ran low; dissension ran high. Spring finally broke the ice, but the starving and homesick men accused Hudson of concealing food.

Mutiny flared on June 22, 1611. The ringleaders set Hudson, his son John, and seven men adrift in a shallop with neither "food, drink, fire, clothing, or other necessaries," and sailed for home. Near the mouth of Hudson Bay, Eskimos attacked and killed the "guilty." An English court acquitted the survivors.

Hudson was never seen again. But the spirit that drove him infected others and helped mold sturdy mariners for an England that now stood on the threshold of empire.

"One of our companie looking over boord saw a mermaid"

HENRY *Hudson duly recorded the incident in his log while off Novaya Zemlya in the Barents Sea: "from the navill upward, her backe and breasts were like a woman's ... they saw her tayle, which was like the tayle of a porposse, and speckled like a macrell."*

Hudson's "mermaid," probably a seal or walrus, was only one of many surprises in northern waters. John Davis, whose strait extended the North American coast on the chart at right, found "white beares of a monstruous bignesse" on the island soon to be named for William Baffin. Martin Frobisher saw "ilands of ise ... of such heigth as the clowds hanged about the tops of them," and fur-clad little men who shot arrows and paddled "small boates made of leather" (top inset).

The weather, "mistie, melancholy and snowie," swallowed castaway Henry Hudson and his son (bottom inset).

GRO

Hope Sanuderson

London coaste

L. Darcies. I.

MESTA INCOGNITA

Desolation

Fretum Dauis

C. Besford

Sanderson towre

Furbishers straights

Reg: E. foreland

Mt. Rayleigh

Cumberlands Iles

ESTOTILAND

Warwicks forelande

Furious Ouerfole

Ths land was discouered by Iohn Sebstian Cabok for Kinge Henry y 7. 1497

Bell Ile

C. grate

Clere ilande

C. bonauista

CANADA

Bacalaos

C. raso

The Lake of Tadouac the boundes wherof are vnknowne

C. britton

I. sablet

I. S. Iohn

VIRGINIA

Croatamonge

Hatorask

Croataon

La bermu

The Gulfe of Mexico

Babaina

Cignales

Mavaguano

Abrecso

Anegada

Mari

Antigua

S. Crux

Dominica

Matalanao

CHAPTER FOURTEEN

Elizabethan sea dogs defy the might of Spain

For Queen and for gain, England's stout adventurers poach in Spain's New World preserve. Drake plunders gold, circles the globe, "synges the bearde" of Philip II. The King strikes back with the mighty Armada. In Captain Villiers' story, the empires clash and pirates spread terror.

SILENTLY, NOW. Don't wake the town! Let the sails bring her in." Francis Drake hisses the orders. Cloaked figures pull in oars, grasp weapons. The swirl of seas along the beach, the sigh of wind in the palms are the only sounds as the boats glide ashore.

Nombre de Dios, the Panama port where Spain's galleons load the gold of South America, slumbers on. No attack is expected from the sea—in this year of Our Lord 1572, is not the Caribbean Spain's? The runaway slaves called Cimaroons might strike, but they would come from the jungle. Only a single sentry paces among the harbor cannon.

The Spaniard hears a rustle and turns to see armed men leap over the parapet. He flees to give the alarm.

Now the great bell in the church tower clangs and keeps on clanging. From the town come the cries of men and frightened women.

Drake sends his younger brother with a dozen men to come in from the other end of the town with all the noise they can make.

"Drummers, trumpeters, sound!" Down the main street march Drake and his men, their flaming pikes held high to strike terror. Defenders form up in the marketplace, lashing on armor, priming muskets. Drake's men open with a volley, charge with their pikes. At the same instant John Drake and his handful burst in on the other flank like a small army. The Spaniards break; but they get one volley away, kill a trumpeter and wound a few others.

The town is Drake's. Now for the treasure!

The heavens cloud over and a tropical rain pours down. It douses the fire pikes and the matches without which muskets are useless. The men take shelter under a veranda.

The rain stops. Drake steps out and pitches on his face. For the first time his men see that he is wounded. They pick him up, carry him to the beach and away into the sunrise.

Drake has failed, but he is not done yet. If Nombre de Dios will now be too strongly guarded, he will snatch the treasure before it gets there. Gold and silver mined in Chile and Peru are shipped to Panama's Pacific coast, then packed by mules across the isthmus to the Caribbean side. Cimaroons show him the route.

Drake's men crouch in the underbrush along the mule track and listen. They hear jungle birds, the ring of shipwrights' hammers from Nombre de Dios, only a few miles away. At last! A distant brassy sound mingles with the murmur of the wind, becomes a swelling jingle-jangle of harness bells mixing with the creak of leather, the grunts of drivers.

"Now—at them!" Men leap for the leading and last mule of each string, hold them fast. Muskets roar. Defenders and attackers topple.

"**I HAVE THE BODY** *of a weak and feeble woman, but I have the heart and stomach of a king." So spoke Elizabeth. Here the victorious Queen, in magnificent raiment of brocade and pearls, holds the world in her hand. Behind sail her victorious sea dogs (left) and the storm-wracked Armada.*

HENRY VIII STANDS PROUDLY *in the waist of his golden-sailed* Henry Grâce à Dieu, *the wonder of her day, as his fleet departs Dover for France in 1520. Dubbed the* Great Harry, *she was "built loftie" with eight decks, bristled with some 385 guns, carried 700 soldiers and seamen. As a boy Henry liked to act "as pilot on board ship, blowing a whistle as loud as a trumpet." As king he built shipyards, established an admiralty, ordered vessels designed specifically for fighting. Dissatisfied with small, man-killing guns on poops and forecastles, he had big, ship-killing cannon mounted on lower decks and hulls pierced for gunports. Broadside batteries revolutionized sea warfare. During reign of Henry's daughter Elizabeth, English gunnery skill helped defeat the "Invincible" Armada.*

111

"HENRY VIII'S DEPARTURE FOR THE FIELD OF THE CLOTH OF GOLD" BY FRIEDRICH BOUTERWEK, AFTER AN UNKNOWN CONTEMPORARY ARTIST, MUSÉE DE LA MARINE, PARIS

FRENCH CORSAIRS, *first on the Spanish Main, carry loot from a flaming town to their ships.*

Finally the Spaniards flee toward Nombre de Dios, where soon that alarm bell clangs again.

Swiftly Drake's men strip the treasure from the beasts and strike out toward the hidden base where their ships wait. At last Drake can say, "Our voyage is made."

WHAT MADE Francis Drake, this preacher's son from Devon, so anxious to "synge the bearde" of Spain's King Philip? As a young man Drake had joined his kinsman John Hawkins on what they considered a legitimate trading voyage to Spanish America. They had brought bales of taffeta and linen, butts of sack and malmsey, pewter, and African slaves to exchange for gold.

Philip forbade such trade with his colonies. But slaves were in short supply, and local officials winked at the English voyages.

Unfortunately for Drake and Hawkins, a Spanish fleet bearing a new viceroy arrived at the Mexican port of San Juan de Ulúa while they were there. The viceroy could not tolerate such flouting of the King's commands. He agreed not to molest the English if they would let him enter the harbor unopposed. But once

in, he attacked. Only two of the six English ships survived, those captained by Drake and Hawkins. Drake swore to return—as a raider like the French who had badgered the Spanish in the Caribbean since the 1520's.

England is ripe for such a man and such a passion. Barred from the New World and the East by Spanish and Portuguese monopolies, opposed in the Baltic and Mediterranean by entrenched trading powers, annoyed by Spanish plots and religious friction, England must have an outlet for her enterprise and her resentment. Queen Elizabeth herself "would gladly be revenged . . . for divers injuries I have received."

Drake is not content to raid the Caribbean. In 1578 his 100-ton *Golden Hind,* "well fitted out . . . a good sailer," slips daintily up the Pacific coast of South America. Her sails, laced with bonnets, billow in a favoring wind. Behind lie the Straits of Magellan, where "most mad seas" and "most intollerable winds" had separated Drake from his other ships, blown him as far south perhaps as Cape Horn.

Now the officer of the watch, a thickset Devonian, stands by the binnacle humming

114

softly to the sailor who toils with the whipstaff. Down in the waist, the watch burnishes weapons, and yarns in broad West Country accents. On the quarterdeck sits a fair-haired lad painting the coastline, carefully stroking in the peaks of the Andes beyond. By the rail leans a dark, brooding figure, the Portuguese pilot Nuño da Silva, kidnapped from his own ship to help Drake interpret stolen Portuguese charts.

A trumpet blares. From the bricked galley marches the cook with a huge tray piled with silver dishes. Two musicians with viols take stations by the cabin door. Out comes a stocky little man, scented and dressed in the height of fashion. He looks aloft first, then around the horizon—a careful look that misses nothing.

Captain General Drake goes in to dine with music. The meal is good: pea soup thick and nourishing, cod soaked two days and boiled.

So it goes, day after day, with religious services morning and evening. Sometimes Drake raids a settlement and takes what's offered—once a ton of silver from the backs of "pretty cows," llamas. Sometimes he overtakes a lonely treasure ship. Spanish vessels along this Pacific coast carry no cannon—only Spaniards sail here.

Northward goes Drake, the sea growth now trailing from *Golden Hind*'s sides like mermaid hair. After a try for the Northwest Passage, he careens ship in California, which he claims for his Queen. Then he heads westward across the Pacific, raising land in 68 days. He takes on cloves in the Spice Islands, runs nonstop 9,700 miles from Java to Sierra Leone (the longest run a ship had ever made), and sails into Plymouth Sound in September, 1530, "after we had spent 2 yeares 10 moneths and some few odde daies beside."

"Does Queen Elizabeth live?" Drake shouts to some fishermen. She does.

The Queen and her ministers have stakes in the voyage and reap dividends of 4,700 percent. Spain is furious: "The Spanish ambassador doth burn with passion against Drake." But the *Golden Hind* comes to Deptford on the Thames, and Elizabeth goes aboard to knight her "pirate," the first Englishman to circumnavigate the world.

Where does "that woman," as Philip of Spain calls Elizabeth, really stand in all this? Temporizing, vacillating, grabbing some of the gold, holding back Drake sometimes, never having to urge him on—the Ruling Redhead is an enigma. She has inherited a reasonable navy, has been warned by Parliament to maintain it "ever in readiness against evil haps," and sees it improved through the untiring efforts of Hawkins on the Navy Board. Yet she never gives it free reign to crush the growing Spanish threat. Even after *Golden Hind*'s provocative voyage she still hopes for peace.

When Philip seizes all English ships in Spanish ports, she simply orders Drake to make reprisals, a quite legal means of redress in those days. And if Drake exceeds his

Grenville and the *Revenge*

SPANISH ships of war at sea! We have sighted fifty-three!" The news stuns Sir Richard Grenville, waiting in the Azores in 1591. He expected treasure ships from the Spanish Main, not another Armada. Hopelessly outnumbered, his consorts slip away to sea. He stays to sail Revenge, *Drake's former flagship, alone into the fray.*

On comes the towering fleet of Spain, thundering, trying to board in this "fight of the one and the fifty-three." Yet in the ballad by Tennyson, "Ship after ship, the whole night long, drew back with her dead and her shame." By dawn "the Spanish fleet with broken sides lay round us all in a ring."

Revenge, *a sinking hulk, could fight no more. In words that ring with Elizabethan pride, the dying Grenville cried: "I have ended my life as a true soldier ought to do, that hath fought for his country, Queen, religion and honour."*

orders—well, "The gentleman careth not if I disown him." Drake sails to the Caribbean, pillages Santo Domingo, Cartagena, and the Florida settlement of St. Augustine. He finds little treasure but carries away 240 guns.

Learning that Philip is quietly assembling an armada to invade England, Drake leads 26 sail into the throat of Cádiz Harbor in Spain. The port is rimmed by batteries, jammed with vessels. Cannon roar, galleys charge. The wind falls and Drake is trapped for 12 hours. But with the morning breeze he sails clear, leaving the wreckage of some 30 ships and the shat-

tered stores that an invading army must have. The Armada is delayed. Fifteen months pass.

VICE ADMIRAL SIR FRANCIS DRAKE paces the quarterdeck of *Revenge*, one of the newer 500-ton English galleons, and ponders. He, Lord Admiral Charles Howard, Hawkins, Frobisher, and the other commanders have taken a great gamble. When the Armada entered the English Channel, they swung around behind it to gain the weather gauge. Now they hang on its heels like sheep dogs. But what if the Spaniards turn suddenly to

"God breathed and they were scattered"

PROCEED *direct to the English Channel . . . there opening communication with the Duke of Parma, ensuring him a safe passage across."*

With these orders the Armada —73 fighting ships and 57 supporting vessels—departs Lisbon on May 9, 1588. Storms force a halt at Corunna, but on July 29 England is sighted. Out from Plymouth come Drake and Howard with 100 sail. In four Channel clashes the Spanish lose two ships. August 6 finds the Armada at Calais awaiting the assembly of Parma's army at Dunkirk. Fire ships drive them out, break their formation. Caught off a lee shore at Gravelines with shot running low, the great Spanish ships are brutally mauled, some mortally.

Painting at left shows the Armada hotly engaged. Spanish galleass in foreground—half galleon, half galley—churns to attack the English galleon at lower right, Lord Howard's flagship Ark Royal.

Fleeing northabout, some Armada ships are dashed by gales on Scotland's rocks (below); others seek shelter on the Irish coast only to be driven ashore. In late September, 66 ships stagger back to Spain. Of the 30,000 soldiers and seamen who once sailed so proudly, perhaps two-thirds perished. A grateful England strikes a medal: "God breathed and they were scattered."

"THE WRECK OF THE ARMADA ON THE SCOTTISH COAST" BY AN UNKNOWN ARTIST, COURTESY MR. REX DE C. NAN KIVELL, LONDON

seize an English port? Could they be stopped?

The Armada is a fantastic fleet, greater than any the world has seen. A mile-wide phalanx of 130 ships—towering galleons, lumbering storeships, great galleasses, and lesser escorts—rolling steadily upchannel to the sounds of trumpets, drums, chanted prayers, and the incongruous neighing of cavalry mounts. Discipline is perfect: "They are determined to sell their lives with blows," Drake writes.

To close with the Armada is folly: its heavy cannon could be murderous at short range, and the ships' waists are packed with Spanish infantry, reputedly the best in the world. Drake and the English, with their swift, low, weatherly galleons, must play the hound: hitting, running, trying to pick off stragglers.

Stores run low: "My Lords, our victuals are not yet come . . . for the love of God and our country, let us have with speed some great shot sent us of all bigness . . . and some powder." The English are desperate, their supply ships always late, always bearing too little. Their furious cannonading, like the Spanish, has little effect. Range is too great. They must get closer, somehow shatter that formation.

The Armada swings away from the English coast and anchors in the open roadstead at Calais. The plan to link up with the army in Flanders has gone awry. The admiral, the Duke of Medina Sidonia, must await word.

The English, anchored scarcely a mile away, see their chance. On the second night they fill eight vessels with combustibles and send them with the wind and current toward the Armada. Now they come like giant funeral pyres—flames crackling from their glaring hulls, masts with flaming sails falling in showers of sparks. Pandemonium!

Spanish captains rush to get under way to escape the hell of fire. Behind is a lee shore. "Cut the cables!" Great axes swing, the hemp twangs at the blows, then bursts as irreplaceable anchors are left behind. Aloft, sails swell swiftly from gaunt masts. Ships jostle and collide as they stagger from the roadstead, all in the hideous glare of fire.

Morning finds the Armada's invulnerable formation broken, wind and tide pushing it slowly toward the Flemish coast, the English closing from windward. The Spaniards cannot work clear of the shoals, dare not try to come about. There is no haven to leeward, no ground tackle left to anchor by. Cornered!

Here off Gravelines, Drake leads the English ships in. At "half musket shot" range his *Revenge* exchanges broadsides with Medina Sidonia's *San Martín*. The fast firing English gun crews aim for the exposed bilges as Spanish ships heel to leeward under a press of sail. Their nine-pound balls punch holes in the stout oak, shatter the upper works, plunge along crowded decks until scuppers run with blood.

The Spanish, their shot nearly spent, try vainly to grapple and board. The end seems very near when a violent squall blows up with lashing rain. The fleets separate.

A providential shift in the wind saves the Spaniards from stranding. They stand away to the north, seeking to return home by swinging around Scotland. The English follow as far as the Firth of Forth. "There was never anything pleased me better than seeing the enemy flying with a southerly wind to the northwards," reports Sir Francis Drake. It is over. England has won her place on the seas.

The shot-splintered Armada holds together up the North Sea and around the tip of Scotland. But once exposed to the full fury of North Atlantic gales, it is torn apart. Some ships founder at sea, some are flung against the outer islands of Scotland.

Other captains, their men wracked by thirst, hunger, and sickness, turn to seek help on the coast of Ireland. But tricky tides, stiff winds, and Spanish ignorance of the coast pile the vessels on a lee shore. Irish looters, bands of English soldiers put survivors to the sword.

Only half of the once-proud ships limp home to Spain, many never to sail again.

ONE RESULT of the Armada's defeat was to encourage bold men to nibble at Spain's far-flung empire. In the early 1600's bands of French and English adventurers set themselves up on sparsely populated islands of the West Indies, were joined by ship deserters, runaway servants, fugitives of all kinds. They hunted wild cattle and pigs on Hispaniola, smoked the meat on wooden racks *(boucans),* sold it to passing ships. The French hunters called themselves *boucaniers,* the English buccaneers. Nearby Tortuga became their stronghold.

Harassed by the Spaniards, tempted by gold, they soon turned to raiding Spanish ships and towns. These "Brethren of the Coast" had their own code—but it did not include pity for victims. Montbars the Exterminator followed normal practice when he tortured citizens of

WITH CUTLASS, PIKE, AND PISTOL, *pirates board a merchantman. Their dark ship lies hove to.*

Maracaibo to learn where they had hidden their valuables. The fiendish L'Olonnois, confronted by a group of close-mouthed prisoners, suddenly cut the heart from one and bit it.

Boldest of buccaneers was Henry Morgan. Attacking Portobelo in Panama, he forced monks and nuns to place his ladders against the walls. In 1671 he stormed the city of Panama, and his men looted, tortured, burned. Yet he was knighted and died a respected Jamaica planter. He operated on land and sea with letters of marque—commissions granted to shipowners allowing attacks on enemy nations' commerce. Once at sea, of course, such a privateer might turn pirate and attack anybody.

Captain Kidd was hanged for just this.

Other sea rovers were pirates pure and simple. Edward Teach, the notorious Blackbeard, plundered and murdered along the Carolina coast. He ended up with his head lashed to a bowsprit. John Avery sailed to the Red Sea and took a treasure-laden ship of the Great Mogul (and rumor said, the Mogul's daughter),

was tricked out of his gain, died in poverty. Tea-drinking Bartholomew Roberts set a record: 400 vessels he is said to have captured.

Pirate strategy was simple. A swift, raffish craft comes out of the dawn or dusk, fires a shot across a merchantman's bow. A broadside wings the victim's rigging, sends it out of control. The pirates grapple, slash through boarding nets, swarm over quarterdeck and waist armed to the teeth. Steel clashes on steel, pistols flash, men grunt, lunge, topple, thud on the decks. A knot of women cowers aft. In minutes it's over; the outnumbered defenders are killed or trussed up. Rum-soaked louts charge about, competing in atrocities.

Merchants both prominent and shady handled the ill-gotten goods in New York, Boston, Charleston, Bristol, even set up receiving stations on pirate-ridden Madagascar.

Among the authorities who worked to stamp out this wanton sea robbery was an untiring official in the Admiralty who kept a secret diary. His name? Samuel Pepys.

119

Designs for defense: naval science replaces old rules of thumb

SAMUEL PEPYS, *Secretary of the Admiralty under Charles II, kept an eye on pirates, but his gravest concern was Dutch admirals De Ruyter and Van Tromp. Commercial rivalry with Holland's "waggoners of the sea" plunged England into three wars between 1652 and 1674. To wrest victory from defeat, she needed all-weather ships with increased firepower, like the 70-gun* Resolution *(above). The greatest problem was to pack three decks of heavy guns into strengthened hulls. Placed too high, they made a ship top-heavy; if too low, seas rolled into open gunports. Crowding guns aboard without increasing length and sail area sank the hull deeper and slowed the ship.*

Here Pepys, at far end of table, takes notes as Lords of the Admiralty study the scale model of a man-of-war, exact to the last detail. A young ship designer points to "the Boddy so clean under watter and her shape so fine above." Apple-cheeked bow lets the ship carry heavy guns without pitching deeply into seas. A veteran shipwright stands by for questions. Many of Pepys's models are preserved at Cambridge and Greenwich.

121

Evolution of the shipborne gun

GUNNERS, make ready your cannons, demi-culverins, bastard culverins, sakers, half sakers, falcons, slings, murderers, passevolants, harquebuses!" So went the order as a three-master beat to quarters in the 1540's. How curious a miscellany had developed since artillery went to sea in the 14th century!

At first guns were a novel addition to pikes and bows, and were stuck on ships not built to accommodate them.

The 15th century *murderer* (below), with two-inch bore, swiveled on the gunwale and blasted boarders with anything handy—stone, nails, bits of iron or glass. A loaded chamber with a handle was inserted in the wrought-iron breech and the charge ignited through a touchhole.

Its low-slung relative, the *lombard* (left top), was mounted on a two-truck (wheeled) carriage and fired through the bulwark. Bundled iron rods or wooden staves formed its "barrel." Improved lombards carried by Columbus hurled a stone ball 1,000 yards. Breeching tackle checked the recoil.

By mid-16th century the cast-bronze *demi-saker* (left center) could take a heavier charge and hit harder with greater accuracy. It was raised or lowered by a wedge under the breech and, like all cannon for centuries, aimed by eye. Flemish bellmakers sometimes melted down church bells plundered in war to make these muzzleloaders.

As ships became floating cannon platforms, cast-iron guns gained favor. They

might burst and kill their crews, but they were cheaper than bronze! The *cannon royal,* largest Elizabethan gun with an 8½-inch bore and a 30-pound powder charge, could lob a 66-pound ball nearly 2,000 yards.

The small *falcon* (left bottom) could reach 2,500 yards, but its ball weighed only three pounds. The notched wooden shoes of its carriage gripped the deck against recoil. But they made it difficult to run the gun forward, even with the training tackle now in use. The wheeled carriage soon returned.

The four-truck *saker* (right top) became the basic shipboard armament in the 17th century. It slammed a nine-pound ball 4,000 yards, sprayed decks with case shot, brought down rigging with chain shot, or fired hot shot to set enemy sails ablaze.

In broadside batteries it transformed the elegant *St. Albans* of James II (above) into a floating fortress. Elaborate oaken wreaths circle the upper gunports.

The *carronade,* aptly called "The Smasher," was a heavy gun of short range capable of battering wooden walls impervious to lesser guns. It came in the late 18th century.

The U. S. frigate *Constitution* and other men-of-war of that period bristled with iron *24-pounders* (right bottom). Such cannon lasted to the Civil War—start of the age of armor plate and rifled guns.

123

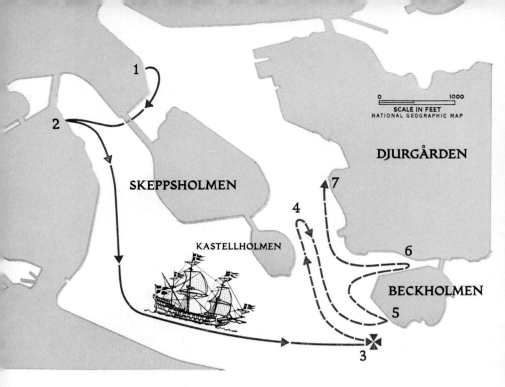

STOCKHOLM HARBOR *saw* Vasa's *brief life and resurrection. Built at the Royal Dockyard (1) and fitted out near the Palace (2), she sank scarcely a mile out (3). Twentieth century salvagers moved* Vasa *to shallow water (4) and floated her. She was towed first to dry dock (5), later to outfitting quay (6), finally to restoration and exhibition site (7).*

CHAPTER FIFTEEN

Warship Vasa: ghost from the deep

She sailed to disaster on her maiden voyage and slept 300 years. Anders Franzén found her grave.

REBIRTH *of the once-proud*

TRULY A PROUD MOMENT, a fine day, this Sunday afternoon in August, 1628. Spectators shout gay good wishes on the quay before the royal palace in Stockholm as seamen warp their country's mightiest warship out into the harbor. *Vasa*—named for the royal family—has begun her maiden voyage.

Sweden, locked in what history will call the Thirty Years' War, welcomes the 1,400-ton galleon to her navy. *Vasa's* big bronze cannon will roar appropriate reply to a German emperor's threat of invasion.

Sailors high in the rigging break out light sails, and *Vasa* ghosts along easily. But off

galleon begins in dry dock. Early salvagers, ships' anchors tore away main deck, masts, and stern.

Beckholmen, not a nautical mile from the quay, a squall ruffles the harbor. It heels *Vasa* drunkenly to port. Surprised, men brace themselves on slanting decks and wait for the ship to right herself. Instead she leans over farther —and stays there, robbed of all grace. Water cascades through the lower gunports, left open for the harbor passage.

On shore, cheers die in thousands of throats. The pride of the fleet of Gustavus Adolphus sinks like a stone in 110 feet of water. Boats pull wildly for the survivors—sailors, marines, visiting wives and children—floundering about *Vasa*'s jutting masts. But 50 die. Loss of the 180-foot warship is a national disaster.

On another fine August day 328 years later, I sat in a motorboat in busy Stockholm Harbor and held an instrument of my own design—a marine core sampler. The six-pound steel cylinder resembles an aerial bomb tipped with a sharp hollow punch. Many times it had fetched up mud and debris from the harbor floor. This time it brought up something different—a plug of black, close-grained oak!

I knew that oak requires at least 100 years of immersion in these waters to turn black. And I knew that only the largest and most important vessels of the 16th and 17th centuries were built of that expensive wood. *"Vasa!"* The thought electrified me. If I'd found her, she

125

OVER GOES MIGHTY VASA *in 110 feet of water as long-haired Swedish sailors scramble to get clear.*

could help fill a gap between the ninth century Viking ships unearthed in Norway and the 18th century *Victory* preserved in England.

For me, finding *Vasa* would climax years of underwater exploration. I had learned that teredos, the most common shipworm, do not thrive in the Baltic: salinity is too low. I reasoned that wooden vessels sunk in these waters would not be damaged by them.

Study of naval history drew my interest to the large, decorated warships of the 16th and 17th centuries. We had paintings of such vessels, but there were questions of design, building methods, and fittings that only blueprints or one of the ships could answer. "Find *Vasa*," a noted historian told me, "and you will have the greatest treasure of them all."

I was not the first to go after *Vasa*. Stockholm's church bells had scarcely ceased tolling for her victims before the first attempt was under way. In the most profitable try, in the 1660's, men descended in a primitive diving bell. Breathing air compressed into the top of the chamber, they grappled 53 cannon and hauled them to the surface. Then for almost three centuries *Vasa* rested in her grave. Eventually, even its exact location was forgotten.

Armed with a huge amount of data, I began a systematic sweep of Stockholm Harbor with grapnels and wire drags. Boat crews laughed when I brought up bedsteads and tires.

Poring over a contour map, I noticed a large hump near Beckholmen. I was told that it no doubt was debris from an old blasting opera-

SALVAGED TOOLS, *tankard, pipe, and slipper mirror 17th century*

A few had brought along wives and children.

tion. I went back to the archives and came on an all-important letter. Dated August 12, 1628, it contained a report on the *Vasa* sinking to Gustavus Adolphus, then fighting in Poland.

It read, in part: ". . . she came to Beckholm-sudden, where she entirely fell on her side and sank in 18 fathoms." Beckholmen!

With my core sampler, I went to the hump and brought up that plug of black oak. Again and again the sampler yielded oak plugs.

The Royal Swedish Navy moved its Divers Training School to the Beckholmen site and let students practice on what I hoped was the wreck. But the first report from the murk and mud 110 feet down was not encouraging.

"I'm standing in porridge up to my chest," the diver told me over the telephone. "Can't

shipboard life. Some kegs (top) still contained butter.

WHEELED GUN CARRIAGES *line the lower gun deck.*
Water pouring in open gunports on this level sank
the ship. Customarily these decks were painted red
to soften crews' shock at sight of blood in battle.
In dry dock a continuous spray prevents drying and
decay. Later, waxy polyethylene glycol will preserve
the blackened oak. It sinks in, forcing out moisture.

Skull crops up (below) as a water jet clears away
mud. Archeologists found 12 complete skeletons.

see a thing. Shall I come up?" Gloomily I agreed. Then I heard an excited whoop.

"Wait a minute!" he cried. "I just reached out and touched something solid . . . it feels like a wall of wood! It's a big ship, all right! Now I'm climbing the wall . . . here are some square openings . . . must be gunports."

We had found *Vasa.*

SIX MONTHS LATER began one of the most complicated and perilous jobs in diving history. Helmeted divers, bubbling to the bottom, used powerful water jets to carve six tunnels down beside *Vasa*'s hull, under her oaken keel, and up the other side. Suction hoses vacuum-cleaned the bottom, pumping debris to the surface to be sifted for artifacts.

As the divers burrowed, valuable objects streamed to the surface—most of them carved figures that had fallen from the hull over the centuries. The divers, as superstitious as any seafaring folk, began grumbling about the antics of *Den Gamle,* the "Old One"—the spirit of a boatswain, they said, who still inhabited *Vasa.* He was angry at having *Vasa* torn from his grasp. Sometimes when they reached out for a bit of wreckage, the Old One snatched it away.

Actually, these tricks were played by vagrant water currents. But the divers began flinging coins into the water to placate the Old One.

Through the tunnels under *Vasa* the divers passed steel cables six inches in diameter. At the surface they secured them to two big salvage pontoons.

By August, 1959, the salvagers were ready to start lifting her so she could be shifted to shallower water. Would *Vasa,* with her cargo

of mud, stand the stress of the lifting cables, or collapse like an eggshell?

Pumps began discharging water from the pontoons. As their buoyancy increased, they strained upward, putting tension on the lines. A diver went down. "*Vasa* has lifted 18 inches, all in one piece," he reported. "All well."

Clear of the bottom but still deeply submerged, *Vasa* "sailed" that first day about 80 yards toward shallow water.

It took 18 lifts and 27 days for *Vasa* to reach the 50-foot depth near Kastellholmen. Now, how to float her? Suggestions flooded in. One inventor wanted to fill the hull with millions of ping-pong balls.

We did it the conventional way. In two years divers boarded up gunports, repaired the damaged stern, and made *Vasa* reasonably watertight. They placed pontoons under her

keel and passed larger cables under her hull. These they secured to huge hydraulic jacks on the salvage pontoons.

The jacks went to work, inching *Vasa* upward. Bulwark stanchions broke the surface, the huge sides became visible, the pumping started, and finally *Vasa* floated. Then, to be preserved and restored, she was tugged to dry dock, close to where she sank. Now in a concrete-and-glass structure she will serve her country again—as an incomparable museum.

Why did *Vasa* sink? Many believe she was top-heavy, likely to capsize. But questions of blame do not trouble me when I stroll beside *Vasa* and relive adventures with the divers. They still mutter about having robbed the Old One. But if I were to encounter the Old One, I would greet him with a short Swedish word: "*Tack.*" It means "Thanks."

GRACEFUL OARS *drive the Doge of Venice in magnificent procession to the "wedding of the sea."*

CHAPTER SIXTEEN

Sunset of the galleys

The oceans were yielding to sail, relates Captain Villiers, yet the Mediterranean still pulsed to the swing of countless oars.

130

"WE WED THEE, our sea, in token of true and everlasting dominion!" So declared the Doge of Venice from the deck of the state galley *Bucentaur* as he tossed a consecrated ring into the Adriatic.

Every year from the 13th century down through the 18th, *Bucentaur,* preserved in Venice's great shipyard, the Arsenal, emerged on Ascension Day. Resplendent in crimson and gold, it carried clergy, senators, ambassadors, and the Doge (chief magistrate of the Republic) out to the "wedding of the sea."

But all the glorious pageantry and martial music could not disguise the fact that this was a marriage of convenience

Venetian convenience.

The "love" was a one-sided love of profit that came from "dominion" over the sea.

"All the gold of Christendom passes through the hands of the Venetians," wrote a medieval chronicler. They monopolized the spice trade, drove hard bargains with everyone, including the Crusaders and pilgrims to the Holy Land.

Napoleon seized last state galley, stripped off gold.

GILDED REMINDER *of past glories, the state barge of Amalfi, Italy, races those of her one-time rivals Pisa, Genoa, and Venice.*

Venice's fortune rode the waves in two specialized ships of ancient lineage—the plodding round ship of trade and the light galley of war. Then about 1300 she began to develop the *galea grossa,* the great galley of commerce.

Longer, beamier, and sturdier than the war galley, it carried more sail and used oars as auxiliary power. It grew as large as 250 tons burden with a crew of more than 200 men— freemen, often small traders themselves.

These great galleys plied to Alexandria, Beirut, and Constantinople, bearing gold and passengers and returning with luxury cargoes. They extended Venice's flourishing trade empire out into the Atlantic, voyaging in annual fleets to England and Flanders.

In 1453 Constantinople fell to the Turks. Then Portugal's discovery of a sea route to the Indies sounded the death knell of Venice's spice trade and her proud merchant galleys.

The fighting galley lived on. Shallow in draft, maneuverable, it long remained the favorite warship of Mediterranean nations. Its human engines were now mostly convicts or prisoners of war. Christians used cutthroats, heretics, Moslems. Moslems used Christians. "There is no fear of mutinies with condemned men, for these are chained to the benches," reported the Venetian director of manpower in 1556.

Savage flogging kept the poor wretches pulling, three to six on an oar. Some biscuit, a skin of water, a rough cloak, and a blanket for the night dews lay at each slave's place. He wintered in a dungeon, rowed until he died. If his galley sank, he went with it.

Galleys fought in line abreast, their three to five heavy guns fixed forward, their light upper decks packed with fighting men who used the armored beak as a boarding bridge. Rush, blast, ram, board was the order of battle.

Greek fire still played a role. This mixture of naphtha, sulfur, and pitch had once spewed from metal animal heads on the prows of Byzantine ships. Now it splashed flaming death from catapulted iron balls or hand-flung earthen pots. Only sand or vinegar put it out.

131

DEATH THROES AT LEPANTO: *Proud lines of cross and crescent crash head on. In the melee, six*

The last great clash of galleys was the Battle of Lepanto in 1571. More than 400 Christian and Turkish galleys charged each other like cavalry, their oars frothing the Gulf of Patras off the coast of Greece.

The Turks had raided commerce, seized Cyprus from the Venetians. The Pope gave his blessing to retaliation by the Holy League — Venetian, Genoese, Spanish, and papal forces, under the command of Don John of Austria.

Now as the galleys closed, their bow cannon roared. Christian arquebuses opened fire.

Turkish arrows whistled back. "The sky could not be seen for the arrows and shot," reports an eyewitness. "It was...dark from the smoke...of many fire projectiles which were inextinguishable even in the water."

Grappling hooks clank on wood. Shouting, scimitar-slashing Turks lock in bloody hand-to-hand combat with men of the Holy League. Amid the carnage, 75-year-old Veniero, a helmeted Venetian noble, waits calmly for his crossbow to be wound up by an aide, then picks off the enemy with iron bolts. A Christian

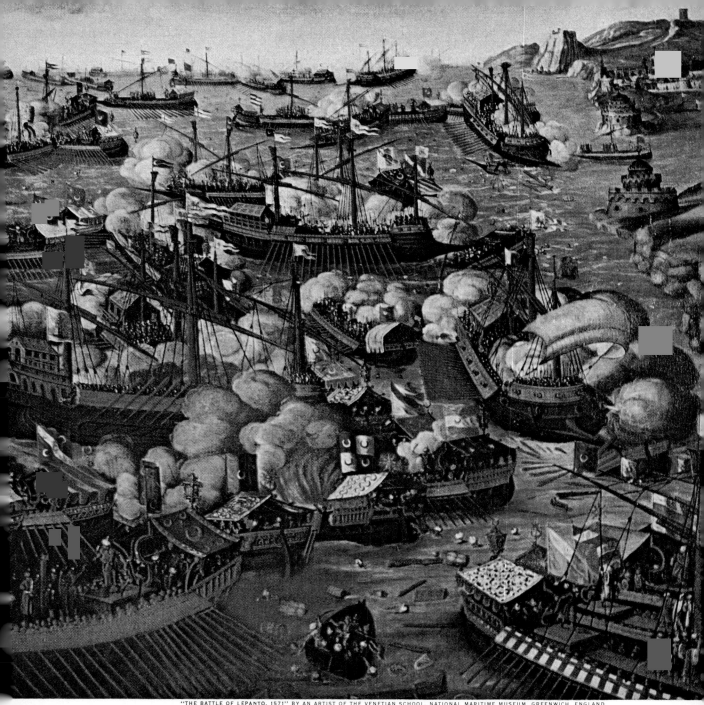

Christian galleasses splintered the Turks with broadsides that foretold the end of galley warfare.

captain, his galley overrun and three arrows in his face, ignites his magazine and blows up himself and the boarders. A young Spaniard, Miguel de Cervantes, rises from a sick bed, joins the action, and receives wounds that nearly cripple his left hand but will not prevent him from writing *Don Quixote*.

"Fire not until the blood of your opponent will splatter you," was the Christian order. And by nightfall the sea ran red from 30,000 enemy corpses. Nearly 8,000 Christians died, but the Turkish tide had been turned.

Galley warfare enabled soldiers to fight at sea as they did on land. Crowds of oarsmen left little space for heavy broadside batteries. Putting more guns forward would force the galley down by the head, jeopardize its mobility in a calm, make it dangerous in a seaway.

Galleys lingered on with the Knights of Malta, the Turks, the Russians in the Black Sea and the Baltic. France and the Barbary corsairs used them till the 19th century. But the deep-hulled, full-rigged ship, a stable, all-weather gun platform, had long been supreme.

134   **DUTCH WARSHIP** *grinds a Spanish galley under her forefoot off the Flemish coast in 160*

HENDRIK CORNELISZ VROOM, 1617, RIJKSMUSEUM, AMSTERDAM

Flailing oars, bow guns, boarders were no match for a tall, heavy-gunned sailing ship in open sea.

HE TURNS OCEANS INTO HIGHWAYS

LONDON'S CUSTOM HOUSE QUAY ON THE THAMES BY SAMUEL SCOTT, 1757, COURTESY FISHMONGERS' HALL, LONDON

A<small>T</small> London and Bristol, bales and barrels thumped ashore to be weighed and tallied. Teamsters shouted and drays rumbled over cobbles, carrying Virginia tobacco, Jamaica molasses, Indian calico, and China tea. Ship after ship nosed into port to empty its hold while scratching quills toted up profits from this "traffick in the remotest countries."

The very prospect of this new trade quickened the pulse of Europe. Why, rich and wondrous cargoes awaited  any vessel that could cross an ocean! Eager merchant adventurers pooled their capital to finance voyages, send colonists who would foster trade. Scientific societies sent naturalists to seek new plants. Improved navigation made the ocean a thoroughfare. Improved navies turned it into a battlefield in wars of conquest and trade.

This heyday of countinghouse and colonies began when English and Dutch merchants founded rival East India companies in 1600 and 1602.

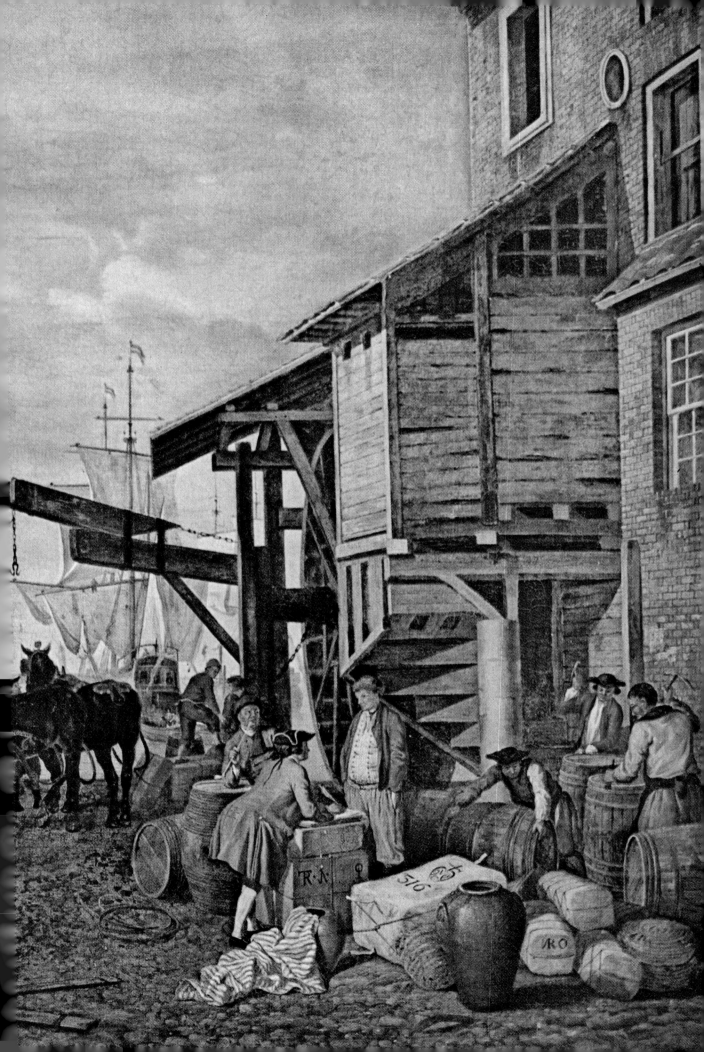

CHAPTER SEVENTEEN

Stately East Indiamen ply the spice trade

A century after Da Gama paved the way to the Indies, Portuguese power was failing. Hardheaded Hollanders elbowed their way into the world's richest commerce. Captain Villiers describes the bluff and beamy ships, holds bulging with profit, that sailed for the Dutch East India Company.

A GOOD VOYAGE OUT took six months at least, so what was the use of hurrying? Placidly the East Indiamen swung at their anchors off Amsterdam or Hoorn or Delfshaven, awaiting a fair wind. And tow-headed boys, gazing wistfully at these imposing ships, dreamed of becoming captains.

For these were the ships that helped make Holland one of the richest nations of the 17th century. And their captains commanded respect. They were seagoing businessmen, veterans of that huge monopoly called the Dutch East India Company, with its more than 100 merchantmen, its warships, its thousands of soldiers at far-flung trading posts.

A captain could make a small fortune. He had rights to cargo space for personal ventures, and no one knew better how to use this privilege. He might sit rich passengers at his table, rent part of his great cabin. Several voyages, and he could live comfortably ashore the rest of his life.

When weather vanes on the red-tiled housetops swung round to a favoring wind, the plump burghers in the countinghouses paused at their windows to watch men climb the rigging, to see the sails flutter and fill. As the ships waddled off toward the cold North Sea, the burghers rubbed their hands and prayed—a prayer for safety and another for profit.

Threading the English Channel was an anxious ordeal for Dutch crews. England had become a shooting rival for the Indies trade, and for years Dutch and English blasted away when they met at sea. But there was plenty of trade for both—and France, too.

Captains and passengers relaxed as the ships swung down the Atlantic. Graceful pyramids of sail stiffened as the trade wind blew with becoming decorum. Southward rode the ships, apple-cheeked bows treading down the blue sea with the dignity of stout bishops, decks sometimes cluttered with clucking fowls and fat domestic beasts like a Dutch farmyard—day after day, week after week, unhurried in a manner now unknown.

Merchants and officials at the captain's table washed down their ample meals with beer and brandy. They walked the poop, watched the crew at work aloft, observed the soldiers enroute to posts in the East. On an occasional ship there might even be music played by buxom young women who hoped to find husbands at Batavia, Company headquarters on Java.

At the Cape of Good Hope the ships put in at the Dutch settlement of Cape Town for provisions and diversion. Then the tempo of life changed. Captains stripped their ships for action, and passengers huddled below, for they were dropping southward to pick up the roar-

OUTWARD BOUND *with a fair wind, Dutch East Indiamen nod their blunt bows in farewell as they pass a busy headland. Stout two-deckers, these ships spurned ornate carvings and gilded embellishments. Their task was to make long voyages and carry huge cargoes. And they could take care of themselves if sea raiders attacked. Speedy* jacht *skips out of the way at left. Fore-and-aft rig made her handy as a dispatch boat and pleasure craft. Her type evolved into the yacht.*

Marten Looten of Amsterdam (left) typifies the venturous merchants who built Holland's empire in the East. Traders first competed in backing individual voyages, then merged in a giant monopoly, the Dutch East India Company.

139

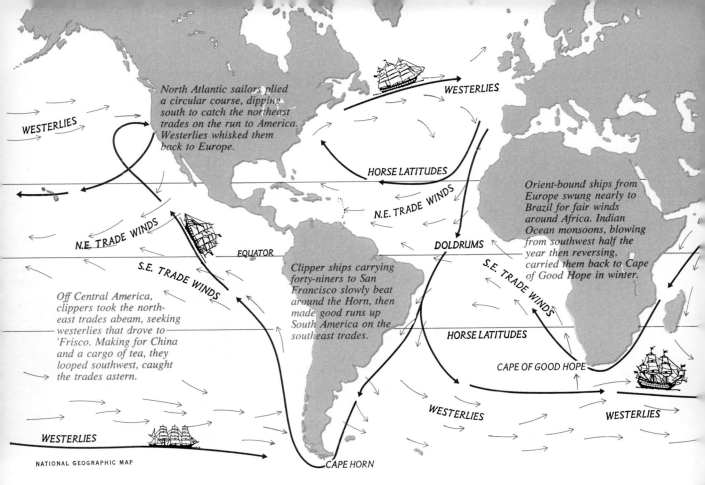

The map contains the following labels:

WESTERLIES

North Atlantic sailors plied a circular course, dipping south to catch the northeast trades on the run to America. Westerlies whisked them back to Europe.

WESTERLIES

HORSE LATITUDES

Orient-bound ships from Europe swung nearly to Brazil for fair winds around Africa. Indian Ocean monsoons, blowing from southwest half the year then reversing, carried them back to Cape of Good Hope in winter.

N.E. TRADE WINDS

N.E. TRADE WINDS

EQUATOR

DOLDRUMS

S.E. TRADE WINDS

S.E. TRADE WINDS

Clipper ships carrying forty-niners to San Francisco slowly beat around the Horn, then made good runs up South America on the southeast trades.

Off Central America, clippers took the northeast trades abeam, seeking westerlies that drove to 'Frisco. Making for China and a cargo of tea, they looped southwest, caught the trades astern.

HORSE LATITUDES

CAPE OF GOOD HOPE

WESTERLIES

WESTERLIES

WESTERLIES

NATIONAL GEOGRAPHIC MAP

CAPE HORN

SAILING SHIP CAPTAINS SOUGHT THE MOST FAVORABLE WINDS, *not the shortest route, when the*

ing forties. Soon they were rushing headlong before these wild west winds, leaping, cavorting, rolling in gale after gale, and always flying eastward. Seamen called it "running their easting down," and it cut weeks off the old explorers' route up the east coast of Africa and across the Arabian Sea.

They had to haul up short not to hit western Australia—some Indiamen smashed on that barren coast with its "wild, cruel, black savages." Turning north, they picked up the southeast trades and sailed the sunlit sea until Java beckoned in all her green loveliness.

There the fleet split up, each ship making for a Company trading station. With a salute from the Company fort, a captain moved ashore. His crew lowered his ship's cargo into waiting praus. Then the capacious hold was stuffed with peppercorns, cloves and cinnamon, bay leaves by the bale, nutmegs and ginger, mace and aloes. Parcels of precious stones, bars of silver and gold found their way to secret compartments. Rich silks and brocades, shuttled from Japan by the Company's inter-island carriers, topped off the bulging holds.

Hatches were secured, the fort boomed fare-

well, and the ship rendezvoused with the others at Batavia. In October the fleet began the return voyage, borne on the winter monsoon.

HOLLAND had trained herself well for her Indies trade. In the 1500's she dominated the North Sea herring fisheries, traded in the Baltic, transshipped Portugal's Oriental imports from Lisbon to the spice-hungry cities of northern Europe. "The sea trade of Europe," noted a French observer a century later, "is carried by 25,000 ships. Of these, 14,000 or 15,000 belong to Holland."

They were good ships with simplified gear. Sir Walter Raleigh reported that a Dutch ship of 200 tons freighted goods cheaper than an English ship "by reason he hath but nine or ten mariners, and we near thirty." And they "build every year near one thousand ships, and not a timber-tree growing in their own country."

Hollanders infiltrated the Portuguese empire in the East. In 1592, Jan Huyghen van Linschoten brought back charts, trade secrets, and the welcome news that Portuguese strength "is nothing so great as heretofore hath bene supposed." Encouraged, Cornelis

140

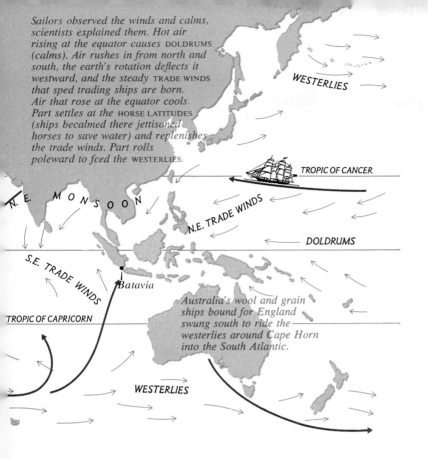

Sailors observed the winds and calms, scientists explained them. Hot air rising at the equator causes DOLDRUMS (calms). Air rushes in from north and south, the earth's rotation deflects it westward, and the steady TRADE WINDS that sped trading ships are born. Air that rose at the equator cools Part settles at the HORSE LATITUDES (ships becalmed there jettisoned horses to save water) and replenishes the trade winds. Part rolls poleward to feed the WESTERLIES.

WESTERLIES

TROPIC OF CANCER

N.E. MONSOON

N.E. TRADE WINDS

DOLDRUMS

S.E. TRADE WINDS

Batavia

Australia's wool and grain ships bound for England swung south to ride the westerlies around Cape Horn into the South Atlantic.

TROPIC OF CAPRICORN

WESTERLIES

plowed the oceans in quest of Asia's spices, silks, and teas.

TEA PICKERS *on Ceylon.*

de Houtman set off on Holland's first East Indies voyage in 1595. He made for Bantam, pepper port on the north coast of Java, and returned with hopeful reports, though two-thirds of his crew died of fever and scurvy.

Soon so many Hollanders had entered the trade that competition was cutting prices. This would never do; the merchants banded together and organized the Company.

The Portuguese still dominated trade in the East, and the Dutch fought hard to push them aside. The Spanish, temporarily ruling Portugal because of a royal marriage, harassed the Dutch from their base in Manila.

But within a few years the Hollanders had founded Batavia, gained control of the Spice Islands, blockaded Goa, grabbed Ceylon, Malacca, Formosa, set up stations at the Cape of Good Hope, in the Persian Gulf, in India, and won a monopoly in Japanese trade.

From Ceylon to the Moluccas, Dutch "factories" rose on tropic coasts. There the agents, "factors," settled down to buy and store the spices, fabrics, and metals of the Orient. There rose the Company forts. And there came the broad-beamed ships to fill their holds.

Searching for even wider areas of trade, Abel Tasman discovered Tasmania and New Zealand and showed that Australia was an island continent. Meanwhile a fleet out of Hoorn struggled around the gale-swept cape at the tip of South America and named it for their home port. It was corrupted to Cape Horn.

ENGLAND had chartered her East India Company 15 months before the Dutch. But the Hollanders, sailing in greater strength, vowed the island trade "should belong to the Company, and no other nation in the world should have the least part." The English company turned to India, where it traded iron, lead, tin, and woolens for cottons, silks, spices, and gems. In time it brought India under its sway, dominated China's tea trade, outstripped and outlived its Dutch rival.

For two centuries the ships of both companies plodded purposefully, doing what they were supposed to do with acceptable efficiency, bringing profit to their owners. Meanwhile a lonely little ship named *Mayflower,* freighted with human hopes, would make a greater mark than all the stately East Indiamen.

141

CHAPTER EIGHTEEN

Sailing *Mayflower II* across the Atlantic

Some called it insanity — to design and build a replica of the Pilgrims' *Mayflower* and sail her to America. But with endless patience, skill, courage, and seamanship the job was done. Here Captain Villiers, master of *Mayflower II* on her epic voyage, describes how he relived the 1620 story.

"THERE SHE IS — the ship that couldn't be built." Stuart Upham's blue eyes lit up as he glanced across his shipyard at Brixham, Devon, to the berth where the new *Mayflower* was growing into a shapely vessel. She was being built as a replica of the Pilgrim Fathers' ship of 1620. With luck she would sail the Atlantic to become a feature of Plimoth Plantation at Plymouth, Massachusetts.

Little is known of the original *Mayflower,* but researchers and naval architects had designed this namesake along the lines of an early 17th century vessel of 180 tons. Then the pessimists opened fire on her. The right wood for her could never be found, they said, nor the shipwrights to work it. And if she were built, no master could be found to sail her nor a crew to man her. How could you sail a ship like that across the fierce North Atlantic? What, no engines? Forget it!

When I read that, I sought out the London promoters of the venture. Had they a master for the *Mayflower,* I asked. They had not. I volunteered — for free — and got the job. And

so I took considerable interest in the shipyard where she was taking form.

The new *Mayflower* was built with the same sort of tools that 17th century shipwrights used. The very accents of the builders seemed to come from history, for these men were from Devon where things change slowly.

"Give her another bang now, Harry. Handsomely! Handsome does it!" An older man in a cloth cap was speaking to the wielder of a sledgehammer who was fitting the last awkward timber to the beak — a holdover from days when ships had rams. Nearby a hammer rang on an anvil. The blacksmith was turning out stout ironwork for the rigging and rudder.

Mr. Upham had scoured the woods of Devon for stout oaks to form the ship's timbers. Often he had to look at night for fear of protests from ardent tree lovers.

So the new *Mayflower* was built — a small, handy bark, primitive in rig but thoroughly sound. All she had to do was sail once westward across the North Atlantic with the eyes of the world upon her — to sail, to survive, to

FEW VOYAGES OF COLONIZATION *had such impact on history as the one that carried a freedom-seeking band of settlers to the New World in 1620. Here, 337 years later, the new* Mayflower *nears the coast where Pilgrim Fathers landed in solitude. A gentle breeze fills the spritsail beneath the steeving bowsprit.*

LUIS MARDEN, NATIONAL GEOGRAPHIC STAFF

B. ANTHONY STEWART, NATIONAL GEOGRAPHIC PHOTOGRAPHER, ABOVE: UNITED PRESS INTERNATIONAL, RIGHT: WIDE WORLD

arrive. Why not? Her predecessor had made it with no fuss at all.

The pessimists were encouraged when the ship was finally floated out of dry dock. She was in shallow water and so could not be properly ballasted or she would have run aground. But without enough ballast, she fell heavily to starboard. "Mayflower Capsizes!" shrieked the headlines.

She did not capsize. As soon as she was in deep water we stowed and secured her ballast of railway iron and she came up nicely.

After a call at Dartmouth, in the wake of the first Mayflower, we went on to Plymouth and sailed from there on an April day. There had been no chance to make any real sailing trials. The ship was eagerly awaited at her American destination, and a date had been somewhat optimistically set for her arrival there.

The sea was completely calm in Plymouth Sound. Under all sail the ship swung as she willed, and for a while headed east toward the Strait of Dover instead of west toward America. Next day Plymouth was still in sight.

It took a couple of days to get out of the channel, and that gave us a chance to learn the ropes and how to use them. The spritsail, rigged from a yard under the bowsprit, proved to be a fine maneuvering sail. It was so far for-ward that its turning power was quite enough to offset the windage of the high poop.

I set three watches, and the mates held sail drill, especially at night. There was no light on deck save an oil lamp in the modern binnacle and a candle lantern for the old-fashioned compass in the wooden binnacle. That old compass was good, but its fitful candlelight made it useless at night. We steered by the other.

IT BEGAN TO BLOW hard on the third morning, and the little ship began to jump in the shallow, choppy sea of the English Channel. How she could jump! She rolled, lurched, pitched, stumbled, all with a wild and unpredictable abandon. Even some of the old Cape Horners among the crew were seasick. The motion in my tiny cabin, high in the aftercastle, was so violent that it was strenuous exercise to stay there, asleep or awake.

Aloft, the motion could be dangerous. Our rope rigging had been well stretched, but the play in it was often frightening. To climb aloft in the topmast rigging was to be flung in circles, for all motion was magnified up there. The rigging alternately slacked, then whipped taut as the ship rolled. It was a bad place to go just after breakfast.

As wind and sea rose, the rigging was work-

MAYFLOWER TAKES SHAPE *in the shipyard at Brixham, England. Ribs (upper left) were hewn from solid oak. Wooden trenails from Devon cider vats fastened the planking. Fifty-eight feet long at the keel, with a 25-foot beam, she stretches 106 feet, 5 inches from ornate beak to aftercastle.*

Fat hempen rigging, smelling of Stockholm tar, coils in the old-fashioned rigger's loft. Huge five-hole deadeye (left) helps stay the foremast; its upper loop embraces the bowsprit. A Scottish firm searched its 200-year-old records to make this cordage. Mayflower's crew had to learn 350 lines, many with forgotten names like jeers, catharpins, and knave-lines.

Mate Godfrey Wicksteed (far left) buys galley stores as authentic as his costume. Beef was salted the old way, and ship's biscuit made by a 17th century recipe.

ALL SAILS SET, Mayflower II *jogs toward Plymouth, Massachusetts, at better than seven knots. She made her crossing in 54 days compared to 67 days for her predecessor.*

American flag signifies she approaches United States waters. James I's Union Jack crackles from her mainmast, the Cross of St. George from her mizzen. Red Ensign flies from the peak of her lateen yard.

Some 125 to 135 persons crowded the original Mayflower, *but regulations forbade Captain Villiers' carrying modern Pilgrims as passengers. He selected his hardy crew from more than 5,000 volunteers. Thirty-one men, two boys, and a cat made the passage. A stowaway was put ashore in England.*

H.M.S. ARK ROYAL *salutes her countrymen. On earlier pass to windward she becalmed* Mayflower.

ing far more than I cared to see. It looked as though the whole lot might go overboard. Masts shifted a foot laterally with each heavy roll, and no setting up of catharpins (old-fashioned gear for drawing the shrouds together and thus tightening them) helped much. Yet we realized that all this working of rigging was commonplace in 1620—a way of accepting stresses as the ship sailed. Everything had a little "give" to it; nothing carried away. Rigidity doesn't necessarily mean strength.

Yet I hated to see how the yards jumped in their gear and how the foremast, stepped in the curve of the cutwater, behaved. It stumbled and threw its rigging jerkily forward like a hardmouthed horse tugging at its reins whenever the little ship tried to stand on its head— which was often. The bowsprit was stepped in the 'tween decks, entirely unstayed and unsupported except for one gammoning (a rope lashed around it). This was historically correct, but just how long was that bowsprit going to stay with us? The big, deep spritsail put heavy strains on it.

Water poured into the mates' cabins, and the 'tween decks leaked. There was seepage into one place in the hold—not serious as yet, but who could say how it might grow if I had to punch into too many hard westerly gales?

I walked the reeling, tiny poop above my cabin, grabbing for support at bulwarks or rail with every turbulent toss or roll. I wondered how wise I was to persist in trying to sail the

northern route. If a bad gale blew up I could be in trouble.

I made my decision. I would go the southern route, the trade winds way. The course added the best part of 2,000 miles, but we had the food, water, and stores to keep at sea for 70 or 80 days if need be.

I fell off a bit and let the ship bound along west-southwestward to pass clear of Ile d'Ouessant and all Biscay Bay. Let me get clear of all land! Land is dangerous, not sea.

The vessel still flung herself about, but now she ran dry and safe before wind and sea and passed the bay with fine runs—140, 150, 155 miles a day, even 164 one day, about the best she ever did. She could have done at least a knot better if she had not been so deeply laden with British goods for exhibition. The sun shone, the decks dried, and Felix the kitten came up on deck and tried out his sea legs.

Felix was young when he joined, but he soon settled to the life. Third Mate Jan Junker made him his own little life jacket and he was brought to lifeboat drills along with the crew.

THE GOOD NORTH WIND took us right to the Canary Islands. By night the moon shone and the ship under her swelling, lovely sails seemed incredibly romantic. The wash of the sea at her round bows and the burbling of her wake were music as she rushed along. By night and day the good wind filled the sails, and the ship did her best to hurry.

CROSS-STAFF, *forerunner of the sextant,*

Looking aft at the quarterdeck and the shapely aftercastle, I could hardly believe that she was real.

The crew settled down very well. Cook Walter Godfrey baked bread three times a week and turned out nourishing two- and three-course meals three times a day. After the 11th day I served out lime juice daily as required under British law to prevent scurvy. Hence the expression "limeys." Everyone, including Felix, drank it. Felix protested, but he had to obey the law.

At first it looked as if we might make a record run by the southern way—and this in a ship that could do little better than 7½ knots! Her merit was her ability to slip along easily in quiet winds.

Then the winds dropped. So did our speed. Sometimes we had perfect calms, and the lads jumped overboard and swam. In two successive weeks we made less than 500 miles. One day we logged 20 miles backwards. This sort of thing upset all our hopes for a fast passage.

We saw golden sargassum weed, and it grew and grew, sometimes into pieces covering more than an acre. We had queer weather at the tropic's edge, sailing the route Columbus sailed. The ominous roll of thunder, the threat of heavy clouds piled high in a gloomy, overcast sky, the odd rain squall bursting down with a temporary puff of fresh wind from the east to hurry us westward—all helped me understand the fears of Columbus's crews. Go back, go back! the dark skies seemed to say.

At last the trade wind freshened again, and we bowled along once more with a bone of white water curling in our teeth. Approaching the West Indies, we saw many steamers. I had avoided their lanes because of the risk of collision by night, for we carried only the few essential lights. But now the French liners *Colombie* and *Antilles* gave us a cheer. And a British Fleet tanker signaled: "You look like a beautiful old painting."

Out of the dawn one June day came two long, gray warships. When they saw us they formed station, one on each quarter, well astern. At 6 o'clock they dashed alongside,

manning ship with all hands fallen in, fore and aft, in spotless whites. As they passed us at full speed in beautiful formation they cheered ship resoundingly, and we dipped our Red Ensign in salute and cheered back, for it is not often a merchantman is so honored.

The ships were the Italian cruisers *San Giorgio* and *San Marco*. They raced splendidly ahead, one on either beam, then slowed down, and each dropped a boat. These came smartly to us, laden with presents of fruits and wine. As the *San Giorgio*'s boat approached our lee channels, the officer aboard threw wide his arms and shouted, looking up at us, "Magnificent! It is magnificent!" We liked that.

Sometimes big swells came down from farther north, reminding me of the wisdom of my decision to take the southern route. These swells spoke of heavy gales elsewhere in the Atlantic—right across our path, had we gone the other way. The high seas picked the stiff little ship up and shook her like a St. Bernard shaking a wet puppy. Everything aboard fell over, even Felix the kitten asleep in the shade under the longboat. Felix quickly learned how to stay asleep while the ship was rolling. He did not bat an eye.

Our *Mayflower* was a happy ship. All hands pulled together, and the ship's spirit was good. It was tested thoroughly in a Gulf Stream gale which blew up, unforecast and unheralded, one day near the end of the passage.

That morning began with the sea lumpy and confused and the air hazy and humid. We had been through a wild middle watch during which the wind had been jumpy with fresh squalls. I had lowered the two topsails and bunted them up but hadn't secured them. They lay in the

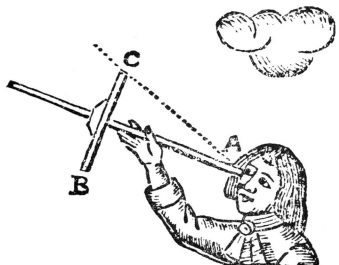

proved too inaccurate for the author. He stuck to modern navigation.

tops, ready for use when the squalls passed. But pass they did not except to return again from some other direction a little harder. I secured the topsails and ran on under courses, spritsail, and lateen. The sea was getting up, and I was sorry that the spritsail was so big. Neither it nor the courses could be reefed.

Nightfall came wild with the threat of growing wilder. I took the lateen in and watched the other canvas anxiously. Would the sunset take the wind and quiet the sea? What could I do if it did not? The squalls still freshened. The mainyard was bending like a wand. The wind roared in the rigging, and the bowsprit was working alarmingly.

I remembered that in Gov. William Bradford's account of the first *Mayflower*'s voyage Capt. Christopher Jones took in all sail in high winds, and the ship lay, as he put it, "a-hull" — just left to herself in the raging waters. We had often spoken of trying it in such conditions. Now we had them.

"Mr. Mate!" I shouted above the wind. "All hands on deck! Port watch for'ard to get the spritsail off her, and then the fore! Starboard watch take in the main! We will lie a-hull."

The mates struggled along the heaving decks to carry out these orders. A mighty squall came down, and the ship leaped up on the crest of a great breaking sea while the wind shrieked with the strength of a full gale!

"Clew lines and buntlines! Haul away now!" shouted the mate from his post.

"Haul up now! Lively there! Aho-o-o-o! Oh haul now! And again!" The boatswain's rhythmic shouts could be heard above the wind.

But the buntlines and clew lines could not haul enough of the sail up to the yard to smother it. Still alive, the canvas thrashed and thundered while the whole bowsprit waved and writhed like a great fishing rod playing a whale.

A spilling line would have to be rove to get control of that deep spritsail. The job could only be done at risk of life, for the ship was leaping like a wild thing. The mate ordered his men to don life jackets.

Out dashed the second mate (in this emergency, all hands had come to get the spritsail in), fighting his way outward along the high-steeved, writhing bowsprit. Out climbed Joe Lacey and Andy Lindsay — my best able seamen. Out leaped Beric Watson from Leeds in Yorkshire, who never had been to sea before.

I feared for them, for if the bowsprit went they died. The ship would run over them. I had no boat to put out in that kind of sea.

But they fought out to the spritsail yard and swarmed on to the footropes. The sail flapped back over them, trying to knock them off. They hung on. In every lull, at each downbeat of the ship as she shook the wind out of the sail, they struggled to rig the spilling line and get its hauling end inboard. At last!

"Heave away again! Heave lively now!"

Up came the thrashing sail, its wilder turbulence quieted, though the whole bowsprit still waved alarmingly. The four lads tore at the sail with their hands, skinning up the canvas, getting the gaskets around.

And so they defeated it, and came in again, and I was proud of them.

With the spritsail in, the two courses came in without great trouble, for there was more gear on them.

"Aloft and furl!" was the order. The mariners swarmed aloft.

"Down helm!"

The wheel spun down — into the wind. Right down, putting the rudder to windward.

This was the crucial test. Would she lie like that, more or less quietly, with the windage of the high poop keeping her shoulder to the sea? Or would she just wallow hopelessly in the great troughs, trying — perhaps successfully — to roll her masts out? We didn't know. No one had tried the maneuver in a ship like that for maybe two centuries.

We need not have feared. She came up, shoulder to the sea, and lay safely and quietly like a duck with its head tucked under its wing.

WE WENT BELOW into the great cabin to splice the main brace. It was peaceful down there, almost as in a church. The stern windows were closed. No spray drove in. No tumult of breaking seas swept across the decks overhead.

"I was never so quiet in a ship in a gale of wind at sea before, nor felt so safe," said Mate Godfrey Wicksteed, in some astonishment.

A NORTHEASTER *heels ship and the windsock stands straight out. Master and*
first mate brace legs on tiny poop deck. Helmsman watches the reeling compass.
Pilgrims on the first Mayflower *were battered by "many feirce stormes."*

NEW YORK *extends a warm, wild welcome to* Mayflower, *driving with only God's good wind for*

This proved to be the last hazard. Soon the sea smiled again and the last remnants of the gale were gone. Under all sail we pitched on toward Nantucket Shoals.

On the morning of the 52d day we were among the swordfishermen and the New Bedford draggers, who gave us a cheering welcome and some lobsters and fish. On the following morning we came at last round Nantucket

Lightship—53 days out from Plymouth, England, having sailed 5,400 sea miles. At daybreak that morning the liner *Queen Elizabeth* came out of her way, slowing down gracefully to blow a salute on her siren, which must have disturbed her passengers at that early hour, and to make us a welcoming hoist of signal flags. For an hour or so there were only three ships together in sight of each other, and two

power. She also visited Washington and Miami, then returned to Plymouth, her permanent berth.

were square-riggers, for the United States Coast Guard training bark *Eagle* came sailing by. The third was the *Queen Elizabeth* — what an odd combination!

The sun shone and the sea flattened, and the little new *Mayflower* put her best foot forward, bounding along with the beam wind at an average of 7.7 knots. Soon we were approaching Provincetown. After a call there we sailed on to Plymouth to moor at a special buoy off famous Plymouth Rock.

The Vice President came to greet us. Indians flew in from Oklahoma, cowboys from Cheyenne, and Pilgrim descendants by the thousands from all over America.

The odd little ship and her volunteer crew had done well. We heard no more of those pessimists, back in England.

CHAPTER NINETEEN

Captain Cook and the seagoing clock

James Cook started as a ship's boy on a coal bark and died as England's greatest maritime explorer. He probed and charted the Pacific, pampered the health of his crews, led naturalists to new worlds of wonder, and tested Harrison's chronometer, the long-sought key to precise navigation.

A ROBUST six-foot figure with bushy brows and small keen brown eyes stood on the quarterdeck of the bark *Endeavour* and watched Plymouth, England, fade from view. It was August, 1768, and James Cook, at 40 a newly commissioned lieutenant in the Royal Navy, was off to write another chapter in the story of Pacific discovery.

Admiralty orders instructed Cook "to observe the Passage of the Planet Venus over the Disk of the Sun on the 3rd of June 1769" at Tahiti. This would help determine more accurately the distance of the earth from the sun. Secret papers told him to search for the legendary southern continent and to "observe the Nature of the Soil, and the Products thereof ... the Genius, Temper, Disposition and Number of the Natives ... the Situation of such Islands as you may discover." Aboard were astronomers and naturalists.

This was a new type of expedition—one dedicated to scientific discovery. And it took a new and rare breed of commander—humane, intelligent, thorough, skilled in navigation.

An 18th century map of the Pacific showed few of the island groups we know, and much of what it did show was wrong. The Pacific covers one-third of the globe; its area is greater than all the continents combined; its width at the equator is nearly half the earth's circumference. Small wonder that Spanish sailors hugged the parallel of 13° N. to insure touching the Mariana Islands on their 80-day voyage to the Philippine Islands.

Cook would hug no parallels. A self-taught mathematician and astronomer, this son of a Yorkshire day laborer had charted Newfoundland and sounded the St. Lawrence. His worry was not navigation but scurvy, a disease that had cut down sailors on many a long voyage. He realized that he must prevent it if he was to reach the remote areas of the Pacific.

At Madeira he sentenced a marine and a sailor to 12 lashes apiece for refusing to eat the onions he bought for them. Sailors in those days were not epicures; scant rations of salt junk and worm-eaten oatmeal made up their diet, and they accepted it stoically. But to ask

JOHN HARRISON, *a Yorkshire carpenter, devoted a lifetime to perfecting the first reliable seagoing clock so mariners could determine longitude. His secret: compensating for temperature change by use of different metals to vary spring tension. Chronometer No. 1 (right), completed in 1735, still ticks off seconds, minutes, hours, and days in the National Maritime Museum at Greenwich, England.*

STANLEY MELTZOFF

"DEATH OF CAPTAIN COOK—FEBRUARY 14, 1779, AT KEALAKEKUA," FROM A PAINTING BY JOHN CLEVELEY, 1787, THE MARINERS MUSEUM, NEWPORT NEWS
BELOW: JAMES COOK IN CAPTAIN'S DRESS UNIFORM BY NATHANIEL DANCE, 1776, NATIONAL MARITIME MUSEUM, GREENWICH

CAPTAIN COOK *won fame and met death in the Pacific he made known to the world. He criss-crossed it with characteristic thoroughness (below). Logging more than 60,000 miles on his second voyage alone, he once spent 117 days out of sight of land in his search for a southern continent.*

During the Revolution, Benjamin Franklin instructed American ships to treat "Captain Cook and all his people with all civility and kindness . . . as common friends to mankind."

A dagger thrust on "Owhyhee" (above), in a dispute with Hawaiians over a stolen boat, ended the explorer's life. His ships completed probes in Bering Strait before returning via the Orient.

FIRST VOYAGE (1768-71) Tahiti, New Zealand, Australia

SECOND VOYAGE (1772-75) Antarctic waters

THIRD VOYAGE (1776-80) British Columbia, Alaska, Hawaii

each man to eat 20 pounds of onions in a week, followed by 10 pounds more a few weeks later — that was too much!

They grumbled their way around Cape Horn and across the broad Pacific. No one knew what the next mess would bring: sauerkraut, coconut milk, sometimes even island grasses that their captain had cooked for them.

On April 13, 1769, Cook reached mysterious Tahiti and began his exploration of the archipelago. Because the islands "lay contiguous to one another," Cook wrote, "I have named [them] Society Isles."

He described the natives in detail—their tattooing, burial rites, four-note musical scale, nostril flutes, and dances wherein they would "shake themselves in a very whimsical manner." He realized the importance of their breadfruit. It could become a foodstuff for Negro slaves in the West Indies. Before leaving Tahiti, Cook planted watermelons, oranges, limes, and other seeds. These and subsequent gifts of poultry and pigs at other places changed the economy of many Pacific islands.

Two of Cook's marines jumped ship at Tahiti, succumbing to the charms that were to lure many later adventurers. Tracked down in the mountains, they were torn from the arms of their new wives. It was a sad return to reality for the men, for a Tahitian maid was trained to gather coconuts and breadfruit for her husband and to feed him silently at mealtime.

COOK DULY TRACKED VENUS, then explored southward for many days before striking westward. After a rough passage he raised New Zealand. Although shocked by the cannibalism of the Maori, he persisted in his policy of fair treatment toward natives. He flogged a sailor for stealing from one, and when the seaman protested that it was no crime to plunder an "Indian," he got six more lashes.

Cook found time to describe bird songs which "seemed to be like small bells, most exquisitely tuned," sketch a huge natural arch, note that the sand contained iron, calculate the timber in trees, and help collect some 400 plant species unknown to England.

The Dutch explorer, Abel Tasman, had sighted New Zealand in 1642 and named it Staten Land. Cook cruised for six and a half months along the coast, charting New Zealand as two main islands. The strait that divides them is named for him. He then headed west to fill in the blank east coast of Australia—

New Holland, as the Dutch labeled it. In April, 1770, *Endeavour* dropped anchor in this land of kangaroos, dingoes, and naked, white-streaked savages armed with "a weapon resembling a scimitar" (a boomerang). Cook called his anchorage Botany Bay for its "great quantity of New Plants." Just north of it would grow the city of Sydney.

Steering northward he named Port Jackson, Bustard Bay, and Cape Tribulation, where he discovered the Great Barrier Reef the hard way. Although she drew only 13 feet of water fully loaded, bluff-bowed *Endeavour* "struck and stuck fast" on the 1,200-mile-long coral reef. Overboard went stores, ballast, even six quarterdeck guns. Still the ship held fast. Every effort to haul her off failed. Leaks increased, and pumps working constantly could not keep pace with the inrush of water.

At the next high tide heroic efforts floated her, but now water poured in faster.

Cook ordered the ship fothered. His crew sewed oakum and wool on a sail, then smothered it with dirt, lowered it from the bow, and dragged it back over the worst of the leaks. Within an hour the ship was pumped free of water. A single pump kept her so until Cook found a favorable harbor for repairs.

Seaworthy again, *Endeavour* sailed through the strait navigated by Luis Vaez de Torres in 1606, touched at New Guinea, and put in at Batavia, on Java. Up to that time her captain had not lost a single man to sickness. Now malaria and dysentery contracted at the Dutch colony cost 30 lives.

When he arrived back in England Cook's conquest of scurvy was acclaimed. Promoted to the rank of commander, he took *Resolution* and *Adventure* toward the South Pole in 1772 to settle for all time whether there was a great inhabited southern continent. Among his companions were naturalists, astronomers, and a small seagoing clock—a copy of John Harrison's Chronometer No. 4.

This was the chronometer's first extended voyage. It always told Cook exactly what time it was at the prime meridian (0° longitude), which runs through Greenwich, England. His sextant and astronomical tables told him the local time. Cook converted the difference (1 hour = 15 degrees) and got his longitude or east-west position.

Mariners had long known how to calculate their latitude or north-south position (page 78). But they never knew precisely how far east or west they were—witness Columbus's wide error. They had no way of keeping exact time. Spring watches in the 16th century improved on the hourglass. But temperature changes rendered them inaccurate.

To Cook the chronometer became "our trusty friend, the Watch" and "our never-failing guide." It weathered the trials of sub-zero temperatures—and so did Cook's men as they entered polar waters and shivered eastward.

Inch-long icicles hung from their noses. They were encased in frozen sleet, as if in armor, while on deck. They worked with rigging so encrusted with ice that human hands could scarcely grasp the ropes.

Yet the sailors kept cheerful and well, though Cook himself came near death. In his convalescence he related, "A favourite dog fell a sacrifice to my tender stomach; and I could eat of this flesh, as well as broth made of it, when I could taste nothing else."

158

The voyage proved that no Antarctic land extended to habitable latitudes. Cook demonstrated this by circumnavigating the globe while cruising southern waters.

How narrowly he missed discovering the continent of Antarctica!

Many were the fruits of this voyage. "We explored the Pacific Ocean between the tropics and temperate zone," reported a shipboard scientist, "furnished geographers with new islands . . . naturalists with plants and birds, and above all the friends of mankind with various modifications of human nature."

REWARDS CAME to Cook. The Royal Society elected him a fellow and asked for scientific papers. For one, on preserving the health of his crew, it bestowed its gold medal. The Admiralty made him a captain and gave him a comfortable shore assignment that would provide an income the rest of

"BEAGLE" AND "ADVENTURE" AT FOOT OF MOUNT SARMIENTO IN TIERRA DEL FUEGO BY CONRAD MARTENS, MEMBER OF THE EXPEDITION; COURTESY COMMANDER JOHN SMYTH, R.N., LONDON

his life. But, dining one day with Lord Sandwich, he was asked to suggest a leader to undertake a new search for the Northwest Passage—this time from the Pacific side. Impulsively he volunteered himself.

He was off again!

Cook left Plymouth on July 11, 1776, rounded Africa with *Resolution* and *Discovery,* and island-hopped to New Zealand and Tahiti. Heading north, the explorers celebrated their second Christmas out by naming a tiny guano island for the holiday. They sailed on to the Hawaiian Islands (Cook named them the Sandwich Islands after his patron), then coasted Oregon and Washington.

They put in at cross-shaped Nootka Sound on Vancouver Island and set up a crude observatory. Cook wrote of the skins of wolf, bear, deer, marten, fox, seal, ermine, and beaver to be had there—prophetic of the days when the great North West Company was to open up British Columbia for its fur trade.

The explorers sailed to Prince William Sound in Alaska and tested Cook Inlet as a possible Northwest Passage. Cook noted the volcanic activity of the Aleutians. He explored the Bering Sea and proved how narrow is the strait between Asia and North America.

Then he sailed back to Hawaii. On February 14, 1779, at Kealakekua Bay, England's greatest explorer died in a clash with natives.

Cook put Australia and New Zealand firmly on the map; removed the mythical southern continent; found numerous island oases in the Pacific; extended the cruising radius of future navigators by conquering scurvy. He "excited the zeal for similar undertakings," and proved the chronometer was a reliable tool.

Two of Cook's subordinates would carry this new instrument on voyages of their own. One was George Vancouver. The other was William Bligh.

159

The *Beagle* and Mr. Darwin

I*N 1832 H.M.S.* Beagle *anchored off Tierra del Fuego. She carried 24 chronometers for precise navigation and surveys—also a seasick young naturalist who would make her voyage historic: Charles Darwin.*

On Beagle's *journey along South America Darwin had found mammal fossils that shook his belief in the stability of species. Now he got his first look at "man in his lowest and most savage state"—the Fuegian native. He watched a woman suckle her child as sleet fell on their naked bodies. He saw stunted men, "their hair entangled, their voices discordant, and their gestures violent." When* Beagle *sailed from the shadow of Mount Sarmiento (left) with the sloop* Adventure, *a scientific time bomb sputtered in Darwin's mind: "Could our progenitors have been men like these?"*

At the Galapagos he discovered that finches and giant tortoises differed slightly from island to island, evidence that new forms of life evolve gradually. Darwin collected specimens around the world on Beagle's *five-year voyage, then studied them 20 years. In 1859 his* Origin of Species, *theorizing that plants and animals were products of natural selection, rocked the world. In 1871 he placed the capstone on his theories with* The Descent of Man.

CHAPTER TWENTY

The *Bounty*: mutiny in the South Seas

Her voyage in quest of breadfruit became a tragic legend. Luis Marden of National Geographic, living among the mutineers' descendants, found her bones off Pitcairn Island.

THE AUTHOR PHOTOGRAPHED THE "BOUNTY" IN REPLICA OFF MOOREA, WEST OF TAHITI.

THE COURSE WAS WNW. The breeze had fallen during the night, and the ship had almost completely lost way. Her sails hung loose from the yards. Cordage slatted against the masts, the blocks creaked, and the chuckle of water at the bows died to a whisper. As the vessel rolled gently in the oily sea the trucks of her masts traced slow arcs against the blazing stars of the southern hemisphere. The moon, in her first quarter, filled the sails with a white radiance.

Distant 10 leagues, under the brilliant blue-white star Vega, the volcanic peak of Tofua rose from a dark sea.

Eight bells struck. Fletcher Christian, acting mate of His Majesty's Armed Vessel *Bounty,* came on deck to relieve the watch. The ship's commander, Lt. William Bligh, was asleep in his cabin below.

"I am now unhappily to relate one of the most atrocious acts of Piracy ever committed," Bligh later wrote. "Just before sun-rising, Mr. Christian, with the master at arms, gunner's mate, and Thomas Burket, seaman, came into my cabbin while I was asleep, and seizing me, tied my hands with a cord behind my back and threatened me with instant death, if I spoke or made the least noise: I, however, called so

loud as to alarm everyone; but they had already secured the officers who were not of their party . . . . Christian had only a cutlass in his hand the others had muskets and bayonets. I was hauled out of bed and forced on deck in my shirt. . . .

"The boatswain was now ordered to hoist the launch out, with a threat, if he did not do it instantly, to take care of himself. . . . Particular people were now . . . hurried over the side: whence I concluded that with these people I was to be set adrift."

So on April 28, 1789, began one of the greatest sea stories of all time: the mutiny in the *Bounty* and its fantastic train of events.

Bounty had sailed from Spithead in December of 1787, under orders to proceed to Otaheite (Tahiti) in the South Sea, there to take on breadfruit for transport to the West Indies as food for slaves. She stayed nearly six months at "the finest island in the world," loading plants, then proceeded toward Torres Strait by way of Tonga, the Friendly Islands.

There, off Tofua, the mutiny took place.

When Bligh returned safely after the mutiny, he became the talk of England: he had navigated an open boat 3,618 nautical miles in 41 days to the island of Timor. He was hailed as a hero and a martyr. Then public opinion

161

changed. Ever since, he has usually been pictured as an unendurable martinet.

There is no doubt that Bligh had a caustic tongue and an irascible nature—and that Fletcher Christian had felt their sting. Though Christian left no written record, a crewman wrote that at the time of the mutiny the acting mate said to Bligh: "I have been in Hell for this Fortnight passd and am determined to bear it no longer.... I have been used like a Dog all the Voyage."

Bligh attributed the mutiny to the charms of the "handsome, mild and cheerful women" of Tahiti. His men wanted to return to the island paradise "where they need not labor."

Bligh returned to Tahiti, and he succeeded that time in transplanting breadfruit to the West Indies. Perhaps the final irony is that when the breadfruit reached the Indies at last —at the cost of mutiny, piracy, shipwreck, murder, and exile—the slaves there found it tasteless and would not eat it.

IRONICALLY, TOO, the mutiny brought only trouble to Fletcher Christian and his men. After they set their captain adrift they tried to settle on the island called Tubuai, about 400 miles south of Tahiti. Hostile natives kept them constantly at war. Malcontents among the mutineers demanded to return to Tahiti "and there Seperate, where they might get Weomen without force."

Feeling his authority weaken, Christian said: "Gentlemen, I will carry you, and land you, wherever you please. I desire none to stay with me, but I have one favour to request, that you will grant me the ship, tie the foresail, and

give me a few gallons of water, and leave me to run before the wind, and I shall land upon the first island the ship drives to. I have done such an act that I cannot stay at Otaheite."

Christian knew the Admiralty had a long arm, and that sooner or later they would send a ship to look for him and his henchmen.

He took them back to Tahiti, and 16 mutineers elected to stay there. True to Christian's fears, an Admiralty ship arrived a year and a half later and captured all mutineers on the island except two who had been killed.

With eight other mutineers, six native men, 12 women, and a little girl, Christian sailed from Tahiti and disappeared. Not until the ship *Topaz* of Boston touched at lonely Pitcairn Island 1,300 miles southeast of Tahiti, 18 years later, was the mystery solved.

Looking for seals on what they believed to be an uninhabited island, the astonished crew found a flock of women and children and a lone aging Englishman—sole survivor of Christian's band. From him they heard a tale of violence and tragedy.

Slipping out of Tahiti, Christian had sailed for weeks with his fellow mutineers and the natives, looking for a hospitable but deserted island where he could live out his life without fear of discovery. He nearly had another mutiny in the *Bounty* before he sighted Pitcairn early in 1790.

Landing stores, plants, and livestock brought from Tahiti, the renegades stripped *Bounty* and burned her. Christian divided the island into nine portions among the other Englishmen and himself, leaving none for the Polynesian men. Their resentment smoldered. Two

162

130° Equator

NEW GUINEA

South

TIMOR

Torres Strait

3 *Fleeing warlike Tofuans, Bligh bears away for the Dutch settlement on Timor, 3,618 miles to the west. The 18 men overload the 23-foot launch to within seven inches of the water.*

4 *Fighting hunger, thirst, burning sun, and the sea itself for 41 days, Bligh brings his men safely to Timor—history's most celebrated open-boat voyage. A Dutch ship carries him homeward. He lands at Portsmouth March 14, 1790.*

Great Barrier Reef

NEW HEBRIDES

Tropic of Capricorn

AUSTRALIA

JEERING MUTINEERS *set their captain adrift to face "a sea where the navigation is but little known, in a small boat, twenty-three feet long, deep laden with eighteen men, without a chart." Bligh had bread and water, cutlasses, compass, quadrant, and his memory of the Pacific. "Cold and Shiverings," starvation, and constant bailing reduced men to scarecrows sprawled on the boat's planking. Green islands beckoned, but Bligh feared native attack. Two weeks: "Some of my people half dead." Three weeks: "saw several Boobies . . . caught one. . . . The body, entrails, Beak and feet I divided into 18 shares." Five weeks: "extreme Weakness, Swelled legs, Hollow and Ghastly countenances." Six weeks: Timor.*

180°   130°

0   1000
NAUTICAL MILES
NATIONAL GEOGRAPHIC MAP

Pacific   Ocean

1 *Mutineers seize Bounty April 28, 1789, off Tofua, set Captain Bligh adrift, and sail to Tubuai, then to Tahiti. To escape the Admiralty's avenging arm, Fletcher Christian searches eastward for a remote island.*

2 *Settling on cliff-girt Pitcairn, mutineers strip and burn Bounty January 23, 1790. Yankee sealers discover the hideout 18 years later; one mutineer still lives. On January 21, 1957, author Marden finds Bounty's bones.*

FIJI ISLANDS

TAHITI

TOFUA

TUBUAI

PITCAIRN ISLAND

years later it burst into flame—over a woman.

The wife of one of the mutineers died in a fall from a cliff, and the widower appropriated the wife of one of the Tahitians. The Polynesians banded together to take revenge. The next few years saw a series of bloody clashes and violent deaths. Fletcher Christian was shot as he worked in his field. Another man threw himself into the sea after drinking too much home-distilled alcohol. Ten years after *Bounty* landed, all the Tahitian men were dead, and of the mutineers only the doughty patriarch discovered by the *Topaz* survived.

THE STORY of the mutiny and its incredible chain of events had long fascinated me. In 1956, 166 years after Christian landed, I sailed for Pitcairn Island. Though I told myself that the chance for success was nearly nil, I was going to dive for traces of the *Bounty*.

Ten days out from Panama on a New Zealand ship, we raised the island. It lay low on the horizon, a slate-colored smudge against the bright gold of the westering sun. As we approached, it rose slowly out of the sea and gradually took on the shape of a crouching lion rimmed with the white of surf.

Three longboats from the island intercepted our steamship. When we stopped they shipped oars and were warped alongside. I stared curiously, for this was my first look at the Pitcairn Islanders. My impression was of friendliness. Every upturned face wore a smile. Some Pitcairners were calling to friends on board.

They swarmed up our dangling Jacob's ladders, first the women, then men who hauled up items for trading: fresh fruits, wood carvings, handwoven baskets. A tall, broad-shouldered

LUIS MARDEN, NATIONAL GEOGRAPHIC STAFF

HARDY SALTS, *mainly from Nova Scotia, man a new* Bounty. *She foots steadily across the cobalt Pacific to Tahiti to take part in a new filming of the Nordhoff and Hall book* Mutiny on the Bounty. *She was built in Lunenburg at the same yard that launched the famed fishing schooner* Bluenose. *Figurehead (left) is a replica of the "woman in a riding habit" that charmed Tahitians when they visited Bligh's vessel in 1788.*

man came up the companion ladder. He wore a crowned palm-leaf hat, and as he smiled white teeth flashed in a handsome tanned face. He held out his hand to the captain. This was Parkin Christian, 73-year-old great-great-grandson of Fletcher Christian and chief magistrate of Pitcairn Island.

"Welcome to Peet-kern," he said when the captain had introduced me.

I watched the Pitcairners on deck. Their features were more strongly European than I had expected. They were tanned, but most were no darker than sunburned, brown-haired Englishmen. The women looked more Polynesian than the men. All were barefoot.

When trading ended, I climbed down into a longboat with the people who would be my hosts. Someone shouted, "A song for the captain!" Seventy voices rose in harmony singing,

"In the Sweet Bye and Bye." As the last strains died away our boat captain called out, "Cast off!" and we moved slowly away.

A voice sang out. "Tillah, tillah! Anybody bin see ah tillah?" The heavy tiller was passed over my head. Then a dozen hands raised the mast, made fast the shrouds, and hoisted our jib and gaff-rigged mainsail.

A man thumped a crate of my air tanks. "I heardsay you gwen dive in Bounty Bay."

I admitted it.

"Man," he said, "you gwen be dead as hatchet." Why a hatchet should be deader than a doornail, or anything else, I never found out, but it signifies utter extinction.

As we approached shore, the darkening island grew taller. In the half light I could see a line of white breakers ahead. The captain shouted, "Down sail!" and stood to his long steering sweep, scanning the breakers. "Pull ahead!" he cried, and long oars bent as 14 rowers dipped in unison. We shot forward, keeping just ahead of a big sea that rose under our stern. At express-train speed we rushed past black rocks, entered a narrow channel, then slowed and gently bumped the shore, where ready hands seized the boat. The man next to me jumped into the waist-high water, turned his broad back, asked, "Ready, mate?" and carried me pickaback to the landing.

As I panted up to the escarpment where the village begins, 250 feet above the landing, the women looked at me with friendly amusement. At the top I followed Fred Christian to his home, where I would be staying. His wife Flora took my hand at the door.

"I hope you be happy here," she said.

"Thank you, Mrs. Christian," I replied.

"No Mister or Mrs. here; I'm Flora."

"Yes," their son Tom said with a grin, "we all use our Christian names here."

It would be confusing otherwise. Of the island's 153 souls, 55 have the family name Christian; there are only half a dozen surnames, three of them representing mutineers.

TAHITIANS *in swarming canoes re-enact the welcome their ancestors gave the original* Bounty. *Bligh later blamed the mutiny on the lush island's "allurements of dissipation . . . beyond anything that can be conceived." Capt. Samuel Wallis of England discovered Tahiti in 1767.*

"Come have a bit o' supper," Flora said. After grace she placed before me a steaming platter of corned beef. I was surprised, because most of the Pitcairners are members of the Seventh-day Adventist Church and the Adventists I knew were vegetarians. Later Pitcairn's pastor told me that vegetarianism is not an inflexible tenet. The islanders' isolation and limited diet gave reason to eat meat.

These mutineer descendants are amazing trenchermen. I thought I could hold my own at table, but I was forced to yield to professionals. At length even Fred, master of us all, had to stop.

"Can I bring you anything?" Flora asked.

"Yes," murmured Fred, "another stomach." He smiled beatifically. "I always say Fletcher Christian find a good place to hide."

The island bell awoke me next morning. When it rings three times all able-bodied men must report to the courthouse for whatever public work the island council decides upon. Today's job was to bring the freight up from the landing. As Fred Christian and I walked down the path he greeted the people we passed:

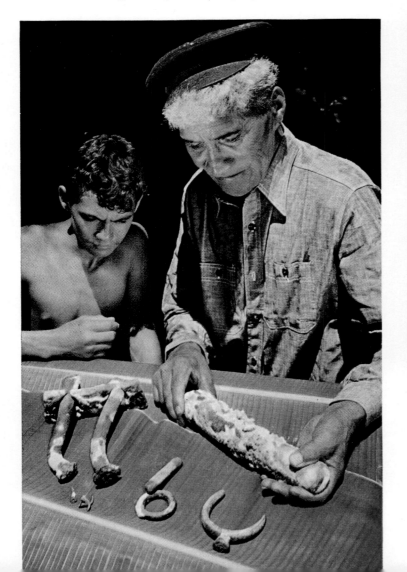

BOUNTY BAY *conceals the bones of the ill-starred ship beneath 20 to 40 feet of turbulent water. Her iron ballast bars lie in the surf. Her rudder was found to seaward years ago. The author believed it had snapped off when mutineers ran*

the ship into the bay to ground her and set her afire. Her skeleton, then, seemed likely to lie on a line between rudder and ballast. Diving for six weeks, he discovered Bounty's resting place and brought up the rudder pintle, oarlock, sheathing nails, and hull fittings that

Fred Christian, great-great-grandson of the mutiny leader, shows young Fletcher Christian at left. Pitcairners live by gardening, fishing, selling souvenirs to passing ships. On return, longboats are winched up a log ramp into thatched sheds beyond reach of the relentless combers.

"Bout yawly gwen?" (Where are you going?) The islanders say this instead of "Good morning." The women answered, "We gwen up ah hill, pick *kumara*" (sweet potato). And to me they said, "Enjoy yourself?" and seemed genuinely concerned.

As the days passed I questioned these kindly people about any visible remains of *Bounty* that might assist me in uncovering her.

Everybody knew that a clutch of iron ballast lay in the surf near the shore. And years ago Parkin Christian had found her rudder farther out. The islanders were convinced that the rest had either been salvaged earlier or destroyed by the relentless pounding of sea.

"It-sa gone," they all said. "Nothing left."

I trained Len Brown and Tom Christian, two Pitcairn youths, to use the Aqua-Lung. Together we tried to picture where the ship lay.

The thing is relatively simple, we decided: *Bounty* was about 100 feet long; the ballast bars are over there in the surf; the rudder was found out there; all we have to do is to draw an imaginary line between the two places, search along it on the bottom, and we are bound to find some trace of the ship.

Search we did; we nearly plowed furrows in the bottom with our chins. But we found no clues to the ship. Standing on our heads on the floor of Bounty Bay, we took a beating. Our heads and shoulders were in comparative calm, but every few seconds the surge of a roller would slam into us, and our wildly kicking feet were powerless to control us. Helplessly we would crash against the sharp coral fingers that clung to the rocks and feel their sting as they scored red lines on our legs.

The days fled, and still nothing. But these were pleasant days among the islanders. With Fred or Tom or Len I strolled over Pitcairn's two square miles, gingerly skirting its almost sheer cliffs, crossing the undulating savanna that fits like a cloak on the top of the island, visiting the wind-powered radio transmitter and the post office run by an American who migrated to Pitcairn years ago.

170

OARS FLASHING, *a Pitcairn longboat, designed like a whaleboat, leaps crashing surf. Outside*

I saw the excitement of mail day, when the bell is rung four times and islanders gather hopefully. They may not have received mail for weeks if bad weather has forced ships to bypass them. Parcels are eagerly awaited by Pitcairners; since there are no shops on the island all buying is by mail. Women regularly order from Sears Roebuck and Montgomery Ward in the United States. I saw cloth-wrapped parcels that contained 65 pounds of fishhooks, ordered from Norway by one man for all the fishermen on the island.

Through the generations, land has been so subdivided through inheritance that by the time I arrived some people owned only four feet. Others are landless. Even individual trees have owners, but no one objects if a hungry man picks an orange or coconut. "All right you pick coc'nut," Fred told me, "so long you eat it under the tree. Cahn't cahly it away."

Pitcairn is only about six miles in circumference, and every prominent rock, cove, or cliff has acquired a name. I had seen one point on the southwest coast marked "Oh Dear" on the map, and I asked Fred how it got its name.

"Well, native man wading 'long shore there, drop his *malu* [loincloth] in water. You know that's all they wear, and he look down and say, 'Oh dear!' "

Then there are old island dishes—humpus-bumpus, china-in-the-milk, Eddie, potta. The last is made from taro greens, the others from bananas. "It's not Eddie the name," Flora told me when I asked about that one, "but they put it that way. Eddie—that's Lucy's husband—he like it, so that's why they call it for him."

SIX WEEKS PASSED, and as far as finding any more of the *Bounty* was concerned, I was beginning to agree with the islanders that "It-sa gone." One day Len and I were out, but we were not enthusiastic. I shrugged into my Aqua-Lung and fell backward, diver fashion, into the sea. Waiting for Len, I cruised slowly over the animate carpet of seaweed. Big jacks swam round me, watching curiously.

171

the breakers, men exchange steering sweep for rudder, step the mast, and sail to a hove-to ship.

LUIS MARDEN, NATIONAL GEOGRAPHIC STAFF

BROAD ARROW, *symbol of the British Crown, was struck into* Bounty's *larger copper and bronze fittings. Luis Marden recovered this relic after it had lain on the ocean floor 167 years. A few days later a young diver from the globe-circling yacht* Yankee *spotted the weed-covered fluke of a* Bounty *anchor (right). When winched up, the 12-foot hook still held fragments of its wooden stock.*

On a bed of weed I saw a crescent-shaped object. It was an old-fashioned oarlock, with one arm longer than the other. Then I came unexpectedly on a long, sandy trench. The end nearest me was covered with white limestone secreted by calcareous algae. I could see little squiggles in the surface, curious markings that resembled nothing so much as petrified worms.

I thrust my face closer, almost touching the bottom. My heart jumped. The squiggles were encrusted sheathing nails, *Bounty* nails—dozens of them!

I drove a cold chisel through the limestone crust of the trench. At each blow a puff of black "smoke" arose—carbonized wood of the ship's planking. I came on a long bolt and carefully chipped it free. Digging deeper, I uncovered fragments of the copper with which the *Bounty* had been sheathed, in good condition and almost an eighth of an inch thick.

Beyond, two other trenches stretched toward the spot where the ballast bars lay in the yeasty surf. These must mark the line of the keel, or one of the main strakes of the hull.

I looked up for Len. He was just above me, staring questioningly. I reached up my hand for his, pumped it violently, and pointed. He grinned and nodded, and we shook hands again.

We had found the resting place of the *Bounty.*

172

CHAPTER TWENTY-ONE

War at sea

Mighty ships in battle line, massive
broadsides at close range marked
the era of fighting sail. Alan Villiers
logs its greatest day — Trafalgar!

"NO CAPTAIN can do very wrong if he
places his Ship alongside that of an
Enemy." Thus Vice Admiral Horatio
Nelson summed up his orders to the British
fleet. His ships were patrolling off Cádiz that
fall of 1805, bottling up Napoleon's fleet in the
harbor. One day soon, as every British captain
knew, the French and Spanish ships would
come out and fight — a long battle line with
gunports open, ready to slug it out, broadside
to broadside, in the accepted way.

Though outnumbered, the British crews
waited confidently for the battle that would
kill hundreds of them. For their leader was
Lord Nelson, the slight, one-armed, one-eyed
genius who added an extra flair — "the Nelson
touch" — to the formula for naval warfare.

The great day came with ominous weather.
Out of the glowering dawn of October 21
sailed the combined French-Spanish fleet, 33
mighty ships of the line, their gilded and brightly
painted hulls gliding under a press of snow-
white sail. Converging on them came 27 British
ships, black with yellow gunport bands.

Perfect in symmetry, the great vessels
looked like sea cathedrals, creations to sail
softly to the glory of God. But the swish of
slow-turning water at their bows, the soft hum
of low wind in taut rigging was suddenly punc-

BOARDERS AWAY! *French seamen leap from
the entangled bow of 20-gun* Bayonnaise *to
capture Britain's 42-gun* Ambuscade. *The
two nations fought almost continuously
from 1793 down to Napoleon's fall in 1815.*

"BATTLE OF THE BAYONNAISE AND THE AMBUSCADE, DECEMBER 14, 1798" BY LOUIS-PHILIPPE CRÉPIN (1772–1851), MUSÉE DE LA MARINE, PARIS

CHEERING CREW *of the British* Belleisle *greets supporting ships. Dismasted by raking fire as she broke the French-Spanish line at Trafalgar, she's still in the thick of it. Ships fought as long as men could serve guns in the smoke-filled hell of gun decks (below). Gun captain signals for elevation, one hand on taut trigger line that trips flintlock and sends a 32-pound shot crashing into the enemy.*

NELSON'S SHIPS *shoulder through the enemy line into a chaos of destruction. A storm struck after the battle, wrecking all but four of the British prizes.*

tuated by blasting trumpets and rolling drums.

Beat to quarters! Flags fly in a flurry of signals. Boatswain's pipes shrill. The bare feet of seamen thud on decks and companionways. Gunports open and light floods the gun decks. The planking is painted red so that blood will not show. Decks are sanded so that blood will not cause men to slip. Powder monkeys stack neat bags of powder. Gun tackles creak as grim black muzzles are run out. Marines in bright uniforms step to their stations.

As the British fleet closes, the enemy battle line heads back toward Cádiz. Nelson forms two lines of his ships. Instead of angling in to meet the foe flank to flank, they aim straight across the line, intending to break it and destroy the rear before the van can maneuver to its aid. This is the Nelson touch.

French and Spanish close up, bowsprits almost prodding through stern galleries. Nelson's tactics give them the advantage of a raking position: their broadsides can sweep the length of the oncoming British ships while only a few

bow guns can answer. But Nelson weighs the danger and accepts it. He calmly walks his quarterdeck with his friend and flag captain Thomas Hardy.

The Admiral wears a frock coat with the stars of his four orders. He refuses to cover them, though he knows that sharpshooters in the enemy fighting tops recognize his flagship *Victory* leading one attacking line and will be watching for a small man with an empty right sleeve and many decorations on his chest.

Vice Admiral Collingwood leads the second line in *Royal Sovereign*. Her copper bottom is clean, and she surges ahead. Her crew now spot the wooden crosses at the ends of Spanish spanker booms. They glance toward *Victory* and read Nelson's signals: "Engage the enemy more closely." And then another string of flags rises to the mainmast head: "England expects that every man will do his duty."

Flickers of crimson brighten the line of enemy ships facing *Royal Sovereign;* smoke wraps their hulls. The first broadside reaches out for

177

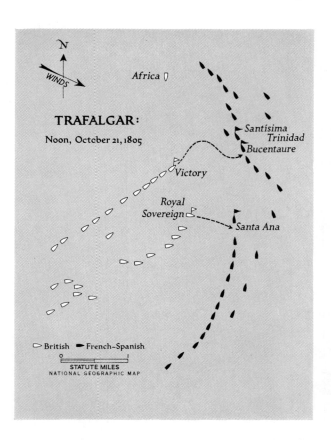

TRAFALGAR:
Noon, October 21, 1805

Africa

Santísima
Trinidad
Bucentaure

Victory

Royal
Sovereign

Santa Ana

◁ British ◀ French-Spanish
STATUTE MILES
NATIONAL GEOGRAPHIC MAP

FATALLY WOUNDED, *Nelson drops on*
Victory's *bullet-swept deck. Top-hatted*
midshipman, scarlet-jacketed marine fire
at enemy tops to avenge him. Captain
Hardy rushes to his side. The hero's
body, brought home in a cask of spirits,
lies in St. Paul's Cathedral in London.
The battle that denied Napoleon the sea
began when fleets converged in light airs
(above) some 12 miles off Cape Trafalgar,
Spain. Nelson's smallest ship of the line,
64-gun Africa, *arrived late, but helped*
dismast 130-gun Santísima Trinidad, *the*
greatest warship built up to that time.

the British and the Battle of Trafalgar begins.

Nelson watches Collingwood engage and rake the massive Spanish ship *Santa Ana.* He continues his leisurely pacing. On *Victory's* lower decks gunners crouch tensely, stripped to the waist, neckerchiefs wound around their heads to deaden noise. Men hone cutlasses. Some, incongruously, dance a hornpipe. There are Americans, Germans, even Frenchmen and Spaniards. All will fight with fury.

A few shots splash about *Victory,* finding the range. Then from four enemy ships a massive broadside flames and crashes — nearly 200 guns slam their metal at the flagship's bow. Shot smashes home. Flying splinters snarl through the air. Torn sails flap; cut rigging twangs and lashes. Nelson's secretary, standing near the Admiral, is killed. Eight marines tumble grotesquely. A splinter shears the silver buckle from Hardy's shoe.

"This is too warm work, Hardy, to last long," says Nelson.

178

"DEATH OF LORD NELSON" BY DENIS DIGHTON (1792-1827), NATIONAL MARITIME MUSEUM, GREENWICH

Yet it seems to last forever. *Victory*'s mizzen topmast crashes, her wheel is smashed. Men rush below to steer by emergency tackle. She faces a wall of blazing guns, and Hardy asks which ship to head for. The Admiral shrugs. "Take your choice."

In a hail of shot, Hardy drives past the stern of the French *Bucentaure,* so close that *Victory*'s main yardarm breaks the vangs of the Frenchman's gaff. Now! A thundering British broadside of double- and triple-shotted guns roars death into that defenseless stern, shot howling the length of the French ship, mowing down men, dismounting cannon. Nelson has broken the line.

Ship after ship heads through the gap; each rakes *Bucentaure,* then swings to engage the following vessels. In a melee of flames, smoke, and dying men, guns roar ceaselessly, masts crash on shattered decks. So close are ships that gunners, leaning through ports to ram home fresh charges, have rammers snatched away by the enemy. Muzzles almost touch opposite hulls. At each shot a seaman flings a bucket of water at the enemy's powder-scorched planking lest it burn both ships. Boarders spring across bulwarks and hammock netting. French and Spanish gunners hastily slam lower gunports to keep cutlass-swinging Britons from stepping aboard.

Victory draws alongside *Redoutable* and hammers her with lower deck guns. Muskets fire from the Frenchman's tops. Yet Nelson continues to stroll with Hardy. The plan has worked. The enemy van cannot now turn in time to help the beleaguered battle line.

WHY DIDN'T those lead ships turn earlier? Perhaps their captains were confounded by dread of Nelson. This strange little admiral was a legend even before Trafalgar immortalized him. At sea since he was 12, he ever sought the heroic role. At 20 he became "the merest boy of a captain," as the future William IV described him.

Wounded during the fight for Corsica in 1793, he lost the sight of an eye. He gave his right arm leading an unsuccessful attack on Santa Cruz de Tenerife, in the Canary Islands, in 1797. Yet it took the Battle of the Nile to make him the public hero that he craved to be.

In 1798, a French fleet convoyed troops to Egypt to launch Napoleon's eastern campaign. Nelson found the ships anchored in line, hugging a shoal at Abukir Bay, near the mouth of the Nile. An "unassailable" position. Whoever heard of challenging anchored ships? Why, with no sails to handle, every man became a gunner! Attack in a defended bay? Madness!

But Nelson noticed that the Frenchmen lay at single anchors, swinging freely. If there was room to swing, there must be room to sail. As night fell he struck. Half his ships squeezed between the enemy and the shoals, where they were least expected. The rest kept to the deep-water side of the French fleet, sandwiching it between two roaring battle lines. The British had hoisted lanterns for recognition, but soon light enough came from blazing French ships. Nelson all but annihilated Napoleon's fleet.

Three years later at Copenhagen he faced a similar problem—a line of enemy vessels moored behind shoals under strong forts. He gathered shallow-draft ships of the line, sloops, fire ships, and bomb vessels, braved the shoals, and battered the foe. Carnage was dreadful. When his worried superior signaled to break off action, Nelson blandly ignored the flags.

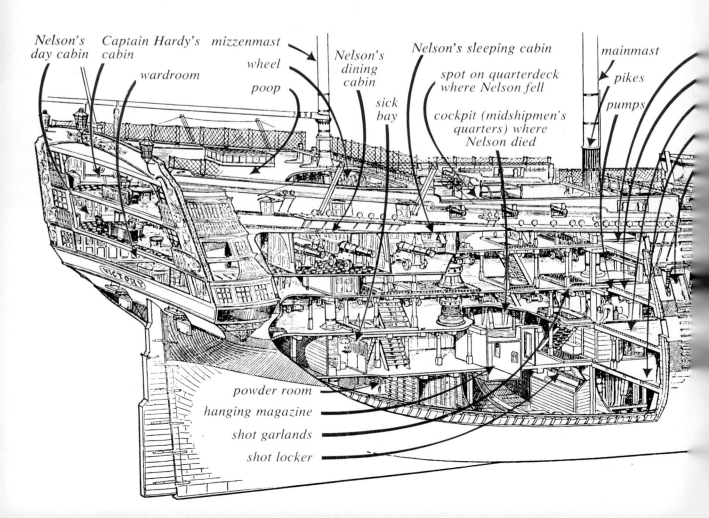

Nelson's day cabin

Captain Hardy's cabin

wardroom

mizzenmast

wheel

poop

Nelson's dining cabin

sick bay

Nelson's sleeping cabin

spot on quarterdeck where Nelson fell

cockpit (midshipmen's quarters) where Nelson died

mainmast

pikes

pumps

powder room

hanging magazine

shot garlands

shot locker

"I have only one eye," he said. "I have a right to be blind sometimes."

Though he was worshiped by his crews and beloved by fellow officers (his "band of brothers"), Nelson's affair with Lady Hamilton shocked those superiors who would have honored him. Of the four orders that adorned him at Trafalgar, only one, the Order of the Bath, had been bestowed by England.

Who knows whether it was this insignia that a French sharpshooter sighted on while Nelson paced his deck? The musket flashed from *Redoutable*'s mizzen top, and the small figure pitched forward. "They have done for me at last, Hardy," he gasped. And at last he covered his orders with a fresh handkerchief that his seamen would not notice who was being carried below to die.

He lay in the crowded cockpit in the bowels of the ship, and over him timbers trembled with the shock of guns, and cheers sounded as enemy ships — 18 of them, finally — struck their colors. Napoleon's naval power was crippled. Britannia ruled the waves.

The little admiral whispered instructions to his captain. Later he murmured, "Thank God I have done my duty." And as *Victory*'s logbook records, "he then died of his wound."

B. ANTHONY STEWART, NATIONAL GEOGRAPHIC PHOTOGRAPHER. DRAWING BY COLIN MUDIE

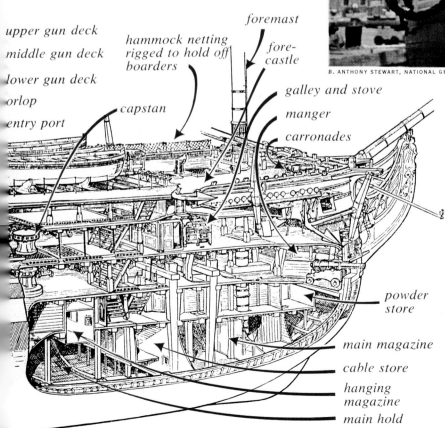

upper gun deck
middle gun deck
lower gun deck
orlop
entry port
capstan
hammock netting rigged to hold off boarders
foremast
fore-castle
galley and stove
manger
carronades
powder store
main magazine
cable store
hanging magazine
main hold

H.M.S. VICTORY, *last of England's "wooden walls," lives on in dry dock at Portsmouth. From elegant figurehead to three-decked stern, experts keep her as Nelson knew her.*

Launched in 1765, she's 2,162 tons burden, 186 feet on the gun deck. Cutaway shows elaborate organization of a 100-gun ship of the line: 12-, 24-, 32-pound guns range three decks, the heaviest below; 68-pound carronades hulk on forecastle. Powder and shot ride deep — below orlop, lowest deck in a ship.

181

The seaman's life in the days of sail

IN Dr. Samuel Johnson's view, going to sea was like being jailed, with the added risk of drowning. Many of Nelson's day agreed, for life in the "wooden walls" was harsh.

Some 850 officers and men crammed a ship of the line. There was little ventilation, no plumbing. Food was deplorable. Any misdemeanor called for flogging. Humane officers eased up on this, but others might make a man run the gauntlet, with every seaman aboard taking a fierce swipe, or order him flogged through the fleet—which killed him.

Little wonder that men who might not step ashore again for years roistered in their home

182

base at Portsmouth, England, (above) until the fleet was ready to weigh anchor.

Usually naval seamen were kept aboard while in port, lest they desert. But wives were allowed—one per man, with no questions asked—in hammocks slung between guns in the jam-packed 'tween decks. The phrase "son of a gun" is said to originate here. Some women quietly slipped to sea with their men, even went into action beside them. An admiral complained of their laundering. "The hold is continually damp and a vapour arising from it highly pernicious," he lamented.

Only a rare career man served willingly. An outstanding captain like Nelson might recruit a few men from his hometown or county. Sure of prize money and glory, they came. For the rest, bounties were offered, jails ransacked, and the press-gang prowled the lanes and streets, nabbing farmhands, shop clerks, anyone who couldn't raise a protest in Parliament or the Admiralty. They even got John Wesley, father of Methodism. But they let him go.

The navy never had enough men. "Fluxes," scurvy, and fevers decimated the crews. Of 176,000 men who shipped out between 1774 and 1780, 1,243 were killed in action, 18,541 died of disease, and 42,069 deserted. Short-handed warships stopped merchantmen at

sea to search for navy men who had deserted for better treatment. The impressment of Americans was a cause of the War of 1812.

Life in the fleet had its lighter moments. A ration of grog (watered rum) and a slice of chewing tobacco made a man forget the weevils in the biscuit, the green scum on the drinking water, the salt pork and beef so hard "it would take a good polish." On one of Nelson's ships just before Trafalgar, officers joined the crew in putting on a play.

Many a sailor wrought ship models from bones or scribed the royal arms on a scrap of ivory. Someone could always wrench a tune from a fiddle, and the men below would raise a song or dance a jig. Work at the capstan came easier with a chanteyman to lead the grunting, heaving chorus.

Jack's clothes came from the slops. The British Navy had no regulation uniform before mid-19th century. A sailor, in the usual striped trousers and short jacket, often carried all his worldly goods in a kerchief (above).

American tars, better paid and better fed, boasted more belongings. Items garnishing a Salem sea chest (below) turned a forecastle into a home: accordion, whalebone ditty box, ship model, knife, pipes, tobacco, letters, medicine bottles. Here are a man's razors and strop, shaving soap, knife and fork, marlin spike, sheath knife, slungshot (lead ball wrapped in string), and fid for splicing. This sailor wore a tarpaulin hat, mended his clothes with a sewing kit and sailor's palm, played cards and checkers, studied navigation with the aid of a quadrant and a copy of Bowditch's *Practical Navigator*, and like a good Yankee read his tiny sailor's Bible.

The British tar was never so lucky. But he fought with a will when the time came. Kipling wrote the best epitaph:

If blood be the price of admiralty,
Lord God, we ha' paid in full!

183

CHAPTER TWENTY-TWO

Fighting ships for a young nation

Colonial Americans had the timber to build ships, the skill to sail them, and the courage to defend them — all in ample supply. Having won a Republic, they combined these seafaring ingredients and produced the United States Navy, a dish that acquired plenty of seasoning in 1812.

A SMALL MAN, impeccably dressed in the uniform of America's Continental Navy, paced the quarterdeck and eyed a distant crowd of sail. The Baltic convoy, he guessed, flocking like sheep under the protection of two warships off Flamborough Head on the Yorkshire coast. A tempting target for John Paul Jones, scourge of British commerce. Those ships carried spars and tallow and other naval stores vital to the British now that the Revolutionary War had cut off supplies from New England.

He shaped course toward the convoy, and a two-decker stood across to meet him. Jones knew her. *"Serapis,"* he said to the knot of officers. "A brand new forty-four."

He also knew the odds. His flagship *Bonhomme Richard* was a converted French East Indiaman on loan to the Americans. Some of her timbers were rotten; many of her 40 guns were condemned. Her crew was a mixture of Americans, Irish, English, Scandinavians, Portuguese, and other nationals. But they were also well-trained veterans, and John

Paul Jones was not the man to avoid a fight.

Briskly the men cleared for action. Drums rolled, calling the French marines to stations in the tops and along the bulwarks. In light airs *Bonhomme Richard* and *Serapis* closed that September afternoon in 1779 to fight one of history's great sea duels.

At the first broadside two of *Richard's* overripe guns blew up, killing their gun crews and wrecking the deck above. Round shot pulverized her timbers, badly holing her. Jones backed sails and filled, jockeying to rake the enemy or at least to grapple. Seizing a dying kick from the evening breeze, he got across *Serapis's* bow. Her bowsprit snagged *Richard's* mizzen shrouds. Jones lashed it there.

The two vessels pirouetted together; then their hulls met and grappling irons hooked on. Yardarm to yardarm the battle roared, British guns blasting away *Richard's* entire gun deck until cannonballs were passing cleanly through that shattered hull. But in the tops Jones's sailors and marines cleared the enemy's upper deck, mowed down every helmsman.

"I HAVE NOT YET BEGUN TO FIGHT!" *shouts John Paul Jones as* Serapis *demands his surrender. He grapples the enemy to keep* Bonhomme Richard *afloat, hurls a pistol at a gunner who tries to strike the colors. Victorious, Jones later learns the British captain was knighted for the action. Next time, he quips, "I'll make him a lord!"*

FIFTH *CONGRESS* OF THE UNITED STATES:

At the Second Session,

Begun and held at the city of *Philadelphia*, in the state of PENNSYLVANIA, on *Monday*, the thirteenth of *November*, one thousand seven hundred and ninety-seven.

An ACT *to provide an additional armament for the further protection of the trade of the United States; and for other purposes.*

DOCUMENT FROM NATIONAL ARCHIVES. SAIL PLAN FROM "THE HISTORY OF AMERICAN SAILING SHIPS" BY HOWARD I. CHAPELLE, W. W. NORTON & COMPANY

Birth of a Navy

BARBARY *pirates spurred the young United States into building its permanent federal navy. Congress boiled over at the depredations on American commerce and in 1794 authorized six frigates. A 1797 act (opposite) called for more vessels. The 38-gun* Philadelphia, *seen amid scaffolding (above), and the 32-gun* Essex *(left) joined the rolls of the new Navy Department by 1800.*

Essex' sail plan shows a mountain of canvas crowded on tall masts to give speed. Yet the graceful hulls of such frigates served as steady platforms for up to 44 heavy guns. Copper spikes like the one (left) from Paul Revere's foundry secured stout planking.

Frigates, the cruisers of their day, were the most powerful U. S. warships until 1814. Then the nation's first 74-gun ships of the line slipped down the ways; they helped persuade Algerian pirates to respect the American flag.

187

Crowds gathered on Flamborough Head, listening to the thud of cannon, watching flashes of gunfire in the night sky. Suddenly a wall of flame roared upward, lighting the high spars and shot-torn sails. A seaman from *Bonhomme Richard* had skipped across the interlocked yardarms and dropped a grenade into the enemy's open hatch. It touched off a magazine. Jones meanwhile had been using his last three cannon—little nine-pounders—to chew away at the British mainmast. It toppled, taking the mizzen topmast with it.

The first tremble of the mast was enough for Captain Pearson of *Serapis*. "I found it in vain and in short impracticable, from the situation we were in, to stand out any longer with the least prospect of success. I therefore struck."

Down came the British ensign. Jones and his crew boarded *Serapis,* thankful to leave a sinking wreck. Their victory cost their ship and the chance to shatter the Baltic convoy. But it gave Americans their first naval hero.

JOHN PAUL JONES had earned a reputation before he ever met *Serapis*. In his ship *Ranger* he had raided the English port of Whitehaven, landed in Scotland and seized the silver plate in Lord Selkirk's manor (he returned every bit of it later), taken prizes, and spread alarm around the British coast. War insurance rates climbed, and a home guard was formed in Liverpool. "Not all their boasted navy can protect their own coasts," said Jones. Had he commanded a fighting fleet he might well have shortened the war all by himself.

But the American colonies had never organized a navy, though their ships and seamen were highly regarded. The hastily built frigates authorized during the Revolution were badly overmatched. Most remained bottled up in home waters. But some 2,000 privateers, superbly handled by American sailors who had been schooled in fisheries and on the whaling grounds, preyed on British commerce to "the very chops of the Channel."

When the Revolution ended, so did thoughts of a navy. There would always be privateers, Congress believed. But American merchantmen were fair game for Barbary pirates of North Africa and for privateers spawned by the French Revolution. So warships were authorized to guard trade routes. In 1798 the frigates *Constellation, United States,* and *Constitution* put to sea. Others followed.

The undeclared naval war with France and the Tripolitan War of 1801-05 tested these vessels and produced a crop of officers whose names ring down through the years: Hull, Decatur, Perry, Bainbridge, Preble, Porter. When America, infuriated by impressment of sailors and seizure of cargoes, declared war on Great Britain in 1812, these men had already forged a tradition of daring seamanship and sharp gunnery. The British navy, supreme over Napoleon's fleet, was caught by surprise.

ON A HOT July afternoon in 1812, *Constitution* drifted past the New Jersey coast. Her captain, Isaac Hull, hoped to join forces with the squadron of Commodore John Rodgers. When he sighted sails he thought he had made that rendezvous.

Instead, Hull had met a British blockading squadron, and it took him two days and two nights to inch his way out of their grasp. His men, gasping in the heat, piled into boats to tow the lumbering frigate, then scuttled back aboard when the wind freshened for a few tantalizing moments. They hauled buckets of water to the yardarms and doused the sails so they would catch the faintest breath. But the breeze died, and it was back to the boats again, this time to try kedging *Constitution,* for the British were creeping up. A light kedge anchor was rowed far ahead, then dropped. Men on deck hauled on the cable, pulling the frigate forward by brute force. The process was repeated again and again. At last *Constitution* escaped—to fight an action that rocked the British Empire on its heels and turned the United States into a naval power.

This time the big frigate was rolling south from near Halifax when Hull spotted topsails and bore down to investigate. She was the British frigate *Guerrière,* one of the squadron that had chased *Constitution* only a month before. The ships closed fast, and *Guerrière* fired a long-range broadside that fell short. Both vessels altered to run downwind, *Guerrière* ahead. Hull's guns were still silent.

Then the American ship cracked on sail and surged forward, right in range. Her big guns, well served by slick gun crews, loosed a terrible broadside that slashed into the Briton and carried away her mizzenmast. It trailed overside, swinging *Guerrière* off course. Hull turned with her, crunched home a second broadside, then wore around to cross her bow and rake her with his larboard guns. That was about all. *Guerrière*'s remaining masts

FLAMES DEVOUR PHILADELPHIA, *and her pirate captors jump for their lives. The U.S. frigate ran aground and was seized while blockading the harbor at Tripoli in 1803, third year of the Tripolitan War. With 84 volunteers, some in Maltese dress, Stephen Decatur slipped alongside under cover of night and burned her to bar her use. Here the Americans strain at the oars to escape with their ketch* Intrepid *from under the harbor's guns.*

Action at Tripoli taught many hard lessons. Philadelphia's officers, among them William Bainbridge and David Porter, even held classes while languishing in prison. One of Decatur's brave midshipmen, Thomas Macdonough (left), won the Battle of Lake Champlain in the War of 1812.

189

crashed down. She rolled helplessly, a smoking hulk, and her captain surrendered.

Hull's victory set the pace. Stephen Decatur in *United States* met Britain's *Macedonian* and smashed her at long cannon range 600 miles off the Canaries. The sloop of war *Wasp* battered *Frolic*. And *Constitution* (small wonder they called her "Old Ironsides"!) pummeled *Java* into a wreck.

Even in defeat the United States Navy found a battle cry. In April, 1813, the British frigate *Shannon,* patrolling Boston Harbor, was challenged by *Chesapeake* under James Lawrence. As skipper of the sloop *Hornet,* Lawrence had just whipped a British brig. Now, with many green hands in his frigate's crew, he faced a skilled enemy.

Lawrence sailed out of Boston, got alongside *Shannon,* and traded murderous broadsides. The British Captain Broke slipped into position and raked *Chesapeake*'s quarterdeck. Lawrence was shot, his crew demoralized. "Out cutlasses and board!" was the British order, and the Americans were beaten.

But Lawrence's dying words, "Don't give up the ship!" reverberated. When Oliver Hazard Perry transferred to a fresh ship to win the Battle of Lake Erie three months later, he carried a flag with those words on it. It hangs now in the Naval Academy at Annapolis.

P RIVATEERS took 1,345 reported prizes— probably many more not reported. They were swift brigs and schooners, specially built. Their sleek hulls were bare of ornament; they carried high, raking masts and stout rigging to support a cloud of canvas. The British admired them and used those they captured as dispatch boats and cruisers.

The privateer brigs *Rattlesnake* and *Scourge* took 40 prizes between them, worth more than $2,000,000—a lot of money in those days.

But as the war went on, American sea trade came near to ruin. Those early defeats caused Britain to improve her navy—with disastrous results for the Americans. Napoleon's overthrow released more British forces. Even privateering ceased to pay: owners of 24 privateers petitioned Congress for relief. They were starving. Some 6,000 American seamen lay in English prisons, most of them in grim Dartmoor.

Peace was signed on Christmas Eve, 1814, and America turned to trade. Now it had a navy to guard those merchantmen that carried the Stars and Stripes to ports the world over.

190

The stirring legend of

KATHLEEN REVIS

A MERICANS *cherish* Constitution, *the famed frigate that Oliver Wendell Holmes immortalized with his poem "Old Ironsides." She's enshrined at Boston (above).*

Her nickname came from a gunner who saw solid shot bounce off her oaken sides when fighting Guerrière *in August, 1812. Her triumph lifted morale, inspired a folk song and a square dance, "Hull's Victory."*

Isaac Hull and British Captain Dacres, old friends, are said to have bet their hats on the outcome of a duel between their ships. It was settled in 25 minutes of cannonading off Nova Scotia, with the war but two months

Old Ironsides

old. Dacres hove to as Hull bore down from windward (1). Setting his main topgallant, Hull closed to exchange broadsides. His 44 guns outmatched Dacres's 38, and Guerrière's mizzenmast went by the board (2). Hull raked, then got clear as the other masts toppled (3) and Dacres surrendered his hulk (4).

Hull, who had split his breeches in the excitement, helped his wounded adversary aboard, refused his sword but remarked, "I'll trouble you for that hat!"

191

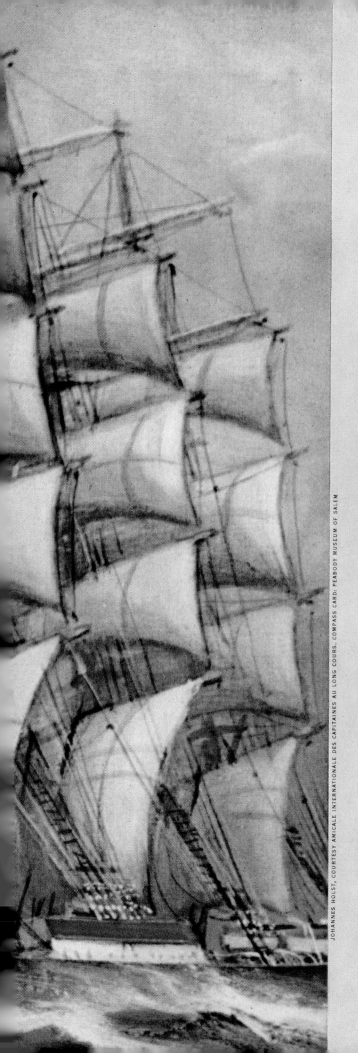

HE PERFECTS HIS SHIPS

HER name? *Preussen*—the greatest sailing ship ever built. Steel to the tops of her five towering masts, she could smash around Cape Horn at 17 knots with more than 6,000 horsepower in those 60,000 feet of gale-stiffened canvas.

This 20th century wind machine climaxed the evolution of sail. Yet she was only the afterglow of a brief and glorious day when the square-rigger touched perfection.

The need for speed produced the magnificent clippers of that golden age. These deep and narrow and clean-lined beauties slipped through calms and rode the wild winds under pyramiding clouds of sail. They were driven relentlessly, faster, ever faster by their Yankee skippers.

America had burst upon the seas with a young nation's vigor. Shipwrights shaped her wooden vessels with a practical eye: the chunky whalers, the trim merchantmen, the fast packets, the rakish privateers.

Gone were the stout galleons, dozing and drifting on their voyages. Smart Yankee brigs snatched fat cargoes from under their nodding bows.

193

Seagoing merchants

Privateering taught the Yankees to chase prizes with vigor and daring. In peace, they pursued trade the same way. Here Alan Villiers presents America's shrewd merchant skippers and their sturdy brigs and ships.

THE SMALL SHIP settled comfortably at her berth in Salem, Massachusetts, as her holds swallowed cargo—dried cod, 128 hogsheads; barrels of flour, apples, and potatoes; 114 cheeses; "5500 Bunches Onyons." In mid-September of 1783 the three-master *Grand Turk,* built as a Revolutionary War privateer, was ready for her first trading voyage.

Her owner, Elias Hasket Derby, strode across his wharf to see that his cargo was secured against storms. His eyes— one blue and one brown—swept the raking masts, the forecastle where the 11-man crew would berth, the bulwarks, patched where guns had been removed.

Satisfied, he drew up instructions for his captain, Samuel Williams.

"I do advise & Order you to sail & make the best of your way for Martinique...sell the most of your Cargo for Cash & there or at Guardalope load the Ship with Sugar Molass⁵ Cocoa & Cotton." Should profit beckon elsewhere,

"Proceed in any way different that you by Calculation shall find more for my advantage."

Off sailed *Grand Turk* for the West Indies. There Captain Williams turned salesman. For Elias Derby had *bought* this New England cargo; he did not merely freight it for others. His captain must be wholesale fishmonger, butcher, grocer, as well as purchasing agent.

Williams sold as expertly as he sailed. He returned to Salem with a cargo that paid Derby 100 percent profit.

From Boston to Charleston, other captains were doing the same for their shipowners. The nation had gone to sea.

Elias Derby eyed more distant markets. In 1784 his ship *Light Horse* carried the U. S. flag into the Baltic for the first time, to sell sugar at St. Petersburg (now Leningrad). In 1785 *Grand Turk* set off for the Indian Ocean. She sped down the Atlantic, calling at Cape Town, then continued to Ile de France (Mauritius). She sold cargo ranging from 50 boxes

JAMES FROTHINGHAM AND (LEFT) ANTOINE ROUX, 1815, PEABODY MUSEUM OF SALEM

ELIAS HASKETT DERBY, *"the first American millionaire," had prospered from privateering during the Revolution. His vessels and others like the jaunty brig (opposite) reaped fortunes.*

CROWNINSHIELD'S WHARF *in Salem, Massachusetts, vied with Derby's in handling cargoes from*

of "Spermacety Candles" to 22 boxes of prunes. Then with hold space chartered by a French merchant, she hustled on to China, following the example of New York's *Empress of China*, the first ship to carry the new American flag to the Orient.

China admitted "foreign devils" to only one port, Canton. At its deepwater anchorage, Whampoa, the 300-ton *Grand Turk* nosed through swarming sampans to nestle among great ships from Britain, Spain, Denmark, Holland, and Sweden. Here was a new world, almost mythical, to these wandering Yankees.

Gongs sounded, robes swirled, and the great official called the Hoppo came aboard to levy custom duties. He measured the ship's length and breadth, multiplied them, added 100 percent for cumshaw (tips), 50 percent more for "Hoppo's opening barrier fee." He asked if *Turk* chanced to carry any "sing songs"—cuckoo clocks or musical snuffboxes. He left with $3,500 in taxes and fees, and several sing

OLD GLORY MARKS CANTON'S *American factory in early 1800's. In this compound, factors traded*

China, India, Mauritius, the West Indies, and Europe. A busy day sees nine vessels alongside.

songs. After much delay, 400 chests of tea were stowed on a flooring of "Table sets Tea & Coffee ditto & Cups & Saucers." Five months later Salem ladies were drinking Bohea tea from Canton china, and Elias Derby was reinvesting another 100 percent profit.

The China trade lured many American vessels to Canton. When the sloop *Experiment* pulled in, the Chinese took her for a tender and asked for the big ship. "We are the big ship," replied her skipper, and started to buy tea.

for cargoes. Sampans bring in tea.

These China traders went out and back around Good Hope. But a Boston ship, *Columbia*, rounded Cape Horn in 1788 and made for the Pacific Northwest, laden with tools and trinkets. She bartered these to Indians for sea otter pelts, then crossed the Pacific to trade furs for tea at Canton. She thus launched another rich traffic—and became the first United States vessel to girdle the globe.

An enterprising Bostonian, Frederic Tudor, hit on the idea of shipping New England's abundant ice to tropic ports. Townsfolk called it "a slippery speculation," and sailors feared the cargo would melt and swamp Tudor's brig. But ice packed in sawdust carried well, and eccentric Mr. Tudor became the "Ice King."

Merchants like Tudor often sent supercargoes—agents educated at Harvard or trained in the countinghouse—to handle business on voyages. Some became shipmasters. But most captains came up "through the hawsehole." They started young and learned fast, ambitious to become officers and take shares in ventures. Nat Palmer of Connecticut shipped out at 14, became captain at 18, sighted Antarctica at 21.

Another young man, Nathaniel Bowditch of Salem, delighted in mathematics. Sailing to Mauritius, he taught navigation to the rest of the crew and uncovered some 8,000 errors in the standard English book of tables. He checked his findings on other voyages and published his *Practical Navigator* when he was only 28. Seamen use it today.

Americans brought new vigor to trade and profited. Another bonanza awaited: whaling.

197

Ships' figureheads:
the woodcarver's art

WHEN I bought the square-rigger *Joseph Conrad* (now preserved at Mystic Seaport in Connecticut) my friend Bruce Rogers carved a figurehead of Captain Conrad for her. A sailing ship had to have a figurehead. The lovely sweeping lines of her cutwater looked wrong without one. Big old windjammers like the *Star of India* (above), now cared for by the San Diego Maritime Museum, might switch to iron bowsprits, even to iron and chain bobstays. But they still wore figureheads.

Figurehead carving grew out of the ancient practice of decorating bows to invoke guiding spirits to dwell in the ship. The skill came to America from England, where families such as the Hellyers of London passed the trade down seven generations.

In the early 19th century almost every American coastal town supported craftsmen like Boston's Levi L. Cushing, whose business card showed a carver at work (right). Or Samuel Winsor, whose Commercial Street sign directed customers "upstairs." The carver usually kept shop in a vacant sail loft near the wharf. Shipbuilders would draw on the floor the lines of the bow to show where the figurehead would go. The carver then chalked the design on his block of pine, and set to work with hammer, chisel, and gouge.

He often carved classic heads like the woman's at right. He sometimes used live models. William Rumney posed his daughter for a figurehead on an East Boston ship.

The vessel's name often dictated the design. The stately eagle at right adorned Donald McKay's clipper *Great Republic*. The twin girls, probably a shipowner's daughters, may have graced a brig with a name like *Twin Sisters* or *Ann and Eliza* 130 years ago.

Indians were popular subjects. The bust of one chief adorned the ship of the line *Delaware*. A bronze copy of it stands at the United States Naval Academy—the famed "Tecumseh" whom midshipmen regard as "god of 2.5," their passing grade. They toss pennies to it.

Such deference is nothing new. When the hat was shot off the ducal figurehead of H.M.S. *Brunswick* during a battle in 1794, sailors ran aft and asked their captain to replace it with his own. He did.

198

CARVER: AMERICAN ANTIQUARIAN SOCIETY, WORCESTER. SIGN: BOSTONIAN SOCIETY

CHAPTER TWENTY-FOUR

The great chase for the whale

In 1857, New Bedford alone had 330 stout whaleships, built to wrest a cargo from the "remotest secret drawers and lockers of the world."

NEW BEDFORD MEN would "hug an oil-cask like a brother," said Ralph Waldo Emerson. When the long jib booms of returning whaleships jutted over Main Street, top-hatted owners rushed down to beam on the big casks being rolled onto the wharf. To the womenfolk, dressed in their go-to-meeting best, the sight of drying sails hanging limply on the oil-soaked barks was more pleasant than a garden full of crocuses. It meant their men had come home at last from the sea.

Wives showed off three-year-old children their fathers had never seen; sisters greeted brothers grown a foot taller; here and there a poor woman realized she was a widow, her children orphans.

The scene was the same at Nantucket, Edgartown, New London, Sag Harbor, or any of the other ports where the bluff ships and their precious cargoes meant livelihoods and fortunes. Oil boiled from blubber was used in lamps and as a lubricant. Spermaceti, baled from the heads of sperm whales, went into candles. Ambergris, odd stuff found in sick sperms, was prized for perfumes. Whalebone, not really bone but horny comblike strips

200

STEPHEN F. ADAMS PHOTOGRAPHED THIS NEW BEDFORD WHALING WHARF SCENE IN 1870

LITHOGRAPHS BY F. MARTENS AFTER PAINTINGS BY AMBROISE LOUIS GARNERAY, C. 1835. UPPER: HUNTING THE SPERM WHALE, THE ALLEN FORBES WHALING COLLECTION,
MASSACHUSETTS INSTITUTE OF TECHNOLOGY. LOWER: HARPOONING THE RIGHT WHALE, SHELBURNE MUSEUM, VERMONT

Of these two prints Herman Melville said:

By far the finest . . . presentations of whales and whaling scenes to be anywhere found, are two large French engravings, well executed and taken from paintings by one Garnery. . . .

"In the first engraving a noble Sperm Whale is depicted in full majesty of might, just risen beneath the boat from the profundities of the ocean, and bearing high in the air upon his back the terrific wreck of the stoven planks. The prow of the boat is partially unbroken . . . and standing in that prow, for that one single incomputable flash of time, you behold an oarsman, half shrouded by the incensed boiling spout of the whale, and in the act of leaping, as if from a precipice. . . .

"In the second engraving, the boat is in the act of drawing alongside the barnacled flank of a large running Right Whale, that rolls his black weedy bulk in the sea like some mossy rock-slide from the Patagonian cliffs. His jets are erect, full . . . so that from so abounding a smoke in the chimney, you would think there must be a brave supper cooking in the great bowels below. Sea fowls are pecking at the small crabs, shell-fish, and other sea candies and maccaroni, which the Right Whale sometimes carries on his pestilent back. . . .

"Thus, the foreground is all raging commotion; but behind . . . a sea becalmed, the drooping unstarched sails of the powerless ship, and the inert mass of a dead whale, a conquered fortress, with the flag of capture lazily hanging from the whale-pole inserted into his spout-hole."

which filled the mouths of the toothless right and bowhead whales, was cut into stays for corsets, collars, hats, skirt hoops, and umbrellas.

A host of dockside trades flourished with the whaling industry. Sailmakers, sparmakers, ropemakers, riggers, coopers, ironworkers, blockmakers, toolmakers all felt a proprietorship in the sea and its greatest animal.

Whaling was no Yankee invention, of course. Eskimos, Indians, Vikings, and Basques beat them to it. The Dutch, Scots, and English had gone after Arctic whales as soon as explorers reported them. Japanese had been whaling a thousand years. But Yankees made the sperm, prize and terror of the sea, their special quest.

Let's go down to the New Bedford waterfront and ship out on a whaler. It's easy to spot one—the comfortable bark rig with single topsails and no kites; the telltale iron hoops lashed near the mastheads of main and fore where lookouts will scan the sea; the tryworks, a pair of bricked boilers on the main deck; the distinctive houses aft—small galley on one side, deck store on the other; the "deck chaser" wheel built on the tiller and moving with it (no helmsman dozed with that tiller nudging his shins!). And, best mark of her trade, wooden davits shaped like gallows—three pairs on the port side, two on the starboard where the whales are cut in. Below them hang the lithe, graceful boats.

We follow a young whaler aboard, a New Bedford boy, Jack or Ned by name. He's a distant relative of the captain, earmarked for the trade. He signs for his "lay," one ninety-fifth share of all oil taken, less 10% for leakage (whether any leakage or not), less a commission for the owner's trouble in selling the oil, less a fee for "fitting out," and a contribution for the medicine chest. Before the skinflint owner can think up other charges, our young friend gets his dunnage aboard in a large sea-bag. He includes at least a year's supply of tobacco to avoid the exorbitant sea prices charged by the captain's slop chest.

Last voyage he was in the forecastle, dark quarters in the eyes of the ship with double tiers of narrow bunks, no headroom, no place to put anything or to eat in comfort, no ventilation except what comes down the steep steps from the ill-fitting scuttle, which lets the sea in too. This voyage, as harpooner and boat steerer in the third mate's boat, he has a better bunk in a two-berth cabin in the steerage.

The whaler needs a crew of 30 to man the five boats properly and provide shipkeepers while they are away. Finding hands is difficult. Too many whaleships have earned bad names. New Bedford and its environs provide the skilled men—master, four mates, four or five harpooners, one cook-steward. For the rest— any farm boys gullible enough to be inveigled aboard by some agent.

"Listen, son. A hundred-and-seventieth part of the full value of all this big ship is going to make ain't enough for you, you say? Tell you what we'll do. We'll make it special, a two-hundred-and-seventieth! Now sign!"

What boy could resist so handsome an offer!

Shore riggers bend the sails. Sharp blubber spades and lances, glinting harpoons with long wooden handles, big wooden toggles and enormous blocks and coils of heavy rope come aboard. Two brand-new boats—spares for the chase—are housed on the skids, bottoms up.

By sailing day the bark has signed on only 18 hands, ten experienced. That is enough. Off she goes, relatives and well-wishers waving farewells. She lopes along with a fine fair wind, a westerly to blow her to the Azores, where she picks up eight good Portuguese whalemen, used to whaling offshore from their own islands. Down to the Cape Verde Islands she runs, spanking along with the northeast trades, and picks up four natives. Now she is full-crewed, and the hunt begins in earnest.

"THAR SHE BLO-O-O-O-WS! And sparm!" "Where away?" This from the captain, jumping for his glass.

"Three points on the lee bow! Big school! Thar she blows, blows, blo-o-o-ws!"

Back the main topsail! Lines in the boats! Away the boats!

Boat falls sing. Boat bottoms smack down on long swells. Men leap into them.

The whales are close, feeding quietly, sensing no danger. Our harpooner stands in the bow, body bent back, one foot braced against a cleat, left thigh jammed into a notched plank. Only he and the third mate at the steering oar can see the whale. Others pull at the long oars, facing aft. The boat shoots down the side of a sea, its bow just clear of a big whale.

Aha now! Strike!

He darts two irons through the soft blubber, just forward of the hump.

"The whale in his pain throws his body half out of the water. With a blow of his flukes he sends spray 20 feet high, then disappears, taking the line so fast smoke rises from the loggerhead." So wrote Herman Melville.

Then Leviathan surfaces, and off he goes, towing the boat on a "Nantucket sleigh ride." The seas fling past, smoking with spume and clouds of spray, rushing by "like gigantic bowls in a boundless bowling-green."

Again the whale sounds. Long minutes pass.

At last the whale rises—"rolls, tumbles, runs his head out of water, snapping his jaws like pistol reports, drops under water with his tail aloft 10 or 15 feet, thrashing the water into foam that spreads for half-an-acre."

He weakens. The third mate runs along the boat, switches places with the harpooner, who now becomes boat steerer. The third mate thrusts the long lance in, twists it until blood flows. The whale flurries.

Starn all!

It is soon over. The beast spurts blood, rolls fin out, dead.

Now the work begins: the tow back to the ship, the cutting in from a platform rigged outboard. With skilled thrusts of spades and flensing knives, men slice the blubber. Green hands strain at the windlass forward, peeling off strips and hauling them aboard. They chop these into small "Bible leaves," the better to yield the oil. Greasy smoke billows from the open tryworks where they render the blubber. (Crews sometimes dunked old bread in the boiling oil to make "doughnuts"!) They haul the severed head aboard, bale out its spermaceti.

Men work until they drop. If they drop too easily they are kicked to their feet again. Hungry sharks rip at the carcass rolling alongside; storms may break it adrift. The work must go on until every drop of oil is stowed below and the reeking ship cleaned up again.

So it goes, week after week, month after month. After the Atlantic grounds—Cape Horn. But the whaleships don't fight as the clippers did for their westward passage there. Buoyant, snug-rigged, they take it easy. In due

AWAY FOR A NANTUCKET SLEIGH RIDE, *"the boat now flew through the boiling water like a shark all fins." Whalers haul on a line "more tight than a harpstring." Harpooner shifts to the steering oar; mate grasps razor-sharp lance he will thrust into the whale.*

ENGRAVING BY J. W. EVANS AFTER A DRAWING BY W. TABER, FROM "THE CENTURY ILLUSTRATED MONTHLY MAGAZINE," AUGUST, 1870

WHALING, JAPANESE STYLE. *Flensers swarm over Leviathan with slashing knives, men strain at*

course they swing along northward with the Humboldt current, hunt whales off Chile and Peru, shift with the Pacific trades to the "off-shore" grounds, wander a year or more around the islands, maybe spend a summer north of Bering Strait chasing Arctic bowheads.

(That was a specially dangerous ground. In 1871, 31 whaling ships were caught in the ice, crushed, and sunk. The hardy whalemen got away. Five years later, when there were only 20 ships there, 12 were caught and ground to pieces. That time some crews didn't get away.)

From Bering Strait to New Zealand and Tasmania, from Hawaii to Timor, the whaling bark wanders. She may go weeks without seeing a whale. Tempers fray. The master is a sad bear with a very sore head. Down in the forecastle the hands no longer yarn. The moment anyone opens his mouth they all shout at him

to stop, for they know the lines better than actors in plays. The food becomes unbearable.

In such circumstances there could easily be mutiny. It struck the *Globe* of Nantucket, Thomas Worth master, on the 26th of January, 1824, when she was two years out. Captain and mates were slain.

All hands aboard the *Inez* of New Bedford took her into Sydney, sold her oil, and sailed her to California after gold. The crew of *Henry Clay* set her afire off the Galapagos because her master would not make for San Francisco.

South Sea islanders, often led by white renegades, were another peril. "The Captain gave orders not to kill any if it could be helped, unless some white man should be in one of the canoes ... kill him on sight," wrote harpooner Nelson Cole Haley of the *Charles W. Morgan*. Gilbert Islanders rushed his becalmed ship

206

WOODCUT BY KUNIYOSHI, C. 1840, KENDALL WHALING MUSEUM, SHARON, MASSACHUSETTS

capstan to rip off blubber. Other whales wait their turn. Hunters continue the chase out in the bay.

with spears and shark's-tooth swords. The whalers held them off with lances and spades until a wind sprang up and the *Morgan* escaped.

"Glory of glories got eight whales," reads the narrative soon after, the attack forgotten.

SOMETIMES the sperm struck back! One August day in 1851 the *Ann Alexander* of New Bedford, John S. Deblois master, lowered unwittingly for a cunning old Moby Dick who had been stung by harpoons before and wanted no more.

The mate got irons in and his boat was off on the usual wild tow. Suddenly the whale turned and smashed it. The whale crumpled a second boat without waiting for irons. The men returned to their ship and kept after him.

"Thar she blows!" The whale sighted the ship the same instant, swung and made a rush.

"Hard down! Hard down!" Captain Deblois flung himself at the wheel. Up came the ship into the wind, her way off, sails shaking. The whale sped by, turned, watched, sounded.

In the day's dying light, the whale was seen rushing straight for the ship at some 15 knots!

The breeze had dropped; no chance to turn! The whale struck below the waterline just abaft the foremast with a shock that shook the ship as if she had run aground, rattled the yards on the masts, knocked pots off the galley stove. The sea rushed in. Pumps were useless. Captain and crew took to the remaining boats. They were picked up the next day.

The *Essex* of Nantucket, George Pollard master, was less fortunate. Twice a giant sperm bashed her, staving in the bows. The crew took to their boats. Six months later a few skeleton-like survivors were picked up thousands of miles away near the coast of South America. They had been forced to turn cannibal.

But our harpooner, spared these dangers, even finds moments of pleasure like the "gams" when two whalers meet far at sea. The crews row over and swap yarns—mail too, if either is homeward bound within six months. Owners might object: "Avoid those ships that wish to spend much time in gamming—as a lone chance is generally best." But the owners are 10,000 miles away and gam all *they* please.

Another delight is the soft-skinned island girls who in many a lagoon come swimming

SAILOR'S MONA LISA *surveys scenes of home and sea scribed on sperm-whale teeth. Making scrimshaw helped men pass long months aboard whalers like the little* Charles W. Morgan *(right). Built in 1841 of live oak, the 105-foot* Morgan *grossed $2,000,000 in 37 voyages down to 1921.*

Last of her breed, she welcomes visitors at Mystic Seaport, Connecticut. Roof shelters try-works. Davits hold whaleboats. False gunports served to frighten off "Feegee" cannibals.

out naked. Young whalemen hung their consciences on Cape Horn outward bound, picked them up when homeward bound. Not all cared to come home. A U. S. consul reported in 1859 that three or four thousand Americans yielded annually to the seduction of the South Seas. Hawaii was their favorite Number One.

Our lad comes back after four years and is paid off—$463.47, less $64.12 charged against him for sundry advances and slop chest purchases, less $74.36 for his outfit plus 25 percent interest. His captain's share is $2,358.75, no deductions, plus whatever he might have made on the side. The owner's share? Some $30,000. But he had no share in the reddest-blooded, most adventurous he-man's life there ever was—deepwater whaling.

WHAT KILLED IT for the Yankees? The Civil War, partly. Steam-driven Confederate raiders burned or seized every whaling ship they came on. *Shenandoah* got among the Arctic whaling fleet in 1865 and burned 25 of them in a week—all after the war had ended. There was no radio then, and *Shenandoah* refused to believe newspapers carried by the whalers.

The Yankees had sunk some themselves. They bought 40 laid-up whalers, bored and plugged holes in them, filled them with stones, then sent them to block channels leading to the Confederate ports of Charleston and Savannah. When the plugs were pulled, the ships sank so deep into mud they blocked nothing.

But the death blow had come even earlier, in 1859 when Edwin L. Drake successfully drilled for oil at Titusville, Pennsylvania. Petroleum offered a cheaper, better fuel for lighting.

Yankee whalers kept on another 60 years, but it was a losing game. The last whalebone cutter did not give up his New York trade until 1920. Pliant steel shut his shop. There was no demand for his products, not even whalebone buggy whips for the "cabbies" of Central Park.

In 1924 the last American square-rigged whaler, the bark *Wanderer,* fitted out at New Bedford for an Atlantic voyage. Twenty-four hours after she sailed, a hurricane got hold of her, flung her on the rocks of Buzzards Bay. In 1925 the schooner *John R. Manta* departed New Bedford. She carried the same old gear, but was a fore-and-after quite unlike the classic whaling ship. She got oil that voyage, but was soon sold into a foreign trade.

She was the last of the Yankee whalers.

"ARIEL AND TAEPING" BY MONTAGUE DAWSON, COLLECTION OF NELSON MOORE, © FROST & REED LTD., LONDON

CHAPTER TWENTY-FIVE

The quest for speed

Make way for the queen of sail, the fabulous clipper ship! A thoroughbred born of the sleek privateer and the hard-driving packet, she raced for California gold and China tea.

W EDNESDAY, *5th September, 1866—A ship since daylight has been in company on starboard quarter,* Taeping *probably.... Have been going 14 knots: royal stunsails and all flying kites set, wind strong from W. S. W."*

Captain Keay of *Ariel* closed his log, looked again at that distant ship skimming along under a press of sail.

He knew *Taeping* well. The two clippers had loaded tea together at Foochow and had sailed the same day. They had met briefly in the South China Sea, then split tacks and lost contact. They had passed Sunda Strait six hours apart; had rounded the Cape of Good Hope a half day apart; had crossed the equator the same day. Now racing up the English Channel, three months and 15,000 hard-sailing miles from Foochow, they were in sight of each other again.

They ran neck and neck like the thoroughbreds they were, knifelike cutwaters slicing through the sea, pyramids of sails straining aloft, graceful hulls now leaping high from crest to crest, now half-smothered in foam.

There was a freight bonus of 10 shillings a ton for the first tea to hit the London docks, and £100 and glory for the captain who put it there. Who would he be: Keay or McKinnon of *Taeping?* Betting had been heavy in the city.

Through the night the clippers raced. At dawn they picked up pilots off Dungeness, *Ariel* first by five minutes. They filled away again, ripped through the Strait of Dover carrying every stitch of canvas perfectly trimmed. Crowds lining the cliff tops watched them overhaul every sailing ship and steamer that wild, sunny morning; seamen in the steamers turned and cheered. They picked up tugs, docked on the

211

THE BALTIMORE CLIPPER *won fame as a privateer and in trades where "deviltry and speed sailed together"—smuggling, running slaves and opium. Developed in Chesapeake Bay shipyards before the Revolution, the lean topsail schooner with its cloud of canvas "clipped along" at 12 knots and better; deep draft helped it sail closer to the wind than other vessels. Rake of the masts lent a swift, smart appearance but added no speed.*

Penn Townsend of Salem (inset) and other masters armed the schooners and raided British shipping in the War of 1812. Outmatched, they'd skip away like Catch Me Who Can, *whose ensign flutters below. Cargo capacity limited, the type faded before 1850. But its sharp lines lived on in the full-rigged clipper ship.*

same tide 99 days out. The slightly smaller *Taeping* drew less water and was first in by 20 minutes. The two Scots captains shared the prize and repaired to the Ship and Turtle Tavern to uncoil taut nerves.

This was clipper racing at its best, a highlight in the 19th century wind sailor's quest for speed—a quest that had begun more than a century earlier in America.

There had always been fast sailers for war and piracy, but the fast merchantman was born of Yankee necessity. In colonial days and after, many foreign ports were closed to American ships. They had to become smugglers, snatching trade from prohibited ports, keeping to windward of the law. From the Revolution on through the War of 1812, Yankee merchantmen were fair game for enemy warships and privateers. Naval protection was scanty; speed was the best insurance.

CATCH ME WHO CAN

Builders on Chesapeake Bay fashioned just the ship to meet the need, modeled on the Bermuda sloop. They produced a schooner with sharp ends, raking masts, and a cloud of canvas. Rigged with topsails, it won fame as privateer and blockade runner, and was copied by shipwrights in the North and in Europe.

With peace, the "Baltimore clipper" was replaced in many trades by slower ships with bigger holds. But speed still counted when carrying fruit and coffee from the West Indies and South America, running slaves and opium, smuggling, and for the U. S. Revenue Marine (the early Coast Guard), catching lawbreakers.

The slaver was a beautiful vessel in an ugly trade. Like a racing yacht, it had a straight sheer, low freeboard, an incredible height of spars, and a deep draft which allowed it to sail close to the wind. It carried a large crew: cruel, hard-drinking men, yet masterful sailors.

213

Imagine the scene: a Baltimore-built brig stands out from the African coast. Below decks lie a hundred pitiful souls chained together, slaves for Cuba's plantations. On the horizon glint the sails of a British patrol ship ghosting in light airs. The slavers set every inch of canvas — studding sails, water sail, ringtail, skysails, moonrakers — until the brig looks like a water bird coming to rest on the sea. It gains speed; the pursuer falls behind, vanishes.

Next time the slavers' luck may run out.

Opium clippers, built on the Baltimore model, engaged in a trade just as despicable. Sleek vessels, decks holystoned white, copper sheathing polished, yards all ataunto, they carried chests of Indian opium to China, returned with silver specie. One voyage might net a fortune for the owner, but crews risked pirates, typhoons, and wreck in the ill-charted China seas. Not all were as lucky as the little British brig *Childers,* which in 1848 reportedly sailed or *jumped* across a line of reef on a mighty wave in a typhoon, and got away with it!

The dainty Baltimore clipper showed the world how much speed sharpness of hull and crowd of sail could give. The Yankees had yet another innovation up their sleeve.

O N OCTOBER 27, 1817, New Yorkers opened their newspapers to see something new in the shipping columns: four little full-rigged sister ships sailing in a row. The oddity was that the owners pledged these vessels would "Sail on their Appointed Days, full or not full."

Hitherto a ship sailed when she was fully loaded and the weather favorable, not before. Square-riggers on schedule — impossible!

January 5, 1818, at 10 A.M. was the first advertised sailing of New York's new packet service, soon to be called the Black Ball Line for the company insignia on the fore topsail. Fare was $200, wines included. There were a few passengers and a hold full of barreled apples, flour, bales of cotton. Not the most profitable cargo but a paying one.

It was snowing bitterly that morning at the East River pier. A few passersby stopped, skeptical that the *James Monroe* (118 feet long, 424 tons) would sail. But the topsails, courses, and fore-and-afters were all loosed and the men standing by.

St. Paul's clock struck ten.

"Sheet fore and main tops'ls! Let go aft! Ease away for'ard!" shouted Capt. James Watkinson in his foghorn voice. Topsails aback, she dropped to the end of the pier, swung on a spring line, filled, disappeared in a squall of snow. The first Yankee packet was away!

Captain Watkinson drove her across to Liverpool in 28 days. Meantime her sister ship *Courier* was thrashing westbound from Liverpool. That bitter feat of windward slogging, that ship-straining, man-killing, sea-swept battle took six savage weeks.

This was the start of a line which became so rooted in sea tradition that more than 100 years later the watch on my Scots bark in the far-off Tasman Sea was still called in its name: *Arise and shine for the Black Ball Line!*

"Packet fever" caught on. The Black Ball Line was followed by the Red Star Line, the Swallow Tail Line, the Havre Line, the Patriotic Line, the Dramatic Line (offering passage in the proud *Shakespeare),* and others.

To meet schedules and competition, packets had to make fast passages. The ships themselves were not sharp-lined, just able and strong. Speed came from Yankee skippers who flung a challenge that the wild North Atlantic had not known before — passages to be made on man's terms, day and night, summer and winter. When a packet skipper got a favorable slant of wind he carried sail until it was impossible to go aloft and take it in. There it was and there it stayed, and the gale could do with it what it willed.

In 1824 Capt. Philip Fox, driving his 352-ton *Emerald* with lee rail under, brought her into Boston only 15 days and 14 hours out of Liverpool. The startled owner thought she had turned back from her outward passage for repairs. Instead, Fox handed him the Liverpool newspapers.

Going the other way, Capt. Pitkin Page slammed his *Washington* past Liverpool Light 13 days and 14 hours after leaving Sandy Hook.

Packet captains were social lions of the day, autocrats of the quarterdeck who could with equal skill tame a gale or charm a debutante on a grand tour. A ship's name was seldom mentioned without the master's. It was "the *Huntsville,* Palmer"; "the *Columbia,* Delano"; "the *Yorkshire,* Bailey"; and so on. Newspapers vied with praise: "The *Queen of the West* is the noblest work of man, and her Commander is the noblest work of God."

The crews of "packet rats," put aboard drunk or drugged by the crimps of New York, or plucked from the Liverpool waterfront and kept in line by bucko mates and belaying pins, might see things differently. Ran one chantey:

'Tis larboard and starboard on deck you
*   will sprawl,*
For kicking Jack Williams commands the
*   Black Ball.*

In the 1850's the proud packets, always at the mercy of the elements, began to lose their struggle against steamships, which could arrive as well as depart on schedule. For all their hard driving, packets sometimes limped in 60 to 80 days out of Liverpool, sails in tatters, passengers haggard, crews worn out, perhaps some men lost. A winter gale killed all officers aboard the Black Baller *Columbia* in 1847. Some ships simply vanished, like *Ocean Queen* with 90 passengers, *Driver* with 372, *Independence, Robert Carnley,* and others.

The packets' last trade was carrying emigrants to America. By the thousands they lined the docks of Europe, clutching their pathetic bundles, their children, their hopes of a new life in a new land. Rates were low, service was meager. They got water, sometimes a fire to cook by, and seven feet by two of 'tween-deck space. Bad weather packed them below closed hatches. Disease and hardship took their toll.

In October of 1853, *Winchester* arrived in New York reporting 79 deaths in the steerage.

DONALD McKAY, *creator of* Flying Cloud, *left Nova Scotia as a boy, learned his trade in New York, by mid-century was America's most famous ship designer. At his East Boston yard (below) he turned out one great clipper after another, 32 in all, but said: "I never yet built a vessel that came up to my own ideal. I saw something in each ship which I desired to improve upon." His 4,555-ton* Great Republic *had masts so tall that youths who climbed them came down wizened old men, some said. Here workers plank the deck and concave bow of* Westward Ho!

American Union, *Calhoun,* and *Antarctic* followed with 80, 54, and 65 dead. The Havre packet *Empire* saw 75 of her 675 emigrants die; *Constellation* buried 100 of her 922 passengers at sea. And so the packets — the windy "railroad route to Europe" — died in hopefulness and in sorrow. But like the sharp-hulled Baltimore schooners, the hard-driving packets had set the stage for the most glorious of sailing ships, the clippers, greyhounds of the sea.

WHAT WAS A CLIPPER? Why did it bloom so dramatically in the 1840's, then wither in a scant two decades? To sailors, three things made a ship a clipper. She must be sharp-lined, built for speed. She must be tall-sparred and carry the utmost spread of canvas. And she must *use* that sail, day and night, fair weather and foul.

She was an uneconomic ship in most trades: cost too much to build, needed too many hands, was too slim to carry much cargo, wore out too soon. She made sense only when taking premium cargoes long distances where speed counted — the China trade, or carrying forty-niners in the mad scramble for California gold.

Some historians call the *Ann McKim* of Baltimore the first "clipper." Built in 1832 on the fast lines of a Baltimore clipper schooner, she was 143 feet long with a 31-foot beam and a draft of 17 feet. Registering 493 tons, she made fine passages to China.

Another "first" was the *Rainbow* of New York, Howland and Aspinwall's 750-tonner designed by John W. Griffiths for the China trade in 1845. With bows that "clipped" the sea as a tailor's scissors clip cloth, *Rainbow* was the first known as an "extreme" clipper.

Actually there was no "first" clipper, suddenly ready in all her racing glory. The clipper ship was not invented; she evolved. Men had her ready when the time and the trade were ripe for her. Men like William Webb, Stephen Smith, Samuel Hall, David Brown, Jacob Bell — and Donald McKay.

In 1850, McKay launched his great clipper *Stag Hound.* Designed and built in only 60 days, she was "the wonder of all who have seen her," sighed the Boston *Daily Atlas.* Her hull stretched 226 feet, her mainmast probed 200 feet into the sky, her spars carried 11,000 yards of canvas. She had a sharp, thrusting bow that arched five feet higher than her stern, and bore as her figurehead a gilded staghound.

She dashed off for California in true clipper fashion, losing her main-topmast and her three topgallant masts in a gale six days out. Her men, true clipper men, rigged new masts and bent new sails as they rushed on.

As more and more gold seekers clamored for passage west, and as those who had arrived offered fantastic prices for supplies from the east, clipper building soared in the '50's.

McKay followed up with *Flying Cloud, Flying Fish, Sovereign of the Seas, Romance of the Seas* — all as lovely as their names, said to have been chosen by his wife Mary, a charming hostess with a taste for poetry.

But there was little poetry in the minds of their sailors as they thrashed around Cape Horn, for the beat to windward there was the toughest piece of sailing in the world. Burly Swedes, catfooted Yankees, and brawny former packet rats, some still wearing their Black

89 Days and 4 hours from

CAPT. JOHN E. WILLIAMS *proudly logged his arrival at San Francisco in 1860.* Andrew Jackson, *built at Mystic in 1855, had bettered* Flying Cloud's *record by four hours! Calms and tricky winds slowed most clippers to 120 days or more. Winds favored eastbound ships:* Northern Light *(1851), Capt. Freeman Hatch, sped from 'Frisco to Boston in 76 days 6 hours in 1853.*

McKay's Champion of the Seas *(1854), Capt. Alexander Newlands, logged the best day's run — 465 nautical miles from noon to noon December 11-12, 1854, in the Indian Ocean. At times she topped 20 knots. His* James Baines *hit 21 knots west of Cape Horn June 18, 1856, enroute from Melbourne to Liverpool. Captain Müller claimed he drove McKay's* Sovereign of the Seas *(1852) at 22 knots on a London to Sydney run in 1854.*

Here are some of the pace-setting American clippers.

SHIP	BUILT	MASTER
Sea Witch	New York, 1846	Robert H. Waterman
Oriental	New York, 1849	T. D. Palmer
Mandarin	New York, 1850	John W. C. Perit
Flying Cloud	East Boston, 1851	Josiah Creesy
Comet	New York, 1851	E. C. Gardner
Swordfish	New York, 1851	Charles Collins
Bald Eagle	East Boston, 1852	A. H. Caldwell
Great Republic	East Boston, 1853	Joseph Limeburner
Sweepstakes	New York, 1853	George E. Lane
Eagle Wing	Medford, 1853	Eben H. Linnell
Red Jacket	Rockland, 1853	Asa Eldridge
James Baines	East Boston, 1854	Charles McDonnell
Lightning	East Boston, 1854	James Forbes

Ball caps, would lay aloft in sleet to fist in icy sails. And if the wind didn't pluck them from the yards, or splitting canvas whip them off, they faced each other's sheath knives in waterfront brawls at voyage end. They were a tough lot, and it took hard men to command them.

Most colorful of the captains was Robert H. Waterman—"Bob" or "Bully" Waterman they called him, according to their likes. He went to sea at 12, commanded a packet at 24, switched to clippers and was given the new *Sea Witch*—a bad name for a ship, the superstitious said. He drove that beautiful black witch from Hong Kong to New York in 74 days, 14 hours, setting the world's first permanent sailing record. New York made him a hero. But hard driving was brutal on men before the mast, and when Waterman later brought *Challenge* into San Francisco he was labeled "one of the most inhuman monsters of this age. . . ."

"Nine of his men are missing," reported the *California Courier,* "and the sailors who are here declare that four were shaken from the mizzen-topsail yard into the sea . . . and five died from the effects of wounds and ill treatment." Waterman barely escaped a lynch mob, then asked for a trial and was found not guilty.

It was a lonely job, and exhausting. Many a captain never slept in his bunk from beginning to end of a voyage. To sleep below was "too far from the ship." So he would lash himself in a deck chair and catnap for an hour or so. The rest of the time he hung with a hand in the weather shrouds or in the shelter of a canvas dodger by the wheel, watching, listening, forever weighing the odds. This high-tuned, yachtlike ship and the lives of all aboard were in his hands. Would she stand all that straining sail? Was it safe to carry on?

The burden of decision weighed heavily on the master. I have felt this burden when I raced my own full-rigged ship, the *Joseph Conrad,* in winter toward the Horn. You live with the ship, *of* the ship. Her every lurch and roll, every slight variation in the wind's roar in the rigging communicates with you. You can detect the note of growing protest, the sudden gesture of alarm, and you are on your feet on the instant.

Clipper captains pressed their luck to the limit, for speed meant passengers, freight, profit, fame. A master prided himself on keeping on sail when others faltered: ". . . passed a ship under double reefs, we with our royals and studdingsails set."

A squall strikes at night. The clipper heels, rail all but buried in foaming water. The mate fights his way to the captain's deck chair, lashed beside the wheel. "Wind's freshened, sir! Shall I get the skys'ls off her?"

"Can ye see the bowsprit still?" growls the captain, opening one eye to see for himself.

"Aye, if you look for it long enough."

"She's a'right then, Mister Mate. Leave her be." And the ship lurches and staggers on. Good wind is the gift of God.

McKay's clippers showed the world how it could be used. Under young Josiah Creesy of Marblehead, the glorious *Flying Cloud,* "Queen of Clippers," rounded Cape Horn in midwinter and passed the Golden Gate in 89 days, 21 hours on her maiden voyage in 1851.

New York

OUTSTANDING RUNS

74 days 14 hours Hong Kong to New York, 1849
80 days 10 hours New York to Hong Kong, 1850
69 days 14 hours New York to Melbourne, 1855-6
89 days 8 hours New York to San Francisco, 1854
76 days 7 hours San Francisco to New York, 1853-4
32 days 9 hours San Francisco to Shanghai, 1853
11 days San Francisco to equator, 1854
15 days 19 hours New York to equator, 1856
74 days New York to Bombay, 1857
83 days 12 hours London to Hong Kong, 1855
12 days New York to Liverpool, 1854
12 days 6 hours Boston to Liverpool, 1854
63 days Melbourne to Liverpool, 1854

"FLYING CLOUD" BY J. AND F. TUDGAY, PEABODY MUSEUM OF SALEM

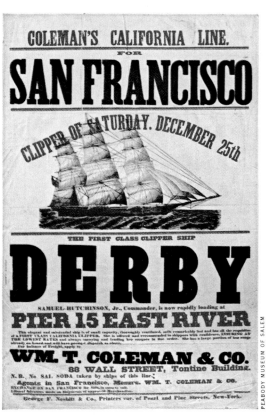

GOLEMAN'S CALIFORNIA LINE.
FOR
SAN FRANCISCO
CLIPPER OF SATURDAY, DECEMBER 25th

THE FIRST CLASS CLIPPER SHIP
DERBY
SAMUEL HUTCHINSON, Jr., Commander, is now rapidly loading at
PIER 15 EAST RIVER

WM. T. COLEMAN & CO.
88 WALL STREET, Tontine Building.

GOLD IN CALIFORNIA *spelled prosperity to clipper owners, who vied for freight and fares with colorful sailing posters. Cape Horn storms kept forty-niners below, but fair weather brought them out on deck to play whist, chat, cook, lounge everywhere, even in the boats (opposite).*

Those who could not afford clipper fare (as high as $1,000) formed joint-stock companies and crowded on slower ships, which averaged about 160 days, could take 240 on the 14,000-mile passage. At San Francisco crews jumped ship to race for the gold fields, left vessels to rot. By August of 1849 the harbor, clogged with nearly 250 whalers, packets, and other ships, was a forest of gaunt masts. Hulks were dragged ashore to serve as warehouses and dwellings for the booming city.

She logged 18 knots during squalls. The following year Donald McKay's six-foot, four-inch brother Lauchlan took the huge *Sovereign of the Seas* to California in 103 days, beating almost all the way through "tremendous seas, southwest gales of almost inconceivable fury, furious snow, and icy rains." She lost two topmasts off Valparaiso, but her master disdained to make port for repairs. Even jury-rigged she made 12 knots. Her crew had a new version of an old song when they wound her to her San Francisco berth with the capstan:

> *Oh Susanna, darling,*
> *Take, oh take your ease.*
> *For we have beat the clipper fleet—*
> *The Sovereign of the Seas!*

McKay's triumph of design, the 335-foot *Great Republic,* largest clipper ever built, burned at her New York berth in 1853 before her maiden voyage. Rebuilt, she had difficulty finding ladings. Demand for San Francisco passages had eased, and freight rates dropped.

McKay's *Lightning* ran between England and Australia, where the Victoria gold rush drew men and supplies—and wild-eyed masters who padlocked the halyards, overawed crews with leveled guns, and shouted "Hell or Melbourne!" On her maiden run *Lightning* logged 436 miles in a day, averaging 18½ knots. Many steamers today cannot do as well!

Dreadnought, built for the California trade but too late for it, actually beat some Cunard steamers on the Atlantic. New York to Liverpool, 13½ days, then 15½ days in 1855; 19 days westbound in 1854—the consistency of *Dreadnought*'s record is astonishing.

So was her master.

Like true clipper drivers, Captain Samuels was at his best by night, declaring that anyone could sail a ship when he could see.

A deck chair was impossible with the wintry sea driving aboard. So he built a shelf to lie on, just inside the companionway on the poop—too short, so he could not sleep if he tried.

But he drove *Dreadnought* once too often, westbound in 1863. A sea knocked him down, gashed his hard head, broke a leg. Worse, it smashed away the rudder. The ship careened out of control, decks and cabins awash.

In agony, Samuels had his leg splinted and was carried on deck to fix a jury rudder. It took three days and nights. Then a ham-handed sailor dropped it into the sea. Undaunted, the "Wild Man" made another and shipped that,

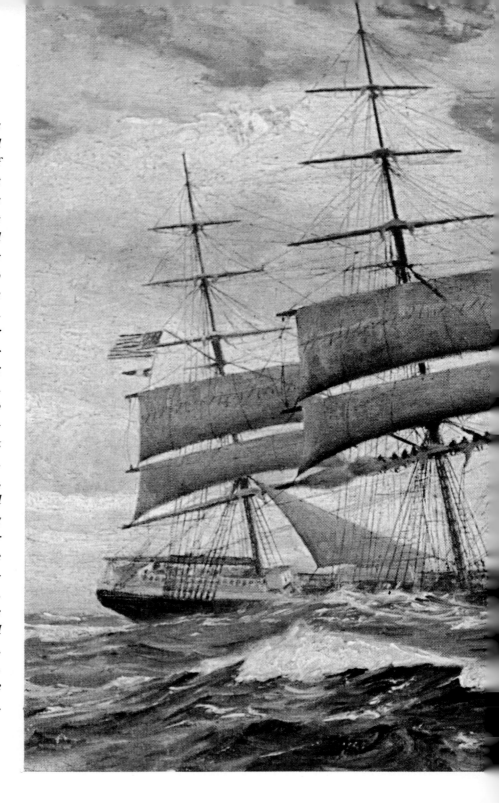

HENRY B. HYDE smashes along under shortened canvas in the sunset of American sail. Launched at Bath in 1884 during Maine's shipbuilding supremacy, this sturdy down easter typified the clipper's successor: not so sharp, greater cargo capacity, no moonrakers or studding sails. Iron straps strengthened her white oak frame and five-inch yellow pine planking; copper sheathed her hull. Built for the San Francisco trade, the 290-foot, 2,462-ton Hyde once made it back to New York in 88 days. She hauled sugar, grain, nitrates; fire in a coal cargo once sent her scudding to the nearest port. Her 24 men before the mast were less than half the crew sail-crowded clippers carried. In 1897 she beat around the Horn with a forecastle full of mutinous Bowery toughs, not a sailor among them. She was wrecked on the Virginia shore in 1904.

meantime controlling his ship by trimming sails and putting out sea anchors.

But Samuels had long since become a legend. On one passage *Dreadnought* made land in a pea-soup fog. Instead of heaving to, the ship stood on. "She's got ship sense," Samuels said with confidence. "She knows the way."

After some time of this, he turned to the mate, so the story goes. "I guess we must be thar," he declared, "or tharabouts. Down sail."

Moments later there was a slight bump. The ship was alongside her East River pier.

BUT NOW the Cunarders were winning. Iron ships, their screw propellers thrusting them forward while smoke belched in dirty clouds from their thin, high funnels, marched over the seas in increasing numbers.

Britain's tea clippers, smaller, not always so desperately driven as the Americans, raced on through the 1860's—ships like *Ariel* and her rival *Taeping*. And *Cutty Sark,* preserved at Greenwich on the Thames. But the Suez Canal, opened in 1869, gave the steamship too great an edge, and Britain dropped her clippers.

Americans, with their eyes turned west and half a continent to develop, held on to their wonderful sailing ships too long—and lost trade to the European tramp steamer and cargo liner. The clipper fattened out to become the down easter, hailing from New England and Nova Scotia. Soon the down easters were gone too. Working square-riggers, in fact, were finished—except for the great steel wagons, heavy-lined and often undermanned, that rounded Cape Horn well into the 20th century.

221

CHAPTER TWENTY-SIX

Rounding the Horn in a square-rigged ship

Even in recent years windjammers could do odd jobs cheaper than steamships. They sailed the roaring forties with Australian grain or Chilean nitrates in their holds and teen-age crews in their forecastles. Alan Villiers, a veteran Cape Horner, recalls one grim 15,000-mile voyage.

D ON'T SHIP OUT in her!" a burly wharf laborer warned. "She's a killer."

We had heard that before. She was supposed to kill somebody on every voyage. But *Grace Harwar* was a beautiful ship. And the sea wind in her rigging called imperiously as she lay at the pier at Wallaroo.

She was a 1,760-ton, three-masted square-rigger hailing originally from London, now from Mariehamn in the Aland Islands of Finland. She was more than 40 years old, and grass and barnacles grew along her waterline, for she had seen no dry dock for two years. Dirty bottoms make slow ships, and slow ships make hard passages. But she was one of the last working full-riggers, a ship with a graceful sheer and no ugly labor-saving devices.

Walker and I had our seabags. We went aboard. Jobs for sailors? She needed half a crew. So my Tasmanian buddy and I signed her articles for the run from Australia around the Horn to Europe, and anywhere else she might be bound in the next three years. That was the way. You signed to serve wherever

your ship could float, and you took things as you found them.

Our ship was loading grain in sacks for the British Isles. She got the cargo because she undercut steamships. She had a small, ill-paid crew and no coal bunkers to deplete — the wind is free. And she had all the time in the world to load. When enough grain had come aboard to give her stiffening, she moved out to anchorage and took on the rest from ketches. That way she saved the cost of wharfage. Every penny counted. She carried one cargo to England from each annual harvest and returned in ballast. Perhaps 20 ships, mostly steel-built, joined this grain trade, turning it into a "race" of sorts with many nationalities represented.

Grace Harwar's crew were mostly Finns, with a Frenchman, a Jamaican, and four Australians. Average age: 19. Besides the master we had a cook-steward, sailmaker, carpenter, and two mates. I don't recall noticing before we left that we totaled 13 hands before the mast. We remembered it well enough afterward!

On April 17, 1929, we dropped our moor-

WATCH THAT SEA! *Shortened down under spray-sodden courses and topsails, grain-racing* Parma *runs for Cape Horn at 12 knots before a full gale. Boy sailors clear decks. Such seas can tear them from taut lifeline and sweep them to their deaths. At every roll clanging washports drain the deck—as another crest smashes aboard.*

ALAN VILLIERS

ings and put to sea. It was coming on winter in the southern hemisphere, and we prayed for a quick run to the Horn. From Wallaroo to Cape Horn is roughly 6,000 miles. If we hit nine knots before strong west winds, we should make it in 30 days—say 35 to 38, allowing for spells of lesser winds and maybe some days hove to if there was too much wind to use. We hoped for strong west winds. If we had to suffer, at least it wouldn't last long.

In six days we passed south of Tasmania and laid course to skirt southern New Zealand. We had our west wind, piercingly cold, with a big sea that the ship was inclined to throw about her open decks. The mizzen topgallant sail blew out of its boltropes, and we had no sail to set on that yard until we could cut and sew one. But we had nothing to fear from westerly gales. They helped us on. It was wind from the east that we feared.

So the wind came from the east. It hurled itself upon us with all the sting of Antarctic ice. We shortened down and hove to, drifting, losing. The wind refused flatly to go back to any point west. We gave the ship the full mainsail in the hope that it would hold her head up a little, decrease her leeway, and give us some longitude toward Cape Horn.

The sea froze where it touched the steel of the bulwarks. Rain and sleet froze into the serving of the footropes. The decks were constantly awash. At night the lookout could not go on the forecastle head, for the seas came over it green and he would have drowned. One of our pigs drowned—we carried two for fresh food since there was no refrigeration.

The east wind gave no sign of ever letting up. Gale succeeded gale. We began to notice how shorthanded we were with six in one watch and seven in the other. Finally we put up the helm to run for Cook Strait, between the two islands of New Zealand. When we reached it a calm fell, and we could not get through.

For four days we lay wallowing with Mount Egmont on one hand and the rocky northern shore of South Island on the other. At last a west wind came and saw us through. We began to think that it meant to stay, and that we would reach the Horn without further misery. But it only got us clear of the Chatham Islands, then faltered and stopped.

When the wind returned it was from the east again, with fog, rain, and gale in succession. Oilskins were useless. There was no dry spot in the ship, nor a dry rag to wear. The forecastle was washed out time and time again. When the forecastle doors were shut, the air was stifling. When they were open, great seas swept joyously in. We kept them shut, preferring suffocation to exposure.

The seas put the galley fire out, so there was often no warm food. We dared not work the freshwater pump, for it was on deck where waves stormed incessantly, and we were afraid of mingling salt water with fresh. So we went thirsty. We were cold. There is no heating system in a full-rigged ship. The very cockroaches retired from active service and might all have died for all we saw of them.

HERE IS AN EXTRACT or two from the diary that Walker scrupulously kept until the day he died: "May 16, 29 days out. Frenchman and I were sent aloft to make fast the fore upper topgallant sail this morning, in a hard squall. We climbed into the shrouds at 6 A.M. in pitch darkness. It was raining steadily and big seas were coming aboard. The wind had a cold sting in it which gradually froze us to the marrow.

"We were up there for nearly two hours, while a cold and cheerless dawn broke over the wind-torn sea, and we fought with the sodden sails until the work became a pain and a purgatory. The rain persistently drove at us, making our caps sodden and our oilskins sodden; the cold water trickled down through crevices which nothing but water could find. Our fingers were stiff and blue with cold and red with blood from tears on jagged wire gear. . . .

"At first we shivered when an icy finger of water found its way down our backs or up a sleeve, but soon we were so wet and so cold we ceased to care. Get wet and stay wet is the best policy for sailing ships. The greatest agony of mind comes when you change into comparative dry, only to know with horrible

STRETCH THOSE HALYARDS! *Oilskinned watch of* Grace Harwar *strains at capstan bars (above) to heave main topsail aloft. "Haul away lively!" bellows the second mate in visored cap (right) as his boys haul brace at main fife rail, squaring a yard. The ship's counter drops into a trough and a giant sea rages astern as she runs on.*

ALAN VILLIERS

ALOFT AND FURL! *All hands take to the shrouds (opposite), always on weather side so wind blows them into rigging, not off. Swarming out on wire footrope below the main yard (above), they fight half-frozen canvas. One man sits, passing a gasket around sail. Cape Horners considered this safer than working on wave-washed deck.*

certainty that as soon as you go on deck again everything will be sodden once more. . . ."

On the 38th day out Walker was killed. It was very simple. We were setting that same fore upper topgallant sail, for the wind had at last something of west in it, and we were giving the ship a little more canvas to help her.

Walker and a Finnish boy went up to loose the sail a little after 4 A.M., the worst time of day. The sail had been made fast with many gaskets to stand against gales. Ice had formed in the gaskets. Any seaman knows it may take an hour to get such a sail loose, but they managed in half an hour.

On deck, five of us with the second mate began the painful process of heaving the yard aloft by the capstan.

When it was halfway up, the second mate saw that a gasket had fouled the weather clew.

He yelled aloft to Walker to go out on the lower topgallant yard and free it. Walker went. He called down to us that everything was clear. We began to heave again. The halyards carried away, and the yard fell on Walker, pinning him in the rigging beneath it.

We rushed up the shrouds and found him between the yards, and we thought he was unconscious. There was no sign of a wound, save for some blood oozing from his mouth. I tried to bring him to with water. But he did not come to. We rigged a gantline, got it under his armpits, and lowered him gently. Captain Svensson took one look. "He is dead," he said.

Nowhere is death more painful than at sea. Ashore there are diversions; one forgets. But at sea there is only the little band of men. And when one goes, no one comes to take his place.

We buried him from the poop next day. The

Finnish ensign flew at half-mast, and the crew were white-faced. At sea you know the "innards" of a man—no subterfuge, no pretense. You see all. We knew poor Walker and we liked him well.

The captain read prayers; we sang hymns. Someone made a short talk. The ship was hove to, the moan of wind in her rigging now stilled by her deadened way, the surly wash of the sea about her decks softened. We carried him to the rail, tilted the hatch, and there was a dull plop. Then we put the ship before the wind once more and we drove her.

ON THE 57TH DAY we came to the Horn. It was June then—midwinter. The sea ran huge, and the cold was almost overpowering. But the old ship ran on and we were glad. Off the Horn we met more gales. The ship began to leak. Water seeped in, and the pumps jammed. Through a night of storm and snow squalls we huddled on the poop, not at all certain that the ship would live to see the morning.

The next day one of the boys was swept overboard by a big sea. There were no falls rove off in the lifeboats, so we couldn't lower. Many men have gone over like this, and in high wind the sailing ship can only run on.

But the wind had quieted a little, and we jammed the wheel hard down and brought her up, moaning and shivering. We rove off new lifeboat falls with mad haste. One of us had gone aloft to the mizzen top to see where the lad had gone—if he was still afloat. We saw he had grasped a lifebuoy flung to him, and he still lived. Night was coming on, with rain squalls and a gale in the offing. But we got the boat over, and six volunteers leaped into it, the mate in charge. No one was asked to go. No one hung back.

We dropped astern. The boat seemed a futile thing, rising and falling in the big seas. We had no idea where the boy was.

It began to rain heavily. None of us had oilskins. Frenchman was in his underwear, just as he had come from his bunk (it was our watch below). Sjöberg, from Helsinki, had been laid up with neuralgia. But now he pulled at his oar, coatless and wet through. We did not want to lose another to Cape Horn.

The mate at the steering oar in the stern sheets swept the sea with his eyes. There was a chance we would not find the ship again if the squall came down heavily and shut her out. That had happened with the Swedish bark *Staut*. She put out a boat to save a boy, a squall came down, and she lost everybody—the boy

228

overboard, those who went to rescue him, the boat. We remembered that.

Then in the last moment of light we saw him. He was on a crest only three seas away! We had been on the point of giving up. Now we lay to heartily and pulled him in over the stern and went back to the ship, which had been watching us and was running slowly downwind toward us. The boy was unconscious and nearly frozen to death, but he lived.

A few days afterward we were around the Horn. Immediately the temperature rose about 20 degrees, and our spirits with it. Off the Falkland Islands we ran into a snowstorm as bad as anything the Pacific had given us, but we were in the Atlantic now and didn't care. Blow on, old gale! We knew that we should quickly come to warmer latitudes and the southeast trades, and so to the line, the northeast trades, the Azores, and to port.

As days and weeks slipped by, we began to forget the early part of the voyage, and the ship made good progress.

But the sea was not yet done with us. The second mate went mad, with awful suddenness. We knew he had worried over Walker's death, for he was officer of the watch. But it wasn't his fault. In the forecastle we had worried too, but we had each other for company.

No one is lonelier than a sailing ship's officer. The captain inevitably keeps to himself. The two mates alternate watches, so when one has the deck the other is below. They must find companionship in their own minds. So no one had seen our second mate approaching a breakdown.

We had an awful time with him. He tried to kill himself three times. We were all sorry for him and kept constant watch lest he succeed. We made for Cape Town to put him aboard a steamship in the shipping lanes. But the wind changed and we couldn't fetch the Cape, and we saw no other ships.

WE FOUND the southeast trades in 30° S. and stood up for the line. Now the days were pleasant and the sun shone, and flying fishes leaped in fear from the bone of foam under our forefoot. Bonito played about, and we saw whales. One whale stayed with us three days. We had no thrashing screw to frighten him away.

On the 100th day we crossed the equator. Here it fell calm for four days, and we made little progress. We were lucky, though. Once I spent three weeks in the Atlantic doldrums.

The wind came again, in cat's-paws at first, and we slipped slowly on. By then the ship's bottom was very foul. Her top speed with a strong wind was little better than seven knots, though she was a fine-lined vessel capable of 12 or 13. So another worry beset us: food.

Each passing day took with it the last of some item of our small sea stock—the last rice, the last margarine, the last sugar, the last bully beef, the last peas. We had some small rather bad potatoes, black sugarless coffee, and bread. There was still the one pig we had been keeping for such an emergency. We killed it, only to find that it was diseased.

Maddening discovery! We tried eating a

GALLANT LADS *of the port watch: two Australians, the rest Finns. Beards belie their ages. All but the carpenter (center) and the mate (right) were under 20. Carpenter stood watch only in bad weather.*

Many lads served seven years in sail as a stepping-stone to an officer's career in powered merchant vessels.

ALAN VILLIERS AND (TOP) NORMAN M. MACNEIL

little of it and were violently ill. But we would not throw the carcass overboard. We put it in a cask beneath the forecastle head. Bad pig was better than nothing at all, or so it seemed to us.

It was now imperative that we speak a steamship quickly and get some food. We had not seen a sign of one until our 104th day at sea, and then it was only a smudge on the horizon. Now we saw none for a week, though we were creeping steadily into the North Atlantic, where we would cross their shipping lanes.

At last we sighted a big passenger liner in the early morning mist, headed down toward Buenos Aires. I don't believe a soul aboard that ship spotted us. All right: there would soon be others, and we would have food.

There were other steamships, later. We ran up signal flags asking them to stop. But they couldn't see our flags, drooping in the calm. We had no other way to attract their attention.

O N THE NIGHT of our 123d day at sea the Scottish steamer *Orangeleaf,* bound in ballast from Invergordon to Trinidad, came in sight. We signaled her with a flash lamp, and she stopped and told us to put out a boat and come across. We pulled over about half a mile of heaving sea. Being a Scot, she did not have much spare food. Being a Scot, she gave us all she had.

She gave us bully beef, flour, fresh vegetables. She gave us a sack of sugar, a case of milk, and half a steer. She gave us tobacco too, but it was in strong plugs, and our boys were too young to be used to it and could not smoke it.

Fifteen days after that meeting we lay at anchor in the harbor at Cobh, Ireland. We had come past the Azores with winds that were sometimes good, sometimes baffling. I was never more pleased to come to the end of a voyage.

From Cobh the ship was towed around to Glasgow to unload its Australian grain. There all of us were paid off, despite the three-year articles. For the poor old ship had nowhere else to go. This was in the depths of the depression, and even a hard-run, penny-pinching windjammer had great trouble finding freight.

As for the grain race, 14 ships had sailed that year, and we were last. But who cared? We had survived.

Thirteen men before the mast! Never again!

FOUR-MASTED BARKS Pamir *(top) and* Parma *both put* Grace Harwar's *jinxed passage to shame. The author sailed in* Parma *in 1932 when she won the grain race in 103 days despite broaching in a furious gale. Bowsprit view shows net rigged to "strain out" lads washed loose in such weather. In 1933 she made it in 83 days; three years later she was scrapped.* Pamir *became a school ship and sank in 1957 with loss of 80 lives. Old salts blamed it partly on the addition of an engine, requiring deck openings.*

Jagged rocks, savage gales took their tragic toll

APRIL, 1912: *The bark* Gunvor *gropes through fog near the Lizard on England's southwest coast. A rending crash. She shudders stem to stern. Seas sweep over her and grind her to pieces, still under working sail (left).*

A year later, same place, same weather, the steel clipper Cromdale *is feeling for a landfall after a long voyage from Chile. Suddenly the rocks have her, the tides dismast and smash her (right).*

The ships were lost, all hands saved.

Slow to respond in light airs, unable to go astern when in trouble, many a fine windship piled on a lee shore. In violent ground swell, lifeboats struggled to rescue the crews (below). But far at sea men went down with ships that foundered, burned, or succumbed to Cape Horn gales. Ocean raiders in World War I sank many square-riggers, for they made good targets.

The splendid Preussen *was fatally rammed by an arrogant Channel steamer that tried to cross her bow in the Strait of Dover. Some vessels like the Danish five-*

masted bark København *and the German four-master* Admiral Karpfanger, *both school ships, simply sailed into oblivion with their crews and cadets. Perhaps violent winds dismasted them, wrenching open their decks to let in the ever hungry sea.*

J. NASH FROM HARPER'S WEEKLY, MARCH 28, 1874, MARINE HISTORICAL ASSOCIATION, MYSTIC. TOP RIGHT AND OPPOSITE: F. E. GIBSON

HER 22 SAILS *barely filling, 1,900-ton Eagle coasts New England. She can top 17 knots. Built to train Hitler's navy, she came to the United States as reparations. Helmsmen (opposite) eye the gyrocompass repeater, hark to the hooded talker linked by earphones to the lookout. Yet the triple wheel takes old-fashioned muscle in a gale.*

234

CHAPTER TWENTY-SEVEN

Summer cruise on a school ship

From Brazil to Indonesia, from Japan to Portugal, a last fleet of square-riggers finds employment — training lads in the hard ways of the sea. Captain Villiers joins United States Coast Guard cadets aboard *Eagle*.

U P AND DOWN, SIR!" was the shout from the forecastle head as the anchor cable came in. "Up and down!" echoed from aft. "Aloft and loose tops'ls! Loose courses!" Pounding feet shook the rigging as eager youths leaped for the high yards.

Crisp orders sounded everywhere. Loose this, haul that. Man the halyards, sheet home the sails, cant the head yards. Break out the anchor! "Anchor's aweigh!"

White sails fell in ordered folds to tauten in the morning wind, curving between the golden yards. Fore-and-afters sang aloft with a jangle of hanks. The main deck swarmed with uniformed boys heaving and hauling as yellow cordage snaked through a hundred blocks. From the bare bones of her masts and yards the bark achieved graceful, sail-clad beauty, standing seaward, swinging in the summer sun. The United States Coast Guard Academy's

G.G. TWAMBLY. BELOW: JOHN E. FLETCHER, NATIONAL GEOGRAPHIC PHOTOGRAPHER. OPPOSITE: ALAN VILLIERS

training ship *Eagle,* manned by some 200 cadets, was off from New London on another long Atlantic summer cruise.

I saw a big lad from Iowa smile quietly as he watched the wake lengthen, heard the wire rigging sing the song of the sailing sea, felt the shapely bark roll and curtsy. "Now I've something to tell my grandchildren," he said.

"Clear up all gear!"

The shouted order broke into reverie, renewing the pace on deck. Aft, the cadet officer of the watch walked the quarterdeck, keeping an eye on the cadets at the wheel, the cadet boatswain, signalmen, radarmen, navigators. The flow of commands never seemed to stop, nor did the work.

That is one reason why *Eagle* is a training ship. She calls for maximum work in full view. "We get a pretty good idea of what our boys are made of before the voyage is over," explained *Eagle's* captain, a four-striper in charge of seamanship at the Coast Guard Academy.

Some 15 other nations agree. They send out a remarkable fleet of about 30 full-rigged ships, barks, barkentines, brigantines, and topsail schooners to train tomorrow's mariners. I began to see how it worked while we slatted along, often with bad winds, on our 20-day run for Santander, Spain.

One evening a severe squall swept over us. The bark heeled in the howling wind, flying spindrift clouding the forecastle head. "Clew up the fore royal!" shouted the upperclass officer of the watch. I held fast to see how the boys would handle this classic stuff of Cape Horn days. The captain watched too, his seabooted feet planted firmly on the wet decks as if he had grown there and belonged, like the masts.

Halyards were thrown off the pin and gear manned. "Lower away! Haul away on those clew lines! Check in the weather brace!"

A few months earlier all this would have been completely unintelligible to many of these lads. Now down came the thrashing royal to be smothered smartly by its gear. Aloft raced four lads; others streaked to take in the main royal. A smart piece of work all around.

After every midday muster, cadets drilled at man overboard, fire and collision, sail handling, or putting the ship about. Sometimes the shapely bark

MANNING A CAPSTAN *the time-honored way, cadets replace the electric windlass to weigh anchor. It keeps them fit. So does steering a towed boat (above) and swarming up the mizzenmast to furl the spanker (right).*

LIKE OLD-TIMERS, *cadets sway on footropes and lie over yard to practice furling. Those*

went through some odd contortions. But the *cadets* were doing the jobs. "I'm never going to command a big sailing ship," said one, "but what I learn here will last me all my life."

At chow time I followed the line through the spacious galley for generous helpings of oven-roasted veal, mashed potatoes, peas and green beans, lashings of white bread and the best of butter, with ice cream to follow. Shades of salt horse and stockfish in the old grain racers! The cadets slept in hammocks (except upper-

classmen, who had bunks) in the 'tween decks, as sailors did in the frigate *Constitution.*

Shore-leave khakis replaced dungarees as *Eagle* moored at Santander. The cadets visited castles and cafes. They saw the former royal palace, and the ancient rock paintings in the caves at Altamira. They did a fine job of showing the flag.

Five days fled, and *Eagle* was off across the Bay of Biscay and through the English Channel. As we picked up the low coast of the Neth-

in the top take in staysail. Handholds on yard add safety. Fuzzy baggywrinkle prevents chafing.

erlands, the boys revved up "Elmer," the diesel auxiliary. Slipping through the North Sea Canal, we passed barges streaming along like trucks on the Pennsylvania Turnpike. We berthed at Amsterdam, and *Eagle* stretched her bowsprit over the waterfront road as the clippers once did along New York's South Street.

Oddly enough the salty youngsters preferred round-the-harbor voyages in rubberneck launches to most other diversions. The big boats could just squeeze through some of the older canals. Their helmsmen edged them slowly past gloriously brilliant flower marts and along rows of stately old homes.

Again time pressed. *Eagle* had more boys to train before fall term. A brief stop at wonderful Copenhagen and we sailed for New London—a good 3,600 miles by the stormy Viking route, past Iceland and the tip of Greenland. We made it in 26 days. Windblown and stalwart, the cadets swung proudly ashore. They had met the sailing ship's sea.

239

240   **HULL DOWN** *behind a comber, Belgian school ship* Mercator *runs with a freshening breeze fron*

tarboard quarter. Topgallant and main gaff topsail await setting. Old Glory tells she's in American waters.

WINSLOW HOMER, 1886, ADDISON GALLERY OF AMERICAN ART, PHILLIPS ACADEMY, ANDOVER

"EIGHT BELLS!" *Yankee skipper and mate follow ritual with a fleeting shot of the sun at its zenith. They order the schooner's clock set at 12. Some down easters claimed they could smell out their position from samples of the bottom brought up by sounding. Artist Winslow Homer settled on Maine's coast, went to sea with a fishing fleet, painted his subjects "exactly as they appear."*

PARADE OF SCHOONERS *awaits dry-dock repairs at Newport News, Virginia. The photographer just missed a two-master under sail but got the three-master* Sallie I'on, *the four-master* Malcolm Baxter, Jr., *the five-master* Jennie French Potter, *the six-master* Eleanor A. Percy, *and the* Thomas W. Lawson, *only seven-master ever built.*

242

EAST COAST WORKHORS

NEWPORT NEWS SHIPBUILDING AND DRY DOCK COMPANY, 1906; MARINERS MUSEUM, NEWPORT NEWS

he three-master carried a simple rig and small crew, but packed large cargoes in her durable hull.

CHAPTER TWENTY-EIGHT

"See how she scoons!"

A lovely lady of uncertain origin, the schooner won the hearts of seafarers plying the coasts and braving the Banks.

A SPITEFUL WIND from Greenland's mountains snarled along the low deck as our Portuguese schooner bashed northward for the fishing grounds off Disko. Her big lowers, staysails, and jibs pulled like Trojans. Smoke from the liver works on the foredeck smutted the nearer sails.

I held her on course, shivering through two layers of woollies, two Iceland jerseys, heavy oilskins, leather seaboots, and a fur cap. It was well that *Argus* was a schooner. She virtually sailed herself while the dorymen split, cleaned, and salted cod with the skill born of 30 or 40 voyages to the Grand Banks and Davis Strait. Cod, cod, cod filling the pounds, piled everywhere, slipping as *Argus* rolled.

Being a square-rigger man, I hadn't thought

DRIVING HARD, *fastest fishing schooners of Canada and the United States race for a trophy instead of top market price.* Gertrude L. Thebaud *of Gloucester leads, but Lunenburg's famed* Bluenose *overhauls to windward. The Nova Scotian won this 1938 contest, defending her title.*

In the 1920's fishermen like Elizabeth Ann Howard, *seen beneath* Henry Ford's *foresail (left), still stretched their broad lowers to boil back to port from the Banks.* Thebaud, *launched in 1930, was too late for sail's heyday. She could do her job as well as any diesel seiner but was judged archaic except for the international race with the old champion* Bluenose. *Both were the ultimate in schooner design, and rivalry was keen since home-port pride rode with them. So proud were Canadians of their spoon-bowed darling that they sailed her to England for George V's silver jubilee, even stamped her image on a dime.*

Bluenose *was wrecked off Haiti in 1946; two years later* Thebaud *smashed on a breakwater in Venezuela while carrying cargo. Other fine schooners had their topmasts trimmed to take nothing more than a trysail, stained by a panting diesel's exhaust. But in ocean-racing yachts the lovely hull lines of the fisherman live on.*

about schooners since I'd seen them at the docks in Melbourne when I was a boy. Four- and five-masters came from America then, stacked with West Coast lumber. With their great sheer—huge wooden hulls shaped like an archer's bow—they had almost no free-board amidships; you wondered whether the timber cargoes kept them afloat. I remember their high masts, perfect sticks of oiled Oregon pine, their long jib booms, the comfortable houses aft, and the small funnels of their donkey engines just abaft the forecastle head.

They had small crews: "One mast, one man—that's the rule," sailors told me. "The donkey engine does the heavy work." Yet those schooners had spotless decks, quarters shining with brass polished like gold.

Schooners were not an American invention, despite the yarn that a Yankee captain named the type with his shout, "See how she scoons!" (skims along), when one was launched at Gloucester in 1713. Fore-and-afters plied the North Sea in the 1600's, skimming over shoals with leeboards raised. But the schooner came into prominence as an American rig, well suited for coastal trade. Sails abaft the masts let these vessels lie close to the wind and tack quickly through narrow waters. Centerboards enabled them to put into rivers and shallow ports for cargoes. Schooners could speed to the West Indies and back, bucking the Gulf Stream, clawing against contrary winds.

As trade increased, they needed larger hulls, hence more sail area. But too much canvas on two masts could be harder to handle than all the sails of a square-rigger. So more masts were added. Three-masters, or terns, were a favorite rig of Canada's Maritime Provinces. Scores of two-, three-, and four-masters were launched in Maine, where locally owned square-riggers were losing overseas cargoes to tramp steamers. Maine still had forests, slip-ways, and know-how. There was still plenty of coastal trade. Towns like Bath, Thomaston, and Rockland produced and sailed big schooners as community enterprises.

They carried lumber from Savannah or Pensacola. They took on coal at Norfolk; some four- and five-masters were built specially for that difficult freight, with heavy planking and keelsons as high as a man. Even so, some worked so much as they aged that in a sea the whole foredeck would "flap" perhaps two feet.

In 1900 the first six-master was built, the 342-foot *George W. Wells.* She could carry

ROBERT BENDICK AND (ABOVE) JOHN MILLS, JR.

246

LUIS MARDEN, NATIONAL GEOGRAPHIC STAFF

LUNENBURG *rivaled Gloucester in fishing and shipbuilding, helped give Nova Scotia the world's largest tonnage per population until the 1880's. Cargo schooners and fishermen rose on its ways before World War II, or nosed in to be caulked (above). Shipwrights now build wooden trawlers but still know how to bang home trenails in the old way to fashion a replica of the famed Bounty (right). Retired skippers rebuild vessels of the past as models (left)—accurate in every detail.*

Chesapeake Bay Craft

Skipjack

Pungy

Bugeye

Log canoe

FAST, STURDY VESSELS, *shallow in draft and easy to handle, developed for the fisheries of Chesapeake Bay.*
Log canoe, *harking back to the Indian dugout, was hewn from several logs and rigged with a leg-of-mutton sail. A yacht version races above, crew member perched on a plank to hold her upright.*
Bugeye, *big offspring of the log canoe, was designed to haul an iron dredge over oyster beds.*
Pungy, *a keel schooner, carried produce to market.*
Skipjack, *a centerboard sloop, is still seen along the Eastern Shore, for Maryland law bars use of power for oystering.*

5,000 tons and touch 15 knots. The six-master *Wyoming,* 350 feet by 50 in beam, marked the limit for wooden sailers. The only seven-master, the *Thomas W. Lawson,* was steel. She was 395 feet long, could carry 11,000 tons, and from a distance looked a bit like a picket fence.

What those masts were named has sparked many a forecastle argument. Usual nomenclature for a six-master was fore, main, mizzen, spanker, jigger, and driver. But the *Lawson's* seven? One of her captains listed them as "fore, main, mizzen, no. 4, no. 5, no. 6, and spanker."

The *Lawson* cost $240,000, what with double bottom for water ballast and a steam engine for steering. But she proved as unwieldy as she was expensive and lasted only five years. Converted into a tanker in 1907, she was wrecked on England's Scilly Islands on her first deep-sea voyage with the loss of all but two of her 17 men.

Steam colliers and tankers and barges towed by tugs finally put the great down east schooners out of business. Sail lasted longer on the West Coast, where a fleet of cargo schooners was built as late as World War I. I remember seeing one, the big *Elinor H.,* at Port Adelaide, Australia, during the depression. She had brought lumber from Oregon and had been abandoned for lack of cargo. She was auctioned as she lay, sails and all, for $2,000.

A DIFFERENT BREED of schooner was the fisherman. Even a high-sterned Marblehead "heel-tapper" of colonial days was sharp and fast; so too the double-ended pinky of the early 1800's. Before the Civil War the fishing fleet began concentrating at Gloucester, linked by rail to Boston and other centers. Close competition emphasized speed. Fishing schooners grew sharper than ever ("too sharp to live," growled old-timers), and in the early 1900's adopted spoon bows and yachtlike hulls—glorious, dramatic vessels.

For all their sleek looks, they had a job to do—wresting a harvest from Georges Bank off Massachusetts and the Grand Banks off Newfoundland. Summer and winter they took whatever the Atlantic served in the way of fog, ice, gales. Sudden storms might drown scores of dorymen. But they were tough as their ships—hard-nosed Yankees, wild Galwaymen, leathery bluenoses from Nova Scotia, "Newfies" from Newfoundland, Portuguese originally from the Azores. They filled their holds with cod, mackerel, halibut, then raced home, topsails and staysail set, a bend in the main boom, lee rail buried in boiling seas. "Drive her, boys, drive her!" And the captain balanced on his heeling deck, sniffed for the smell of Cape Ann, and figured the price for the first cargo to hit the fish pier—only a shade better than the others but worth the wild voyaging.

Portugal's fine steel schooners still brave the Banks and venture into Davis Strait for cod. As I steered *Argus* that bitter day I realized that these were among the very last sailing ships to earn their keep on the sea.

Around the world man wrests a living from the sea

S HE'S NO BEAUTY—a rust-stained bucket of a ship, reeking of diesel fumes and fish, slamming and creaking out to the Banks in the same heaving sea that graceful schooners once sailed. She's a modern Gloucesterman— a trawler. She's a bit more than 100 feet long and throbs with power, for she must drag a weighted net 100 feet wide at the bottom, 80 at the top, along an uneven sea floor 90 fathoms down. She's fitted with radio, radar, loran (long-range navigation), depth sounder to outline the contours of the bottom, a fishscope to find schools of fish.

She needs these electronic aids. Once on the Banks, she may be surrounded by streamlined Soviet trawlers taking home huge catches that are cleaned, processed, and frozen aboard ship. She must find some for herself—redfish or haddock, probably; cod is no longer king. She must stay out in savage weather until she has filled her holds. Only a full load pays off.

Fishing goes on everywhere in the world in an infinite variety of stout vessels, each evolved for its own type of job.

The Great Lakes gill-netter has a heavy superstructure to protect the crew in cold weather. The Buzzards Bay swordfisherman has a pulpit jutting from the prow where the harpooner poises to strike his quarry. The California tuna clipper cruises fast and far. Its crew jerk the big tuna aboard, two or three men to a line.

The North Sea drifter nets herring by drifting over the schools. The inshore shrimp boat fleet leaves its Gulf Coast port in the evening and returns at sunrise. The Maine lobsterman works the other way round. Every artist along that spruce-lined coast has painted these clean-lined boats with high bows and low freeboards chugging seaward from their rocky havens at the first light of day, come light fog or the threat of a northeaster.

Most fishing vessels share certain features: an able hull, seaworthy whether loaded or not; a big deck for working area; bulwarks to hold the catch when it comes aboard; maximum space below to store it, and minimum crew space; low freeboard amidships or aft so men can handle the nets; a dependable engine that is economical yet will hurry the ship back to port for a good price at the fish auction sales.

Japan, China, Peru, the Soviet Union, the United States, and Norway lead the world in commercial fishing. But whether a man fishes from a sampan or a long line trawler he is a special sort of seaman. He can wrestle with the bulging cod end of a net while the deck is standing on its edge in freezing waves. He can rise before dawn and still be dressing down the catch past midnight. He is tough.

Among the toughest are dorymen like Antonio Rodriguez (below) of Fuzeta in the south of Portugal. He and 3,000 other Portuguese still catch their cod from those little 14-foot slab-sided wooden boats that heel to the oarlocks if you look at them, yet don't quite go over. The men stay six months at a time on the North Atlantic, taking to their dories each day. And they find a certain contentment in following one of man's oldest careers.

ALAN VILLIERS AND (OPPOSITE) KOST RUOHOMAA, BLACK STAR

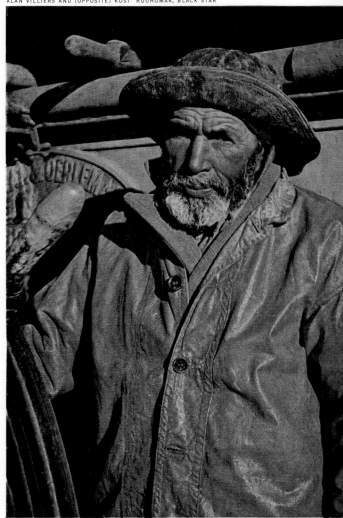

HE EM-PLOYS THE POWER OF STEAM

WHISTLES scream, pistons slam in metallic chorus, paddles slap the water in mechanical cadence. Here is steam, man-made power, at work after centuries of man's dependence on God's good wind.

On the Mississippi, the steamboat was the darling of the 1850's, the powerful, elegant symbol of man's ingenuity. Not always was it so. The first steam vessels clanked and hissed to the sound of jeers, clung to sheltered rivers and bays as had the first sailing craft. But soon steam came of age. Nations vied for the fastest transatlantic service; tramp steamers took cargoes from clippers; ironclads ended the windship's role in war.

Progress quickened: wooden hulls gave way to iron, then steel; paddle wheels to propellers; reciprocating engines to turbines; cordwood and coal to oil and atomic power. How great a stride separates the nuclear ship *Savannah* from that earlier *Savannah,* first to steam on the open ocean!

253

WEIRD AND WONDERFUL *were the ways of early steamship inventors. Jonathan Hulls designed his tugboat (right) in 1736 but never tried her out. A single-acting cylinder, filling with steam, lifted a weight. The weight then returned the piston for the next stroke. Ratchets kept the paddle wheel turning in one direction. By the eighth century, Chinese were turning paddle wheels with coolie power. The American John Fitch tried upright oars (below). In 1788, a later model with oars at the stern began plying between Philadelphia and Burlington, New Jersey. In 1661, Thomas Toogood and James Hayes suggested "a particuler way of forceing water through the bottome or sides of shipps belowe the surface ... which may bee of singuler use and ease in navigacon." The first water jet! In 1807, Robert Fulton's well-designed Clermont (bottom) proved that steam could be commercially successful.*

The steam

Man spent centuries planning ways to move ships against wind and tide. But from primitive paddle-wheeler to twin-screw liner took only about 80 years. Alan Villiers tells of the surge of steam.

254

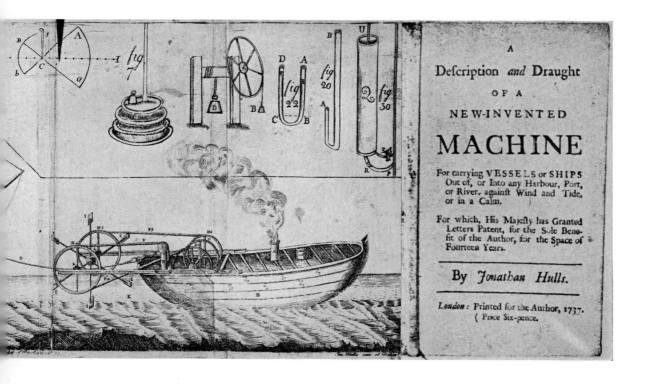

A
Defcription *and* Draught
OF A
NEW-INVENTED
MACHINE
For carrying VESSELS or SHIPS
Out of, or Into any Harbour, Port,
or River, againft Wind and Tide,
or in a Calm.

For which, His Majefty has Granted
Letters Patent, for the Sole Bene-
fit of the Author, for the Space of
Fourteen Years.

By *Jonathan Hulls.*

London: Printed for the Author, 1737.
(Price Six-pence.

engine takes to the water

"SHIP AFIRE, SIR! Starboard bow!"
The captain of the British revenue cruiser *Kite* grabbed his glass, steadied himself, and took a long look.

"No doubt about it," he declared. "Bring her up! Head for the smoke. Poor devils—fire at sea. Worst thing you can have."

The cruiser bounded through the gray sea off the Irish coast. But the burning ship made steadily away, smoking intermittently as if the fire found fresh fuel at regular intervals. Her wake had an odd appearance, a beating of the water unlike the clean wake of most ships.

It took a shot or two across her bow to bring her to. And to the astonishment of the British crew, she proved to be an American steamship.

That is the story told of *Savannah*, a 100-foot ship built at New York in 1818 and fitted with an auxiliary steam engine and paddle wheels that could be folded up and stowed inboard when not in use. She carried 60 tons of coal and some cordwood to stoke her boilers.

She used steam power only about 80 hours during her 29-day Atlantic crossing.

Her captain, Moses Rogers, had no intention of wasting the wind with this newfangled device. The engine was for harbors and calms, when it gave a top speed of about five knots. Obviously, it was wildly impractical for long voyages. Why put a space-wasting engine in a ship that did perfectly well under sail? Why carry a lot of expensive fuel to do what the wind did for nothing? *Pay* for motion at sea? The idea was absurd.

The little vessel crossed the Atlantic to see if she could stir interest in Liverpool. She also tried St. Petersburg, Russia, then went home under sail. Her engine was removed and she resumed life as a coasting packet. Few people realized that almost by accident she marked an epoch. She was the first vessel to venture across an ocean with a hull crammed with heavy machinery and to use it at sea.

Steam had been a long time coming. Heron

255

SAVANNAH, *putting to sea in 1819, looses canvas to take over from steam. In a moment her* *paddle wheels in their removable housings will slow and stop. Crew will fold and stow them* *aboard. Smoke will fade away from the angled funnel that guides sparks away from sails.*

of Alexandria, an ancient philosopher and mathematician, experimented with a simple steam turbine and described how steam could blow a horn and how the pressure of heated air could be harnessed to open temple doors. A 17th century Frenchman, Salomon de Caus, realized that if steam had force enough to drive water far up a tube, it could probably move ships at sea. His English contemporary, David Ramsey, may well have contemplated steam as one of many "newe apt formes" which could "make boates runn upon the water as swifte in calmes, and more safe in stormes, than boates full sayled in greate wyndes."

But it remained for a Scot, James Watt, to produce an effective steam engine in 1765 and make the steamship possible. His separate condenser allowed the piston to do far more work than merely pump water. When James Pickard invented a connecting rod and crank system in 1780, the steam engine was ready to take to the water.

Before long, John Fitch, a Connecticut Yankee, was boldly predicting that sailing ships would soon give way to steam-driven vessels on the Atlantic. Fitch had wanted to build a steam carriage, but the roads of his day were so terrible he turned to steamboats instead. His first two boats had vertical paddles linked to an engine that dipped them in and out along the side. His third boat was propelled by three stern paddles that looked and acted like a duck's legs. The *Experiment* logged more than 2,000 miles on the Delaware River, but Fitch lost his backers. He tried in France and failed there. His inventiveness merely impoverished him. Still predicting success for steam vessels, he killed himself in Kentucky. "Poor fellow," said his few friends. "What a pity he was crazy."

In 1802 a small tug called *Charlotte Dundas* churned along the Forth and Clyde Canal (linking the two Scottish rivers), towing two barges. She had a single paddle wheel turning through a well at her stern, and she ran her trial at a smart three miles per hour.

Charlotte Dundas was the work of William Symington. Years before, he had started designing steamboats around primitive open-topped steam cylinders whose pistons rose under steam pressure, then dropped by gravity. The rise and fall tugged at two chains, each hitched to a revolving drum. Instead of rocking back and forth with the alternating tug of the chains, the drum rotated more or less steadily by means of ratchets.

It was an awkward device, nothing like as good as the crankshaft that drove *Charlotte Dundas*. She was so successful that canal owners with an interest in horse-drawn barges complained of her wash and hounded her off the water. Symington died in poverty —the frustrated inventor of a perfectly workable steamboat.

Robert Fulton was a Pennsylvanian of Irish parentage. A civil engineer of broad talents and interests, he painted landscapes, including probably the world's first panorama, and wrote a book on canals. He invented an early submarine, *Nautilus,* and displayed it before a

Bostonians free *Britannia* from their icebound harbor

O<small>N</small> *a winter run in early 1844*, Britannia, *first of the regular transatlantic Cunard liners, arrived in Boston along with a cold snap. Harbor ice locked her in, upsetting the schedule. Citizens deluged her captain with dinner invitations, then rallied to help him out. They cut a seven-mile channel through the ice from* Britannia's *East Boston dock to open water. They cheered her lustily as she eased through it, produced this picture of the great event, then hastily suppressed it as a bad advertisement for the port.*

Americans welcomed the Cunard Line when it began in 1840. Poet Henry Wadsworth Longfellow toasted the new age: "Steamships! The pillar of fire by night and the pillar of cloud by day, that guide the wanderer over the sea." Emerson agreed that sea voyaging enjoyed many advantages, "but security is not one of them."

For many years Cunard had little opposition. Its liners became Atlantic ferries, noted for reliability, disciplined crews, constant improvements. Today the mighty Queen Elizabeth carries Cunard's flag at more than 30 knots.

GREAT WESTERN LEAVES BRISTOL, *bound for New York in 1838. A seagoing extension of Britain'*

commission appointed by Napoleon. Fortunately for the British at Trafalgar, the Consul did not buy. Fulton turned to steamboats, built a more or less successful one in France, then returned to America to construct *The North River Steamboat of Clermont.*

Beset by troubles — "Never did a single word of encouragement or bright hope or a warm wish cross my path," said Fulton — *Clermont* was finally ready for a trial trip up the Hudson to Albany. Scoffers lined the banks to laugh at "Fulton's Folly." With hissing boiler and groaning piston, *Clermont* began to move, her paddles dipping steadily, smoke belching from her funnel. One farmer took a hasty look and

ran home, telling his wife he had seen the devil on his way to Albany in a sawmill. Witnesses recalled *Clermont's* night passage on that 32-hour trip: "a monster moving on the water, defying the winds and the tide, and breathing flames and smoke." Sailors on other vessels cowered as she came on at 4½ miles per hour.

Clermont made her first run in August, 1807. She plied the Hudson for seven years — the first commercially successful steamship. Following her example, scores of riverboats and tugs churned up and down American inland waters. This was where steam was needed, said Americans, not on the ocean where sails answered well enough. No steamer could

Great Western Railway, she was the first ship built specifically to cross the Atlantic under steam.

possibly make regular transatlantic voyages, said the conservatives.

The British disagreed. Two years after *Savannah*'s voyage home, they sent the auxiliary full-rigger *Rising Star* around Cape Horn to Valparaiso—the first steamship to enter the Pacific. How much she used her two-cylinder engine, no one now knows. Britain built vessels for the Irish Sea, the Channel, and the coastal trade. By 1838 British shipowners were ready for the Atlantic.

April 23 of that year was a big day in New York. Britain's little *Sirius* wheezed up to an anchorage off the Battery, and no sooner had her engine stopped than word reached the

cheering onlookers that yet another steamship was plowing into the harbor, billowing smoke. This was the 1,320-ton *Great Western*. The city went wild.

Sirius, designed to run between England and Ireland, had been chartered for this Atlantic voyage in order to reach America ahead of *Great Western*, the product of a rival company which was after a mail contract. *Sirius* had done well—18 days from Cork, Ireland, her paddle wheels driving her at an average of more than six knots against head winds. She had beaten an American packet ship.

But *Great Western,* starting late, had crossed from Bristol in a fabulous 15 days, steaming at

259

better than eight knots. She was built like a ship of the line—hull trussed with iron and wood diagonals and sheathed with copper below the waterline—built to smash her way headlong through wind and sea, immune to the thumping of the giant engines in her innards, the pounding of the great paddles at her sides. It took about 30 tons of coal a day to keep pressure in her four boilers. Her bunkers could hold 800 tons. She would eventually make 64 Atlantic crossings. With her, the days of the oceangoing steamship had arrived.

"How this glorious steamer wollops and gallops and flounders along!" declared an enthusiastic passenger (£30 the ride, wines included, plus £1 10s. for service). "She goes it like mad . . . puffing like a porpoise, breasting the waves like a sea-horse, and, at times, skimming the surface like a bird."

She was the product of an odd genius, Isambard Kingdom Brunel, engineer of railroad systems, bridge builder, and visionary. Had he been an American, railroading would have absorbed all his energies. But in England the tracks soon reached land's end, and Brunel looked upon the sea and pondered the notion of a steamship. *Great Western* emerged from his drawing board.

Brunel followed her in 1845 with the 322-foot *Great Britain,* first big screw-propelled steamer, and the first iron ship to cross the Atlantic. Conservatives were aghast at using iron. It was "contrary to nature," and vessels built of it would sink like stones. But shipbuilding wood was getting scarce in England, and there were limits to the size of a wooden hull. *Great Britain* had six watertight compartments, six low masts. Her engines of about 1,000 horsepower (a term invented by James Watt) drove a six-bladed 15½-foot propeller that gave her 11 knots on trials and an average of better than nine on her maiden voyage. She could carry some 360 passengers with room for cargo.

"Confessedly the most splendid experiment in shipbuilding ever submitted to a British public," declaimed her publicity agents. And with some reason, for that iron hull proved to be just about indestructible. *Great Britain* ran ashore on the coast of Ireland and lay stranded for the best part of a year, pounded by gales. But she came off with hardly a scratch, went on the Australian run for 30 years, became a four-masted sailing ship, and survived a tempest off the Horn. Until 1937 she stored coal in the Falkland Islands, then was beached. I saw her iron hull not long ago. "Contrary to nature," it's still intact.

NEXT TIME Mr. Brunel designed a ship, the whole world sat up and took notice. For this was the fantastic *Great Eastern,* a monster of about 22,-500 gross tons, so ahead of her time in the 1850's. Not until 1899, when the liner *Oceanic* was launched, was her 693-foot length exceeded. Her tonnage wasn't topped until 1904, by the White Star's *Baltic.*

"To make long voyages economically and speedily by

FIRST OF THE FLOATING CITIES, Great Eastern *took all winter of 1857-8 to launch. Windlasses were to check her momentum; as she inched toward the Thames, one spun, hurling workers sky-high. Christened* Leviathan, *she was called "Leave-her-high-and-dryathan" by hooting onlookers, got her final name by popular demand. Isambard Kingdom Brunel (left) designed her five times the size of any other vessel of the day— too big for available engines, too wide for the Panama Canal had it been built.*

steam, vessels must be large enough to carry the coal needed for the entire voyage.... Vessels much larger than have been previously built could be navigated with great advantage from the mere effect of size," Brunel explained.

No single means of propulsion existed powerful enough to move *Great Eastern* at useful speed. So she was designed to take 58-foot paddle wheels driven by 1,000-horsepower engines, and a 24-foot propeller turned by a 1,600-horsepower engine. Six masts could spread 6,500 square yards of sail. Since no pair of ordinary tugs was capable of handling such a ship in harbor, Brunel planned that she would carry her own—two 100-foot steam tugs slung abaft the paddle boxes. (They were never built.) She could carry enough coal for a round trip from England to Ceylon at an average of 15 knots. She had room for 4,000 passengers or 10,000 troops.

"She will never pay as a ship," said author-shipowner W. S. Lindsay to Brunel after looking her over on the stocks at Millwall on the Thames. But he pointed out that "her hold would make magnificent saltwater baths and her 'tween decks a superb hotel, with an elegant restaurant, smoking and dancing saloons." Brunel was not amused.

Great Eastern grew on ways laid parallel to the river, for she was considered too big to be launched stern first. The big day was to be November 3, 1857. But the inclines down which she was to slide gave way under the 12,000 tons of her bare hull. Hydraulic rams burst. A windlass crumpled. Massive iron chains snapped. Brunel tried again and again to inch her into the water, but not for three months did she float, and then only because of an extra high tide. The monumental cost of that launching, added to the fortune that had gone into her as she lay six years a-building, broke Brunel and ruined the company that his backers had formed. Brunel started a new company which bought the ship and got her to sea in September,

LAYING THE ATLANTIC CABLE: *the right job, at last, for the white elephant* Great Eastern. *Her huge interior, stripped of cabins and saloons, held some 3,000 miles of wrist-thick insulated wire.*

Cyrus Field first linked Ireland and Newfoundland by telegraph in 1858, using U.S.S. Niagara *and H.M.S.* Agamemnon, *whose propeller was guarded by an outrigger (right). The ships met in mid-ocean, spliced cable, paid it out east and west from storage spools (left). Queen Victoria and President Buchanan exchanged greetings. Insulation soon wore out.*

Field tried again with Great Eastern *in 1865, and laid a lasting cable the next year. The great ship then spun other telegraphic webs until 1873.*

1859. On her trials an explosion killed five men —and Brunel, who died upon hearing the news.

In the summer of 1860 she crossed to New York with only a handful of passengers to wander through her white and gilt grand saloon or stroll the vast expanse of deck they called "Oxford Street." America went wild over her; rubbernecks flocked aboard. But the net profit from sightseeing was pitifully small. And it remained about the only source of income. The demand for ocean transport just wasn't big enough for such a leviathan.

She made a few voyages, barely rolling when small ships were forced to lie to. But when she was enroute to New York from Liverpool in 1861, a gale smashed her paddles and rudder and pitched two cows through a skylight into the ladies' saloon. With jury-rigged steering gear she made it to Queenstown (now Cobh), Ireland. It was another huge financial loss for her backers—but Great Eastern survived.

Off Long Island on another voyage, she ripped her outer hull on an uncharted rock— Great Eastern Rock it is now called—and was repaired by means of a cofferdam. While riveting new plates over the damaged hull, workers reported a mysterious tapping within the dead space. Crew members listened white-faced, for legend had it that a shipwright had been sealed in alive while Great Eastern was being built. A worker found that the hammering came from underwater tackle. The ghost was forgotten, and the ship returned to service with another repair bill.

From 1865 to 1873 the great ship found a job laying transoceanic telegraph cables. She did it handsomely: her gaping holds could stow cable by the mile, and "Oxford Street" provided a fine working area. But after laying the Bombay-Aden link of the London-Bombay cable (she dared not enter the reef-strewn Red Sea), she found herself unemployed. True to

"MONITOR AND MERRIMAC" BY J. O. DAVIDSON, PEABODY MUSEUM OF SALEM, UPPER RIGHT:
MATHEW B. BRADY, LIBRARY OF CONGRESS. BELOW: HARPER'S WEEKLY, DECEMBER 6, 1862

IRONCLADS *slug it out in Hampton Roads,*
Virginia, in March, 1862. Confederates
raised the sunken Merrimac *armored it with*
sloping sides of iron rails, and played
havoc with Union shipping, shooting and
ramming. Monitor, *the "cheesebox on a*
raft," steamed down from New York in time
to give battle. Both strange craft were
intact after their dingdong fight, but the
world's "wooden walls" had crumbled.

Monitor's *builder, Swedish-American John*
Ericsson (above), designed rotating turret
armed with two 11-inch naval guns (below).

the half-joking prophecy of W. S. Lindsay, she
ended her days as a sideshow.

In 1889 at Liverpool, the tedious—and expensive—job of breaking her up began. Deep
inside her double hull, wreckers found the
skeleton of the riveter who, said old salts, had
jinxed her for all her 31 years.

SAMUEL CUNARD, a Nova Scotian, bought
a little steamship named *Royal William*.
In 1833 she crossed the Atlantic from
Canada to England, and Mr. Cunard was not
far behind her, eager to found a transatlantic
steamship service. With the help of a British
subsidy, he got the Cunard Line operating on
the North Atlantic by 1840 with dependable
steam passenger vessels. It's still going strong.

Cunard concentrated on safety and reliability. The first vessel built by the line, *Britannia*,
set the pace—a steady 8½ knots, day and night,
fair and foul. Fresh milk came from seagoing

265

cows. And as an "Important Notice" pointed out, "The ship's Wine and Spirit Bar will be opened to passengers daily from 6 A.M."

One passenger, Charles Dickens, found his stateroom an "utterly impracticable, thoroughly hopeless, and profoundly preposterous box," and trusted it must be "a pleasant fiction and cheerful jest of the captain's, invented ... for the better relish and enjoyment of the real state-room presently to be disclosed."

The *Africa* and *Asia* joined the fleet in 1850. They were built with two thick skins of English oak, the space between filled with rock salt to prevent dry rot.

Soon the Cunarders were built of iron. Officers were superbly trained. Mark Twain said: "The Cunard people would not take Noah himself until they had worked him up through all the lower grades and tried him ten years."

But the ships were not always the fastest on the Atlantic. "We expect to see the day," noted the New York *Herald* in 1847, "when a traveller will be able to leave New York and, going eastwards all the time, will be enabled to make the circuit of the earth ... in the summer interval between two sessions of Congress, spending a month or two in the Mediterranean on the way."

Such a voyager, to gain time, would have started off by America's Collins Line. Like Cunard, this was a subsidized venture and it cost the American taxpayer a lot of money.

THE SUEZ CANAL *opens to Europe's crowned heads in 1869. Empress Eugénie of France in her yacht Aigle leads a parade of royal vessels past a wooden obelisk raised to mark the Port Said entrance.*

Fulfilling an age-old dream, Ferdinand de Lesseps, French diplomat-engineer, pushed the 100-mile sea-level ditch from the Mediterranean to the Red Sea in ten years. It clipped 4,500 nautical miles off the London-Bombay voyage (map).

Europe turned to steamships; Red Sea navigation was too tricky for sailing vessels. Liners flourished; the grand tour stretched round the world. Passengers on the sweltering trip to India vied for the shady side of the ship — "port out, starboard home," abbreviated as "posh." The expression still denotes the height of luxury.

In mid-20th century nearly 12,000 ships a year steam across the desert (below).

The first subsidy approved for the new steamers built by Edward K. Collins was $19,250 a voyage.

Collins was a shrewd and able ship-owner. He induced Congress to help on the grounds that Cunard's service between Liverpool and Boston via Halifax was the only "medium of regular steam navigation between the U. S. and Europe."

National pride was stung. And *Arctic, Baltic, Atlantic,* and *Pacific,* pioneers of the Collins Line, came off the ways, built of live oak and pine planking and strengthened with a lattice of iron bands. They were big side-wheelers that could do better than 13 knots. In 1851, *Baltic* made it from Liverpool to New York in nine days, 18 hours—the first mail ship

267

to battle westward in less than 10 days. Even the British voiced congratulations:

> *A steamer of the Collins Line,*
> *A Yankee Doodle Notion*
> *Has quickest cut the mighty brine*
> *Across the Western Ocean;*
> *British agents, no way slow*
> *Her merits to discover,*
> *Suggest we buy her, just to tow*
> *The Cunard packets over!*

Passengers crammed the Collins liners, basking in steam-heated cabins, gaping at bathrooms, "smoke-rooms," and barbershops. But costs outgrew the subsidy, and before the lawmakers would raise it they asked for more speed. To increase a vessel's designed speed can double or treble costs. The liners were caught in a financial whirlpool.

Bad luck hastened their end. In September, 1854, *Arctic* came belting along through a fog off Cape Race, Newfoundland—no slackening of speed in those brave days, come icebergs or fishing schooners—and was rammed by the French steamer *Vesta*. At first little *Vesta* seemed more seriously damaged. *Arctic's* men lowered a boat and went to her aid, helping to quell the panic aboard. Passengers and crew had rushed her boats and launched two, swamping one. Some drowned. The French captain shored up his collision bulkhead and made for St. John's, where he arrived safely.

Arctic's help was ironic. For as it turned out *Arctic* had been fatally gashed below the waterline. The sea got up. Inrushing water first put her fires out, then sank her with the loss of about 300 lives. Mr. Collins's wife, son, and daughter were drowned.

Within less than a year the Collins liner *Pacific,* also with passengers and valuable

freight, sailed from Liverpool bound for New York, and vanished. Probably she collided with an iceberg.

Despite these appalling losses, shareholders put up more capital to build two better ships, and passenger figures mounted. But the British fought back. New Cunard liners edged ahead of Collins. By 1863 the 400-foot *Scotia* was running from New York to Queenstown in a little more than eight days. She was the last and best of the transatlantic paddle-wheelers. By then the Collins Line had folded—Congress had withdrawn its subsidy.

Cunard had plenty of other competition— fast German liners, luxurious French liners where, beneath gently tinkling chandeliers, diners delighted in the elegant cuisine. Britain's Inman Line flourished for a while. Its clipper-bowed ships bore big deckhouses that would grow into the superstructures that mark the modern liner. The line devoted itself to the increasing emigrant traffic across the Atlantic. The steerage had always been miserable—bare shelves for bunks, and meals cooked on deck by the individual. Inman liners improved these primitive conditions and sped the newcomers to New York in reasonable comfort. The later ships had twin screws.

Yet Cunard flourished. In 35 years of service it lost not a passenger's life nor a single piece of mail. Here was the transatlantic ferry, and Americans used it gladly. The costly failure of their Collins Line discouraged them from further large-scale competition. The Civil War put a lid on it for years to come.

But there was plenty of work for steamships on the inland waterways of this rapidly growing country. Just as the little *Clermont* had prospered on the Hudson, great gaudy paddle-wheelers were thriving on the Mississippi.

A SLEEK INMAN LINER, CITY OF NEW YORK *nudged 20 knots with her twin screws. Propellers had proved powerful and economical since 1845, when the Royal Navy tested its screw-propelled* Rattler *in a tug-of-war with the side-wheeler* Alecto. *Paddles churning,* Alecto *was towed backward. Twin screws allowed repairs to one engine while under way, could steer a rudderless ship.* New York *and her sister* City of Paris *ushered in the age of the Atlantic greyhounds. Launched in the late '80's, they lasted until 1922.*

CHAPTER THIRTY

"Steamboat a-comin'!"

Paddle wheels thrash, roustabouts chant as riverboats make a turnpike of "Ol' Mississip'." John J. Putman brings to life their golden age.

JOHN PEMBERTON, chief engineer of the paddle-wheel steamer *President,* pulled a pipe from his dungarees, thumbed in tobacco. His hands were thick and strong. They had worked with wrenches and ball peen hammers and great engines for 50 years.

We stood in the shade of the pilothouse. Forward, thin ribbons of smoke curled from the twin stacks of the oil-fed boilers. Below us, on the New Orleans wharf, tourists studied the big signs: HARBOR TRIPS — 150 WONDERFUL SIGHTS! Beyond them, olive-green trolleys pivoted at the foot of Canal Street, click-clacked back past the palm trees and elegant black lampposts which line their route.

On the mud-yellow Mississippi, giant tankers, freighters, and stub-nosed towboats spoke with their whistles.

"Used to be," said Mr. Pemberton, "you could stand here and see the river lined with

WORLD'S LARGEST STERN-WHEELER, *the* Sprague

steamboats. Big Memphis packets, smaller boats from the Red, Cumberland, Atchafalaya—all those rivers and bayous. The landing then was open field and wooden platforms. You'd see thousands of cotton bales sitting under canvas, hogsheads of tobacco from Tennessee, barrels of sugar waiting to go north.

"Farmers sent their produce down the river: potatoes, turkeys, hogs. Bulls and mules were the hardest to load. I've seen roustabouts grab a young mule by his legs and carry him on.

"Packet boats were just like jitneys. They would take anything offered. I guess it's always been that way on the river."

Always? Well, almost. Flatboat- and keelboatmen had a lively business carrying all sorts of farm products to New Orleans as early as 1809, when Nicholas J. Roosevelt and his wife came floating down the Ohio to the Mississippi. Roosevelt had joined Robert Fulton in a plan to introduce the steamboat to the rivers west of the Appalachians.

Like any Easterner, he was filled with wonder at the mighty current charging down the heartland of the continent. The Mississippi was a mile wide in some places, her brown surface alive with boils and whirlpools. She swept fallen trees along like chips of wood.

Keelboaters told Roosevelt that in spring the Mississippi rose as much as 50 feet. They said no newfangled machine could push a boat against that five-mile-an-hour current. Put eight men ashore with a rope and they could pull a boat—that and poling were about the only ways to get upstream. Roosevelt kept on with his soundings, inquired about freight possibilities, and made up his own mind.

The next year he began building the 148-foot *New Orleans* at Pittsburgh from Fulton's plans. On sailing day there were tears as well

PITTSBURGH, 1911: *Steam marks 100 years on the Western rivers. Packet with gangplank out, big*

as cheers. Local ladies feared Lydia Roosevelt would never survive such a hazardous trip. And in *her* condition! But Lydia waved bravely, the paddle wheels turned, and pilot Andrew Jack swung the boat in a wide arc, then headed her for New Orleans — 1,800 miles away.

Soon, towering bluffs and endless forests seemed to glide by an arm's length away. The only sounds were the slap of the paddles, the panting of the less than 100-horsepower engine. Now and then a farm clearing came into view, and running, shouting children waved while parents rubbed their chins in amazement.

At Cincinnati and Louisville, Roosevelt was congratulated. But everybody said he would never make it back upriver. So he invited Louisville dignitaries aboard for a sumptuous dinner and quietly got under way. His startled guests rushed to the rail to see the *New Orleans* bravely chugging against the current.

Lydia had her baby at Louisville. A few weeks later heavy rains swelled the river, giving the *New Orleans* five inches of clearance over the Falls of the Ohio, dreaded rapids below the city. With two pilots on the bow and a full head of steam, the boat shot the Falls and came to anchor. While she lay there, the anchor cable began to tremble, and some aboard felt "a nausea resembling sea sickness."

Weeks before, a great comet had appeared. Since then the sky had been dull and misty, the sun like "a globe of red hot iron." Now began the greatest series of earthquakes in American history, centered at New Madrid, Missouri.

The quakes did not deter Roosevelt. Down the lower Ohio and into the Mississippi plunged the *New Orleans*. Like Noah's family, those aboard saw the world seemingly end in watery cataclysm: bluffs collapsed, islands vanished, fields became lakes. The earth heaved and shuddered. Clouds of birds darkened the sky. Indians raced downstream in canoes and hurled oaths at the "fire canoe" that had apparently upset their world.

Landing for wood, the Roosevelts found pitiful survivors who pleaded to be taken away. But there was not enough room, or food. Aboard, few spoke. The Roosevelts' dog Tiger "prowled about, moaning." At last the boat passed the earthquake area, and on January 10, 1812, steamed proudly around the river's crescent at New Orleans. One field hand expressed the sentiments of all when he shouted, "Ol' Mississip' done got her master now!"

THE *New Orleans* served the lower river until 1814, when she hit a snag near Baton Rouge. She and other Fulton boats were never at home on the Mississippi. Built by Easterners with seagoing ideas, they had heavy keels, carried their machinery in deep, rounded hulls. "Ol' Mississip'" with her hidden sandbars, submerged forests, and wildly fluctuating levels called for something else.

Westerners like Henry M. Shreve and Daniel French helped develop a boat as practical and as American as barbed wire. They moved the machinery to the main deck and made the hull wide and shallow to ride *on* the water, not in it. They discarded the single, low-pres-

downriver towboats, small Monongahela boats crowd sharp-bowed replica of pioneer New Orleans.

sure condensing engine for a pair of high-pressure machines—riskier (boiler explosions killed more than 1,000 persons in a four-year period) but stronger and lighter.

By 1850 the classic Mississippi steamboat had arrived—"an engine on a raft with $11,000 worth of jig-saw work around it." The *Eclipse,* built at New Albany, Indiana, in 1852, was a paragon of her day. The sight of her on her Louisville to New Orleans run was one a plantation boy never forgot.

At first, far around the bend, rises a dark column of smoke. Twin chimneys poke above the trees. Then she rounds into view, a white palace gliding across the yellow water. With clang of bells and hiss of steam she nuzzles the wharf. Chattering families step ashore. Negro roustabouts grab sacks of cotton seed,

ROBT. E. LEE *and* Natchez *race up to St. Louis. The* Lee *won, averaged 11.58 miles per hour.*

PHOTOGRAPH C. 1870. BELOW: CABIN DIAGRAM OF "JAMES LEE," BUILT IN 1898. BOTH FROM COLLECTION OF LEONARD V. HUBER

"ABOUT TWICE AS COMFORTABLE *as Willard's Hotel"—thus one traveler described a Mississippi packet to a Washington, D.C., friend. Great Republic's 300-foot saloon (above) was flanked by 54 staterooms, lured passengers with "an air of elegance which borders on magnificence." Carpeting marked ladies' area aft, farther from boilers' heat and danger of explosion. Lightly built "floating palaces" averaged five years' service. Steam tonnage on Western rivers exceeded that of British Empire from 1830's to '50's.*

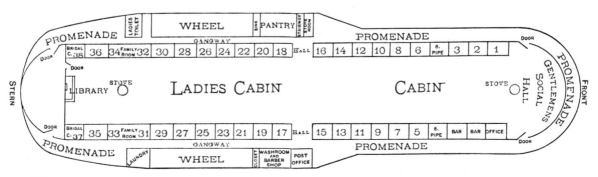

274

swing them into the hollows of their shoulders. As they run-shuffle over the gangplank, it whips up and down like a loose fiddle string. The rouster who loses the stride is bounced off. Songs keep the rhythm:

Ol' roustabout ain' got no home,
Makes his livin' by his shoulder bone!

The main deck is piled high with freight—dry goods and ironware from Pittsburgh, sacks of flour from up the Missouri. Chickens cluck and flurry in their crates. Deck passengers sprawl in the shade.

Forward, men heave four-foot logs into the furnaces. Big steam pipes lead aft to two engines, each with a single piston 36 inches in diameter. An engineer stands by each engine, hears the jingle of bells from the pilothouse, opens a throttle. Giant pitmans flash back and forth, turning 40-foot paddle wheels. The *Eclipse* backs out, heads downriver.

In the 300-foot saloon on the second deck, white-coated stewards set up tables, lay out pearl-handled cutlery. Ladies swish across Brussels carpeting, admire gilded chandeliers, frescoes, and stained glass skylights aglow from the setting sun. Above the murmur of voices the barkeeper asks: "Brandy smash, gin sling, mint julep—what'll it be?" A sharper approaches a drummer clad in a tight-fitting suit: "Ever try three-card monte?" The captain greets planters warmly: "Good year, Mr. Wallace?" "Satisfactory, Captain."

After a meal of a dozen courses, passengers wander out on the promenade deck. Chairs scrape, cigars glow. A boy hugs the rail, close to his father, watches the darkening woods glide by, smells the earthy smell of the river, listens to the thump-thump of the engines, the roar of steam from the 'scape pipes. The river seems a lonely place.

The big boat stops at Greenville, Milliken's Bend, Vicksburg, Hard Times, Waterproof, Cole's Creek. Then, with a blast of her whistle, she bumps against the wharf boat below the bluff at Natchez, Mississippi. Men spill ashore, for here is the rowdy-town of the river.

"NOTHING DOWN THERE nowadays," the old-timer told me as we stood on the bluff and looked down on a jumble of tin roofs half-hidden by trees and bushes. "A few people, maybe. But they're not part of Natchez. Reckon they don't belong to anywhere—'less it's to the river."

I walked past a ROAD CLOSED sign and down the steep asphalt lane to Natchez-Under-the-Hill. Hounds yapped as I passed shanty houses silent with sleep. On one porch an old woman paused in her rocking to eye me closely and nod. Two Huck Finns played on a rusted pickup truck, too busy to notice me. Close by, half-drowned willows nodded and quivered in the river.

The *whoooomp* of the railroad ferry's whistle seemed to stir ghosts in a deserted building. I looked in. Tin cans and cobwebs shared a room that had known the laughter of proud men. I could imagine how it used to be.

Saloonkeepers, gamblers, and gaudy women would come filing out of their haunts to greet the packet. "Wet yer whistle in here, boys!" Those who heeded the cry entered a dark world smelling of cigar smoke and stale "likker," throbbing to the rhythm of banjo and rinky-tink piano, alive with the shouts and curses and bragging of steamboatmen. No night was complete without a "knock-down" fight in the dust of the street.

Natchez on the hill reflects another side of steamboat life. The comfortable, white house of Capt. Thomas P. Leathers sits on a tree-shaded lane close to the mansions of his planter and banker friends. A captain was usually full or part owner of his boat. He had to drum up freight and credit as well as have "sufficient polish to commend him to his passengers." Navigation of the boat was in the pilot's hands; he alone knew the twisting river channel.

Bluff, red-bearded Leathers won great popularity with his series of *Natchez* packets before the Civil War. Afterward he faced a challenge from archrival John W. Cannon. The wily Cannon was a friend of Gen. U. S. Grant but wooed cotton shippers by naming his fire new boat the *Robt. E. Lee.* She promptly began setting records.

Leathers went up to Cincinnati and ordered the finest *Natchez* yet—303 feet long, with eight boilers to drive her 34-inch pistons. People said she looked like a great white swan and that her whistle, mounted inside a stack, sounded like a gigantic bumblebee.

A race wasn't long coming. On the afternoon of June 30, 1870, the two boats left New Orleans minutes apart, bound for St. Louis. Both men denied that they were "going out for a race," but Cannon loaded no freight, carried only a limited number of passengers. Leathers, ever confident, loaded as usual.

TICONDEROGA, *a classic inland steamer, welcomes visitors to Shelburne Museum in Vermont. She*

The boats were well matched, except that the *Lee* had pistons six inches greater than the *Natchez*. They soon took the *"Hoppin' Bob"* out of sight. Cannon ran nonstop, tied on to refueling barges while under way.

Leathers stopped for freight, gambled that he could make up the lost time. At Cairo he was only an hour and a few minutes behind. Then he ran into fog. "Tie her up," he said. Cannon, with four pilots aboard, pushed on.

The *Lee* steamed into St. Louis three days, 18 hours, and 14 minutes out of New Orleans —a record that still stands for the 1,250-mile run. Leathers arrived six hours later, in time for his rival's gala celebration banquet.

The *Lee* and the *Natchez* had raced in the sunset of an era. Railroads were crisscrossing the nation, taking passenger and parcel business. More and more the river belonged to stern-wheel towboats that, despite their name, *pushed* fleets of barges laden with bulk commodities like coal. But then all America was changing at the turn of the century. The West, which the steamboat had served so well, was settled. Some Americans were even looking overseas for new challenges.

...aversed Lake Champlain 47 years.

EVENING LINE OF STEAM BOATS

FOR

PHILADELPHIA,

VIA NEWCASTLE & FRENCHTOWN RAIL ROAD.

The Steam Boats and Cars of this Line being now in complete order, have commenced their regular trips between Baltimore and Philadelphia.

Leaving Bowly's Wharf, Baltimore, at 6 o'clk. P. M.

" Dock-st. " Philadelphia, 1, " P. M.

DAILY EXCEPT SUNDAY.

The subscribers take great pleasure in assuring the public, that the care, attention and comfort so much admired heretofore by the passengers in this Line, will be strictly adhered to.

PASSAGE THROUGH $4. ALL BAGGAGE AT ITS OWNER'S RISK. MEALS AS USUAL.

Freight by this Line will meet with despatch, care, and attention, and at moderate prices.

T. SHEPPARD, *Agent.*

Baltimore, March 1839.

Printed by Lucas & Deaver, Corner of Calvert street and Lovely lane, Baltimore.

STEAMBOATS *and steam locomotives joined to link Atlantic seaboard cities in days long before autos and trucks. Eastern boats like the Hudson River steamer* America *had sharp, shiplike lines. After end of diamond-shaped "walking beam" was thrust up and down by low-pressure engine; forward end transmitted power to paddle-wheel shaft. In the gilded age from the '70's to World War I, steamers serving Long Island Sound, New England, and Chesapeake Bay reached 400 feet in length, carried up to 6,000 day passengers.*

CHAPTER THIRTY-ONE

Blue Riband liners and eight-inch guns

Armored cruisers blacken the sky with coal smoke and raise the muzzles of their long turret guns to feel for the range. Majestic four-stack liners, portholes agleam, speed across the Atlantic in five days. James Dugan writes of great ships in the changing years from Manila Bay to Jutland.

IT WAS EARLY APRIL, 1898. The battleship *Maine* had lain two months in the mud of Havana Harbor. In faraway Hong Kong men of four United States cruisers and two gunboats fretfully awaited the inevitable war with Spain. Gunners were drilled to automata; the white ships had been repainted gray.

In the flagship *Olympia*, Commodore George Dewey, 61-year-old sea dog with a moustache like a bow wave, paced the turkey rug between his wicker chair and the breech of an eight-inch gun that trespassed on his quarters. A third of a century had passed since he saw action at New Orleans as a lieutenant in Farragut's fleet. Now he was near retirement in this obscure Oriental duty. But another chance was coming, and he was ready for whatever President McKinley might direct.

Two days after the Spanish-American War was declared, Dewey got his orders: "Proceed at once to the Philippine Islands. Commence operations at once, particularly against the Spanish fleet. You must capture vessels or destroy."

Last reminders of peacetime duty were cleared away. Chests, ditty boxes, mess tables, even the Commodore's rocker were stored ashore or thrown overboard. Joined by a fifth cruiser, the fleet moved. Near Luzon all hands watched for the dons. No sign. So in yellow moonlight, the midnight before May Day, Dewey raised Corregidor, guarding the narrow entrance to Manila Bay. Its forts reminded him of the ones he had run on the Mississippi back in '62.

He blacked his ships down to stern lanterns, parked his colliers outside, and slipped past the island in line of battle. At dawn he sighted the enemy—seven cruisers, five gunboats, two torpedo boats—nestled in Cavite Harbor. He closed in, took his line past, and opened fire, shattering the morning stillness. Back and forth *Olympia* led the battle line, edging closer at every turn, pouring a stream of four-, six-, and eight-inch shells through a thickening haze of powder smoke.

In the hot, miasmal morning, gunners stripped to the waist and hopped on melting deck seams. Below, in hellish heat, stokers fed furnaces as gun vibrations showered them with soot and

"FIRE AS SOON AS YOU GET READY, GRIDLEY," *shouted Commodore Dewey to his flag captain as flagship* Olympia *closed range at Manila Bay. White-moustached Dewey was not on the open conning tower but on the bridge. Gridley had the con.*

"DEWEY AT MANILA" BY R. F. ZOGBAUM, 1899, COURTESY STATE OF VERMONT

"DESTRUCTION OF U. S. BATTLESHIP MAINE IN HAVANA HARBOR, FEB. 15, 1898,"
CONTEMPORARY PRINT IN CHICAGO HISTORICAL SOCIETY. ABOVE: U.S.S. "OLYMPIA" AT HER
PERMANENT BERTH IN PHILADELPHIA; KARL F. LUTZ. RIGHT: U.S.S. "CONNECTICUT"
DOING 19 KNOTS DURING HER 1907 TRIALS; MARINE HISTORICAL ASSOCIATION, MYSTIC. FAR RIGHT:
STOKEHOLD OF "OLYMPIA" BY VICTOR PERARD, FROM "LIFE AND LETTERS OF ADMIRAL DEWEY."

Gleaming ram-bowed warships made the United States a naval power

FLAGSHIP *of the Great White Fleet, U.S.S. Connecticut voyaged around the world with 15 other battleships in 1907-09. The vessels and their 14,500 officers and men were dressed in peacetime's spotless white, for this was a goodwill tour, the fond idea of President Theodore Roosevelt. They also served to show off the new steel muscles of the United States Navy. Though the ships retained a vestige of the ancient ram and burned sooty coal that sweating stokers (below) fed them, they could hit 18 knots and were well armored—far better than the* Maine, *which had blown up in Havana Harbor in 1898 with a loss of 260 men. That blast (left) set off the Spanish-American War. Experts predicted defeat for the small American fleet, but Dewey, in* Olympia *(top left), proved them wrong.*

281

GREAT BLACK FLEET, *new battleships and unseaworthy ironclads, made the incredible seven-month voyage under Vice Admiral Rozhdestvenski (inset). Object: to relieve Port Arthur, Manchuria. At night in the North Sea, the nervous Russians, thinking Japanese torpedo boats were attacking, riddled British trawlers. Coaling at sea, they inched sootily around Africa, learned Port Arthur had fallen, steamed on toward Vladivostok, Siberia — and the waiting Japanese fleet.*

RUSSIANS *left Kronshtadt (1) in the Baltic, October, 1904, hit British trawlers off Dogger Bank (2) in the North Sea. From Tangier (3) lighter ships took Suez route, rejoined the others at Madagascar (4). Reinforcements (5) caught up off Indochina (6). Fleet died near Japanese island of Tsushima (7).*

RUSSIA'S BALTIC FLEET SAILS TO DISASTER IN

The Battle of Tsushima

MAY 27, 1905

NATIONAL GEOGRAPHIC MAP

steam from shaken pipes. When the battle smoke became a pea-soup fog, Dewey broke off and moved across the bay for breakfast and naps.

Spanish Rear Adm. Patricio Montojo y Pasarón did not disturb the rest period. His ships had been badly hurt, and he thought the battle was over. But soon the American gunners were back in action. Sweating men heaved 100- to 250-pound shells into smoking guns and fired them as the breechblocks slammed. Projectiles tore jagged holes in the steel plates of Spanish ships. Jets of flame and smoke marked the hits. With two ships sunk and eight burning, Montojo struck his colors. He counted nearly 400 casualties. Dewey had a few men wounded. His shattering victory and the equally decisive battle at Santiago, Cuba, two months later knocked Spain's dispirited navy out of the war.

THE WORLD had to wait until 1905, a century after Trafalgar, to see a grand fleet action in the open sea with full use of all the new weapons—rifled 12-inch guns, explosive shells, rangefinders, heavy armor, and wireless. The testing ground was in the strait between Japan and Korea, northeast of the island of Tsushima. There the great naval battle of the Russo-Japanese War flamed and roared.

Japan, to establish herself as a Pacific power, had sent Adm. Heihachiro Togo to smash the Russian naval base at Port Arthur, Manchuria, and bottle the vessels within. The Czar dispatched his Baltic fleet to the Pacific. It was an ill-assorted armada that Vice Adm. Zinovi Petrovich Rozhdestvenski led on this incredible—and doomed—adventure. More than 40 warships and auxiliaries, black with golden stacks, lum-

WHITE-BEARDED ADMIRAL TOGO, *Japan's naval hero, awaited Russians off Korea. His fleet was speedy, his crews trained along British lines. Though the Czar's battleships had more 12-inch guns, the Japanese fired more powerful shells with devastating accuracy. Of the 37 Russian ships engaged at Tsushima, only nine escaped.*

283

bered and blundered down the North Atlantic. Some broke off to go through the Suez Canal; most ploughed miserably around the Cape of Good Hope to Madagascar, suffering more than a hundred breakdowns. They filled their bunkers at sea from colliers stationed along the route. Coal was stored everywhere—even in officers' cabins. Coal dust wrapped the fleet in a black pall. The ill-trained crews alternated chills of despair and fevers of mutiny. Scores died of disease, by firing squad or suicide during the seven-month, 16,000-mile ordeal.

As the "Great Black Fleet" left its last anchorage in Cochin China (South Vietnam), the whole world knew its fate was near. Port Arthur had fallen. Rozhdestvenski must now force his way to Vladivostok, right past Togo's fast warships and veteran crews. The Japanese could sail rings around the weedy Russian ships, could hurl shells seven times as destructive as the best Russian 12-inchers. Togo, knowing his opponent's limited fuel range, placed his force across Tsushima Strait, the shortest route to Vladivostok. And on May 27, 1905, Rozhdestvenski sailed into the strait, his men ready for action, blessed by their chaplains, warmed by their tots of vodka.

Togo met the Great Black Fleet and within gun range ran up an amazing signal that should have lost the battle for him then and there: he ordered his ships to turn across the Russian course, each vessel swinging on the same pivot point at two-minute intervals. In such a turn a ship loses way; its gunners cannot maintain accuracy. All the Russians had to do was pick them off, one by one.

The half-trained gun crews scored hits, but the Japanese got through their turn. Togo raced on a parallel course and opened fire. At that range his four-foot-long, 12-inch shells (the Russians called them "portmanteaus") could be seen somersaulting as they arched toward the Czar's ships. Very soon they were running true and exploding murderously. One burst in an observation slit in the flagship's command turret, ringed by 10-inch armor. Fragments screamed around inside and felled the Admiral. Sailors rolled him down their backs to the deck

of another vessel. By now the Japanese were using armor-piercing shells that punched deep into a ship's vitals before bursting. Ship after ship was sunk or crippled. The destroyer bearing the wounded Rozhdestvenski surrendered. The battle was over; 5,000 Russians had died.

Overnight Japan had become a naval power. The United States reacted by building a Pacific fleet and hastened to realize the old dream of a canal through Central America. This would allow ships to go from coast to coast without having to round Cape  Horn. Before the Corps of Engineers could dig the Panama Canal, the Medical Corps had to conquer yellow fever. The disease had ruined an earlier attempt by Ferdinand de Lesseps of Suez fame. But under the urging of President Theodore Roosevelt the fever was beaten and thousands went to work with picks, barrows, and steam shovels.

They moved 211 million cubic yards of earth, built three sets of locks, and pushed the big cut 50 miles across the Isthmus of Panama. It was opened in 1914, a $380,000,000 project that knocks about 9,000 miles off the voyage from New York to San Francisco (see map).

A transit of the canal is unforgettable. Electric locomotives called "mules" tow ships into the locks, which raise them to the level of the lakes that lie in Panama's interior. In Gatun Lake you will often see dozens of ships lying at anchor, taking a freshwater cure. The mountain water destroys the saltwater weeds and barnacles on their hulls and saves the cost of dry-docking and scraping.

On the Pacific side of the lake the Gaillard Cut leads through the mountains. Dredgers are constantly at work to clear it of landslide debris. More locks then lower the ship to the Pacific. The level here varies considerably, for the tide is 12 times as great as at the Atlantic

GAILLARD CUT, *nine-mile channel across Panama's spine, proved a tough problem for canal diggers. Volcanic soil kept sliding back in as steam shovels gnawed through the hills. Photograph of August, 1913, shows the 300-foot-wide corridor almost finished. A year later, S. S.* Ancon (*lower*) *made the first passage between the continents, voyaging from Atlantic to Pacific.*

BROWN BROTHERS. DRAWING FROM "A HISTORY OF TECHNOLOGY," OXFORD UNIVERSITY PRESS. BELOW: SCIENCE MUSEUM.

LUSITANIA, *early turbine liner, leaves on 1907 maiden voyage. U-boat sank her*

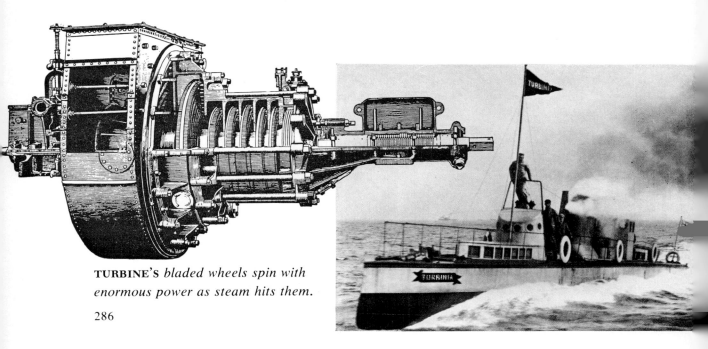

TURBINE'S *bladed wheels spin with enormous power as steam hits them.*

in 1915 with loss of 1,198 lives.

A SHARP CRAFT *disrupted
Queen Victoria's Diamond
Jubilee fleet review in 1897
by threading between crack
British warships at an unheard-
of speed of 34½ knots.
Stunned authorities found she
was Charles A. Parsons'
Turbinia, powered by three of
his steam turbines. Turned
down by the Admiralty for
years, the inventor chose to
prove his engines dramatically.*

end of the canal. Another long cut leads past the towns of Balboa and Panama to the open sea. You enter the Pacific slightly *east* of where you left the Atlantic

As NAVIES GREW in the early 20th century, so did the world passenger fleet, prospering from two extremes of customers, the cosmopolite in first class and the emigrant in steerage. From Naples, Fiume, and Hamburg the freedom-seekers embarked. Names that sounded strange back then are now the names of famous Americans: Sarnoff, DiSalle, Berlin, Callas, Dubinsky, Friml, Musial, Rickover, Salk, Saroyan, and a host of others. The passenger liner might be, for its elegant clientele, a hotel grander than all hotels, a restaurant eclipsing all restaurants. For the humble masses below it was also a tabernacle of hopes and dreams.

Almost always the great liners had four stacks This became such a status symbol of North Atlantic travel in days of hobble skirts, hard collars, and suffragettes that some ships added an unnecessary fourth stack just to be in the swim.

These were steel ships. Steel had been used in shipbuilding as early as the 1850's, but not until the late 19th century had its quality improved enough for general acceptance. The Cunard Line's *Servia* of 1881, the first steel mail ship on the transatlantic run, was lit by electricity. She carried her 1,100 passengers in some comfort at a steady 16 knots, and provided a pattern for the great four-stackers that followed.

Fast passages paid off for the steamship lines, so speed inched upward at the turn of the century. Competition for Britain came abruptly from Germany in 1897 — the *Kaiser Wilhelm der Grosse,* with triple expansion engines and two big screws that gave her better than 20 knots on her maiden voyage. She was the pride of the Fatherland — glistening white, with a wireless that carried 25 miles.

The Cunard Line countered ten years later with two liners that became memorable: *Lusitania* and *Mauretania.* They were by far the world's largest ships — 790 feet long by 88-foot beam — and carried steam turbines designed to give them 24½ knots. This proved an underestimate. On her trials *Lusitania* averaged more than 25 knots and immediately began setting records across the Atlantic. *Mauretania,* launched a little later, was even faster than her sister. In 1909 she crossed from Queenstown, Ireland, to Sandy Hook in four days, 10 hours, 51 minutes, averaging more than 26 knots. She won the Blue Riband for speed supremacy on the Atlantic and kept it 22 years. After she lost it to Germany's *Bremen* in 1929, *Mauretania,* "Grand Old Lady of the Atlantic," came back with an outward passage averaging just under 27 knots and a homeward trip bettering that blistering pace.

Battling the competition of Cunard and the Germans, Britain's White Star Line had been concentrating on speed since it was formed in 1869. But its reply to Cunard's twin racehorses was the launching of two graceful four-stackers that forsook speed for size and luxury. *Olympic* appeared in 1911, the new "largest ship in the world." She was followed a year later by an even bigger sister, a floating city with ebony sides and white

287

superstructure topped by the line's buff and black stacks. Her name was *Titanic*.

She caught the world's fancy, what with her 883-foot length, bulkheads that made her "unsinkable," triple screws—two driven by triple expansion engines and one by a turbine—and her appointments, including a complete Turkish bath. The press dubbed her "Millionaire's Special," and crowds watched her slip out of Southampton on April 10, 1912, the start of her maiden voyage.

She moved easily, finding herself, satisfied with 20 knots. On the evening of April 14 she was running through smooth seas and receiving radio reports from other ships: watch out for ice. "We seem to be stuck in it, almost completely surrounded," said one vessel.

The horizon was hard to make out that night, and the air felt strangely chilly. But at 11:40 a lookout saw something that chilled him even more. A hulking ghost rose, it seemed, from the sea directly ahead of *Titanic's* bow.

"Ice! Dead ahead! A big berg!"

The first officer, on the bridge, ordered the helm hard over and rang up full astern on the engine room telegraph. The great liner barely veered, then crunched along the broad underwater base of the berg.

The ice tore a 300-foot gash in her flank, and water flooded six of her watertight compart-

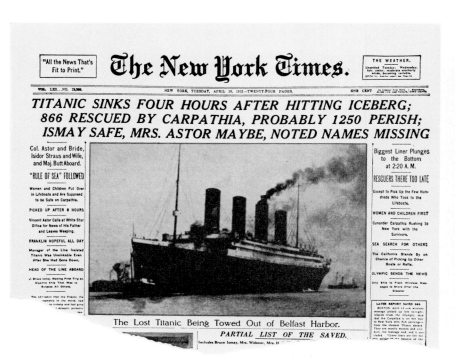

The Lost Titanic Being Towed Out of Belfast Harbor.

"UNSINKABLE" TITANTIC UPENDS; *her 20 lifeboats keep clear. The great hull echoed with the thunder of engines, boilers, furniture tearing loose and crashing forward. Then her lights went out and she slipped under. Survivors sang to drown out the terrible cries of the last helpless victims. Alert Cunarder* Carpathia *caught* Titanic's *sos and radioed "coming hard." She raced through the ice field, picked up the boats. The steamer* Californian *was wisely hove to in the ice a few miles from the stricken White Star liner. Her wireless operator had turned off his set at the usual time and gone to sleep, unaware of the disaster. The New York* Times *headline proved optimistic: only 712 were saved. The enormity of the tragedy spurred long-needed safety measures—adequate lifeboats, a 24-hour radio watch, weather broadcasts, and formation in 1914 of the International Ice Patrol.*

288

ments. Strangely, had the lookout been asleep, had *Titanic* smashed head on into the iceberg, she probably would not have sunk. Dancers in the grand ballroom might have been sent spinning, and card players in the smoking room would have lost the thread of their game in the confusion. But only the bow compartment would have flooded. The ship would have seemed truly unsinkable.

She went down about 2:20 A.M., taking 1,503 people with her. Lloyd's of London, the famous marine insurance organization that was founded in a coffeehouse in 1689, had considered the odds a million to one against *Titanic* sinking because of collision with an iceberg. Now the *Lutine* bell, traditionally rung at Lloyd's to announce portentous news, tolled for the worst maritime disaster on record.

FOUR YEARS after the *Titanic* tragedy and just a decade after the Battle of Tsushima came the last naval engagement to be fought in the classic manner of massed fleets trading massive broadsides. Some 250 British and German ships clashed in a battle the British call Jutland, the Germans call Skagerrak, and the trawlermen of both nations more accurately place north of Dogger Bank in the North Sea: about 57° N. by 6° E.

A bold German admiral, Reinhard Scheer,

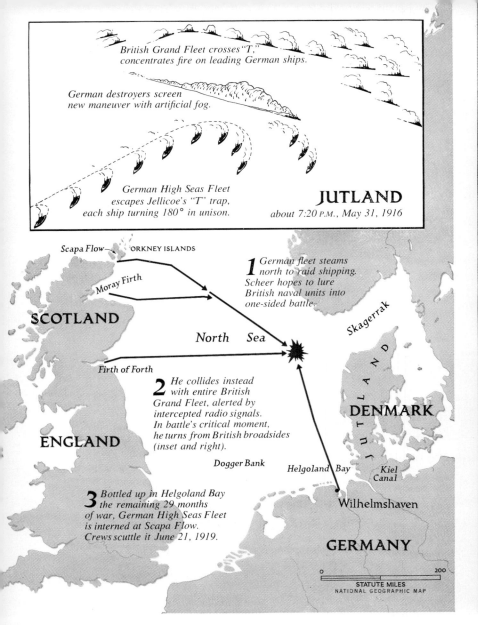

British Grand Fleet crosses "T," concentrates fire on leading German ships.

German destroyers screen new maneuver with artificial fog.

German High Seas Fleet escapes Jellicoe's "T" trap, each ship turning 180° in unison.

JUTLAND

about 7:20 P.M., May 31, 1916

Scapa Flow — ORKNEY ISLANDS

Moray Firth

SCOTLAND

North Sea

Firth of Forth

Skagerrak

1 German fleet steams north to raid shipping. Scheer hopes to lure British naval units into one-sided battle.

2 He collides instead with entire British Grand Fleet, alerted by intercepted radio signals. In battle's critical moment, he turns from British broadsides (inset and right).

ENGLAND

Dogger Bank

3 Bottled up in Helgoland Bay the remaining 29 months of war, German High Seas Fleet is interned at Scapa Flow. Crews scuttle it June 21, 1919.

DENMARK

Helgoland Bay

Kiel Canal

Wilhelmshaven

GERMANY

0   200

STATUTE MILES
NATIONAL GEOGRAPHIC MAP

was trying to break Britain's blockade of Germany. Though outnumbered three to two by Adm. Sir John Jellicoe's British Grand Fleet, Scheer determined to venture out, engage part of the British force, and destroy it. In May, 1916, he led the German High Seas Fleet out of Helgoland Bay, looking for trouble.

British wireless monitors alerted Jellicoe of activity at Wilhelmshaven. From Scapa Flow, Invergordon, and Rosyth his Grand Fleet put to sea. About 80 miles from the Danish peninsula of Jutland his battle cruisers, commanded by Adm. Sir David Beatty, met the German vanguard of Rear Adm. Franz Hipper. Now came the test of dramatic new ship design.

In 1906 Britain had produced a tremendous battleship built around an armament of ten 12-inch guns. Turbines drove her at better than 20 knots. Heavily armored, she served as a stable platform for long-range, precision firing. Her name was *Dreadnought,* and she inspired imitation, especially in Germany. Both nations supplemented these giants with new battle cruisers, nearly equal in firepower but faster and less heavily armored.

Dreadnoughts and battle cruisers mounted their big guns two abreast in revolving turrets. Inside, men yanked open the breech and hydraulic rammers thrust home a half-ton shell brought up on a lift from the magazine. Men then shoved in silk bags of powder—a 400-pound charge. Loading took about ten seconds.

High in the superstructure a gunnery officer gave a signal; all the right guns in the turrets fired, then all the left guns. Shells screamed 11 miles at 1,500 miles an hour. The first salvo dropped long, the second short. Corrections

290

were made; the third salvo (hopefully) hit home.

Hipper's superbly trained gunners scored quickly, blasting the midship turret of Beatty's flagship, H.M.S. *Lion*. A Royal Marine officer, both legs blown off, saw flaming debris falling down the barbette, dragged himself to the voice tube, and shouted, "Flood the magazines!" He saved the ship.

Less fortunate were the *Indefatigable* and the *Queen Mary*. As the two battle cruiser forces raced on parallel courses, snaking to avoid salvos, shells hit both ships, exploding their magazines. They sank with 2,200 men.

Beatty led his survivors northwest to rendezvous with Jellicoe's main force. Scheer and Hipper gave chase, unaware that they were charging into the British lion's mouth.

So the great fleets met, Jellicoe with the advantage of being in position to "cross the T"—to lead his battle line across Scheer's bows and bring all his broadsides to bear against only Scheer's forward-firing guns.

It looked like the end of the German Imperial Navy. Then German destroyers stormed at flank speed between the fleets, trailing chemical smoke. Behind the screen Scheer ordered the new and hazardous maneuver of turning in line simultaneously. In three minutes the German fleet swung 180° without collision, and when the smoke cleared, the British saw only enemy fantails passing out of range.

Once again Jellicoe tried to cross the T. Once again Scheer baffled him with smoke and buttonhook turns, and under cover of night steamed back to his base. Scheer had escaped, but he never ventured out in force again.

The battleship had seen its day of glory; the next war would be fought differently.

CHAPTER THIRTY-TWO

World War II: a sailor's story

These flaming years saw battleships yield their rule to aircraft carriers, convoys keep open a supply pipeline despite U-boat attack. Each man fought his own war, and landing craft commander Alan Villiers tells of his.

THERE ARE 96 U-boats on the plot between you and Gibraltar," said the staff officer at Bermuda. "Hope you make it. Sorry about no escorts."

I didn't mind. Escorts advertise the weakness of the escorted. I thought my welded sheet-steel craft might do better on their own. Each was driven by eight bus engines and carried four 20-mm. Oerlikon guns, a couple of smoke floats, and two depth charges. They looked like orange crates, were called LCI(L)'s — Landing Craft, Infantry (Large) — and I had 24 of them, bound across the Atlantic. It was early 1943.

A Washington brass hat had inspected my fleet (it was called a "flight," but I never knew why, except to add to the confusion) and noted how short it was on experienced seamen. So I was given four — one for each corner of the five-column formation I'd worked out as best for open sea.

BATTLESHIPS DIED *in a war of bombs and torpedoes. Japanese carrier planes knocked out seven in attack on Pearl Harbor, December 7, 1941 (upper). Earlier, Hitler's mighty* Bismarck *broke into Atlantic to raid convoys. Hounded by British, she sank the* Hood *with 1,500 men, was battered by ships and planes. Cruiser's torpedoes finally sank her with 2,300 men (lower). In last battleship duel, October, 1944, Americans smashed a Japanese force in Surigao Strait in the Philippines.*

293

"Another thing," the officer added. "You're on the secret list, so keep clear of shipping. You look mighty like submarines at a distance."

I led my odd ships down the channel at Bermuda, formed them up with some difficulty, and headed east along a dogleg course which would keep us clear of friendly ships. Most of the time I was glued to my bridge—three steps across and two back, with a compass and a couple of voice pipes. The steering was below in a protected wheelhouse. There was no other armor except gun shields.

I kept the columns wide and short so I could control them. In blacked-out nights I couldn't see them, and by morning some vessels would

not be there. It is a scary thing for a young watchkeeper to try to keep station all night jammed in among 24 ships. The one ahead is too close; suddenly it looks frightening. Its wake is right in your bow wave! And the dark shapes on each side are veering off course, yawing to slice right into you! Better fall off, drop back. Better lose station than drown. So every morning I had to round up the strays.

I had been briefed that a 40 percent loss was not only acceptable but almost expected. I wanted to keep that down. But there was a bad moment not far from the Azores.

"Wolf pack is shadowing you, contemplating attack!" The radio crackled with the cheer-

AIR ATTACK! *Japanese planes scream down on a carrier task force in a typical Pacific Ocean fleet action. Helmeted sailors man antiaircraft guns fringing flight deck, pour devastating fire at low-level attackers. Smoke plumes mark death dives of stricken aircraft; some are being downed in snarling combat high above the fleet, for carriers' fighter squadrons have scrambled to intercept. "Jill" torpedo bomber, dragging one wheel because of a ruptured hydraulic line, takes a pasting as it flashes overhead aiming for one last target. Off its starboard wing another Jill bores in through geysering shell splashes. Gunners (below) feverishly feed 40-mm. clips into hungry guns hammering at attackers.*

U. S. NAVY. LEFT: CARRIER GUNNERS ON THE "YORKTOWN," APRIL, 1944, BY WILLIAM F. DR   U. S. NAVY

ful news, and suddenly the Atlantic looked a nasty big piece of water to drown in. What could I do? If I knew where the subs were, I could turn toward them and put up a show. Up came the operator again with a piece of paper: "Attack imminent."

I thought quickly. Only the operator could pick out these signals and decipher them. No one else in the flotilla was worried. If I ordered them to scatter I would advertise to the U-boat commanders that I knew they were there and that I was afraid of them. But these Germans were only fellows like myself doing the best they could. They obviously didn't know what my funny little ships were, for they could

have surfaced outside our 20-mm range and had a little gun practice at us. I decided to keep my mouth shut and hold to the course.

Nothing happened. Months later we learned through prisoners that the U-boat had seen us and shied off. Our unfamiliar silhouettes looked dangerous to them: a new weapon, perhaps, for destroying them. They quietly dropped astern and went after targets they knew—tankers, freighters. We made our transatlantic passage with little trouble. All but one of my 24 ships got across. I was glad we had not been ordered to join a convoy.

Those early months of 1943 were touch and go in the Atlantic, where the war was well defined: convoys versus submarines. The British fleet had sunk or bottled up Germany's proud new warships, but U-boats came *very* near breaking the lifeline of escorted merchant ships that supplied the Allies with troops, trucks, tanks, planes, fuel, all the fodder of victory. In the first ten days of March, 41 vessels went down; in the next ten days 44. But gaps in air coverage for the convoys were being filled by planes from escort carriers. Escort vessels were getting better search devices, better weapons. More and more U-boats were not returning to base.

Though the balance was slowly swinging toward the convoys, it was plain hell to serve on them: day after day, night after night at action stations, watching for U-boats and enemy planes. The lumbering ships, deeply laden, tried to keep station. Some were quick on the helm, some as sluggish as fat oxen, yet they had to zigzag violently even on stormy nights.

Once 40 U-boats attacked a convoy for days while ferocious weather grounded escort planes and threw surface vessels about like flotsam. I knew the master of one of those merchantmen. He told me he saw his son's tanker blow up. Of course no ship stopped for survivors—she'd be a sitting duck. This skipper saw a lifeboat drift close by and in it was his son, a 17-year-old apprentice. The boy looked up as the crest of a sea flung the boat high, and he smiled. He was never seen again.

THE GRIM CONVOY WAR was finally going our way by the night in June, 1944, when I led another "flight" of LCI(L)'s down the mineswept lanes of the English Channel. We were headed for the Normandy beaches in what Navy men had dubbed "Operation Bloodbath." Now people call it D-day.

The weather wasn't too good. Already there had been postponements, and I was surprised that this time we were on our way. I wondered about those nasty Channel tides sweeping in on the beaches. I wondered about a lot of things. But no one seemed worried. Wherever I looked I saw strange craft: pontoon sections and concrete slabs snaking along behind tugs, things that looked like big drums unreeling themselves across to France, and everywhere ships, ships, ships—fat LST's and low-slung LCT's crammed with tanks of all kinds, including some that could swim off the ramps and others that flailed great chains before them to explode land mines. High overhead the bomb-

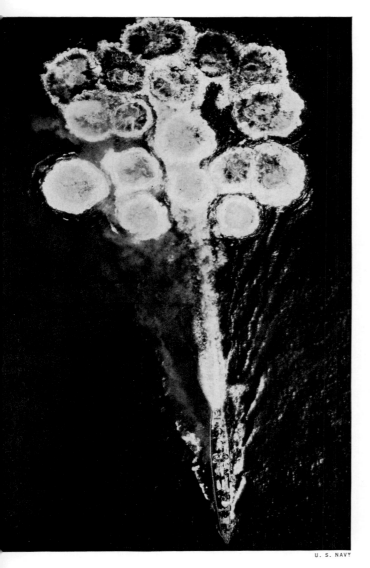

U. S. NAVY

DEPTH CHARGES *blossom symmetrically astern of a speeding destroyer. Fatal to a submarine if they exploded within 20 feet, they helped bag 781 U-boats during the war. Sonar picks up propeller sound or spots a submerged hull from echoing sound waves. Charging overtop, the sub hunter looses a rosette of "ash cans" fused for various levels, then watches for oil rising from the quarry's ruptured hull. Sub sometimes escapes by lying still at maximum depth.*

ers shuttled back and forth. Inshore, battleships opened with 16-inch guns, silencing German batteries.

I was carrying British Eighth Army men, Gordon Highlanders, Black Watch, Seventh Lancers, all of them veterans of the Mediterranean campaigns since El Alamein. A Gordon Highlander was blowing lustily on the bagpipes with an awful din. Hunting horns blared from an LCI astern. We would be rushing at a heavily defended beach in a couple of hours. Odd fish, these soldiers.

My thoughts drifted back to Dunkirk, just four years before. What a difference between these high-spirited, confident men and the bewildered troops, bone-tired, who had waited so patiently to be taken off those smoke-hung beaches after the Germans had broken through in France. Every British boatman, yachtsman, fisherman, and seaman who could find a craft had crossed and recrossed the gray Channel to rescue the soldiers. You'd hear cheerful voices: "Push 'er orf, Alf! All aboard the *Skylark,* lads. 'Op in!"

So it went aboard many a *Skylark* — the name is a favorite for those Channel launches that carry summer tourists on ten-minute "sea" trips. No skylarking at Dunkirk. Bombs crumped down as the snarling Stukas dived toward the littered beach. And the Alfs and Berts and 'Arrys of all the *Skylarks* kept going until they dropped, exhausted — and then got up again and carried on. You soon learned that most bombs miss. If one hits, you don't really have much left to worry about.

They'd told us that with luck we might get 50,000 men out of Dunkirk. We didn't count them. But when it was over, the total came to nearly 350,000. A few days afterward, I came out of the Portsmouth dockyard and passed the big green. The locals were playing cricket, all in their best whites, as if they hadn't a care in the world. There was scarcely an effective weapon left in England. But there they were — and, good Lord! That was Alf, skipper of the *Skylark,* now stepping up to bat!

S HOULD BE a minesweeper's dan buoy coming up to starboard, sir, about 20 yards away." The voice of the sublieutenant in charge of our electronic navigation gear snapped me back to Operation Bloodbath. Mine-cleared lanes were marked like streets. You entered a circular zone called Piccadilly Circus and followed it to the right. PT boats

U. S. SUBMARINES AND AIRCRAFT *crippled Japanese supply lines by sending eight million tons of shipping to the bottom. The sinking Japanese destroyer, seen through the periscope of U.S.S.* Wahoo, *had closed to depth-charge the sub, patrolling off New Guinea in 1943, but got torpedoed first. Dive bomber pilots (lower), emotions still at full throttle after a raid on Wake Island, fill in the air intelligence officer in a carrier's ready room. They claimed a tanker and 65 planes destroyed at a cost of 12.*

CONVOY *reaches the English Channel under an escort's protecting guns. Lumbering across the Atlantic no faster than its slowest ship, this flock of freighters has run the gauntlet of*

U. S. DESTROYERS *in a fleet action*

lay at each exit, flying flags with big numbers. When you reached your number, you took your road to France.

Our lane led to a huge marshaling area off the French coast, the starting point for the race to the beach at H-hour. I had studied charts and photographs of my beach. I knew its pill-boxes, the church spires and prominent buildings rising beyond its dunes, even the kind of sand to expect.

Now, as we left the marshaling area, I could finally see my beach, low and misty in the summer morning. It looked just like the photographs.

It was half tide, and I could make out the German obstructions on the sand, pilings with mines stuck on them, barbed wire farther ashore.

Suddenly a pillbox flashed and barked briefly. Big brother battleship opened up with a roar. End of pillbox. Big guns from somewhere near Le Havre fired on us. As we plowed forward we passed the keels of upturned ships, barges, landing craft. How new they looked!

Stand by to beach!

Soldiers crouched. They wore light rubber waders pulled up to their armpits. Gear was slung around them—everything from weapons to self-warming soup.

Let go!

Away goes the stern anchor. Out runs the wire. In comes the tide, and the sea leaps with it. What tides they have on this French coast! The beach is very close. We hit.

Down ramps!

They splash down, and the soldiers dart down them, hunched, hurrying. The water is deep, with waves a foot or

298

COMBINE. ELC... ARTHUR BEAUMONT, 1941

submarine wolf packs. Now it faces attack by bombers, torpedo boats, and long-range guns.
U-boats sank 2,775 merchantmen, but more than 300,000 cargoes kept the lifeline open.

dash from a smoke screen at 37 knots to attack with five-inch guns and torpedoes.

two high. Men are knocked down, they struggle back up, stream away carrying rifles and submachine guns above their heads.

From the LCI's all along the beach they rush ashore. But a craft in my flotilla hits a mine. Her stern blows off, spilling out fully laden soldiers. Her anchor is gone, and she swings broadside toward the beach. Will she hit me? Another of my skippers gets stuck fast. And there goes another mine! One of that fellow's ramps is wrecked, but he carries on unloading with the other one.

The LCT's are beaching, and mine-clearing tanks waddle ashore, their great chains thrashing in front of them. Then come the broad-tracked heavy tanks, turrets open, gunners watching for targets.

A penetrating whistle grows in frightening crescendo and ends in a series of smashing explosions. It is a stick of bombs from some German who got through our air cover. He hits nothing but sand. As the gray fleets come churning in from the sea and grind ashore, their ramps crashing down, I wonder what has happened to the opposition. Troops, tanks, and transports swarm up the beach. Are the Germans all gone?

Bullets snap by me. I glance around to see the sublieutenant, the nice young lad who looked after the electronic navigation, sink slowly to the deck. His smooth face wears the astonished expression that those who are shot so often have—as if amazed that God has suddenly chosen them to die.

D-DAY, NORMANDY, was not the end of my war. After the landing came the buildup of supplies and reinforcements, the slogging work of keeping things going at any price. The price had been high at the landings in Italy—Salerno and Anzio. At our sector of Normandy we were lucky.

BEACHHEAD, NORMANDY: *LST's disgorge tanks and trucks. Transports crowd offshore.*

Then we were withdrawn to Oban, Scotland, for an extensive refit. What now, I wondered. A landing in Norway? That seemed about the only enemy territory reasonably convenient. But our refit turned out to be "tropicalization." Next stop: the Arakan coast of Burma. Would this war never end?

In the Pacific a totally different kind of sea war had been going on. Japan called the tune on December 7, 1941, with the surprise air attack on Pearl Harbor that temporarily knocked out the battleships of the United States Pacific Fleet. But within months America was fighting back with the same technique — carrier planes striking at Japanese warships. The Battle of the Coral Sea in May, 1942, was the first naval engagement in history when surface vessels did not exchange a single shot.

Then in early June of that year Japanese Admiral Yamamoto approached Midway in the North Pacific with four carriers, all veterans of the Pearl Harbor raid, 11 battleships including the monstrous *Yamato* with nine 18-inch guns, a fleet of supporting vessels, and an armada of landing ships. The United States met him with not a single battleship. Yet dive bombers from the carriers *Hornet*, *Enterprise*, and *Yorktown* sank all four of the Japanese carriers for the loss of *Yorktown*. It was the first clear-cut tactical as well as strategic victory for the United States in the Pacific War. Those great Japanese battlewagons stood by while the empire suffered its first decisive naval defeat in 350 years — and no a shell left their big guns. At no time were they within 100 miles of a possible surface target.

This was a war of carrier strikes, of furious night actions in which cruisers, destroyers, and PT boats dodged through narrow straits in the Solomons and the Philippines; of American subs picking off Japanese ships, of Japanese kamikaze pilots smashing themselves and

301

Largest armada in history, 5,000 ships and landing craft took part in the 1944 invasion

UTAH BEACH ON D-DAY, JUNE 6, 1944 U. S. COAST GUARD

their bomb-laden planes on the decks of American carriers. Only in the island-hopping Allied invasions did battleships play a major role, stunning the defenders with their salvos so the landing craft could reach the beach.

The plan was for us to make landings in Burma, continue to Malaya, swing into the South China Sea and northward for the final assault on Japan. In Europe, landings brought on massive, wild fighting for a stretch of beach. Then it was over, the beachhead secure. In the Pacific, landings often seemed ominously quiet, but when the Japanese were brought into play they hung on literally to the last man. One by one they had to be burned out and cut down. We didn't relish the idea.

I was very glad when the Japanese surrendered on September 2, 1945. The best part of a year later I handed the survivors of my little fleet over to the United States Navy at Olongapo in the Philippines. Each of my odd vessels had taken part in at least three assault landings, steamed at least 30,000 miles, landed an average of 10,000 men.

When I'd taken them over at Norfolk, Virginia, back in early 1943, I'd been as much as told that they were expendable. For expendable ships, they had done pretty well.

HULL SHAPES *reveal the types of U. S. Navy vessels kept in the mothball fleet at Norfolk, Virginia. Twin stacks and bridge well forward mark big Fletcher-class destroyers at upper left. Long, narrow hull of the heavy cruiser* Salem *in the next slip indicates speed. Broad beam of the battleship* Massachusetts *gives her 16-inch guns a stable firing platform. Gun mounts enclosed in metallic cocoons, hulls sealed and dehumidified to prevent corrosion, ships could quickly be readied for sea. They rest among fuel and utility barges and tugs. Battleship* Missouri *(opposite), aboard which the Japanese surrender was signed in Tokyo Bay, lies at Bremerton, Washington.*

302

Naval profiles
1798 - 1963

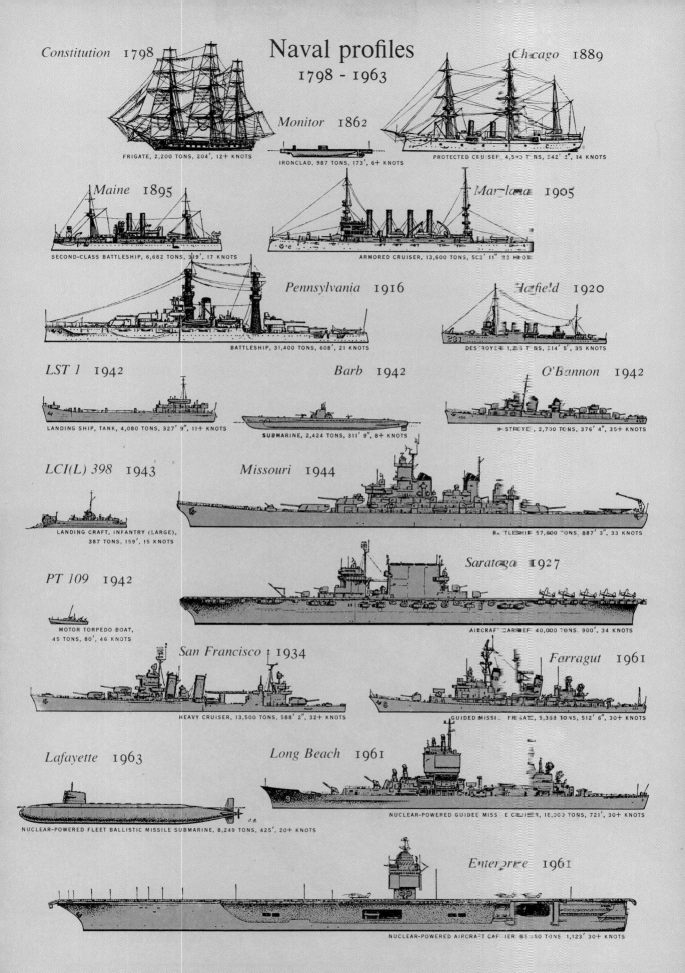

Constitution 1798
FRIGATE, 2,200 TONS, 204', 12+ KNOTS

Monitor 1862
IRONCLAD, 987 TONS, 173', 6+ KNOTS

Chicago 1889
PROTECTED CRUISER, 4,500 TONS, 342' 2", 14 KNOTS

Maine 1895
SECOND-CLASS BATTLESHIP, 6,682 TONS, 319', 17 KNOTS

Maryland 1905
ARMORED CRUISER, 13,600 TONS, 503' 11", 22 KNOTS

Pennsylvania 1916
BATTLESHIP, 31,400 TONS, 608', 21 KNOTS

Hatfield 1920
DESTROYER, 1,215 TONS, 314' 5", 35 KNOTS

LST 1 1942
LANDING SHIP, TANK, 4,080 TONS, 327' 9", 11+ KNOTS

Barb 1942
SUBMARINE, 2,424 TONS, 311' 9", 8+ KNOTS

O'Bannon 1942
DESTROYER, 2,700 TONS, 376' 4", 35+ KNOTS

LCI(L) 398 1943
LANDING CRAFT, INFANTRY (LARGE), 387 TONS, 159', 15 KNOTS

Missouri 1944
BATTLESHIP, 57,600 TONS, 887' 3", 33 KNOTS

PT 109 1942
MOTOR TORPEDO BOAT, 45 TONS, 80', 46 KNOTS

Saratoga 1927
AIRCRAFT CARRIER, 40,000 TONS, 900', 34 KNOTS

San Francisco 1934
HEAVY CRUISER, 13,500 TONS, 588' 2", 32+ KNOTS

Farragut 1961
GUIDED MISSILE FRIGATE, 5,358 TONS, 512' 6", 30+ KNOTS

Lafayette 1963
NUCLEAR-POWERED FLEET BALLISTIC MISSILE SUBMARINE, 8,249 TONS, 425', 20+ KNOTS

Long Beach 1961
NUCLEAR-POWERED GUIDED MISSILE CRUISER, 16,000 TONS, 721', 30+ KNOTS

Enterprise 1961
NUCLEAR-POWERED AIRCRAFT CARRIER, 85,350 TONS, 1,123', 30+ KNOTS

ALL DRAWN TO SAME SCALE, 1":180'   DATE: COMMISSIONED   TONS: DISPLACEMENT, FULL LOAD   LENGTH: OVERALL   SPEED: MAXIMUM
SUBMARINE DISPLACEMENT AND SPEED: SUBMERGED

MISSILE-LADEN F8U CRUSADER ROARS FROM U.S.S. "RANGER" IN PACIFIC. BELOW: COMBAT INFORMATION

CHAPTER THIRTY-THREE

Today's Navy: in the air, under the sea

Giant carriers, globe-circling submarines.
supersonic missiles have brought the
Atomic Age to sea. Thomas Y. Canby,
a wartime naval officer, takes a look
at the new wonders in his old service.

"LAUNCH AIRCRAFT!" Voice lost in the scream of jets, the catapult officer speaks, with the saber thrust of his arm. The catapult piston crashes forward, slamming a plane down the carrier's flight deck in a blur of speed. The pilot is flattened against the backrest belly against his spine. In 2½ seconds he is moving 150 miles an hour and is safely airborne.

Below, in the quiet twilight of the combat information center, radar spots the streaking plane. Seconds later another blip appears as the next plane takes off. More dot the radarscope as they boil out like hornets; a full air group of some 90 planes can be launched in about 15 minutes. The control officer tracks their positions and directs them to their target.

The long arm of the aircraft carrier can strike anywhere with supersonic speed. The carrier can launch and land planes at the same time, thanks to her angled flight deck. Steam catapults, powerful enough to hurl an automobile a mile and a half, have no trouble getting a 35-ton attack plane up to flying speed while the ship is racing into the wind at better than 30 knots. Rugged arresting gear can snag a big jet fighter, howling

305

in for a landing at 140 knots, and stop it safely within a few yards—a "controlled crash," the pilots sometimes call it.

HOW DID CARRIERS get their start? In the fall of 1910 an exhibition pilot, Eugene Ely, flew a plane held together by bamboo struts and piano wire off the deck of an anchored cruiser. A platform had been rigged over the forecastle. Ely ran its length, dipped as he reached its end, brushed the water, final-

ly managed to stagger into the air. His was the first successful takeoff from a ship.

Two months later the same daredevil pulled off another significant stunt. Flying low, he approached the stern of the armored cruiser *Pennsylvania*, anchored in San Francisco Bay. He set his plane down on a 120-foot wooden deck that had been built to receive him. Three hooks below the plane snagged ropes that had been stretched across the deck and weighted with sandbags. Ely came to a safe, if tooth-

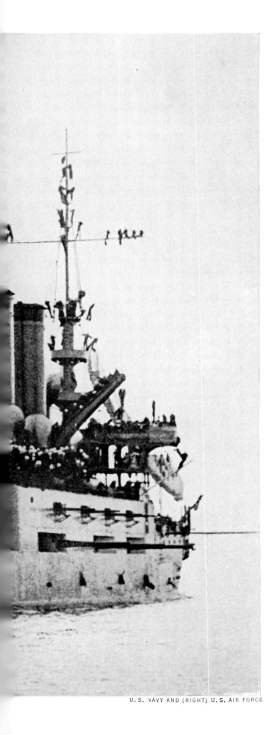

"**MOST IMPORTANT LANDING** . . . *since the dove flew back to the ark,*" *said U.S.S.* Pennsylvania's *captain after Eugene Ely landed on his deck in 1911, proving the feasibility of aircraft carriers. In the early '20's, Gen. Billy Mitchell dramatized air power by testing his bombers on condemned warships. U.S.S.* Alabama *(right) and two other battleships were hit and sunk.*

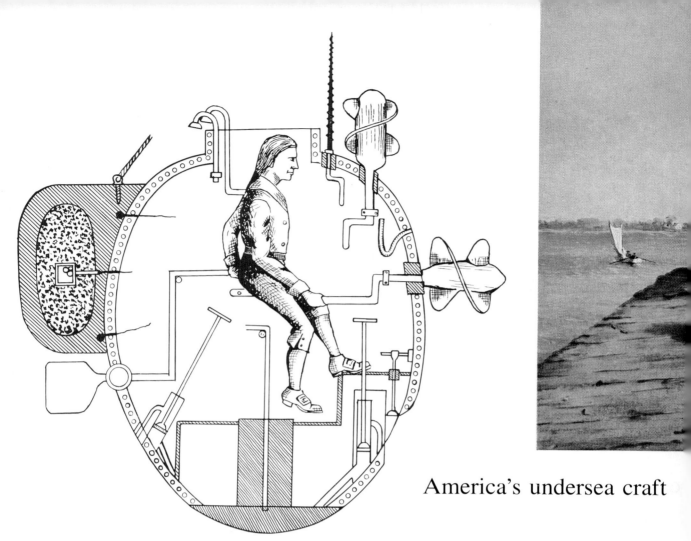

America's undersea craft

jarring, stop. He had accomplished the first "carrier" landing—with the first arresting gear.

In the last year of World War I, Britain commissioned the first real carrier, H.M.S. *Argus*. Not even a funnel broke the sweep of her flush flight deck. The United States followed suit by converting the collier *Jupiter* into a carrier, U.S.S. *Langley*. She trained a new breed, the carrier pilot. When *Lexington* and *Saratoga* joined the fleet in 1927, they were served by fliers who could navigate to their floating base and slap their landing hooks faultlessly on her heaving flight deck.

World War II saw the carrier come into her own. Task forces built around flattops wrote blazing history; small escort carriers hunted submarines and covered amphibious landings. As postwar planes grew heavier and faster, carriers became more powerful, more efficient. Fifty years after Ely landed on the *Pennsylvania*, the nuclear-powered U.S.S. *Enterprise* was commissioned. More than 1,100 feet overall, she became the world's longest ship.

A second great offensive arm of today's navy, the submarine, has a longer history. A Dutch doctor, Cornelis Drebbel, is said to

have built one in 1620 of wood covered with greased leather. It took in air through tubes.

The one-man submarine *Turtle*, built by David Bushnell of Connecticut during the American Revolution, was certainly the first to go to war. Sgt. Ezra Lee bobbed up to an anchored British warship one night in New York Harbor, ducked beneath her, and tried to set a drill into her planking with a time bomb attached. The copper sheathing that the King's ships boasted in those days foiled him. He bounced back to the surface and wallowed toward shore with his hand-cranked propeller, while the enemy rowed after him. The bomb, cast adrift, exploded with a roar. It did no damage, but the British moved to a less exciting anchorage.

During the Civil War, Confederates used boiler plates to build the cigar-shaped submarine *H. L. Hunley*. She swamped twice, drowning all but her skipper, then foundered with him as well. Raised, she rammed the blockader *Housatonic* with a spar torpedo in Charleston Harbor. The blast sank the Union ship—also the *Hunley*, first sub to make a kill.

Ten years after the Civil War ended, the

date from the Revolution

Navy was offered a submarine design and promptly turned it down. But this plan was the work of a stubborn man, John P. Holland, and nothing kept him from trying again and again. In 1900 the Navy bought Holland's latest model and started its submarine fleet.

The 53-foot *Holland* had a 50-horsepower electric motor for running underwater, a 45-horsepower gasoline engine for the surface and to recharge the batteries. Diesels later replaced gasoline engines. But Holland had set the pattern for subs for 50 years.

One problem nagged submariners. Submerged, they could only use battery power—and batteries needed recharging, usually a nightly routine. In World War II, the Germans adopted the snorkel, long air and exhaust tubes that let the diesels "breathe" and so keep running while submerged. Snorkel subs played a large role in the undersea blockade that almost brought Britain to her knees.

U NDER WAY on nuclear power!" Flashed from the submarine *Nautilus* in 1955, the words signaled the birth of the atomic navy. The big sub's reactor, needing

TURTLE, the first American submarine (opposite), held one busy man. Using both heels and an elbow, he had to steer, crank her forward end up and down, pump water ballast, and drill into his victim's hull.

Eight men cranked the Confederacy's Hunley (above); an officer conned her on surface from an open hatch. Destroying a Yankee ship, she swamped.

John P. Holland (below) used an electric motor underwater. For the surface he tried steam, but diving was slowed because fires had to be doused. So gasoline drove the sub he sold the Navy.

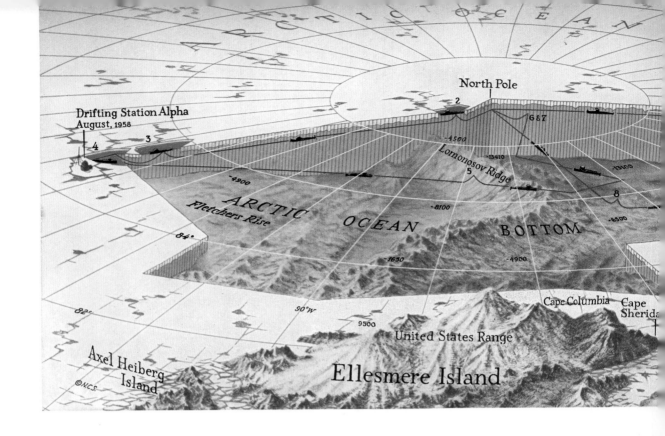

no oxygen, severed her dependence on the atmosphere, made her a true undersea craft. At speeds and depths that are still classified, *Nautilus* knifed through more than 62,000 miles of ocean on her first small core of uranium fuel. She demonstrated that the length of time an atomic sub can remain underwater is limited only by her crew. She carries equipment to extract oxygen from the ocean and to remove impurities from the air inside her. As long as food and the morale of her men hold out, she is completely independent of land.

With the dark undersea world suddenly opened to it, the United States Navy eyed the Arctic Ocean. A sea lane under its massive ice cap would clip some 4,000 miles off the run from Tokyo to London. Though the least used, it is potentially the world's most strategic ocean.

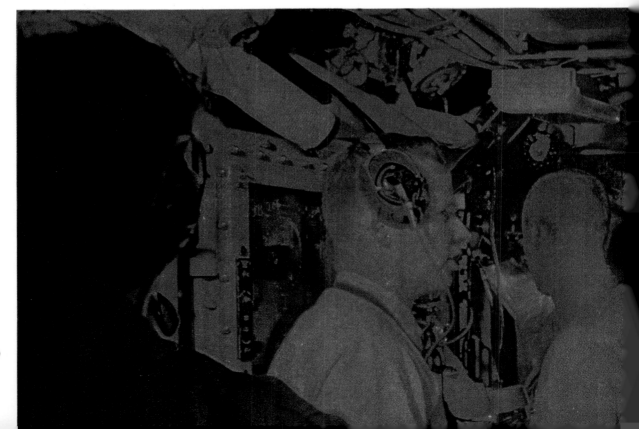

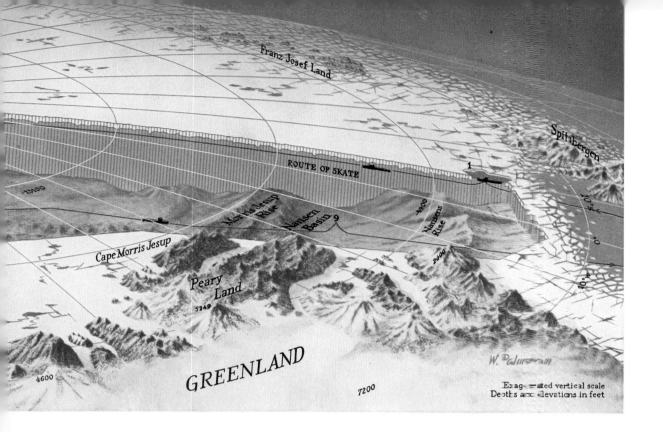

So in the summer of 1958, *Nautilus* dived beneath the Arctic ice on the Pacific side and crossed under the North Pole to the Atlantic, blazing the Northwest Passage of the Atomic Age. She proved that the Arctic Ocean could be traversed in its depths. Now came *Skate*, third U. S. atomic submarine, to see if she could actually surface within the pack ice.

Skate bore 106 submariners and scientists

DIVING UNDER THE ICE *between Greenland and Spitsbergen, Skate surfaced in nine open-water polynyas on her first Arctic voyage. A week after Nautilus, she reached the Pole, rose within 40 miles of it. Seven months later she broke through the ice ten times, once at the Pole itself.*

Attack center's red glow (below) adapts eyes to night vision through the periscope.

BREAKING THROUGH ICE *300 miles from the North Pole, U.S.S.* Skate *proved that a nuclear*

up the Norwegian Sea, Atlantic gateway to the frozen north. She took a final bearing from Spitsbergen. Comdr. James F. Calvert, her captain, spotted the long white line of the Arctic pack stretching ahead and ordered the dive. Down she went, heading for the Pole.

The depth recorder traces the ocean floor nearly a mile below. The ice detector bounces electronic impulses off the solid ceiling above, picking up pressure ridges that lance down dangerously. Suddenly it shows open water — a *polynya* or unfrozen lake — overhead. The crew has gathered for Sunday service. Calvert calls them to station. "We'll have church later; right full rudder; station the plotting party!"

Watching the ice detector, they plot the shape of the lake and stop *Skate* under it. They rise slowly. Still more than a hundred feet down, Calvert raises the periscope. The water is incredibly clear. He can see jellyfish and other marine life. There is a chance that new ice may cover the lake and not show up

submarine can surface in frozen Arctic Ocean leads, or "skylights," even in winter.

on the detector. It could damage *Skate*'s delicate "sail" with its periscopes, antennas, and ventilation pipes. Calvert raises a buggy-whip antenna and watches its tip. If it bends it will give warning. It continues to stick straight up.

Free of motion forward or aft, *Skate* rises foot by foot. Suddenly the antenna tip disappears in a circle of ripples. Open water.

"Prepare to surface!"

Tanks are blown. *Skate* rises to the surface. Taking the bridge, Calvert looks out on a world of white. The sub rices in a lake that seems too small for it. A polar bear pulls himself out of the water, shakes himself off, and stares solemnly at his first atomic submarine.

Diving again, *Skate* probed toward the Pole, her skipper relying on inertial navigation at this latitude. Delicate instruments, feeling the direction of the earth's rotation, indicated east and west. They also sensed the decreasing speed of rotation as the sub neared the earth's axis, thus could tell how close *Skate* was to

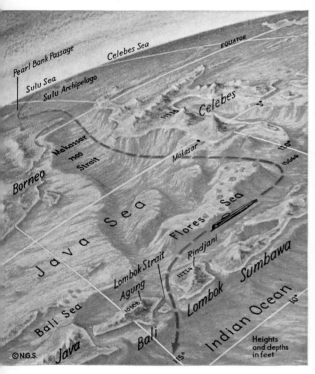

CAPE HORN *loomed dark and stormy through the periscope of nuclear submarine* Triton *on her submerged voyage around the world in 1960. Radar gave a clearer view (top right). Electronic soundings (lower) along her 26,723-mile track revealed an uncharted Pacific peak. In Lombok Strait (left), currents pulled her down 125 feet in 40 seconds. "It was as though we had hit a hole in the water," said skipper Edward L. Beach (above, center). The 61-day endurance test led past Spain, where Magellan set sail on the first circumnavigation.*

the top of the world. In the small hours of an August night, inertial navigation showed all rotational force focused at a single point. They had reached the North Pole — far below the ice.

Skate's next goal was Drifting Station Alpha, an encampment on the pack that the United States had established for scientific observations. A message from Alpha informed Calvert that there was a polynya right in its front yard, and that its personnel would run an outboard motorboat around it. If *Skate*'s sonar could pick up the sound, it would guide the sub to the lake.

Sure enough, the sonarman soon heard the soft mutter of the outboard. The huge vessel zeroed in on the sound until it seemed to come from all directions at once. The ice detector showed an opening. Up came the sub slowly, and Calvert found his periscope trained on a small motorboat, its occupant madly waving his hat. In a few moments one of Alpha's scientists was chiding the crew: "The Arctic has always had a beautiful privacy. Now it's gone. You people will be popping up all over this ocean before long!"

Skate fulfilled the prophecy. She popped up nine times in Arctic lakes, then set out to prove that a modern submarine can break six to eight inches of ice and surface just as whales do. With a strengthened sail, she cruised under the ice pack in winter, found a frozen lead, rose under it, and bumped it with her 3,000-

ton mass. She rebounded gently, tried again a little harder. A television camera was trained on the ice canopy; the men were watching the screen when the picture suddenly disintegrated into splashing water and shattering ice. *Skate* had broken through. Calvert took a walk around her to check for possible damage.

"It is not every day," he noted, "a skipper can walk away from his ship and contemplate it from a distance while it is a hundred miles from land, in water more than a mile deep."

Reaching the North Pole again, hundreds of feet down, *Skate* waited for a thin spot or "skylight" to pass overhead in the slowly drifting ice canopy. At last the faint emerald green of a long narrow crack appeared on the surface.

Again and again the great submarine maneuvered into position only to find the lead had drifted away. But finally the sail crunched home.

From the bridge, men looked out on a dark twilight, for the sun was below the horizon this March day in 1959. The wind roared at 30 knots. Blowing snow cut visibility to a quarter-mile. It was a wild, forbidding scene that greeted *Skate*, first ship in history to rest on the surface of the Arctic Ocean at the Pole.

ATOMIC SUBMARINES have given the United States Navy a tremendous new striking force. Some carry Polaris missiles armed with nuclear warheads. To avoid radar detection the subs launch them from below the

Monster from the deep

TRITON'S *undersea voyage around the
world was secret. Capt. Edward L. Beach
raised the periscope furtively. But in the
Philippines he found himself looking into
the eyes of the fisherman above.*

*As the Filipino stared back, Captain Beach
logged a description of the "moon-faced young
man"; photographer Roberts snapped a picture.
"Down periscope!" Seconds later it was raised
again. There sat the "impassive Asian, staring
with curious concentration." Captain Beach
kicked* Triton *ahead. When he slowed for a
second look, the fisherman was "paddling
rather strongly in the opposite direction."*

*With only the picture and log entry as guide,
the National Geographic set out to find the
fisherman through a Society member in the
Philippines. Finally came a triumphant cable:
"Have found needle in haystack." The needle:
19-year-old Rufino Baring.*

*When he saw the periscope, Baring thought
it a piece of wood. Then its wake suggested a
fish. As it vanished, he decided his eyes were
playing tricks. When it reappeared, he feared
he was sharing the bay with a sea monster.*

*"I tried to get away as fast as I could," he
said. To ward off monsters, he painted saints'
names on his canoe. His dread vanished only
when he was told what he had really seen.
Baring was the only outsider to detect* Triton.

surface. They can reach deep into a continent.

Fleet ballistic missile submarines are the
giants of the undersea world. The *Lafayette*
stretches 425 feet, displaces some 7,000 tons.
Each sub carries 16 combat-ready missiles.
The explosive punch per sub: greater than all
the bombs dropped during World War II.

Two crews—the blue and the gold—alternate on 60-day patrols. The men must be of a
special caliber—stable and good-natured as
well as efficient. Cramped living tries tempers.
Bunks may perch next to an atomic reactor
or a deadly missile. On the long, submerged
cruises night differs from day only because the
electric lights are dimmed.

BESIDES supporting its own submarines,
the Navy must know how to destroy
those of an enemy. Antisubmarine warfare (ASW) has stepped into the Atomic Age
along with the submarines themselves. The
system for finding and hitting undersea raiders
is based on the hunter-killer group (HUK), a
combination of aircraft, subs, destroyer types,
missiles, and electronic detectors. The team-
work dates from World War II, when U-boats
sank a thousand merchantmen in a year.

Today, HUK groups train constantly.
Tracking planes roar off carrier decks. A
tracker's radar picks up a periscope or snorkel;
its "magnetic anomaly detector" senses a
metal hull beneath the surface. Word flashes
back. Helicopters from the carrier hover over
the area, lower their "dunking sonar" to pick
up an echo from that hidden hull. Destroyers
churn in, sonars sweeping.

Suddenly a copter hears the telltale echo
from its sonar "ping." Contact! The copter
drops a bomb. Or from a destroyer an Asroc
missile flashes. It delivers either a nuclear
depth charge or an acoustic homing torpedo
capable of zeroing in on a submarine miles
away by "listening" to it.

Aircraft carry their own brands of missiles.
The Sparrow traces its radar beam to a hostile
plane. The Sidewinder homes in on the hot
engine of an enemy aircraft. The Bullpup is
guided by radio from its parent plane to knock
out tanks, bridges, or truck convoys.

Guided missiles are supplanting guns on
surface ships, ending the 400-year reign of
naval cannon. Cruisers carry the Talos, a
supersonic missile guided by radio to targets
a hundred miles away. The Terrier and Tartar,
smaller antiaircraft missiles, bristle on carriers

316

and other surface vessels. Submarines can blast enemy subs with the Subroc, which roars up from underwater, arches, dives into the sea near its submerged target, homes in on it, and destroys it.

Only one battleship remains in commission in the 800-ship surface navy: the shattered hulk of *Arizona* flies the flag in memoriam for the dead at Pearl Harbor. Two have been given to states as museums, the *North Carolina* at Wilmington and the *Texas* at Houston. The others lie mothballed or await scrapping. Most cruisers are being converted into missile launchers; a new one is nuclear powered. Destroyers carry guided missiles. The term "frigate," revived from days of Old Ironsides, now applies to sleek escort vessels, some with nuclear power.

Motor gunboats, big, fast descendants of the famous PT boats of World War II, will be ready to dart along enemy coasts. Assault ships, resembling small carriers, can launch a landing force by helicopter behind a beach-head. And all attack vessels will take orders from command and communications ships which sprout forests of antennas on their flush decks and still have room for helicopters.

In support will be drive-on cargo ships which can lower ramps and disgorge a parade of supply vehicles; oilers to refuel the fleet at sea; and submarine tenders which can feed Polaris missiles, spare parts, or frozen foods to three subs at once.

More than half a million men and women now serve in the United States Navy. They man the ships, planes, and electronic gear. They keep supplies flowing. They live around the world on some 300 shore installations. With all its computers and guidance systems, the Navy still depends on flesh, blood, and devotion.

POLARIS STREAKS SKYWARD *from the nuclear submarine* George Washington, *submerged off Cape Canaveral, Florida. Compressed air hurls it from sub; contact with air ignites solid-fuel propellant; self-contained guidance system directs the roaring missile to preselected target. Tested with a nuclear warhead in May, 1962, Polaris hit "right in the pickle barrel" at nearly 1,400 miles. Lafayette's missiles are designed to fire 2,500 miles.*

317

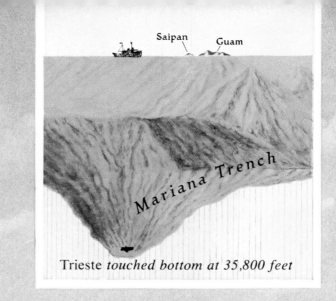

Saipan   Guam

Mariana Trench

Trieste *touched bottom at 35,800 feet*

UNDERSEA EXPLORERS *burst into sunshine atop the U. S. Navy bathyscaph* Trieste *after completing man's deepest dive. Crammed in a steel sphere suspended under the hull, Piccard and Walsh in 1960 descended to the floor of the Pacific's Mariana Trench (inset), a mile deeper than Mount Everest is high.* Trieste *carries 32,000 gallons of lighter-than-water gasoline. She starts down by flooding air tanks. If descent lags, gasoline is jettisoned. In cold depths the gasoline contracts, lets in more water to equalize pressure, and descent speeds.*

The men slow it by releasing iron shot held in two ballast containers by electromagnets. Propellers, run by battery, can drive the craft ahead or astern. At the bottom, pressure on the sphere equaled the weight of five battleships.

Oceanographers probe the undersea world

Two men drop inside *Trieste*'s conning tower. They climb down her escape tube and squeeze into a spherical gondola hanging beneath the sausage-shaped bathyscaph. Lt. Don Walsh, U.S.N., and Jacques Piccard, son of the bathyscaph's inventor, close the heavy hatch and let seawater flood the tube. Her buoyancy reduced, *Trieste* sinks slowly into the Mariana Trench, nearly seven miles deep, in the Pacific off Guam.

650 feet: Darkness closes in, revealing the phosphorescence of minute plankton.

1,500 feet: The black water outside chills the cabin. The cold is penetrating.

13,000 feet: Torrents of plankton seem to rise past the porthole.

24,000 feet: The two explorers pass the greatest depth ever reached by living man.

THOMAS J. ABERCROMBIE AND (INSET) GILBERT H. EMERSON, BOTH NATIONAL GEOGRAPHIC STAFF

They descend about a foot a second. They turn on the sonic depth sounder, wait anxiously.

32,500 feet: There is a dull cracking sound; the gondola trembles but continues its descent.

35,500 feet: At last the sonic depth finder records bottom only 300 feet below.

In ten minutes *Trieste* touches the ivory colored floor—"the last extreme on our earth that remained to be conquered." A searchlight picks out a solelike fish, and all doubts of whether life can exist at such depths are an-swered. The men measure the water tempera-ture: 38° F. They test for currents and radio-activity. Negative. On a special undersea telephone, without wires or radio waves, they talk to the surface. They discover the cause of the shock—a porthole had cracked as it contracted from cold.

After 20 minutes the men, first visitors to the black world of 35,800 feet begin their 3½-hour ascent. It ends in the day's finest dis-covery: sunshine and fresh air at the surface.

UNDERWATER EXPLORER *Jacques-Yves Cousteau traces sonic echoes from a phantom bottom, the "deep scattering layer" often 900 to 1,500 feet down. A stratum of sea life, or changes in temperature or salinity may cause it.*

BERING SEA TIDES *are recorded on a cylinder at Amak Island, Alaska, in study by the U. S. Coast and Geodetic Survey.*

HAROLD E. EDGERTON. LEFT: J. BAYLOR ROBERTS, NATIONAL GEOGRAPHIC STAFF

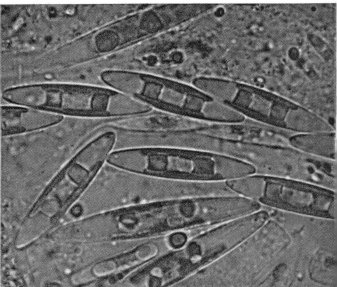

PAUL A. ZAHL, NATIONAL GEOGRAPHIC STAFF

DIATOMS, *here magnified 300 times, are the grass of the sea. The one-celled plants contain chlorophyll, manufacture carbohydrates. These feed other plankton, which support sea animals eaten by fish. Oil from diatoms enriches fish livers. Their silica shells carpet the ocean floor, in places as thick as 1,400 feet. One diatom may have 100 million descendants in 30 days.*

TRIESTE's plunge dramatizes man's quickening interest in the 70.8 percent of his world that is covered by water. Oceanographers are going to sea in gear-crammed ships to explore the great basins that hold the seas in place. With sonic depth finders they chart drowned mountain ranges and vast depressions. With core samplers they gather sediments—clues to earth's history. They search for ocean currents—subsurface rivers, some a thousand times mightier than the Mississippi.

More than a century ago Matthew Fontaine Maury, an American naval officer, induced ship captains to jot down observations of winds, waves, tides, currents. Piecing together the reports, Maury drew up pilot charts—mosaics of wind and water conditions crisscrossed with recommended shipping routes. The U. S. Navy Hydrographic Office, outgrowth of his work, continues these surveys today, with the aid of other oceanographic centers.

Chemical engineers now extract thousands of tons of magnesium and bromine from the ocean's fabled treasure-house. In time they may develop economical ways to "mine" its potassium, cobalt, manganese. Gold is there too—one ounce per eight billion tons of water.

Oceanographers know that fish thrive where cool subsurface water, rich in nutrients, rises to replace a warm top layer. By studying where and how this happens, they can often point the way to new fishing grounds.

In floating laboratories, biologists scoop up diatoms and other microscopic plants to observe the green magic of photosynthesis, the process in which chlorophyll enables chemicals and the sun's energy to be converted into carbohydrates, a basic stuff of life. Ocean vegetation produces two to four times as many billion tons of carbohydrates as the land.

Farming this fertile ocean promises an abundant source of food, given new techniques. Ocean fish may someday be husbanded like livestock. Some scientists suggest plankton as table fare. Alain Bombard, who ate it while crossing the ocean alone on a raft, reported that it "tasted like lobster, at times like shrimp, and at times like some vegetable."

DIVING SAUCER, *on a National Geographic-*Calypso *Expedition, gives her two-man crew windows on the Caribbean floor. Rudderless, she navigates by water jets. Scientists from Woods Hole Oceanographic Institution bring up coring tube (right) with cross section of sediments from Atlantic bed two miles below.*

CHAPTER THIRTY-FOUR

Tankers, freighters, and the luxury fleet

Longing to ship out on a freighter or fashionable liner, this university student got purser's papers and made the rounds until he found his berth. Merle Severy's dream ship turned out to be a tanker, bound in ballast for the Persian Gulf to bring back 100,000 barrels of black and smelly oil.

IT WAS NIGHT, and drizzling, when I arrived at the dock in Norfolk. Big black hoses snaked off the gray ship, lying deep in the water. A couple of men were turning valves on the well deck; an officer leaned on the catwalk railing. The *Mascoma* was no beauty, but I felt a thrill as I carried my gear aboard.

"Sparks," the young radio operator from Miami, took me up to meet the "Old Man."

The captain, deeply tanned and built like a wrestler, fixed on me a noncommittal stare, then wrapped his fist around mine. "You will like this ship, Bob," he said in a thick Norwegian accent. (To the captain, all pursers were "Bob.")

All that night the ship pumped her cargo ashore. By morning she rode high and empty. Water ballast was now taken on to trim her for sea. Stores were coming aboard. Replacement crew members filed into my cabin amidships with their union assignment slips and chits from the company doctor. An able-bodied seaman from Tennessee, an electrician from New York, a messman from Puerto Rico, a wiper from Saudi Arabia—on they streamed, in dungarees or khakis, T-shirts or loud sport shirts, some boozed up, some sober, until the crew list of 47 was filled.

The first mate checked for stowaways, the gangplank came aboard, whistles shrilled, lines slapped the water, and I felt a throb beneath me.

As the ship moved out into Hampton Roads, I worked frantically at forms and reports. Sparks stuck his head in the porthole: "Pilot's coming off the bridge, Purse." I stuffed papers in fat envelopes and handed them to the pilot as he swung down to his boat.

In the wheelhouse the engine telegraph jingled. The breeze tugged at my clothing, wisps of spray flicked me as our ship headed out to meet the Atlantic swell. Our voyage had begun!

Life on a tanker centers in two "islands." Amidships stand the bridge, wheelhouse, chartroom, gyro room, radio shack, and deck officers' quarters. Aft are the galley, messrooms, engine officers' and crew's quarters, and the engine room. A catwalk above the low well deck joins the two islands; crossing it in heavy seas calls for a 190-foot dash.

But we had fine weather. Chipping hammers chattered as the bosun kept the deck gang at their endless war against rust. A seaman daubed the naked steel with red lead.

Below in the boiler room no "hairy apes" shoveled black coal into raging fireboxes— only a fireman-watertender in unsoiled dungarees adjusted flaming oil jets, kept an eye on the water level in the twin boilers.

In the engine room an oiler was lubricating reduction gears, a wiper soogeeing the gratings.

ROBERT F. SISSON, NATIONAL
GEOGRAPHIC PHOTOGRAPHER.
LEFT: A. AUBREY BODINE

WHISTLES *tooting,*
tugs jockey a freighter
from her berth.
Harbor pilot conns her
through the channel;
when he swings
down the Jacob's
ladder into his boat,
she is on her own.

The second assistant engineer left his panel of dials to explain the turbo-electric machinery driving us across the Atlantic at 16 knots.

The eyes of a windjammer sailor would pop at the quarters these men take as a matter of course. Our forecastle was aft—one to four men to a cabin—airy, clean, steam-heated, with fresh linen supplied by the steward.

At supper I interrupted my thoughts of the good old days of hardtack and salt horse to turn to the messman at my elbow: "Make that steak rare, will you?"

Officers and crew ate the same food, prepared in the spick-and-span galley between the two messrooms. We had fresh fruits and vegetables, juices, eggs, fresh-baked bread. But we did run out of ice cream—the crew raided the freezers too often.

They were a young bunch, averaging about three years' sea experience. After a couple more years many would drift away to shore jobs. One boy wanted to buy a farm; another was saving to start a charter-boat service.

I got to know them well. I'd chat with the lookout at night at the bow; or the quartermaster, who stood by on the bridge while the iron mike steered a gyrocompass course. I swapped English lessons for Spanish with our Ecuadorian second cook-baker, a fine fellow who was serving five years on U. S. ships to qualify for naturalization as a citizen. (An American-flag ship is U. S. soil, I learned.) He'd bring a delicious pie hot from the oven when he came for the lesson.

Other crewmen came amidships to buy clothing, toilet articles, cigarettes, and candy when I opened the slop chest. They knocked on my door when they learned I had a footlocker full of books. And they were always coming up to get pills or penicillin or to have me bandage their cuts and bruises in the ship's hospital.

Seeing me check the surgical instruments early in the voyage, the captain reminisced on gory penknife surgery he had performed in his windjammer days. "Now I have a purser to do the operating." Never did my Coast Guard first-aid course seem so incomplete!

I asked Sparks: "What happens if someone needs an appendectomy at sea?"

"Simple," he said. "I radio a doctor. He says to slice the man open. I ask, 'What next,

Doc?' He tells me and I tell you. Nothing to it." I was relieved when we raised Gibraltar.

MY FIRST GLIMPSE of the famous strait was on radar. It was at dusk, and the rotating sweep on the scope brushed in Cape Trafalgar in Spain and Cape Spartel in Africa. I went out on the wing of the bridge and watched the lights wink on Tangier, then Ceuta to starboard; Tarifa, Algeciras, then Gibraltar to port, its ghostly fortress rock looming above the town. The lights receded and we sailed on into blackness.

On our five-day passage the Mediterranean was the way I had always pictured it—blue water, clear skies, warm sun, cooling breezes. My binoculars swept Cape Bon, Tunisia; the island of Pantelleria with its mountain terraces spilling into the sea; the limestone cliffs of Malta golden at sunset. But joy was tempered by the knowledge that we were to transit the Suez Canal with no port time en route.

Then news came from Sparks that the economizer on our port boiler had burned out and that the home office had radioed us to make repairs in Port Said, Egypt.

Even before our anchor clattered down in a cloud of rust, the ship swarmed with swarthy bumboatmen—peddlers of everything from camel-leather hassocks to "fee thy pictures." When you went to throw them off, they all claimed to be officials, agents of the ship chandler, canalmen, supervisors of supplies, and assistant supervisors. They'd flourish official-looking passes and letters extolling their honesty and dependability. Some were in Arabic (indecipherable to me), some in English (which they couldn't read). I did a double take on one: "Don't have no dealings with this no-count bum."

They would sullenly retreat to their bumboats, shout "Hey, Brooklyn!" (a sailor from South Carolina), toss up a cord, and start a brisk trade—giraffe-skin handbags, inlaid trays ("See how beautiful—the workman went blind making it"), gimcracks going up by basket; cash, cigarettes, soap going down. Every price was "just for you special." To lower a price we'd unfasten the cord and turn away.

The captain brought out his black briefcase for official ship's business, tucked in bonded

---

SEAS SWEEP A TANKER *bearing Texas oil to New York. Tankers account for almost 40 percent of world merchant tonnage; largest carry more than 900,000 barrels.*

bottles, and invited Sparks and me to join him and the chief engineer at the Eastern Exchange Hotel after I had completed port and canal papers and given the crew a pay advance.

Port Said, crossroads of the East! An ancient freighter lay at anchor, barges alongside. Lights shone upon lines of dark figures running up the gangways, baskets of coal on their shoulders, to feed yawning bunkers, then hastening back—a crisscross of motion like passing streams of ants. So men labored in Egypt to build pyramids. And so they labor still to nourish thousands of horsepower of engines.

Ashore I walked past stately buildings with wrought-iron balconies and arcade shops on palm-shaded avenues. I entered tenement alleys throbbing with life. Nasal Arab music wailed from open-front cafes packed with men in fezzes and pajamalike robes.

Sent back to the ship each day to check on how the boiler repairs were coming, I sought out the first assistant, grimy, streaming sweat, bleary-eyed from round-the-clock work. "Don't hurry on my account," I told him.

I tweezered glass out of a seaman whose spray gun had blown up in his face. I got a doctor to sew up a man stabbed in a brawl. The rest of the time I gloried in my first Eastern port.

On the third day I brought word to the captain that repairs were completed and the pilot would be aboard at noon. Convoys left punctually from either end of the canal so that they could pass in the Bitter Lakes—the canal itself had one-way traffic.

The captain was loath to let a little thing like time get in the way of a farewell drink. We boarded about ten minutes after 12. The pilot had gone. Our next turn for the passage was at 3 A.M. The captain swore mightily. Then he winked and told me to come ashore with him to make a protest. I brought his black bag. Soulless ships run with cold efficiency on strict timetables? In a pig's eye. But we did manage to leave at three.

As dawn broke, our ship was moving at 7½ knots in a column down the ribbon of water. I scrambled to the crow's nest to savor crossing a desert by ship. Soft contours and gentle colorings sharpened. Shadows shortened, and the sand dazzled my eyes.

We passed some squalid huts, made a sharp turn past the garden settlement of Ismailia, its thirst quenched by the Sweet Water Canal that flows from the distant Nile. Then our bow anchor clattered down in Great Bitter Lake,

where we waited for ships from the Suez end to file by. Several of us, ignoring the blue jellyfish that dotted the water, dove over the side ("bitter" is the word for that supersaline water evaporated by the desert sun) and swam to a freighter anchored nearby. Soon sharp blasts of *Mascoma's* whistle summoned us back, and the convoy got under way. At Suez we slowed to let the pilot off, and as dusk fell headed down the Gulf of Suez.

Official sailing directions for the Red Sea area state that heat and humidity make it one of the most unpleasant spots on earth. I agree. For three July days and nights we sweltered.

A mist hung over the water, not only moisture but sand, coating the ship with fine yellow grit. I did my paper work at night, sitting in a pool of sweat, soiling every form I touched. At 2 A.M., with blowers and fan going, my cabin cooled down to 101°. I couldn't sleep, couldn't read. I stood at the rail watching the bow knife through phosphorescent water. Not a breath of air stirred even there. The wind came with us from the north, so we carried along our doldrums.

What a relief to pick up the southwest monsoon in the Arabian Sea! But at 5 A.M. three days later I was almost knocked out of my bunk by a wall of heat. We had rounded Ras al Hadd into the Gulf of Oman. Through binoculars I studied the coast of Arabia—eroded mountains hemming in the burning desert.

That night we entered the Persian Gulf—again the temperature rose. At 6:45 A.M. I was routed out to tend a case of heat prostration.

W E EDGED in to an oil dock standing a couples of miles off Bahrain, and hoses came aboard. No shore leave —but I hadn't come halfway around the world just to watch the barracudas go by. And one of my patients needed a laboratory test.

"Official business? Good idea, Bob," said the captain and joined us in the agent's launch.

Hot desert wind seared us as we drove past the tells of ancient settlements, and clusters of date palms and huts.

From the hospital the captain headed off into town. With the lab test over, I looked for him down dusty alleys, past hawk-nosed men in burnouses, black-robed women veiled to the eyes, overloaded donkeys, water vendors bent under bloated goatskins.

I gazed at a minaret, watched a filigree maker by his charcoal flame, peered into cubicles where merchants lay atop their baskets of grains and curry, boxes of trinkets, old tin cans, beat-up kettles, Persian rugs ("made in Manchester," read the labels).

Swatting flies, shrugging off beggars, I entered the market square. There was the captain, wearing a multicolored skullcap— "Makes me feel native," he explained.

We walked out on the jetty where dhows were unloading, drove to the crumbling fort, reminder of days when Da Gama and his successors made the Eastern seas a Portuguese lake. Then back to the ship. Loading was finished.

After supper I settled on my cot on deck as we slipped out to sea. Lulled by a breeze, I watched stars come out. The sun awakened me, and I moved into the shadow of a lifeboat for a few minutes more of untroubled sleep.

CATALOGING some 7,000 charts kept me in the chartroom much of the trip back. The jovial second mate would pause while plotting our course to reminisce about the U-boats and dive bombers on the Murmansk run, ammo ships blowing skyhigh. He liked tankers: they were always at sea. "The land burns my feet," he said.

The third mate was a quiet one, kept to his cabin when not on the bridge, said he hated the sea. One day he showed up in full uniform at mess. "Who's he kidding," snickered an engineer in shorts. "He ain't going nowhere."

The junior third mate enjoyed boasting of his prowess with women. Listening to such waterlogged Romeos, I worked out the first law of tankeromantics: the shorter a man's port time the taller his stories.

The first mate was in charge of maintenance and loading. After a day of painting the ship gray he liked to paint bright watercolors. Why only seascapes and harbor scenes? "I don't know how it looks inland!"

I staked a claim to the flying bridge, highest deck space on the ship, and there in Olympian solitude I watched the surge of waves over the bows, the sea of glass under a blazing sun, the sea of silk on moon-drenched nights. the woolly carpet of our wake unrolling astern.

The sound of Italian opera there off the coast of Arabia told me that the first assistant was playing his records again. He'd sit at his desk thumbing through engine parts catalogs. But when the tenor soared to a ringing high C, this Irishman in dungarees would clench his fist in ecstasy and mutter, "Sonuma beetch!"

Standing orders on the bridge were that the purser was to be called anytime we made an interesting landfall or passed another ship. "Shea's travel service," the A.B. on watch announced as he roused me to see distant

YOUNGSTERS LEARN *the seaman's trade aboard the* John W. Brown, *one of 2,700 Liberty ships mass-produced during World War II. Now a New York public school she lies in the East River. At nearby Kings Point, the U. S. Merchant Marine Academy trains officers.*

Mascoma 1944
T-2 (TANKER), 21,880 TONS, 523' 6", 16+ KNOTS

Mormacbay 1960
C-3 (CARGO), 18,365 TONS, 483' 3", 19+ KNOTS

John W. Brown 1942
LIBERTY SHIP, 14,120 TONS, 441' 6", 11+ KNOTS

California 1962
C-4 (CARGO), 21,900 TONS, 565', 20+ KNOTS

Charles W. Morgan 1841
WHALING BARK, 351 TONS BURDEN, 105' 6", 12 KNOTS

Willem Barendsz 1955
WHALE FACTORY SHIP, 44,300 TONS, 677' 5", 14 KNOTS

Preussen 1902
8,000 TONS DEADWEIGHT, 433', 17+ KNOTS

Ambrose 1952
LIGHTSHIP, 540 TONS, 128', 5,500,000 CANDLEPOWER

Edward L. Ryerson 1960
GREAT LAKES ORE CARRIER, 34,000 TONS, 730', 16+ MPH

Manhattan 1962
SUPERTANKER, 137,068 TONS, 940' 5", 19+ KNOTS

Mount Sinai at dawn. We exchanged whistle salutes with passenger liners bound for Melbourne or Bombay, freighters headed for Singapore or Hong Kong—lucky dogs with lots of port time while their dry cargo is being winched on and off. Mostly we passed tankers on runs like ours.

Four days from Norfolk I unlimbered my adding machine. Two days out we radioed the payroll estimate and crew replacements needed. Then it was round-the-clock work.

I did the payroll over twice just to be sure. (The captain is charged for overpayments.) And when the company paymaster handed out $39,690.74 without a penny being off, I felt pretty good—but tired.

FOURTEEN MONTHS I stayed with *Mascoma*. We carried Texas oil from Port Arthur and Houston to Norfolk and Providence, we fought through a hurricane to Charleston. Breakfasting on flying fish that landed on deck, we cruised the Caribbean to Aruba, with its stunted trees twisted into question marks by the trade winds that carried refinery smoke over the harbor. We delivered oil to lush Panama, to chill Newfoundland; 13 hours here, nine hours there, with the boon of a five-day repair job in New York, two weeks' annual dry-dock overhaul in New Orleans—and 16½ hours delay in Key West trying to round up enough sober crew.

We lost men in every port. Some replacements would stagger aboard to take the cure between binges. One engineman parboiled himself when he wrenched open a live steam line. We lowered him into a Coast Guard launch, and he got to a hospital in time. One by one, mates and engineers missed watches and were fired. Then—a stowaway!

We were a day out of a New Jersey port when we discovered her sunning herself on deck—the chief engineer's wife. The captain went through torments, for the chief was his best friend. He slumped on the edge of my bunk, head in hands. Should he radio a report and cost the chief his job? Should he turn the ship back and cost the company $3,000 a day? Could he hush up the entire affair and quietly slip the woman ashore at our loading port?

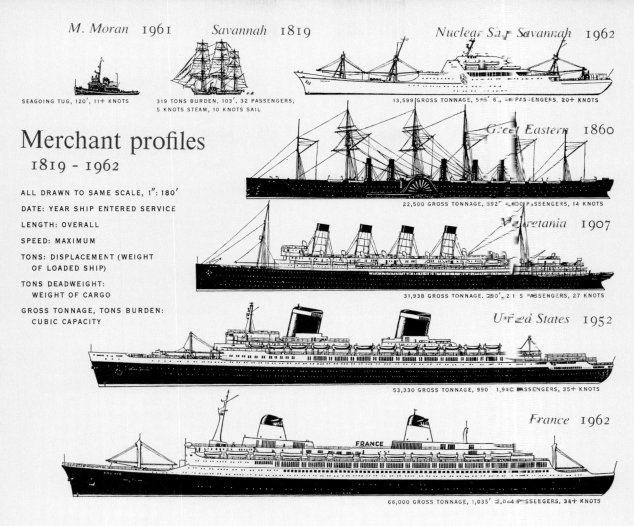

M. Moran 1961   Savannah 1819   Nuclear Ship Savannah 1962

SEAGOING TUG, 120', 11+ KNOTS   319 TONS BURDEN, 103', 32 PASSENGERS,   13,599 GROSS TONNAGE, 595' 6", 60 PASSENGERS, 20+ KNOTS
                                 5 KNOTS STEAM, 10 KNOTS SAIL

Merchant profiles
1819 - 1962

ALL DRAWN TO SAME SCALE, 1": 180'

DATE: YEAR SHIP ENTERED SERVICE

LENGTH: OVERALL

SPEED: MAXIMUM

TONS: DISPLACEMENT (WEIGHT
OF LOADED SHIP)

TONS DEADWEIGHT:
WEIGHT OF CARGO

GROSS TONNAGE, TONS BURDEN:
CUBIC CAPACITY

Great Eastern 1860

22,500 GROSS TONNAGE, 692', 4,000 PASSENGERS, 14 KNOTS

Mauretania 1907

31,938 GROSS TONNAGE, 790', 2,165 PASSENGERS, 27 KNOTS

United States 1952

53,330 GROSS TONNAGE, 990', 1,930 PASSENGERS, 35+ KNOTS

France 1962

66,000 GROSS TONNAGE, 1,035', 2,044 PASSENGERS, 34+ KNOTS

PROFILES BY OSWALD BRETT. BELOW: VOLKMAR WENTZEL, NATIONAL GEOGRAPHIC STAFF

FRESHWATER GIANT, Sparrows Point *loads 19,400 tons of iron at Superior, Wisconsin. Though ice cuts their year to eight months, Great Lakes boats carry five times the tonnage of seagoing U.S. and Canadian merchant fleets. Lakers "speak" with 300 whistle signals.*

329

Six days I watched him wrestle with his soul—and do nothing. When we reached Texas his replacement met us; the stowaway's family had let the secret slip. The spirit went out of the ship when the captain left. Our new skipper, all business, and his mate, a driver, soon were at loggerheads with the crew.

For seven months and 14 days we were on a shuttle run between the Persian Gulf and Japan. Three days in a blinding sandstorm waiting to load at Ras Tanura, Arabia; out-of-the-way ports in Kyushu at the other end. Day after day we lurched in the troughs of monsoon seas, crashing from side to side with maddening regularity, until you'd give your eyeteeth if the ship would only miss a beat. Bewildering changes in routing orders caused us to miss mail and supplies—we were down now to canned goods and powdered eggs. The card game in the crew's mess went day and night; paper debts mounted. With no shore time, 47 men confined in a 523-foot steel prison gnawed away at each other.

The mate took it out on the deck gang. They heaved the pneumatic chipping hammers over the side, pulled a slowdown, petitioned the captain "that in the future the Mate be more courteous and helpful in his relations with members of the crew." Two men were put ashore in handcuffs for threatening the captain.

A break came in the grinding monotony—we cracked our hull in a typhoon off Japan. I was in the sick bay bracing against the wild pitching to give a messman a hypodermic. I heard a sharp crack. Then the alarm bells clanged: "To the boats!"

On my way up I saw Sparks tapping out an SOS. On the bridge I shouted to the third mate, "How far are we from land?"

"Two miles," he shouted back. I looked out, saw nothing but

THOROUGHBREDS OF THE SEA *crowd New York's Hudson River piers*—Independence, America, United States *(whose stacks obscure the* New York), Liberté, Queen Mary, *and the new* Mauretania. *To meet tight schedules, crews and hundreds of shore hands swiftly groom and provision these luxury liners, pump aboard tons of oil and water. A festive farewell like that aboard the* Queen of Bermuda *(below) and they're off!*

wild ocean. Then his thumb made a great arc. "Straight down," he added.

Life-jacketed, we stood by the boats, drenched by spray, buffeted by howling wind, and I wondered what we'd do with them if we ever got them over the side.

Luckily we did not split in two; oil oozing through the 16½-foot gash amidships laid down the waves a bit. Then Fujiyama's snow-capped cone poked above the storm clouds. Never did a mountain look so good. Soon we limped into the shelter of Tokyo Bay.

Ten days in dry dock at Yokosuka gave me 1,200 miles of sight-seeing in Japan. Then Sparks leaked out word that our orders read "San Francisco." The ship went crazy, the whistle almost shook loose from the stack.

A 7½-month payroll is a frightful thing to contemplate, but I didn't mind it, for the Pa-

cific miles were going by outside my porthole. I didn't even mind a seaman's interrupting for a handful of aspirin.

"Got a headache?" I asked.

"Not yet. But I'm going to have a helluva one tomorrow about this time."

As I watched these men beeline for the gangway at San Francisco, I knew that that $100,000 would melt away like the piles of jellyfish on the Port Said beach. Soon many would be back aboard a tanker making their unsung runs from nowhere to nowhere.

SHOWERS OF CONFETTI, blizzards of paper streamers, popping flash bulbs, gay music sent me off on a recent voyage. This time I rode a luxury liner, and with me was my wife Patricia. We shared with fellow passengers the poignant moment when throb-

SUN AND SEA AIR *work their magic on the voyager whether roaming bright, wonder-filled decks with an officer or splashing in the pool. Aboard the 45,000-ton* Canberra *(above), a "floating luxury hotel" whisking more than 2,000 passengers across the Pacific and Indian oceans, teen-agers frolic at the Pop Inn, tots romp in supervised playrooms, adults dine, dance, enjoy movies in air-conditioned comfort or sport in windproof game areas. Engines and streamlined funnels are aft to minimize noise, vibration, and smoke.*

bing engines and chuffing tugs draw the great ship away from its New York berth and snap the fragile, kaleidoscopic bonds that tie one to friends and family ashore.

What a different world! I thought of *Mascoma*'s pinched companionways as Pat swept down the grand stairway in a stunning evening dress; recalled the steel-chaired mess as we entered the elegant dining salon.

We basked in the camaraderie of newfound friends, indulged in a round of delightful shipboard activities, had chamber music for afternoon tea, danced into the wee hours. We toured fashionable ports of call, saw postcard views, scanned other ships at sea.

"Look," said Pat one day as we lounged by the pool. "What is that ugly ship over there?"

"That," I said with a lump in my throat, "is a tanker."

Atoms at sea

Aboard N. S. *Savannah,* Alan Villiers
reports the historic sea trials of
the world's first nuclear merchantman

COMMODORE Gaston R. De Groote, in the wing of the bridge, ordered the engine room telegraph to "Half Ahead." He looked over his streamlined ship to the flurry of white water as the propeller began to turn.

"This," he said with a smile, "is history."

It was Friday, March 23, 1962, off Yorktown, Virginia. The sun shone; the York River flowed quietly past familiar landmarks, just as

RAKISH LINES *reflect the surging power*

on any other morning. But in response to that telegraphed order, for the first time anywhere a merchantman headed to sea on nuclear power.

I stood on the *Savannah's* swept-back superstructure as she moved out into the Atlantic. She slipped along at an effortless 17 knots on only 60 percent power. I heard no noise save the swish of water along her sides. She was clean as a sailing ship; the nuclear plant gave off no smut or smoke or exhaust.

Soon Gulf Stream weed drifted by in long lines on the blue sea, which rose and fell in gentle swells. There was a slight haze on the surface, but overhead the sky was perfect.

We cruised for hours at only 60 percent of her power, and she purred along at 20 knots. Gradually we increased speed 21 knots ... 22 ... 23. It was full power now, better than 23 knots, and still no strain, scarcely any vibration. As a trial we emergency stopped her from full speed ahead in 2,600 feet, and from full astern in 900 feet.

Our voyage was the first real test of what the new ship could do. She ran like a fine clock.

This is the ship that may revolutionize the world's merchant fleets. Atomic freighters

below decks as funnel-less Savannah *sets out to show the world what an atomic freighter can do.* 335

SGT. CHARLES PRESTON, U. S. ARMY SIGNAL CORPS

like her will be able to go wherever there is water to float them, with no wayside stops for fuel, no waste of space for coal or oil. The *Savannah* may bring back to the sea the freedom and endurance of sailing ships that seemed forever lost when steam took over.

I realized that atomic power for ships was not new. It drives U. S. Navy ships, a Russian icebreaker, and Russian submarines. But now N.S. (Nuclear Ship) *Savannah* was sailing the seas alone to show that the atom could carry cargo to the peaceful ports of the world.

W HAT MAKES this incredible ship go? What is at work behind the mysterious lights and dial needles I watched flash and flicker on the engine room console? The answer: heat, just plain heat, lots of it. This heat comes from what I regard as a piece of the sun—fissioning uranium 235—man pro-

duced and man controlled, locked in a reactor.

Water circulates through the reactor. It absorbs heat but does not boil because it is under great pressure—nearly 2,000 pounds to the square inch. It then moves on to give up heat through an exchanger to water in the boiler of a secondary system. This water does boil, and its steam drives turbines that transfer energy through reduction gears to the five-bladed screw, developing 22,000 shaft horsepower.

I went into the engine room, where turbines and gears were hard at work. Cylinders hid moving parts. Only the huge propeller shaft, deep in the bowels of the ship, revolved in view.

With a single fuel load—only 110 pounds of uranium 235—the ship can sail three and a half years without refueling. I smiled as I thought of the first *Savannah*, the little pioneer steamship of nearly a century and a half before. Packed to the gunwales with wood and

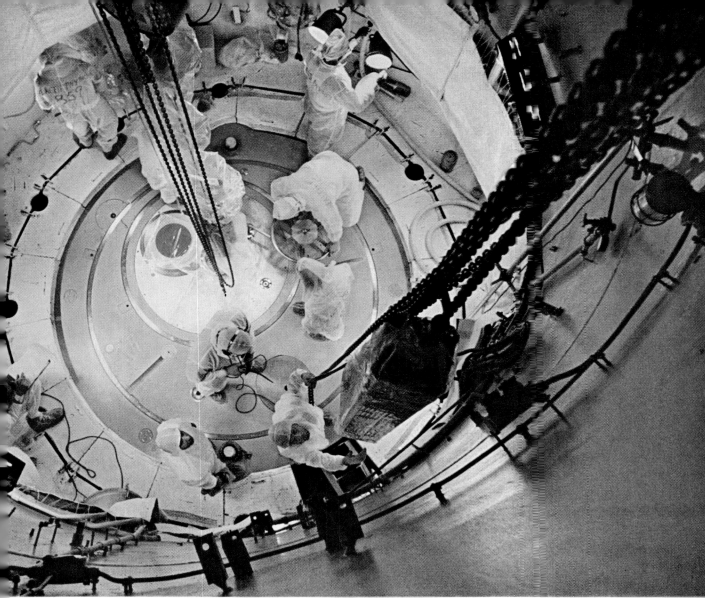

JOHN E. FLETCHER, NATIONAL GEOGRAPHIC PHOTOGRAPHER, FOR AEC-MARAD

coal, she could chug along less than four days.

The strange, blustering power of the little paddle-wheeler attracted some, scared off others. So does the new, silent power of this big atomic merchantman. Most people can't wait to get aboard her just for the thrill of it. But some fear there might be radioactivity or the danger of an atomic explosion.

Radioactivity—tasteless, odorless, invisible —is a specter that could haunt an uninformed visitor. But I learned that automatic monitoring instruments sniffed the air night and day in search of its presence. Crew members constantly prowled the decks, taking smear tests. All during the cruise, I—and everyone on board—wore small film badges clipped to shirt, belt, or jacket. Nobody's film showed a trace. In fact, I was told I would have absorbed more radiation by sitting out in the sun awhile.

I had learned about the safety precautions built into the *Savannah* when I visited the shipyard in Camden, New Jersey, a year earlier. The ship, bows flaring like an aircraft carrier's, was afloat inside an enormous covered dock high enough for her masts.

Aboard, all was seeming chaos, as it usually is in shipyards. Electric cables snaked everywhere. Shipwrights, riggers, welders, electricians, and joiners, wearing colored helmets, swarmed over the ship. Water sprayed from fire-fighting equipment under test. Giant derricks swung back and forth, up and down.

"We know the reactor is safe," my guide told me. "But some people may still be concerned about nuclear ships."

"Here's one," I said.

He looked me in the eye. "Forget it. *Savannah* has the safest nuclear power plant ever devised. It has to be. The ship will dock in dense population centers. She will carry pas-

337

sengers and cargo, and she'll get bounced about in storms at sea. We have made the reactor safe even in the event of the maximum credible accident."

"What's that?" I asked.

"The worst thing, or combination of things, that could possibly happen, like the most powerful ship afloat bashing into her reactor hold at full speed.

"She could flood at least two of her 11 watertight compartments and stay afloat. The reactor can be shut down instantly by pushing the SCRAM button. She can stand a more serious collision or other mishap than any other merchant ship."

He explained that the nuclear plant was sealed off by massive layers of steel, polyethylene, and lead. Outside these is a collision mat of steel and redwood two feet thick. Then comes concrete—more than a thousand tons of it. To break into the reactor, a colliding ship would have to penetrate 17 feet of material designed for resilience as well as strength.

Suppose that by some unlikely disaster the *Savannah* should sink in deep water. Would the pressure cause the containment vessel to collapse and permit radioactivity to leak out? No—special manholes would open and equalize pressures, thus preventing seepage. Even the fish will be unharmed. The United States government is so sure of the *Savannah's* safety that it has pledged half a billion

BLIPS, BUZZES, AND BLINKS *help guide* Savannah *safely through fog or darkness. The loran system (above) picks up signals from shore stations. The navigator takes two bearings, marks the lines on his chart. They intersect, showing the ship's precise longitude and latitude.*

True-motion radar (left) gives a chartlike picture of the ship's own motion in relation to land and nearby vessels.

Depth sounders, stabilizers, course and distance recorders, and other electronic instruments help navigate this nuclear ship. But watch officer at bridge console (right) makes the crucial decisions.

once sailed in cockleshells. I thought of the sweat and hardship that had for centuries been the seafarer's lot. From the slavery of oars and the uncertainty of sail to smooth and infinite power from a handful of nuclear elements—here was progress dramatized.

"She has been practically flawless," said the young chief of construction when we arrived back in Yorktown after three days of trials.

"Do you know how much fuel we burned in 750 miles?" another official asked. "A little more than a teaspoonful."

SUPERCAVITATING PROPELLER, U.S. NAVY

STABILIZER FIN ON THE "SAVANNAH,"
JOHN E. FLETCHER, NATIONAL GEOGRAPHIC PHOTOGRAPHER

the hull. The vessel slices through chop with little pitching or rolling; no one gets seasick.

In Europe hydrofoils make speedy police boats and ferries. The *Freccia del Sole* whisks 75 passengers across the Strait of Messina between Sicily and the Italian mainland in ten minutes. The regular ferry takes 50 minutes. In Norway, the trim *Vingtor* flies between Bergen and Stavanger almost three times faster than its surface competitors. Russian hydrofoils ply the Volga. America's 95-ton, aluminum-hulled *Denison,* with an 18,000-horsepower gas turbine, will carry 60 passengers at 60 knots between Florida and the Bahamas.

Submarines escape surface drag and turbulence by descending to the calm ocean depths. New whale-shaped hulls and finlike conning towers ("sails") cut resistance. Nuclear power opens the door to long-range undersea cargo carriers; subs may someday tow oil in great plastic bags.

Surface ships, too, are changing shape. Superstructures are being streamlined. Smokestacks, once the status symbol of the seas, are going the way of paddle wheels. Oddly, the sharp bow is often designed with a bulb jutting out below the waterline. This reduces wave drag by creating a low-pressure system—a hole in the water—ahead of the bow, and a wave system to cancel out the wave system set up by the bow. It takes less energy to plow through this "hole," so bulbous bows increase efficiency five to 15 percent, sometimes more.

Many a deck-chair seafarer thanks science for stabilizers, now standard equipment on luxury liners. *Savannah*'s electronic fins cut 90 percent of the roll; she is the first freighter to boast these underwater ailerons. When not in use they fold like jackknife blades.

Even propellers are getting a new look. The standard cloverleaf propeller tends to cavitate—create a vacuum, losing power. Scientists are experimenting with a spiral "supercavitating" type with a wedge-shaped blade that gains thrust from this vapor pocket.

Some ships increase maneuverability with a small electrically driven propeller in the rudder itself. The P & O-Orient liner *Oriana* has a new technique for getting in and out of tight berths. Water jets near bow and stern kick her sideways. A new command may well be in order: "Full speed to starboard!"

341

CHAPTER THIRTY-SIX

Keeping the sea safe

Coast Guardsmen track icebergs, rescue the shipwrecked, enforce maritime law. Phillip M. Swatek joins a cutter on weather patrol.

Out of the snow squalls and darkness of the North Atlantic a towering wave rolled down on the U. S. Coast Guard cutter *Half Moon,* a white chip on an empty winter sea. She lifted her bow toward the mountain of water. There was a strange hush in the dark ocean valley. But at the crest, wind tore at radio wires and shrieked through the radar antenna at the masthead. Frozen spray rattled the length of the 311-foot ship.

Sickeningly, she nosed down the other side.

On the bridge the captain gripped his chair. Lookouts locked fingers around handholds. In the galley amidships, cooks held anxiously to trays of bread dough ready for the oven. Far below, an engineman grabbed for a railing.

Then the next wave hit.

Half Moon could not lift for it. Her bow plunged into solid water. A deep boom like an underwater explosion rammed back through the ship. She recoiled and shuddered. Men caught their breath or gave the trembling vessel a soft word or two as tons of green water tore across her ice-crusted decks. A column of sea vaulted from the bow to burst against the bridge and stun the windshield wipers. Instantly ice glazed each wedge of glass.

Wearily the cutter rolled from under her load of seawater. Vibration eased. The wipers thrashed again, friendly as crickets in the night.

MEN OF THE CUTTER "PONTCHARTRAIN" CLEAR ICE FROM THE FORECASTLE. U. S. COAST GUARD

The captain fussed with his pipe. Men below breathed again. The sailor with the red beard said, "Come on, play the card."

From wave to wave the black hours passed. At midnight the captain moved back to the navigator's table. "Hold your course until morning if you can," he said, "but keep her into the sea. I don't want to take any of this broadside."

The navigator looked at the spot on his chart he had seen a thousand times: ocean station Bravo, a 210-mile square in the frigid storm track between Newfoundland and Greenland. Bravo, named after the second word of the international phonetic alphabet, is the coldest of nine Atlantic stations patrolled by ships of six nations. They stand by to rescue downed planes and distressed vessels, serve as signposts to navigators, and relay communications. Most important are their weather observations, made in the storm rookeries of the Atlantic.

Half Moon carried four U. S. Weather Bureau observers, who worked in pairs around the clock. Even this savage storm did not disrupt their schedule. At four bells two of them forced themselves up the swaying ladder to the bridge and stood uneasily while their eyes opened to the gloom and the stare of green-eyed dials. They watched how the rolling ship was taking the seas, on which side the wind carried heaviest spray. "I don't think there's much choice," one said, "unless it's getting back in the sack."

They lurched below, waited by a watertight door until a deck-drenching wave rushed past, then hurriedly unbolted the door and fought their way aft on the open deck to the weather shack over the cutter's fantail.

There they hooked a helium gas nozzle to a limp yellow balloon and swelled the bag to seven feet in diameter. They attached a radiosonde. No larger than a shoebox, it contained instruments to gauge temperature, humidity, and air pressure, and a miniature radio transmitter that would send readings back to the ship. The observers strung on two crosses of aluminum foil as targets for the ship's radar.

In good weather the launching drew an audience. It was one of the events of the day. And there was always the possibility of a take-off crash, hilarious to the sailors. But this stormy night the weathermen were alone as they sidestepped out to the balloon-release platform, holding the thrashing yellow globe high to keep it clear of ice crusts. As the bow rose to a crest, one shouted, "Now!" Carefully they boosted the rig up and out. It hung for

an instant, then swept away into the black sky.

Inside the weather shack a receiver was already getting signals. The radarman announced, "I just picked up your toy balloon," and began calling off the distance and direction of the climbing wind-driven sphere.

From this progressive plot weathermen learn wind velocity at successive altitudes. Eventually the balloon explodes in the stratosphere.

After two hours one of the haggard observers handed a weather report to the radioman. "If you've got nothing to do later on, send this singing telegram, will you?"

These reports, which affect everyone, are vital to aviators. Back in 1947 only a few of the planned ocean stations were regularly patrolled. Then a passenger-laden flying boat, laboring west across the Atlantic against violent and unreported head winds, burned too much fuel to reach Newfoundland or return to Ireland. It ditched in the open sea beside a Coast Guard cutter patrolling station Charlie. In waves two stories high, all 69 persons were rescued. Now ships ply all the stations.

THE NIGHTMARE of the North Atlantic is rime ice. It forms from breaking spray that freezes the instant it hits. A heavy coating could capsize *Half Moon,* but she was able to shed it until the last few days of her three-week patrol. A storm struck, and we found her taking 12 seconds to recover from a 60° roll. Normally she took seven.

Two feet of ice coated the decks. Ice swelled the lifeline cables to a foot in diameter, and crushed the sides of a lifeboat. The captain hove to so that less rime-forming spray would come over the bow. Men could not break it off. They would not have survived on deck in that 75-knot wind.

Next day the sea was quieter. Every sailor not on watch manned steam jets, hot-water nozzles, wooden mallets. All day they hosed and smashed away ice—some 400 tons of it.

Free of this burden the cutter headed home. Everyone took great interest in the diesels, and the oil-smeared men who ran them gained new importance. Then, near New York, "channel fever" struck the crew, reaching its peak as mooring lines were being secured.

It isn't in the nature of seamen to harbor lofty purposes when the gangway is down and shore leave awaits. Ours whipped salutes at the quarterdeck and were gone, to forget for awhile their three weeks patrolling Bravo.

PERCHED ATOP A BREECHES BUOY, *Navy man swings to safety above the California surf where his patrol boat grounded in a fog. Coast Guardsmen shot a line to the wreck, now haul the buoy back and forth with whip lines. Airmen (below) from a ditched Navy bomber climb thankfully aboard the cutter* Coos Bay, *patrolling Atlantic station Echo.*

NORTH SEA GALE LASHES ENGLAND'S NORTH PIER LIGHTHOUSE NEAR NEWCASTLE; PHOTOGRAPHED BY H. S. THORNE
INSET: HENRY WINSTANLEY'S ENGRAVING OF HIS "LIGHT HOUSE ON YE EDYSTONE" IN 1699; MACPHERSON COLLECTION, NATIONAL MARITIME MUSEUM, GREENWICH

Solitary sentinel: the lighthouse

IT STANDS ALONE, feet in the sea, passive to the endless onslaught of the waves. The fangs of flung-up rocks torment giant rollers until they break and roar against its slender flanks a hundred feet high. Twenty miles at sea a weary navigator sees its staccato wink or slow beam. With its flash, the light identifies itself. The mariner relaxes; he now knows where he is.

Nature gave beacons to Mediterranean seafarers: the volcanoes of Etna, Stromboli, Vesuvius. About 280 B.C., Egyptians built the Pharos to mark the harbor at Alexandria. One of the Seven Wonders of the World, it is said to have risen 450 feet. A wood fire burned at its pinnacle.

Beacons dotted the Roman Empire, dimmed in the Dark Ages, flamed again when Renaissance Europe took to sea. With lights came wreckers, whose false signals lured ships ashore to be plundered. Sometimes they hung a lantern on an ox and walked it along a beach near dangerous rocks to simulate a ship sailing safely through a channel.

Early lighthouses marked headlands and harbors, not offshore shoals and reefs. First to rise atop wave-swept rocks was England's famed Eddystone Light, built in the Channel in 1696-8 to warn ships approaching Plymouth from the southwest. Henry Winstanley raised it during mild summer weather. But in the first winter of operation heavy spray flew right over the 80-foot structure, buffeting the lantern.

Winstanley strengthened and enlarged the tower, and it was lit again in 1699. This lighthouse (inset) lasted four years, though keepers claimed that gales rocked the crockery from the table. Some got seasick.

Winstanley went out to repair it, declaring himself ready to stay on through the wildest storm. Alas, this came—a gale that wrecked some 150 ships—and that was the end of Winstanley and his tower. Two more lights were to rise at Eddystone before the present one, erected in 1882.

Bostonians built America's first "Light Hous & Lanthorn" in 1716 and paid for it by charging ships a penny a ton. Today more than 300 manned lighthouses line United States coasts and lakeshores, along with nearly 41,000 buoys, fog signals, radio beacons, day beacons, and loran stations. Steel towers standing on stilts in the sea are superseding the long-familiar lightships. Electronics has replaced sperm oil or candles to guard the mariner.

CHAPTER THIRTY-SEVEN

The frozen frontier

Iron men in wooden ships had long fought ice-choked seas. Their quests: Northwest Passage, North Pole, the southern continent. Alan Villiers now recaptures the 20th century triumphs of Peary, Amundsen, and Byrd, the courage of Shackleton, the tragedy of Scott. He portrays Antarctica today.

A CREAKING SHIP laden with blubber, coal, and yapping dogs made her way up Davis Strait west of Greenland. Ahead lay endless ice, indescribable hardship, perhaps death from scurvy, starvation, exposure. Ahead lay the North Pole, challenge of three centuries. No one knew this challenge better than Comdr. Robert Edwin Peary.

The tall, tough-as-rawhide naval engineer had spent most of his adult life wresting secrets from the Arctic. He had lived with the Eskimos, learned their language and their way of life.

He knew that when the time came he could depend on them to brave the fiercest blizzard, the grimmest terrain, and to drive dog teams like no one else.

He knew too that he could rely on his *Roosevelt* to carry him as far north as any ship could. He had designed her himself—the first vessel ever built in America for polar exploration. The schooner-rigged steamship had wooden sides 2½ feet thick to withstand tremendous ice

BROWN BROTHERS AND (RIGHT) REAR ADM. ROBERT E. PEARY

THE FEARLESS EYES ... *In them the Pole!" Peary, exhausted, triumphs after 20 years exploring the Arctic. His* Roosevelt, *masts piercing the aurora, bore him within 500 miles of his goal.*

pressures. Commanded by Capt. Bob Bartlett of Newfoundland, the *Roosevelt* now reached her farthest north at Cape Sheridan on Ellesmere Island in September, 1908.

She had been "kicked about by the floes as if she had been a football," battered by 1,000-ton bergs, and driven against the shore. Peary blasted her out with dynamite. After six days of touch and go, the *Roosevelt* was safely moored inside the pack.

Her cargo was landed, then sledged to Cape Columbia, the northernmost tip of the island. Here on March 1, 1909, Peary began his trek to the Pole.

Blizzards shrieked like evil spirits. Snow blew into nostrils and eyes. A six-day gale played havoc with the sea ice, opening it here, smashing the edges together, overriding them, then falling calm to let the whole distorted mass freeze.

The cold took its toll. Donald B. MacMillan, a schoolteacher from Worcester, Massachusetts, had to turn back when Peary saw the "frosted heel with which

he had been worrying along for several days." Other members of the expedition turned south after bringing up supplies.

Last to turn back, some 130 miles from the Pole, was Bob Bartlett. He had broken trail and set up supply depots for the final dash. But he was also needed aboard the *Roosevelt*. A ship held in moving ice can be quickly crushed and ground under, or flung a twisted wreck on her side. Captain Bob's cunning, born of years of sealing and Arctic work, had saved *Roosevelt* many times. He was bitterly disappointed to have to go back. But he understood.

Peary, the Negro Matthew Henson, and four Eskimos floundered on, slipping, sliding, fighting for each step.

April 6, 1909: "The Pole at last." Peary shook hands with his men, "a sufficiently unceremonious affair." He fixed the position, unfurled the Stars and Stripes, built a cairn, stayed 30 hours.

Later explorers have flown over the Pole, have drifted there on ice islands, or have come in through the depths by nuclear-powered submarine. But no one else has ever sledged there.

BEFORE **PEARY** conquered the North Pole, Roald Amundsen had tackled that other great Arctic problem—the Northwest Passage. The hawk-nosed Norwegian became a polar seaman serving in tough little sealers. At 25 he sailed with the Belgian Adrien de Gerlache in the polar ship *Belgica* on a voyage to the Antarctic. She was the first ship ever to spend the winter frozen in the pack there.

Amundsen returned to Norway in 1899 and promptly called on famed Fridtjof Nansen with an idea thought out during the long Antarctic night: to take a small ship and drift, drive, and sail through the Northwest Passage. Nansen had done some drifting and driving in Arctic seas himself aboard the specially built polar ship *Fram*. He believed in small ships for this kind of work. His *Fram* was 400 tons, *Belgica* half that. The great man approved.

Amundsen bought an old fishing sloop of less than 50 tons. She had a clumsy gaff-and-boom rig, an old-fashioned bowsprit and jib boom, a bit of cabin aft, a minute forecastle, and little else. Her name was *Gjöa*. Amundsen gave her a square yard and a 13-horsepower motor, and put in a few tanks. These Norwegian coastal and Arctic fishing vessels were very strongly built. *Gjöa* needed to be.

Amundsen packed enough food and equip-

STORM JIB FLYING, *mainsail reefed*, Gjöa *rides*

ment into her to last his party of seven, all Arctic veterans, for five years, and left Norway in June of 1903. By late August, *Gjöa* was through Baffin Bay and among Canada's eastern Arctic islands.

Slowly the little sloop drove with the pack ice toward the Pacific. Storms, fog, impassable ice, tortuous channels among the islands, groundings that nearly wrecked the ship, and once a fire in the engine room—these were the hazards. Though "a mighty flame, with thick suffocating smoke was leaping up from the engine-room sky-light," *Gjöa* did not blow up. It was well she didn't, for she might not have been missed for a year or more.

Gjöa wintered in a harbor on King William Island northwest of Hudson Bay. Two years she stayed there, for the ice never opened in 1904. Amundsen used the time well, surveying, making scientific observations, sledging to the vicinity of the north magnetic pole.

What a life! Seven big men, one little ship alone against a frozen world day after day,

an Arctic gale. Amundsen fought ice three years to bring her through the Northwest Passage.

week after week. No radio, no communications. Pemmican or seal meat for dinner, hoosh (made of pemmican) or dried codfish for supper; if you wanted something else, then off into the winter night you went with rifle to hunt for it. Eskimos for friends, great polar bears for company. The taciturn Norsemen were ideal for this stick-it-out, the-hell-with-the-hardships voyaging.

At last, in August of 1905, the ice parted. Working her way westward through that chain of ice-jammed straits and gulfs along the northern coast of the American continent, *Gjöa* navigated "the hitherto unsolved link in the North West Passage." Then her men beheld a strange sight—another ship!

Could she be from the Pacific? Amundsen hoisted his Norwegian flag. But the stranger didn't answer. A derelict? Then up went her colors: the American flag! She was a Yankee whaler from San Francisco, after bowheads. Amundsen was overjoyed. For all practical purposes, he had made the Northwest Passage.

Ice locked in *Gjöa* one more winter, on the northern coast of the Yukon. It was August of 1906 before the little sloop passed Bering Strait and came romping down into the free waters of the blue Pacific. A tumultuous welcome greeted her at Nome, Alaska.

Gjöa, preserved, can be seen today in Golden Gate Park at San Francisco.

Since Amundsen's epic voyage United States and Canadian ships have mastered the Northwest Passage. Royal Canadian Mounted Police Sgt. Harry Larsen piloted the Arctic patrol ship *St. Roch* both ways through the Passage—eastward to Halifax in 1940-2, westward back to Vancouver in 1944. The rugged, 104-foot auxiliary schooner, pride of the Mounties, rests at Vancouver today.

As for Amundsen, he returned to Norway and plotted his next move—an assault on the North Pole. But even as he was fitting out Nansen's old *Fram,* the news came of Peary's triumph. Here was Amundsen with his ship all ready and no place to go. He had no interest

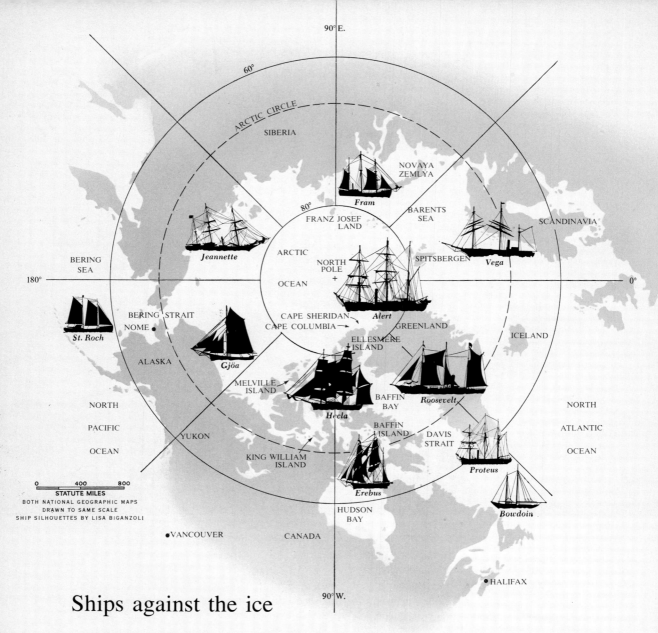

Ships against the ice

SHIPBORNE EXPLORERS *pushed back the frozen frontier in search of the Poles, the Northwest and Northeast passages, and geographic secrets. Epic voyages by Peary in* Roosevelt, *Scott in* Terra Nova, *Amundsen in* Gjöa, *and Byrd in* Bear of Oakland *are described in this chapter. Here are other memorable voyages and ships.*

TO THE ARCTIC

HECLA—*Lt. William E. Parry (Great Britain) rammed his 375-ton bark halfway through the Northwest Passage, wintered on Melville Island, 1819-20; ice turned him back.*

EREBUS—*Sir John Franklin attempted the Passage in 1845. His party perished after finding link with western channel. In 1859 searchers found skeletons, but the auxiliary bark and her consort* Terror *had vanished.*

VEGA—*Adolf E. Nordenskjöld (Sweden) steamed north around Siberia to Japan, 1878-9, first through the Northeast Passage west to east.*

ALERT—*Capt. George S. Nares (Great Britain) forced his steam bark up the coast of Ellesmere Island to 82° 27', farthest north by a ship to that date (1875).*

JEANNETTE—*Lt. Comdr. G. W. DeLong (United States) tried to reach the Pole from Bering Strait, 1879-81. Ice carried the bark-rigged steam yacht westward, sank her north of Siberia. DeLong and most of his party perished.*

PROTEUS—*Lt. Adolphus W. Greely crunched north to Ellesmere with a U. S. meteorological team in this iron-bowed steam barkentine, 1881. She was lost two years later bringing supplies. Only Greely and six of his party were found alive when relief ships broke through in 1884.*

FRAM—*Inspired by* Jeannette's *drift, Fridtjof Nansen of Norway put his round-hulled schooner in the ice north of Siberia, 1893, sought to drift across the Pole. Ice lifted and bore her to 85° 57', farthest north for any ship. She broke out near Spitsbergen, 1896.* Fram *rests at Oslo.*

BOWDOIN—*Veteran of more than 30 years of Arctic exploration, Rear Adm. Donald B. MacMillan's auxiliary schooner is preserved at Mystic Seaport, Connecticut.*

TO THE ANTARCTIC

HERO—*Nathaniel Palmer, American sealer, discovered Palmer Peninsula in his 47-foot sloop, 1820.*

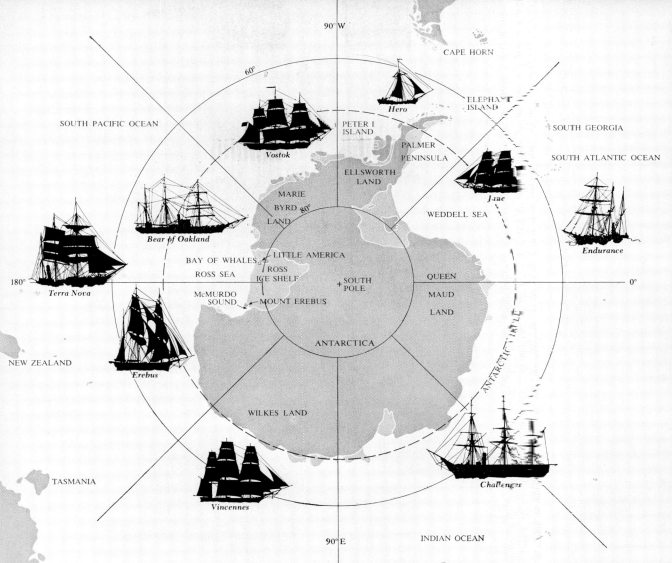

90° W

CAPE HORN

60°

SOUTH PACIFIC OCEAN

Vostok

PETER I
ISLAND

Hero

ELEPHANT
ISLAND

SOUTH GEORGIA

SOUTH ATLANTIC OCEAN

PALMER
PENINSULA

ELLSWORTH
LAND

MARIE
BYRD
LAND

80°

WEDDELL SEA

Jane

Endurance

Bear of Oakland

LITTLE AMERICA

BAY OF WHALES

ROSS SEA

ROSS
ICE SHELF

+ SOUTH
POLE

QUEEN

MAUD

LAND

0°

180°

Terra Nova

McMURDO
SOUND

MOUNT EREBUS

ANTARCTICA

NEW ZEALAND

Erebus

WILKES LAND

ANTARCTIC CIRCLE

TASMANIA

Vincennes

Challenger

AUSTRALIA

90° E

INDIAN OCEAN

VOSTOK — *Russian explorer Bellingshausen circled the polar region in this 500-ton ship, 1819-21; was first to sight land within the Antarctic Circle — Peter I Island.*

JANE — *James Weddell, British sealer, penetrated the Weddell Sea in this 160-ton brig, 1823.*

VINCENNES — *In 1840, Lt. Charles Wilkes skirted Wilkes Land in this U. S. sloop of war, was first to establish that Antarctica was a continent.*

EREBUS — *Capt. James C. Ross, Scottish explorer, pushed through pack ice into the Ross Sea, 1841, found the jumping-off place for dashes to the Pole. An engine was added to the bark for Franklin's Arctic expedition.*

CHALLENGER — *During a British oceanographic expedition, the 2,306-ton corvette under Captain Nares was first to steam across the Antarctic Circle, 1874.*

ENDURANCE — *Locked in Weddell Sea ice in 1915, the 144-foot barkentine (right) drifted north for 282 days. Sir Ernest Shackleton and his men abandoned the crumpled ship and camped on a floe 165 more days. When the ice broke up, they took to boats (page 355).*

in being second man anywhere. If America was first at the North Pole, why not try the South Pole?

Two great British explorers were already determined to reach that. One, former merchant seaman Ernest Shackleton, was then trying. The report of his splendid failure—he had to turn back only 97 miles from the Pole—arrived while Amundsen was still in Norway.

The second was Capt. Robert Falcon Scott of the Royal Navy, a veteran of the Antarctic. As Scott was about to sail from New Zealand for the Ross Sea in *Terra Nova,* he received a portentous cable from the Madeira Islands: "Am going south. Amundsen."

No sluggard at any time, Amundsen sailed directly to the Pacific pack, broke through into the Ross Sea, and made for the Bay of Whales in the great ice barrier.

Two approaches to the Pole—through the Weddell Sea from the South Atlantic, or through the Ross Sea from the South Pacific—could get men to about latitude 78°. In the ice-choked Weddell Sea a ship would have to be lucky to make it. Beyond a deep belt of pack ice the Ross Sea was open in summer. Either way ships went, the last 800 miles was a walk. It was also a climb, for the South Pole lay on a mountain-girt plateau 10,000 feet high. Shackleton had found that out.

On February 22, 1911, Scott learned that the Norwegian was established at the Bay of Whales. *Amundsen!* The name is underlined in Scott's diary. "There is no doubt that Amundsen's plan is a very serious menace to ours," he wrote. Like it or not, he was in a race for the Pole. Nevertheless, he was determined that his scientific program would proceed as planned. It did. And it killed him.

SCOTT'S INCREDIBLE MARCH is a classic. He chose the route across the Ross Ice Shelf near the mountains; chose, too, to climb the Beardmore Glacier to the polar plateau, chose to rely on manpower from that grim point onward. He used Siberian ponies at first. They couldn't take it and needed lots of fodder. He had dogs, but they died. Some-

how the British never got the knack of handling the fierce huskies.

The going is brutal. *One sinks to the knees at every step.... The travelling has been very hard.... Weather is beginning to look dirty again.... Oh! for a few fine days!* Scott and four companions walk, ski, stumble, stagger, flounder on. Their sledge bumps continually over wavelike ridges of snow. *Only 27 miles from the Pole. We ought to do it now.*

Ten miles from the Pole they see a flag marker, the tracks of dogs and sledges. On January 17, 1912, they reach the Pole. Then they find a Norwegian flag, and a letter from Amundsen for Scott to take to King Haakon.

"Great God!" scrawled Scott's frozen fingers, "this is an awful place and terrible enough for us to have laboured to it without the reward of priority.... Now for the run home.... I wonder if we can do it."

One man, worn out, "nearly broken down in brain," died at the foot of Beardmore Glacier. Another, a soldier named Oates, found his frostbitten feet could carry him no longer. Lest he become a fatal burden to his companions, he stumbled off alone to die in a blizzard.

A few miles from a supply depot and safety, Scott and the two others holed up while a storm raged. Food and fuel gone, weakened— they had dragged geological specimens collected on the march—they awaited the end. "... I do not think I can write more—" reads Scott's last entry in his diary. "For God's sake look after our people."

AMUNDSEN had been first to the Pole by 34 days. His expedition had gone like clockwork. His dog teams could average 20 miles a day on the plateau where Scott's man-hauling was lucky to do 12. His Norsemen were, after Eskimos, perhaps the finest polar travelers in the world. But even with this new triumph he could not rest.

In 1918-20 he sailed the Northeast Passage across the top of Asia in the *Maud*, following the track of Nordenskjöld in the *Vega*. In 1926, in a dirigible with Lincoln Ellsworth and Umberto Nobile, he flew over the North Pole

Shipwrecked Shackleton braves Antarctic seas

THE JAMES CAIRD *slides into the surf at Elephant Island (left). Waves thump her on a rock, almost capsize her. She fights clear. Sails are set, and the west wind fills them at once. In minutes she is out of sight. It is April 24, 1916: Sir Ernest Shackleton has begun one of history's most daring voyages.*

The indomitable Irish polar explorer had planned to march across Antarctica. But floes crushed his auxiliary barkentine Endurance *in the Weddell Sea. Salvaging supplies and three boats, he and his 28 men drifted on the ice, sledged, and sailed to Elephant Island.*

Shackleton asked for volunteers to sail for help to the island of South Georgia, 800 miles away. All wanted to go. Shackleton chose five. They covered the 22-foot Caird *with a canvas "deck," loaded a month's rations, two casks of water, a cooker, a few gallons of kerosene. Ahead raged the stormiest seas in the world.*

Caird *leapt, rolled, flung herself about as if stung to madness. "As the sea broke all around us the boat was lifted dizzily upwards, and we would heel.... At these moments we could see for miles ... nothing but grey, grey, grey."*

Always one of the six fought the tiller, watched the compass, kept Caird *to her course. South Georgia was a pinpoint easily missed.*

For a week there was no sun. The boat tossed, iced up, did her dreadful best to fling the men off. One man froze to the tiller "stiff as iron." It took an hour to thaw him.

A storm struck. Seas filled the cockpit. The men bailed desperately. Then they ran out of fresh water: "Our thirst was a torment."

After 14 days they sighted the mountains of South Georgia. Then another gale sprang up. In these wild waters land was a menace.

Caird *clawed off. Ninety-mile-an-hour winds ripped at her, pushed her toward the cliffs. Ten minutes from death, the wind dropped. They coasted to a landing in King Haakon Bay.*

Shackleton trekked to a whaling settlement, obtained a steamer, returned to Elephant Island. Said one of the rescued men, "We knew that somehow Shacky would make it."

355

just days after Byrd. Two years later he was lost while searching in an airplane for Nobile, whose dirigible had crashed on Arctic ice. In the air there were no trusty *Frams*.

First to fly over the Poles—the North in 1926, the South in 1929—Richard E. Byrd also knew the snap of a mainsail, the sting of salt spray, the feel of a shuddering deck as the *City of New York* crunched through pack ice. He had bought her, a veteran Norwegian sealer, on the advice of Amundsen, then had refitted her. "The stout old *City* rode the seas like a duck," noted a correspondent with Byrd's 1928-9 Antarctic expedition. She pushed through the ice into the Ross Sea and the Bay of Whales until she could go no farther. Not far away Byrd established his first camp and dubbed it Little America.

On his second Antarctic expedition Byrd used the steel-sheathed *Jacob Ruppert* (which carried his plane) and the celebrated old bark-entine-rigged *Bear of Oakland*. The *Bear* had rescued survivors of the Greely Arctic expedition in 1884, had policed sea routes to the Yukon gold fields in the '90's. Now in 1934, she was punching her way through Antarctic ice. "A plucky old ship," Byrd called her.

Thrice more Byrd returned to the Antarctic, the last time in 1955 aboard the U. S. Navy ice-breaker *Glacier,* 100 times more powerful than his old *City*. As Officer in Charge of United States Antarctic Programs, Byrd pioneered the modern era of polar exploration—the all-out assault by mechanized expeditions. The White Continent at last had become accessible to questing man in his wonderful ships.

BYRD SAILED *Antarctica's "dangerous unknown waters" in the* Bear of Oakland *(above) in 1934. Later that year he nearly died of fumes from his stove (below) while keeping a solitary vigil at a weather station on the frozen continent.*

Antarctic ice frames Scott's Terra Nova *(left). She steamed back to England in 1913 without him.*

BYRD ANTARCTIC EXPEDITION, ABOVE: WILLARD R. CULVER. OPPOSITE: HERBERT G. PONTING

Science rides

WEATHER INFORMATION: *Antarctica's chief export. Glacier crew members release a balloon that will tell wind velocity and direction. Supplies for Operation Deep Freeze burden steel cargo ships steaming through the ice-choked Ross Sea.*

ALBERT MOLDVAY. INSETS: DAVID S. BOYER AND ANDREW H. BROWN (BELOW), ALL NATIONAL GEOGRAPHIC STAFF

GLACIER *chops out a berth before Mount Erebus, landmark of explorers. With 21,000 horsepower behind her bows, the 8,625-ton U. S. Navy icebreaker can shatter ice 15 feet thick. In 96 hours she chiseled out an estimated 32,844,000 tons of it. Helicopters scout for leads in the ice field.*

nickel-steel bows to an icebound continent

ARMOR-PLATED ICEBREAKERS plow a furrow in a field of ice. In the lead, U.S.S. *Glacier* smashes, lurches, screams with metallic protest against the stubborn pack. She charges up onto thick ice to crush it with her own weight, shudders to a halt, pulls astern, rams ahead again.

How does it feel? "Like a marathon ride on a Manhattan subway," reports National Geographic staff man David S. Boyer, an old *Glacier* hand. "I was always clutching for a swinging strap that was never there."

Trailing icebreakers *Eastwind* and *Burton Island* bite into sides and widen the channel.

It's slow going—a mile or two a day—but nickel-steel bows bash through the Ross Sea months earlier than wooden ships ever could. Thin-skinned cargo ships follow with supplies,

machinery, and
precious fuel oil.
Through here in 1961
the U. S. Navy supply ship
Arneb brought the Atomic Age to
Ice Age Antarctica: a prefabricated
nuclear power plant and an atom-
powered weather station.

Inspired by Byrd, "Admiral of the Ends of the Earth," the United States spearheaded Antarctic exploration. Expeditions led by him tore the veil from half the continent. In 1955 he stood on the bridge of the new *Glacier* and witnessed Operation Deep Freeze, the United States' part in the international assault on Antarctica's secrets.

With the "old sense of excitement," he watched the seven-ship task force unload on the ice at McMurdo Sound at the edge of the Ross Sea. "I like the clatter of tractor trains, the whir of helicopters, and shouts of men wrestling with vehicles and gear," he said.

Above all, Rear Admiral Byrd liked the challenge—"for Antarctica still plays for keeps."

The 1957-8 International Geophysical Year saw ships and scientists flock to the continent from 11 other nations: Argentina, Australia, Belgium, Chile, England, France, Japan, New Zealand, Norway, South Africa, Russia. All established IGY stations.

The United States built six research stations, one at the exact geographical South Pole. Rear Adm. George J. Dufek, commander of Operation Deep Freeze, and six other Navy men were first to set foot at the Pole since Scott's day. A ski-equipped plane landed them there. Later, transports flew in a construction crew—and Dr. Paul Siple, veteran of Byrd's five Antarctic expeditions.

He and 17 volunteers were first to winter at the South Pole, first to feel the sting of 102° below zero weather. In 1958 homesteading Americans greeted trailblazing Britons led by Sir Vivian Fuchs. His caravan of Sno-Cats and weasels was first to cross Antarctica by land. Man, with the harnessed atom, is in Antarctica to stay. He has found deposits of coal, traces of gold, silver,

copper, manganese,
tin, lead. He sees in shrimp-
size krill, teeming in Antarctic waters,
a source of food. He studies winds, temperatures, barometric pressures, and their effect
on world weather. Byrd's words still ring true:
"The things we can learn there will have a
profound effect upon the lives of us all."

359

CHAPTER THIRTY-EIGHT

With a modern whaler in Antarctic waters

Blåst! Blåst! shouts the Norwegian lookout — a far cry from the old Yankee's melodic "Thar she blo-o-o-ws!" Factory ships hungry for blubber, chasers churning amid spouting blues, gunners firing explosive harpoons — this was Alan Villiers' life on the first whaling voyage to the Ross Sea.

D AYS LENGTHENED; nights shrank to brief twilight. The 12,000-ton factory ship *Sir James Clark Ross,* with five whale chasers in tow, steamed south through the pack ice — sometimes a level white, sometimes a crazy pavement where floes had jostled and grappled. Here and there loomed giant bergs.

Churned-up floes, smashed by our green-heart-sheathed bows, swirled in our wake and crashed into the small chasers. I wondered that they could stand it.

We came to solid ice. Bang! The jolt whipped the foremast, shaking our ice pilot up there and sending the helmsman stumbling against the wheel. The ship stopped, throwing the five chasers into confusion. We backed, then charged again. With a wild floundering of the propeller and a grinding and crashing ahead, the ice opened. Broken floes swept back on other floes. Shuddering and groaning, the steel ship flung herself south.

Once we were really stopped, held by the ice so that no amount of going full astern freed the *Ross.* "Out on the ice!" came the order. Whalemen — burly Norwegians and young Tas-manians — clambered down rope ladders. Axes, crowbars, long saws were passed down. We cut a wide trench around the bow and sides — a hundred of us working furiously, throwing off our fur caps and heavy clothes. Penguins slithered on their bellies to gather in excited knots and chatter about the strange scene.

The trench ready, back we scrambled aboard. This time full sternway brought us clear, leaving in the ice the shape of our ship.

We steamed on. Extra lookouts watched for the first sign of swell. For beyond all this ice lay open water, thousands of square miles of it, and that was where the whales were supposed to be. Explorers Amundsen, Scott, and Shackleton had seen a bay in the Ross Sea full of them — the Bay of Whales. But how could soft mammals break through to it, I wondered. They had no greenheart bows.

We were a week in that pack ice. It was mid-December, 1923. The *Sir James Clark Ross,* former cargo liner renamed for the discoverer of the Ross Sea, was the largest whale factory ship in the world, and the largest vessel to cross the Antarctic Circle up to that time. This was

"HELL'S GATE" YAWNS *for world's largest mammal, being winched tailfirst up factory ship's stern ramp. On flensing deck knives and whining saws mince 100-ton blues for fiery boilers 'tween decks. White "balloon" is air-filled tongue.*

the pioneer whaling expedition to the Ross Sea, one of the last strongholds of the whale.

The *Ross* was fitted out at Sandefjord, Norway. Her cargo holds were compartmented for whale oil; her 'tween decks bulged with conveyor belts, pressure cookers, and machinery; her extra forecastle, steam-heated and commodious, could house 100 men; her main deck was overlaid with thick planks to make a flensing platform where men would strip blubber from dead whales.

The ship steamed out around Good Hope to Hobart in Tasmania to ship additional hands. Here I signed on as seaman-whaler at $20 a month plus a lay of two Norwegian öre a barrel—one-twelfth of an American cent. No one had been to the Ross Sea except a few explorers. It seemed too good a chance to miss.

At the Bay of Whales we found nothing but ice. It was a bad season, said Capt. Carl Anton Larsen. He had been south before, with the Swede Otto Nordenskjöld's Antarctic expedition of 1902-03. He had organized shore-based whaling from the island of South Georgia, then pushed on to the South Shetlands with factory ships. Now he was pioneering again.

We sent the five chasers scouting. They were lean little steamers with high natural-draught funnels, tall bridges, and grim guns on the platforms at their upswept bows. The gun flings a bomb-headed harpoon far beyond hand-held range, dispatching enormous blue and finback whales with deadly efficiency. In square-rigger days these species were safe, for men hunted only the floaters—humpback, sperm, and right (the "right" whale for the whaleboatmen). Now they could take whales that sank when killed. But modern expeditions with factory ships and chasers have to find fat whales in large numbers to show a profit.

BLIZZARDS BLEW, chilled us to the marrow. Moisture in our nostrils and eyes froze. Beards gummed up painfully. The great ice barrier, 200 feet high, blocking the cold continent's rim, calved icebergs into the sea. Heavy pack jammed McMurdo Sound. A chaser exploring there was locked in for six days.

Then the whales came, thick and fast. The big ship steamed near them. The chasers steamed among them. I watched the hunt.

A little chaser stalks her prey. She dodges, twists, stops, moves ahead again, now slowly, now at speed. She can turn in her length. She pitches in the swell, rolls heavily as she turns.

Twenty whales spout, all blues.

The chaser's captain runs along the foredeck to the harpoon gun. The mate is in the lookout barrel. An able seaman has the bridge. Legs astraddle, oilskins glazed with ice, the captain-

GUNNER TRIGGERS SIX FEET OF DEATH *at arching finback whale. Harpoon cannon and chaser,*

harpooner swings the stubby gun on its swivel. A fine blue blows, arches its great back slowly to sound. The gunner waves a mittened hand. The chaser swings. Slowly the whale turns and sounds. Will the gunner never fire?

It is a skilled business, shooting whales. At no time does the whale show much of his bulk. The bomb must go in behind his ribs, tear into his vitals. Forefinger squeezes the trigger.

Crash! With a spurt of flame and cordite wads, the six-foot, hundred-pound harpoon hurtles over the waves. Rope snakes after it. Has he hit? No sign of the whale now.

Of course he has hit. Down, down, down goes the whale, the manila running out furiously over the steel bow wheel, singing through the protesting blocks slung from the masthead. The gunner watches the deep before him. Seamen hastily reload the gun.

A dull thud from the depths signals the bomb burst. The chaser backs in a flurry of foam.

Still the stout line runs out.

"Steady the brakes there! Hold him a little!" The line slows, slackens, suddenly is limp. "Heave up! Heave up!"

In comes the line. The gunner stands ready.

Now the whale breaks the surface, blowing blood. He hauls the chaser forward for five, ten minutes. His blood blast thickens. At last he stops. He flurries violently, beating the bloodstained sea. The gunner gets him in his sights. Another harpoon? It is not necessary.

The whale rolls over on his back—sinks slowly out of sight. The chaser hauls back her line, brings Leviathan alongside. He is longer than the 90-foot chaser. His gray-blue body is mottled with white that speaks of thick blubber.

The men lop his flukes and cut a notch to indicate one harpoon (harpoons are expensive, must be recovered and used again). They thrust in a hollow lance and blow compressed air through it to make the carcass float, mark it with a flag, cast it adrift, and go after more.

THE WHALES were towed to the factory ship, lying in the open Ross Sea. We stripped the blubber while they lay alongside. Flensers in small boats sliced off strips which were winched up on wires by steam. Another wire, secured to the outside flipper, turned the whale. It was cold work down at sea level, bitter cold on deck too where the blubber was fed into the boilers.

Motion of the ship and the whale soon made open-sea work impossible. Wires carried away. Flensers were tipped into the sea, hauled out half-frozen. We had to find shelter. Captain Larsen took the ship into Discovery Inlet, named for Scott's ship in 1902. It was a poor harbor, this long crack in the ice barrier west

both developed in Norway, revolutionized the industry. This gunner shot 23 whales in one day.

C. E. ASH

of the Bay of Whales. Ice broke off, sometimes in 10,000-ton blocks. Blizzards roared down suddenly. If calm, the sea froze.

Here we shivered for three months. The huge whales, tongues extended like balloons and corrugated bellies blown up like enormous igloos, froze so hard that axes barely dented them. Flensers, working barehanded, cut into whale flesh and thrust their hands into the warm blood to thaw out frozen fingers.

The whales were there. Many days we couldn't work them. The steel ship was sheeted with ice. Winches froze up. Steam from the boilers froze wherever it touched. I felt sometimes as if my blood was freezing too, as I manhandled jawbones and chunks of blubber. Life in the little chasers was intolerable.

All January, all February, and well into March we stuck it out, working when possible. The continuous daylight and ice glare strained our eyes. It was hard to sleep, though we worked a 12-hour day—longer if the whales could be flensed. Danger was always with us. Often we had to steam to stay at anchor. Once we fetched up right under the dreadful barrier face. In that white hell we could not see.

At Discovery Inlet we were about 800 miles from the South Pole—as close as I ever got. I will settle for that.

By mid-March the whales had left. We had caught 228, most of them blues, the biggest over 100 feet long. These yielded 17,000 barrels of oil; we had hoped for at least 40,000, with luck 60,000. We steamed back to New Zealand. I was paid off at Port Chalmers with just enough for my passage home.

The expedition lost heavily. But the following year Captain Larsen was back again with stronger gear. It was a good season—and his last. He died in the ice. But his pioneering had shown that Antarctic whaling made financial sense.

Ships were built especially for this work, with ramps to haul whales aboard, enormous flensing decks, and steam-driven saws. But the slaughter of whales, hunted with ruthless efficiency on such a scale, was soon too great. International agreement has had to limit the kills, restrict the season to 100 days.

Today many factory ships steam to the Antarctic from Europe and Japan. They keep to sea, stay out of places like Discovery Inlet. They swiftly process not just the blubber but all the whale. Oil from the flesh will go into soap, glycerine, and margarine; the best meat is frozen or canned; bones and residue make chicken feed and fertilizers. Nothing is wasted, not even the squeal, for the poor whale makes no squeal.

"If the whales cried out, I couldn't carry on," a gunner once told me. But the whales die silently.

C. E. ASH

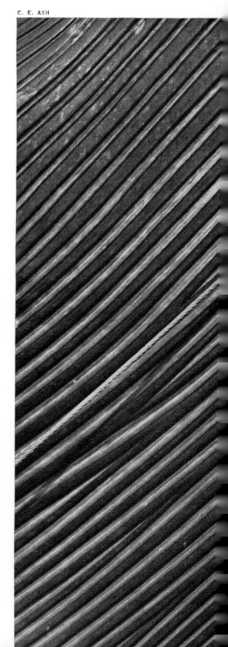

FLENSER UNZIPS *big blue's corrugated belly and peels off foot-thick blubber. The flesh also oozes oil. Giants like this yield 150 barrels, keep a factory ship at "full cook."* Balaena *of London (above), 535 feet, 21,000 tons deadweight, can process one an hour round the clock. Oil, meat, meal, by-products top $5,000 per whale. Crew's quarters stacked high fore and aft, twin funnels set wide apart give maximum clear deck space. Auxiliary vessel refuels alongside.*

364

MAN SAILS AGAIN FOR PLEASURE

THE yawl heels to a freshening breeze, lee rail awash, crew alert to any whim of wind and wave. Proud heir of caravel and longship, clipper and galleon, she is sailed with the knowledge and skill of centuries.

She is a yacht. She offers neither gold nor glory—only the song of taut rigging, the tang of salt spray, the freedom and adventure of the sea.

Rewards enough. In a complex, mechanized world, men seek the sense of fulfillment that comes from pitting brain and brawn against nature's forces.  Businessmen, factory workers, housewives, students take to the water in a vast armada— tall sloops and tiny dinghies, catboats and catamarans, runabouts and houseboats, cabin cruisers and skiffs.

Vacationers sign on as forecastle hands for windjammer cruises. A bold few face the deep alone in frail craft. Yachtsmen tune their thoroughbreds to perfection, drive them in classic races across storm-tossed oceans.

366

CHAPTER THIRTY-NINE

A classic ocean race: Newport to Bermuda

The boom of a starting gun sends 89 sailing craft toward a speck of land 635 miles over the horizon. The yawl *Finisterre* bobs among them, one of the smallest yachts in a race that pits men against their old adversary—the sea. Her owner-skipper, Carleton Mitchell, logs the story.

OUR START was inauspicious. In fact as the gun echoed that Saturday noon in June, we were moving backward, becalmed off Rhode Island in the grip of a tidal current sweeping past Brenton Reef Lightship. Our sails hung limp and useless. Fine way for *Finisterre* to go after the Bermuda Trophy!

Then a faint breath struck in from the southwest, and we set our big nylon balloon jib. *Finisterre* crept past the lightship. Within minutes the wind freshened and hauled farther west, so we broke out a spinnaker, an even bigger and lighter sail. A few more minutes and the wind swung again, and back up went the ballooner. Working that way without cease, we gradually moved through our class. At dark we seemed to be leading.

We were a crew of seven, a well-salted group who had spent much of our lives in small boats. I was skipper and in charge of the starboard watch. Mate and port watch officer was Richard H. Bertram of Miami. His skill and seamanship guaranteed me peaceful sleep during my turns below. Henry K. Rigg and Edward B. Freeman filled out the starboard watch,

Lockwood M. Pirie and Corwith Cramer, Jr., the port. Henry Davis, our professional seaman, was responsible for maintenance.

"What do you do at night?" is the question asked most often of ocean-racing yachtsmen. The answer: You sail. The ocean never rests; neither can you. Even if you could, the open sea is too deep to anchor. Besides, there is an axiom: "Races are won at night."

The moon was bright that first night. *Finisterre* glided quietly over a silver sea, only the roiled water and trail of bubbles in her wake showing the miles spinning astern. A warm breeze still smelling of the land shaped the sails like carved ivory. The barometer held high and steady. The watch below drowsed off to the occasional click of winch pawls, the thrum of taut lines, the creak of blocks and bulkheads, the splash of bow waves.

We used the "hot bunk" system, each watch rolling into the warm bedding abandoned by those on deck. Over each bunk was slung a Pullman-type hammock for clothes just removed; underneath was a drawer for spare clothes. Every cubic inch of space must be

UNDER RACING SAILS, Finisterre *drives in the style that won the Bermuda Trophy three times for the author. He says that the red-topped spinnaker picks up the sun's heat on still days and generates thermal currents that move the boat.*

ONE EYE ON THE COMPASS *and one on the wind, the helmsman feels his way through a rolling sea. Sails snap a warning as the helm comes up, then settle back to work as he holds her off. Watch below relaxes with tea from galley (right) on seats that turn into bunks. Folded table on gimbals stays horizontal despite boat's rolling.*

B. ANTHONY STEWART, NATIONAL GEOGRAPHIC PHOTOGRAPHER, AND (ABOVE) CARLETON MITCHELL

used efficiently to cram aboard seven men and all their needs: food, water, and gear.

At dawn only three of the 89 starting boats were in sight, one close abeam, two appearing as tiny triangles of sail on the horizon. It was a reminder of the ocean's loneliness.

Our strategy for the race was based on the best possible way to cross the Gulf Stream. The U.S. Navy's Matthew Fontaine Maury, pioneer scientist of ocean navigation, described this vast Atlantic current as "a river in the ocean: in the severest droughts it never fails, and in the mightiest floods it never overflows; its banks and its bottom are of cold water, while its current is of warm; the Gulf of Mexico is its fountain, and its mouth is in the Arctic Seas. It is the Gulf Stream. There is in the world no other such majestic flow of waters. Its current is more rapid than the Mississippi or the Amazon, and its volume more than a thousand times greater."

Our plan was to steer to the west of the rhumb line, or direct compass course, until we reached the Gulf Stream. Then we would change course to bring the current on our beam, so that we would cross at right angles and not buck its five-knot flow. If our plan was sound, the stream would then carry us back to the rhumb line on the far side, helping rather than hindering us.

We took temperature readings of the water every half hour. An abrupt rise would mark the Gulf Stream. As we sailed over the deepening waters of the continental shelf, the water gradually rose from 61° to 69° F., where it remained constant.

The wind freshened. A veil of cloud slid under the sun, and the barometer began to fall. The sky took on the hard look that to a sailor means trouble. Crests began to slap on deck.

During the late afternoon I watched our jib carefully. It was the same gossamer nylon ballooner which had ghosted us past the lightship at the start. Now it bulged dangerously, but it was still the most effective sail on the boat. With any other jib we would lose speed.

Dick Bertram, coming on watch, asked, "What about the ballooner, Skipper?"

It was a difficult decision. If the wind went soft near the finish we might need it even more than we needed it at the moment. Yet the falling barometer, rising wind, and look of the sky seemed to indicate an advancing front which would bring still more wind.

"Let's take a chance on its holding," I said.

Two hours later I was awakened when the sail split to ribbons along the seams.

I came on deck as the port watch was muzzling the tattered remnants and hoisting a heavy Dacron genoa jib. *Finisterre* lurched to lumpy seas, and spray pelted the sails.

BUT SHE HAD BEEN BUILT for this, my dream ship: to carry sail and drive hard, to go anywhere in safety and in comfort. All my life I have sailed, and all my life thought of the perfect vessel. She had to be small enough to be handled by me alone and to lie snug in tiny harbors, yet spacious enough below decks to accommodate a crew in harmony for extended periods. She must be rugged enough to cross an ocean; fast enough to be exciting to race, yet easily handled, stable, and sea-kindly.

In short, she had to be a ship which had never existed and never could, in theory. I knew all too well the accepted dictum of marine design: "Every sailing vessel must be a compromise." And I wanted everything!

I had dreamed, and gradually a little ship had taken form. She would be a centerboard vessel, her retractable bronze plate dropping through a lead keel to increase draft when desired. She would have aboard every comfort that could be crammed into a small hull, yet incorporate every feature on deck and in her rig to make her the most advanced of racing craft. Weight would never be saved when it contributed to strength.

Her name had materialized years ago while I was looking on a chart at the cape at the northwestern corner of Spain.

Finisterre! When Roman legionaries first looked out over the vastness of the Atlantic from the headland's heights, legend has it that they thought they had come to the boundary of the earth. They called it "end of the land"— *Finis terrae.* A perfect name for a ship.

While *Finisterre* was under construction, experts shook their heads. She was to be 38 feet, 7 inches overall and 27 feet, 6 inches on the waterline, yet have a beam of 11 feet, 3 inches. Being only a little more than twice as long on the water as she was wide, my dream ship looked remarkably like a watermelon.

Into her capacious interior went a refrigerator, an automatic pilot, a shower bath, bookshelves, a depth finder, a radiotelephone, even a hi-fi and innumerable other items contributing to a good life but usually not found in a

CROSSING THE TURBULENT GULF STREAM, *a small boat is a lonely challenger of mighty elements.*

boat intended to race, where weight is considered fatal to speed. An engine was provided for motive power in calms, to generate electricity, and to turn the icebox compressor. In a race the propeller is clamped to keep it from turning. Use of it, except to recover a man overboard, would disqualify us.

As I stood on deck watching my little ship rush through the night, I was content. My dream of a perfect boat had at last come true.

AT 11 P.M. SUNDAY the half-hour water temperature reading jumped from 69° to 79°. The Gulf Stream! It was almost eerie to picture that great flow of warm tropic water under us sliding inexorably to the north and east, influencing the character of all the lands bordering the North Atlantic.

In the lash of big-boat weather, wave crests douse the decks, and a man is never dry.

Immediately we altered course. Here conditions were different, as sailors have found through the centuries. Because of the current, the seas are steeper and more confused; because of the difference in temperature, squalls of wind and rain are frequent.

Ghostly bursts of foam gleamed through the darkness as waves broke. Water thundered heavily over the lee deck. Rain became continuous, but we hardly noticed it because of the spray. Jet black squalls dotted the sky like raisins in a pudding.

So it went through the night and next day, even after we were past the main flow of the current. The climax arrived about midnight Monday. Bunny Rigg, huddled beside me in the cockpit, suddenly called, "Bad squall coming, Skipper. Looks like the worst yet!"

Racing yachtsmen battle
the clock as well as the sea

W HILE *skippers tune their yachts for an ocean race, officials handicap vessels to give each a chance, regardless of size or rig. The Cruising Club of America rates craft according to length, beam, ballast, sail area, and other factors. The starting gun sends each class on its way. At the finish line handicaps are subtracted from elapsed times; the yacht with the best corrected time wins.*

Since it began in 1906, the Bermuda Race has been a popular contest—but no picnic. One year ten out of 44 yachts were disabled en route. During the 1956 race that Carleton Mitchell describes, a vessel struck a coral reef and sank. Her crew clung to wreckage for more than six hours until rescued.

Ocean racing lures deepwater sailors to courses around the world: the long voyage from Los Angeles to Honolulu, the stormy one from Sydney to Hobart, Tasmania, the famous one from Cowes, England, around Fastnet Rock off Ireland, and back to Plymouth.

HAMILTON'S BUILDINGS *beam on little*

I had been watching it. An ominous arch extended across the sky, dark even against the ebony background. As we looked, it seemed to writhe and flatten.

"Can't hold course!" gasped Ned Freeman from the wheel. "We're getting a shift!"

The squall struck with a roar. Rain and spray blasted in our faces as from a high-pressure hose, physically painful. Lightning flared continuously, while simultaneous crashes of thunder shook the deck under our feet. *Finisterre* lay over, forced down by an enormous weight of wind. In the lurid light the sea looked calm, momentarily knocked flat.

Ned did a superb job of following the shifting wind. An accidental jibe could have cost us the main boom or mast or both. Within minutes the wind veered 180° as the front passed and the new weather system behind took charge. We were heading away from Ber-

muda as fast as *Finisterre* could travel. At nearly nine knots we porpoised and plunged from crest to trough with crashes that felt and sounded as if we were bouncing over sunken rocks. All hands joined to jibe ship, and we came back on course. Moments later the genoa blew out with a roar, and another sail had to be hoisted in its place.

After this walloping the wind held fresh from the east. *Finisterre* stormed along under almost full sail when many larger boats nearby were well shortened down. Finding the islands became our main worry. Clouds prevented our taking sun or star sights.

Tension mounted. In few other sports is suspense so long maintained. By Tuesday midnight we knew we must be making the crucial final approach if our dead-reckoning calculations were correct. Suddenly there was a patch of open sky. Corey Cramer, our navi-

Finisterre *(foreground). To right of big Bermudiana Hotel lies the pink Royal Bermuda Yacht Club.*

gator, had gone below exhausted after hours of waiting. In desperation I seized a sextant and sighted Polaris and Altair while Bunny Rigg kept me from going overboard. The calculation put us 40 miles ahead of our reckoning. We altered course and before dawn picked up the loom of lights.

At 9:10 A.M. Wednesday, Bermuda time, *Finisterre* swept across the finish line off St. David's Head, carrying full sail. Suddenly tension was gone, and we were tired. We dropped our spinnaker and hoisted a small jib for the sail to Hamilton.

As we made our way among the reefs a motorboat plunged toward us. A man in the stern held up one finger, then tried to balance himself to make a photograph.

"He means we won!" exclaimed Woodie.

We had all been fooled into premature celebration before. "Ask him," I said.

"Did we win?" yelled Woodie.

"You did fine!" the man called back.

"Who did win?"

"You have a chance!" came the reply.

"Don't ask again," growled Dick Bertram. "He'll put us back to last!"

Two hours later we sailed through Two Rock Passage into the natural amphitheater of Hamilton Harbor—blue water, a backdrop of white, pink, and pastel houses, the Royal Bermuda Yacht Club at center stage. When we were escorted through the anchored fleet to the place of honor nearest the club, we knew we had won—by 14 minutes!

It had been big-boat weather, the hardest race for 20 years. Many boats were still at sea —some would not finish for days. Yet *Finisterre* set a corrected time record of 64 hours and became the smallest craft ever to win the modern Bermuda race.

CHAPTER FORTY

The golden age of yachting

From Newport to Cannes, everyone who was anyone had a yacht in Victoria's day. Some staked fortunes on a race for the *America*'s Cup. Edwards Park finds the old fever still mounts at the drop of a challenge.

A NASTY CHOP kicked up Rhode Island Sound, and the fleet of spectator yachts reacted according to size. Clipper-bowed oceangoing dowagers out of Newport nodded graciously to one another; sloop-rigged debutantes twisted energetically at their anchors. Our little cabin cruiser flung herself about senselessly. She had no business being this far offshore, and we knew it. But we were young and brave—and determined to watch the cup boats.

The first sight of them was unbelievable—two ghostly mountain peaks bearing down on us, dwarfing every vessel that lined the course. They passed us so fast that I have only a faded mental snapshot to remember them by: long, slippery hulls barely twitching in those waves; towering, translucent sails; a score of white-clad men lying prone on each deck. And the sound! A great stage whisper of speed and power that rose and then fell away.

These were the mighty J boats, 135-foot racing machines spreading more than 7,500 square feet of sail, that fought it out in the 1937 *America*'s Cup series. T.O.M. Sopwith's blue-hulled *Endeavour II*, the British challenger, lost to Harold S. Vanderbilt's *Ranger* that day, as she did on the other three days of the best-of-seven match. *Endeavour II* was a fine sloop and well sailed. *Ranger* was a wonder, the best J boat ever built—and the last.

War came, and *Ranger* was scrapped. So ended an era when millionaires staked fortunes on tremendous yachts just to compete in 30-mile races for a potbellied piece of mid-Victorian silverware.

RACE SPECTATORS *in the '80's gently applauded from sumptuous steam yachts. White-jacketed steward serves owner and elegant guests on the awninged afterdeck.*

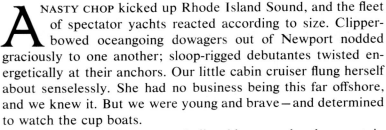

AMERICA *won the $500*

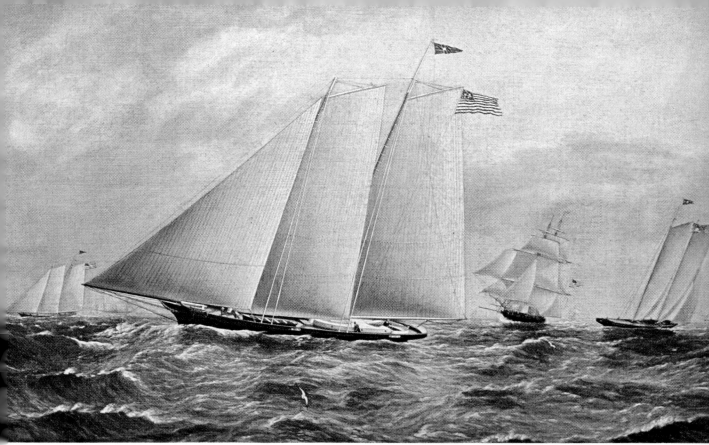

THE YACHT "AMERICA" BY JAMES E. BUTTERSWORTH, AND (BELOW) "SEEING THE YACHT RACE" BY T. DE THULESTRUP, HARPERS WEEKLY, 1886;
BOTH MARINE HISTORICAL ASSOCIATION, MYSTIC. LEFT: LIBRARY OF CONGRESS

urn (left) off England's Isle of Wight in 1851. Since then $30,000,000 has been spent racing for it.

America's Cup Defenders

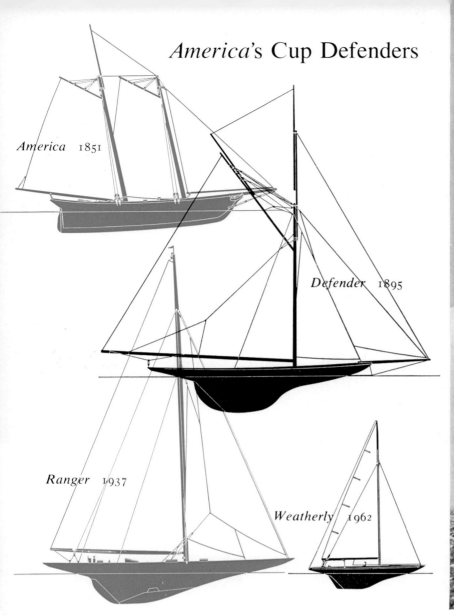

America 1851

Defender 1895

Ranger 1937

Weatherly 1962

TOWERING J BOATS *race for the finish in 1937 Buzzards Bay regatta.* Ranger *leads*
Rainbow, Endeavour I, Endeavour II, *and* Yankee. *Her 18,000-square-foot parachute*
spinnaker, largest sail ever made, dwarfs crew. Designer Nat Herreshoff gave sharp-lined
Defender *(lower left) a deep fin keel ballasted with 85 tons of lead to keep her stiff*
in a breeze. Lightly built, she lasted only seven years. Rugged schooner America
(upper left) served on both sides in the Civil War, was not broken up till 1945.

It all started in 1851 when a group of New Yorkers sailed their new schooner to Cowes to try her against the finest English yachts. *America,* just over 100 feet, with raking masts and a gilded eagle on her transom, finally entered a chaotic regatta with 14 vessels. She started poorly, passed the fleet, and breezed home with a healthy lead. Queen Victoria, on the royal yacht, was informed of *America's* prowess.

"Oh, indeed! And which is second?"

"Madam, there is no second."

There was, actually: a little cutter named *Aurora* which would have come close to winning if there had been such a thing as corrected time. But *America's* turn of speed startled the British; some hinted that she concealed a propeller. They gave her a 100-guinea cup. In 1870 they began trying to get it back.

These were the days when sportsmen raced in big vessels piled high with canvas and weighed down with trappings of the good life. The cabin of *Galatea,* challenger of 1886, boasted potted plants and leopard-skin rugs. Such vessels symbolized affluence. As J. P.

379

COLUMBIA, FIRST OF THE 12-METER DEFENDERS, *marked the modern trend to less expensive cup races. Owned by a syndicate, she sailed to victory in 1958 with an amateur crew led by Briggs Cunningham (right). About 69 feet overall, the 12's can compete for years with far less maintenance than the huge, fragile J's.*

Morgan said, "If you have to ask what it costs to run a yacht, you can't afford one."

Bitterness often haunted the cup races. The Earl of Dunraven, who challenged twice in the 1890's, howled about unruly spectator boats, suspected Yankee trickery in waterline measurements of the *Defender,* refused to heave to after fouling her.

Then in 1899 an Irish-born Scot with an endearing manner and a determined love of racing sailed into the fray aboard his steam yacht *Erin.* Sir Thomas Lipton, the tea king, built five beautiful sloops, all named *Shamrock,* tried five times to lift "the ould mug," and won instead the lasting affection of the American people. An English lady once suggested to him that the Americans "put something in the water over there which makes you lose."

"I completely agree with you, madam," replied Lipton. "It is a better boat."

When *Shamrock V* sailed over for the 1930 races, it seemed that all America wanted "our Tommy," then 80 years old, to win. All but one. Harold Vanderbilt of the defender *Enterprise* was loath to go down in history as the first skipper to lose the *America*'s Cup. His J boat was a marvel with 162-foot duralumin mast, flat-topped "Park Avenue" boom to give the foot of the mainsail an aerodynamic curve, and below, winches run by an eight-man "black gang" that never saw a race. She and her skipper were too good for the dainty *Shamrock V.*

"I canna win," admitted Lipton. But in an eruption of American sentiment, $16,000 was raised and the old gentleman was given a gold cup. On it was etched a picture of the old mug.

Today's cup races match 12-meter sloops about half as big and half as expensive as the $600,000 J boats. I watched one being built in a quiet old New England boatyard. Some 30 men were smoothing down her outer skin of Honduras mahogany. In this age of precision tools and measuring instruments, they used block planes and sandpaper as did their grandfathers before them, pausing now and then to squint along those lovely hull contours, to caress the smooth flank with gnarled, knowing hands. It was good to see.

I watched her slide down the ways and bob free of her cradle, coming to life as surely as does a newborn baby. And I felt a little of the fever that has come upon men for more than a century when their big, gleaming vessels aim sharp bows at that ugly old cup.

WEATHERLY SOARS HOME *to win the first race of the 1962 Cup series. "Horns shrieked, cheers roared from spectators packing excursion boats," recalls Melville Bell Grosvenor, National Geographic's editor. Astern of the contestants wallowed a mass of small boats—"More than I've seen since Dunkirk," remarked an Australian come to urge on Gretel, the challenger. The Aussie 12-meter competed courageously, won one race. But Bus Mosbacher (lower right) skippered Weatherly to four wins off Newport, successfully defending the Cup for the United States.*

383

YANKEE DISPLAYS HER WARDROBE *atop a long Pacific swell. A lad works on fore-topsail yard.*

CHAPTER FORTY-ONE

Yankee's wanderworld

Irving and Electa Johnson love sailing, adventure, and young people. Seven times they have combined these joys, cruising the world, nosing their beloved *Yankee* into seldom-seen ports, always with a new crew of boys and girls. Here they go on a typical 18-month, 40,000-mile voyage.

IN GLOUCESTER our crew of green hands had taken one dizzy look at *Yankee*'s cloud-scraping rigging and vowed, "Boy, you'll never catch me up there!" But as we left Massachusetts and romped past Cape Hatteras toward the Caribbean and Panama, our amateur Magellans quickly became old salts, setting sails with the mates, driving *Yankee* 1,300 miles the first ten days. It was a fast start for a voyage around the globe that would last 18 leisurely months.

We Johnsons had with us three mates, a ship's doctor, the cook (the only paid hand), and a score of boys and girls just beyond high-school age who shared the work and expenses. We chose those we would like to have join our family for a long voyage. The family included our 11-year-old son Arthur.

We were living on *Yankee* in Gloucester when he came aboard at seven weeks. At 22 months he climbed *Yankee*'s rigging alone, at sea. Now his pleasure was to dance on the foot-ropes; his sorrow to sit at his desk and study. Often his classroom was high in the rigging.

Yankee, a steel-hulled former North Sea pilot schooner, 96 feet overall, is rigged as a brigantine—square sails on the foremast, fore-and-aft on the mainmast, and staysails between. When we set all 7,775 square feet of canvas and nylon, *Yankee* was a noble sight.

Fair breezes saw us into the Caribbean. By then our young crew had picked up the lingo and the rolling gait of their new calling. When we snapped the fore-topmast in a sudden squall, they hit the deck like veterans to help secure the wildly swinging wreckage in driving rain and inky darkness. It took us all morning to lower the ton of tangled gear.

Threading the Panama Canal, we headed into the Pacific. As we approached Salinas, Ecuador, Arthur had his 12th birthday. While exploring the rigging for hidden gifts, he forgot about school until offered a cake frosted with the words, "Happy birthday, scholar."

From Ecuador we sailed 520 miles west to the Galapagos Islands. Named by the Spaniards for the giant tortoises found there, these volcanic eminences support a tiny band of settlers who like to be left alone, a few Ecuadorian convicts who want to be elsewhere, and a freak show of strange animals.

Old whalers once dumped the turtles into their holds as fresh meat for long voyages. Survivors share their domain with dragonlike three-foot iguanas. Seals and penguins coexist, cooled by the Peru Current. We captured a baby seal and put it in the ship's bathtub, where it flopped around happily. We called it *Yankee*'s official seal.

Post Office Bay still has its "mailbox"—a barrel on a pole. The whalers, often at sea for two or three years, left letters here to be picked up by others homeward bound. We tried it, and a passing yacht deposited our mail in the States some months later.

On the way to Easter Island, 14 days and 1,700 miles to the southwest, we became familiar with the Pacific—its long swells, sometimes 200 yards from crest to crest, rolling unceasingly past. The four-to-eight watches

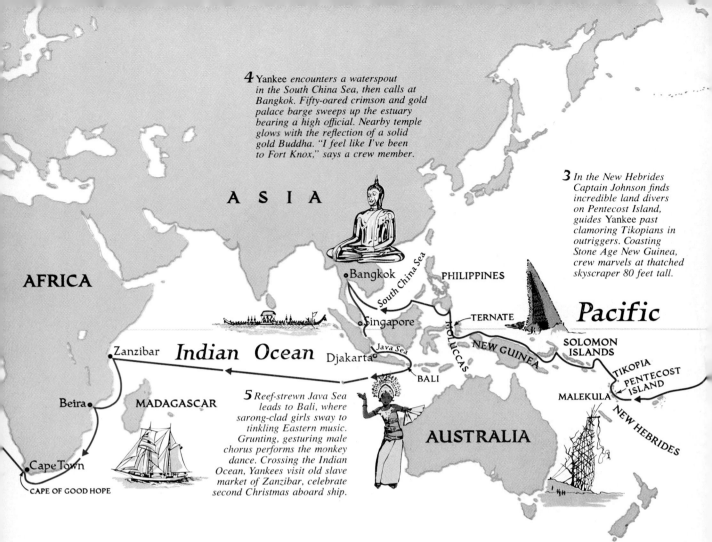

4 Yankee *encounters a waterspout in the South China Sea, then calls at Bangkok. Fifty-oared crimson and gold palace barge sweeps up the estuary bearing a high official. Nearby temple glows with the reflection of a solid gold Buddha. "I feel like I've been to Fort Knox," says a crew member.*

3 *In the New Hebrides Captain Johnson finds incredible land divers on Pentecost Island, guides* Yankee *past clamoring Tikopians in outriggers. Coasting Stone Age New Guinea, crew marvels at thatched skyscraper 80 feet tall.*

ASIA

AFRICA

Bangkok

PHILIPPINES

South China Sea

Singapore

TERNATE

Pacific

Zanzibar   *Indian Ocean*   Djakarta

Java Sea

MOLUCCAS

NEW GUINEA

SOLOMON ISLANDS

TIKOPIA

PENTECOST ISLAND

Beira   MADAGASCAR

BALI

MALEKULA

NEW HEBRIDES

5 *Reef-strewn Java Sea leads to Bali, where sarong-clad girls sway to tinkling Eastern music. Grunting, gesturing male chorus performs the monkey dance. Crossing the Indian Ocean, Yankees visit old slave market of Zanzibar, celebrate second Christmas aboard ship.*

AUSTRALIA

Cape Town

CAPE OF GOOD HOPE

Yankee, riding the winds of adventure, carries young Magellans

CAPTAIN JOHNSON *plots his brigantine's course.*

came to breakfast with enthusiastic accounts of better sunrises than ever, and after supper almost everyone would gather on deck to see what the sunset would be like that night. Sometimes we had gorgeous shows of phosphorescence in the water alongside.

Life is never dull on such stretches. One day Lorita the parrot was moved aft in her cage and set on some oil drums along the lee rail. Suddenly the ship took a quick jump, and Lorita, cage and all, went over the side.

"Parrot overboard!" we yelled.

Looking astern, we could see Lorita, very distressed, perched in one corner of the cage, bobbing up and down in mid-ocean.

"All hands on deck!" The ship must be put about to save Lorita. At top speed the crew took in the light sails. The skipper climbed aloft and directed *Yankee* toward that small speck.

As the ship rounded up, the tallest sailor, hanging from the bobstay under the bowsprit, reached down and scooped up the lifesaving

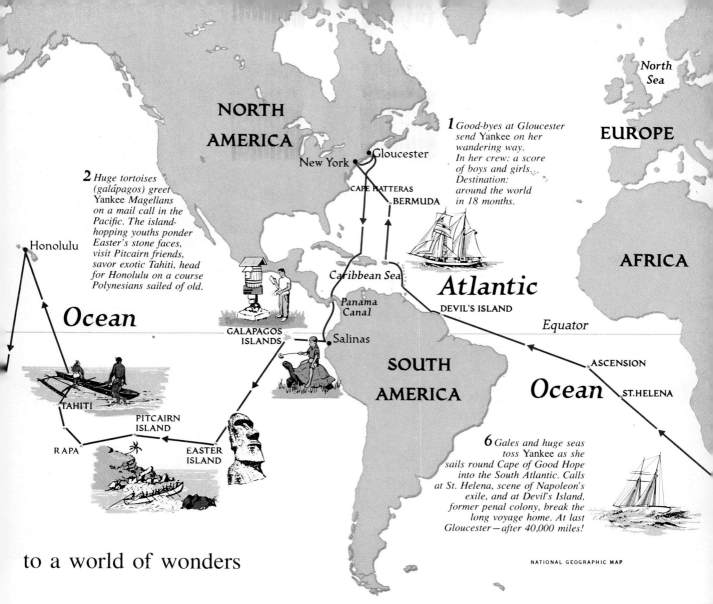

NORTH AMERICA

Gloucester
New York

1 *Good-byes at Gloucester send* Yankee *on her wandering way. In her crew: a score of boys and girls. Destination: around the world in 18 months.*

EUROPE

North Sea

2 *Huge tortoises (galápagos) greet* Yankee Magellans *on a mail call in the Pacific. The island-hopping youths ponder Easter's stone faces, visit Pitcairn friends, savor exotic Tahiti, head for Honolulu on a course Polynesians sailed of old.*

CAPE HATTERAS
BERMUDA

Honolulu

AFRICA

Ocean

Caribbean Sea

Atlantic

DEVIL'S ISLAND

Panama Canal

GALAPAGOS ISLANDS

Salinas

Equator

ASCENSION

SOUTH AMERICA

Ocean

ST. HELENA

TAHITI

PITCAIRN ISLAND

RAPA

EASTER ISLAND

6 *Gales and huge seas toss* Yankee *as she sails round Cape of Good Hope into the South Atlantic. Calls at St. Helena, scene of Napoleon's exile, and at Devil's Island, former penal colony, break the long voyage home. At last Gloucester — after 40,000 miles!*

to a world of wonders

NATIONAL GEOGRAPHIC MAP

cage with a soaked parrot inside. Screaming but unharmed, Lorita dried herself in the sun.

Easter island is now just one big sheep ranch. We inspected the famous stone statues, carved from a crater wall during a vanished golden age. Some weighing 30 tons or more had been moved several miles to stand guard over huge burial platforms, or *ahus*. How they were transported across this rolling, practically treeless country remains a mystery. A few 18th century navigators, among them Captain Cook, witnessed native festivals connected with the statues, but later, clan warfare swept the island and the stone sentinels beside the ahus were overthrown.

In 1862 more than a thousand Easter Islanders were carried off in a slave raid to work on Peru's guano islands. When protests finally availed, a hundred survivors were sent home. But smallpox broke out at sea and only 15 reached the island. The disease spread; population shrank. As the culture languished, so did all knowledge of the great stone statues.

From Easter, *Yankee* sailed to Pitcairn Island, where we visit on each voyage. We have made fast friends among the descendants of the *Bounty* mutineers. One year we temporarily marooned most of our crew with the hospitable Pitcairners and took aboard 45 island men for a special trip to Henderson Island, 110 miles away. Here they cut logs of miro wood, used to build their famed longboats, to make furniture, and to carve curios. They have exhausted the supply on Pitcairn, and must make this long and sometimes dangerous voyage every year or so. *Yankee* served them well as a "freighter."

It was on a later visit that one of our crew, diving off Bounty Bay, discovered the *Bounty*'s stern anchor in 50 feet of water (page 172). Wrenching it free was like pulling teeth.

Yankee now bore us to the magnificent crater harbor of Rapa and on to Tahiti, fragrant with

387

FROM THE MAIN SPREADER, *girls gaze at Rapa's volcanic spires, as steep as the topmast. The island proved a South Sea paradise—for boys. Local youths were working in nearby Tahiti; their belles were in a mood to kidnap any handsome male.*

At Galapagos, Yankee's crew touch up the old barrel post office established by whalers. Stopping by during the War of 1812, Capt. David Porter of U.S.S. Essex *read British mail, learned the whereabouts of enemy ships, and captured 12.*

What culture fashioned the strange statues of Easter Island? With pursed lips the idols (left) guard their secret.

388

IRVING JOHNSON. UPPER LEFT: MALCOLM EVANS. LOWER: LYDIA EDES

tropical flowers. We stole into tree-fringed Papeete and tied up to the main street. Who can fail to love this island's bright lagoons and mountain streams? Its people, full of little graces, combine the best of France and Polynesia. We never saw them worry.

At dinner, Americans, French, British, Polynesians, and Chinese made a gay, garlanded company. A dreamy Tahitian orchestra played hula music under a pale moon. Bashful Americans were pushed onto the dance floor and compelled to do the hula. Arthur, attending his first stay-up-late party, was an exception; no one had to urge him. Shining with joy, he danced with the hula girls to his heart's content. During pauses he sat between a grass-skirted girl and a handsome guitar player. Good boy! If he can remember this all his life, who will have a Tahiti souvenir to compare?

Squalls beset nearly every watch on the 2,300-mile run to Honolulu. Night and day we were in and out of oilskins. To avoid falling out of our bunks we propped up the mattress edges. *Yankee* proved her North Sea pedigree. Often driving at ten knots, she ran 175 miles on her best day and averaged 140.

WE WONDERED how the Polynesians had made this South Sea-to-Hawaii run in their double canoes hundreds of years before Captain Cook. At Honolulu we found the answer in a 40-foot replica of the old catamarans. We found both canoes decked over. Each was deep enough to stand upright in. Four below-deck bunks surprised us.

A flat section shaped like an airplane wing bridged the twin hulls. Here we lay, stripped to swimming trunks, when we took a ride. Up went the sail. We skimmed past Waikiki and Diamond Head and got out in the channel. "If we go any faster we'll take off," yelled our first mate, grabbing a lifeline.

Indeed, the catamaran at times did take off, leaping airborne from crest to crest. We figured her top speed at 25 knots or more.

A long stretch at sea followed Hawaii, and

389

AT TIKOPIA, *north of New Hebrides, outriggers swarm alongside as natives vie for trade. Warily,*

we could sense our young crew's dreaming of dances, porterhouse steaks, and other landlubber luxuries. They craved excitement. Malekula in the New Hebrides was just the place for it. Malekula is the home of the undefeated, uncivilized Big Nambas. Until recently they had a reputation for murder and cannibalism.

A French planter told us about the tribesmen. "Pigs mean everything. Not for pork but for prestige. And it is not thoroughbred pigs that count, but those with circular tusks. The wives feed the pigs, even cook for them. Husbands have been known to strangle women for carelessness with pigs."

Sixteen of us, with native carriers, trekked to Amok, a Big Nambas village. The girls in our party were horrified by the beaten look of the Big Nambas women. They shrank out of

ALAN PIERCE

Captain Johnson let only a chief and his aide aboard (left). Just such throngs greeted Captain Cook.

our path. In lieu of a wedding ring, each wife had two upper front teeth knocked out.

We watched 64 dancers being decked out. Makeup artists painted their bodies black and orange, tied rattles to their ankles, and tucked tail-like fans of leaves under their belts. The dancers donned four-foot headdresses, each with a thousand feathers.

Boom! boom! boom! went the village tom-

toms. With balletlike precision the dancers moved in columns, squares, and circles. With each step 64,000 feathers shook, 128 ankle castanets rattled, 64 tails swayed. The women shrank back like seaweed in a current whenever the men neared. We saw that this was a form of politeness, like a bow. A woman's head must never be higher than a man's.

Darkness set in, and we withdrew for sup-

ROGER BELLINGER

per. The dancers took no intermission. Bon-
fires gleamed; drums beat louder than ever.
We tried to sleep. Torches borne past our shelter and the ominous tom-toms kept us awake.
Three shadowy figures came in. We watched
like children pretending to be asleep. They
moved from one of us to another, feeling our
flesh as though judging the quality of beef. No
one dared speak, but the skipper grasped his
heavy flashlight as a club and prepared to sell
our lives dearly. At last the natives seemed
satisfied and withdrew. In the morning we attempted a polite good-bye. The savage mob,
now finished dancing, ignored us — a breach
of manners we gladly overlooked.

AT PENTECOST ISLAND, a near neighbor of
Malekula, we witnessed an incredible
performance by land divers — natives
who leap headfirst from tall towers, not into
water but onto land. Carefully measured vines,
attached to their ankles, check them just as
their heads touch the softened earth and keep
them from breaking their necks.

We were led to the tower, a maze of tree
trunks lashed with vines, on the side of a
cleared jungle hill. At various heights platforms jutted from it like diving boards. From
each board looped long, curling vines.

The ceremony began with chanting, whistling, cheering dancers; then the jumpers
climbed the flimsy-looking tower. First came

GOING DOWN! *A land diver of Pentecost
Island plunges headfirst toward the ground
to prove his manhood. Trailing vines
lashed to his ankles are just long enough
to allow his head to touch the soft,
spaded earth of the landing spot. When
he reaches the end of his rope the diver
is snapped back by the vines and the recoil
of the rickety, fiber-bound tower. With
skill, he will land on his feet.*

*Yankee's crew learned that the daredevil
New Hebrides custom began with an unfaithful
wife who leaped thus from a palm tree to flee
her vengeful husband. Not to be outdone,
the island men adopted her trick.*

*Dour New Guinea natives (opposite) show
their status with shells and parrot wings.*

an eight-year-old boy, determined to risk his neck to prove he was a man. A relative bound the frayed, softened vine ends to the slender ankles, and the youngster advanced to the end of his platform, 25 feet high. He forced a smile, bravely waved a spray of leaves and cast it earthward. Then he followed it into space.

At exactly the right moment, the vines tautened. The platform took the shock, then partly collapsed. This slowed the boy's fall. As his head touched earth, the tensed vines recoiled, snapped the lad back, then dumped him on the ground, unhurt.

As the jumps got higher, excitement mounted. Near the day's end the bravest jumper of all climbed to the topmost platform and stood, lonely and slim, against the sky. He made a little speech to the crowd, then tossed his spray of leaves as if in gallant salute. Calling up the final spark of his courage, he leaped off and out, an arching drop of 78 feet!

Timed to a split second, the platform absorbed the shock and braked the diver's fall. His head touched the earth, the elastic vines convulsed and pulled him back into the air.

One vine broke! But with the dexterity of a cat he landed on his feet. Women rushed up, tugged at his hair, and splashed water in his face, Pentecost's treatment for the brave.

FAIR WIND brought *Yankee* to exotic shores in the Solomon Islands and along the north coast of New Guinea toward the Moluccas. On this leg we crossed Wallace's line, named for Alfred Russel Wallace, British naturalist whose theory on the origin of the species by natural selection was presented at the same time as Charles Darwin's. Studying the fauna of the Malay archipelago, Wallace found that an invisible line, sometimes only a narrow channel between islands, divides the domain of Australian animals such as kangaroos from that of Oriental beasts like tigers, elephants, and rhinos.

In Ternate, one of the Moluccas, we were definitely at the threshold of the East. Proof positive was Scheherazade (her real name), daughter of a sultan. She spoke English and called herself Rinny, pronouncing it Ree-nee. Only 17 and beautiful, with smooth Malay skin and huge brown eyes, she took the boys on a jeep tour of the island and completely captured their affections.

They plagued her with questions: "Can you marry anybody you wish? Does he have to be a Moslem? Why don't you come to the United States?" We heard one lad say, "Gosh, if the fellows back home could hear me calling you 'Princess,' it would fracture them!"

In her father's palace Rinny put aside her Western ways and became the Malay princess, presiding over a retinue of servants and wearing a batik sarong, embroidered silk jacket, and dangling diamond earrings. But on our final day in Ternate we found the sultan's daughter down under *Yankee*'s keel in dungarees, navy shirt, and diving helmet. The boys were showing her the wonders of a coral formation. After we cast off, Rinny jumped into her jeep and drove away. As *Yankee* slipped past the palace, we saw her, a lonely little figure, waving good-bye from a balcony.

Another parting awaited us in the Philippines, for Arthur had to go back to school in the States. His grandmother came out by liner, picked him up, and deposited his nine-year-old brother Robert, whose turn it was to join us.

We crossed the South China Sea to Thailand and berthed a delightful two weeks in Bangkok, with its fascinating bazaars and temples. Then on to Singapore, Djakarta, and finally Bali, land of palms and paddies, of handsome people and smiling faces.

Here we saw the *ketjak*, the monkey dance. Straight from the Ramayana, the poetic bible of the Balinese, it tells of the monkey army that came at the king's command and rescued his beloved from the forces of evil.

About 150 men dancers sit in the firelight,

YANKEE POKES HER NOSE *into a Solomon Islands village, built on a reef to foil fierce mountain tribesmen who cannot swim. In Bali, tightly clad dancers speak with their hands (right). Here cremation is believed to release souls. Bodies are carried in towers (far right) by 150 men, then placed in ornate wooden bulls, blessed, and burned.*

hands and arms writhing. "Aaaaaaaah UH!" they chant, rising and jumping.

"Chuk!" sputters one side, and "Chuk!" comes the answer from the other. "Chuk! Chuk!" The cadence quickens, the antiphony never breaks. "Chuk-chuk-chuk-chukchuk-chukchukchukchukchuk!"

The *ketjak* ends, the dancers disperse. You are irrationally surprised to find them men, so perfect is the monkey illusion.

H EADING FOR ZANZIBAR, *Yankee* sailed for 25 days across the vast and lonely Indian Ocean. We wrote letters, overhauled gear, and painted ship. We even found time for a bridge tournament.

The ship driving steadily along felt good to us and generated the familiar feelings that make sailing fascinating. There is the sensation of lying in a groove instead of a flat bunk as the vessel heels over, and the equally familiar jolt when you suddenly forsake that groove as the ship comes about and leans the other way. Your ear, a foot from the blue ocean overside, grows used to the sound of seas roaring past. You identify the activities of the crew over-

IRVING JOHNSON. BELOW RIGHT: ALAN PIERCE. OPPOSITE: STEPHEN H. JOHNSON

LIFE ABOARD YANKEE: *barefoot and busy. Louise Stewart knitted in oilskins during foul weather, did a man's job swabbing down in fair. Cook Don Crawford, pictured off Easter Island, replied to critics, "My bread will rise in the roughest sea." With sextant and charts the skipper (far right) taught navigation. The Johnsons made their last cruise aboard* Yankee *in 1957-8.*

head by the deck noises. A sudden rush of many feet forward means something has let go in the headsails. A roar from the officer of the watch—the helmsman has wandered off course. The tune of the rigging tells the force of the wind. And the impression that someone is trying to jump through the deck only means that his feet are cold.

On deck, noontime brings out the navigators with sextants. During the early evening someone is consulting the Light List and noting peculiarities: red flashes, white flashes, varying intervals and candlepower.

Bright moonlight flooded white Arab buildings as we arrived at our African destination at two o'clock one morning. The island of Zanzibar was once known as a clove plantation, an ivory emporium, and a slave market.

We saw some curving ivory tusks carried on naked black shoulders, but a blight called "sudden death" had struck the clove trees. The island's slave trade was no more, though barred windows suggested slave times, and some houses were considered haunted because slaves had been sealed alive in their masonry.

Exploring Zanzibar, our boys wandered into alleys so narrow that they could touch buildings on either side. Bearded Arabs, curved daggers at their waists, strode by, dressed in robes belted with silver. Porters with huge loads shouted for passageway. Moslem ladies veiled themselves in baggy black until only their dark eyes peeped out of cloth cages.

WE WERE ROUNDING the Cape of Good Hope when a southwester of almost hurricane force tested *Yankee* as she had never been tested before. We doused all but two tiny sails, but these were enough to heel the brigantine over until her lee bulwarks dipped under. Wind pressure on the main staysail's steel traveler bent that two-inch rod six inches out of true! But *Yankee* rode every sea. Most of the time her deck was dry; we never had to close the companionways.

We touched at hospitable Cape Town, at the St. Helena of Napoleon's exile, at Ascension Island, at the emerald islands of the West Indies, and then struck for Bermuda.

Our last visit was to New York. Coal dust, the first encountered in 18 months, settled on deck. Some New Yorkers, habitually blasé, did not look up from their newspapers as they churned past us on office-bound ferries.

Finally we set all sails and flew home to Gloucester. "Down stuns'ls! Furl t'gallant! Down fisherman! Down mains'l!" On shore, parents had been waving since we hove in sight; now tears sparkled in their eyes.

Yankee's first line hit old Rocky Neck dock just 18 months and 4½ minutes from the time she left. The skipper apologized for being late!

397

"ALL I ASK IS A TALL SHIP. . . ." *But the author made do with a leaky dugout and awning sails.*

CHAPTER FORTY-TWO

Sea fever

"I must down to the seas again, to the lonely sea and the sky. . . ." The haunting lines of Masefield's "Sea Fever" lure 18-year-old John E. Schultz into making an incredible 13-month voyage from the Andes, down the Amazon, across the Caribbean to Miami—alone in a dugout canoe!

IT WAS spring and the summer was open for travel. When I reread that poem by John Masefield I felt an irresistible call. I too would go "down to the seas again." In my case, though, it wasn't "again," for I knew little of the ocean.

I was visiting my family in Ecuador when I heard the summons to adventure. My reply was simple: I would start eastward from Quito, the capital, and somehow reach the University of Chicago in time for the fall quarter. As it turned out, I was a year late for school!

Early in May, I started walking over the Andes. I carried an old double-barreled shotgun, a 50-pound pack, a few charts, a compass, some sandwiches, $21—and a wealth of misconceptions. The first few days over a rough mule trail and through a 13,000-foot pass were discouraging, although the Indians were friendly and I had no trouble buying food. After a week—and some 130 miles—my feet were raw. But I had reached the headwaters of the Rio Napo, which flows through the jungles of Ecuador into Peru to join the Amazon.

I bought a dugout canoe from a native. Sixteen feet long and as many inches wide, it would turn over at a sharp glance. Copying the short, choppy stroke of the natives, I learned to paddle in the first hundred miles of rapids. I passed the home of primitive Aucas, Indians with a reputation for killing white men. I didn't see one, nor was I favored with a spear flung from a riverbank.

My vague charts indicated that I had walked and paddled nearly a thousand miles when I arrived at Iquitos, Peru, my money almost gone. Five weeks working as a mechanic enabled me to buy a more stable Indian dugout of the *casco* (shell) type. Seventeen feet long, it cost $11 and was destined to take me more than 5,000 miles in ten months. I christened her *Sea Fever* after the poem.

Nowhere else have I heard of this type of dugout—one with a beam much greater than the diameter of the tree used. The builder hollows a log of light *cedro* (South American cedar) through a narrow slit, then heats it over a fire, open side down. The opening is gradually stretched to the right width.

Sea Fever left Iquitos on August 4, headed down the Amazon toward the distant Atlantic. Even as far upstream as Peru the muddy, slow-moving river is often more than a mile wide. In late afternoon I would usually be too far from shore to find an Indian hut, so I'd tie up to a floating tree or a hyacinth raft, sling my hammock under a mosquito net, and sleep while drifting. Sometimes I awoke 30 miles downstream. Never once did I drift into the wrong channel, for floating debris found the strongest current.

On August 25, the day before my 19th birthday, I arrived at Manaus, Brazil. Having paddled 2,050 miles downstream, I was ready to try sailing. A friendly carpenter helped me brace *Sea Fever*, raise the sides to add eight inches of freeboard, and install a centerboard and rudder. I had heard that a yawl rig was good for single-handed cruising, so I stepped two masts. With the help of an awning maker,

I fashioned the mainsail, mizzen, and jib out of blue-and-white striped awning canvas. They were still in fair shape nine months and 4,000 miles later. I got several books on sailing. Luckily I met an officer on an American cargo ship, moored up the river to take on Brazil nuts. Aghast at my scanty plans and equipment, he gave me a plastic sextant, a nautical almanac, and a copy of *American Practical Navigator*. I must confess I wasn't very impressed by the importance of his gift just then.

Sea Fever sailed from Manaus on September 21 with several hundred pounds of iron ballast and a variety of canned food. At first I had trouble bringing her about. The wind was always from downstream and I had to tack. But soon, with my usual overconfidence, I felt I knew everything about sailing.

Six days out of Manaus and 450 miles away, I met a stiff breeze and learned differently. In my ignorance I had put all my sheets on the same cleat, the mainsheet underneath with a knot on top! Suddenly an eddy swung *Sea Fever* around, putting all the sails aback. I found out rather quickly one doesn't tie down the sheets on a small boat! Before I could free the first one, I capsized. I thought of the ballast, grabbed a knife, and started cutting it loose as the canoe sank. Luckily, I managed to free enough weight to bring her back up to the surface. A villager saw me standing on my overturned canoe, waving a pair of pajama pants. He towed me to shore.

REFITTED, I continued down the Amazon. Quite a few squalls struck me, some of them heavier than any I met on the ocean. One night a squall blew me to the river-bank. I jumped into the water to hold *Sea Fever* off. Suddenly I felt a sharp, tearing bite at my ankle and quickly scrambled back in the boat. I found a small hole in my leg, probably the bite of a piranha. These small, vicious, carnivorous fish usually travel in schools of hundreds, even thousands, that can quickly skeletonize a man. Apparently I ran into one that had stepped out alone for a midnight snack!

At the town of Macapá in the immense Amazon delta my canoe was decked and fitted with a high coaming, a heavier rudder, and a canvas cover for the cockpit. I was given a good four-inch Navy boat compass and a small pump. The pump turned out to be far more important than the compass. I took on ten pounds of crackers, 100 oranges, several tins of jam and chocolate, ten cans of tomato juice, and ten gallons of water. For some reason I firmly believed my staple was going to be raw fish. I somehow neglected to consider the possibility that I might not catch any.

On December 13, I sailed into the open Atlantic, setting course for Trinidad. I immediately hit an offshore chop as the river current bucked the head wind. *Sea Fever* never worked too well to windward, and I found it very hard to get away from the coast. Also, I immediately became seasick. I took in my mainsail, sailing under only the jib and mizzen. Constant plunging loosened *Sea Fever*'s caulking; she leaked badly, and I was forced to pump every half hour or so.

That first day was a nightmare. I fought the temptation to turn and sail downwind to the shelter of the river and the hospitality of new-found friends. When night fell I was still working out to sea.

Everything was adrift, and I was too sick to lash things down very well. To sleep I could only curl up with my legs around the center-board trunk and poke my head under the thwart. Sloshing water would wake me in time to pump again. In the morning I found that I was only three miles offshore and within sight of the river mouth I had left 24 hours before!

For the next three days it was the same—constant tacking away from the coast, regular pumping, and the agony of seasickness with nothing to retch. On the fifth day the wind eased. There was no land in sight. I was no longer seasick, but was not very hungry.

I managed to read a booklet, *Lifeboat Navigation,* and learned to my surprise that the only way to find longitude is to use a clock—an accurate one at that. I had a watch of a sort; it had cost $4 and gained two and a half minutes a day until it got wet and stopped. But

"A WILD CALL AND A CLEAR CALL" *led Schultz past stilt-legged river landings (upper) where Indians paddle canoes from the bow, into a maze of Amazon channels (center) writhing through Brazil. He found that floating debris chose the main stream and showed him the way. Off Trinidad, his 17-foot vessel almost swamped while in tow (lower). Schultz cast off and made it on his own.*

in a day or two I could take meridian altitudes of the sun and find latitude to within five miles.

After six days I saw an island. I was very weak and covered with saltwater boils, so it seemed best to go ashore. Not until I was greeted in French by a man dressed in red and white pajamas, the prison uniform, did I realize that I had hit Devil's Island, the French penal colony. My boils were treated by a trusty who had been a Parisian pickpocket.

For several days after leaving the penal colony *Sea Fever* ran into squally weather. By this time I was very weak; raising and lowering the mainsail became more and more of an effort. The regular pumping, the spreading infections, and—surprisingly for the tropics—a constant chill caused by continual dampness caused a good bit of suffering.

On New Year's Day I landed at the U. S. Naval Base on Trinidad. I was almost out of money again, so I wangled the job of removing some old pilings that were a navigational hazard. I bought 100 pounds of dynamite and a booklet, *How to Use Dynamite*. In a few days I had done the job and earned about $500.

Sea Fever sailed on May 4 and made 90 miles to within sight of Grenada in a day. But contrary wind and water kept me tacking 24 hours to go the last five miles. Seasick again, I began to retch blood. Under the circumstances it was something of a shock to read the port officer's return and find the voyage listed as a "Pleasure cruise" and *Sea Fever* dignified as a "Canoe yacht."

After several days on Grenada I sailed north across the Caribbean. Of course I became seasick, and saltwater boils broke out all over my body. Heavy weather struck and I had to take down my sails and lie to a sea anchor. *Sea Fever* was still leaking badly and I was often cold. Strangely, my suffering didn't seem important. It produced a kind of abstraction allowing me to think clearly, independent of pain, though any activity required much concentration. I felt a sort of spiritual elevation.

One morning I saw land that I could not identify. The obvious thing was to use an ancient and extremely accurate method of navigation—I went ashore and asked where I was. It was the British Virgin Islands. I went to the nearest hospital. Since no one was on board to pump, *Sea Fever* swamped at the dock.

A N EASY SAIL carried me to Puerto Rico, where I gave several lectures on my voyage. Five days out of Puerto Rico I suddenly struck something—hard. The boat heeled over, and water streamed in as I pounded on a reef. I had hit Silver Bank, coral reefs 60 miles from the nearest land. I spent all night pumping. In the morning I found that the reef had torn a hole in the bow below the waterline. I cut a wooden plug that stopped much of the leaking.

Single-handed skippers made perilous voyages and

FLORIDA
Miami
Atlantic
Ocean
GREAT INAGUA
CUBA
SILVER BANK
VIRGIN ISLANDS
PUERTO RICO
Caribbean Sea
GRENADA
TRINIDAD
0   600
STATUTE MILES
NATIONAL GEOGRAPHIC MAP
DEVIL'S ISLAND
Quito   EQUATOR   Macapá
ECUADOR   *Napo*
PERU   Iquitos   *Amazon*   Manaus
B R A Z I L

JOHN SCHULTZ's *daring voyage in Sea Fever (map, left) added his name to a select group of men whose solitary exploits challenged both the sea and the imagination. Alfred "Centennial" Johnson, to celebrate the 100th birthday of the United States, wrestled a dory from Gloucester, Massachusetts, to Liverpool, England; Bernard Gilboy sailed an 18-foot skiff from San Francisco to Australia in 1882-3; more recently Harry Pidgeon built a 34-foot yawl, taught himself navigation, and girdled*

On the tenth morning out of Puerto Rico I found myself eight or nine miles north of my intended landfall, Great Inagua Island in the Bahamas. This ten-day passage was the longest I had had between landfalls. As *Sea Fever* was rolling wildly, a little brown seabird landed on my bare head. This noddy tern had little fear of me and grasped my hair tenaciously at each lurch of the canoe.

Finally sighting Cuba, I tried to find a way through the barrier reef that guards its northeast coast. I spotted an islet and thought I saw a passage to it. There wasn't any! Breakers smashed *Sea Fever* against the coral reef. She filled with water, but waves washed her into the lagoon and I got ashore on the island.

There I spent three happy days with fisherfolk, joining the father and son in turtle fishing with big nets set in ten fathoms of water. I was deeply impressed by the tranquillity of soul I saw in this family, their acceptance of whatever comes. Those who depend on something as capricious as wind, weather, and fish seem to have a better outlook on life than many in the city with more possessions but less quietness of heart.

Saying good-bye, I headed north. On June 30, I sailed into Miami's quarantine station. When I was asked the valuation of my boat and answered $11, the customs officer did a double take. He finally listed her not as a boat but as my "personal baggage."

"A STAR TO STEER HER BY" *proved hard to shoot at sea. Schultz lashed himself to mast before using sextant.*

tasted high adventure on lonely seas

the globe twice. But the greatest single-hander was Joshua Slocum, a retired sea captain who in 1895 resolved to see the world again. Although 51 and unable to swim, he set out alone from Boston in the 37-foot sloop Spray *(right). He escaped a pirate felucca off Morocco; repelled Fuegian natives with tacks sprinkled on his deck; narrowly missed destruction by a whale in the Pacific. He navigated by intuition and the stars, lived on potatoes and salt cod, talked to fish and birds. Lashing the helm, he let trade winds spank* Spray *toward the setting sun while he read Robert Louis Stevenson. He reached Newport, Rhode Island, in 1898 after logging more than 46,000 solo miles.*

OSWALD BRETT

CHAPTER FORTY-THREE

Small boating: everybody's sport

Millions of Americans know the pleasures of turning skipper for a day or a weekend. Veteran yachtsman Carleton Mitchell invites you aboard the nation's recreation fleet, the vast array of boats that go to bed at night.

IT WAS A WEEKEND in July when I invited my friend Jim for his first sail. We crept out of the city in an endless procession of automobiles. Heat came up in waves and mixed with the smell of exhaust fumes. We broke away on a side road and were soon at the waterfront. It was cooler, but more important was the sense of tranquillity. We had left behind the hustle-bustle of the workaday world.

Loading ourselves down with gear and supplies—one of the inevitabilities of small boating—we trudged to the dock. Jim noted a power cruiser of ancient vintage. Brightly painted and with windows that showed lamps and potted plants inside, she had something of the air of a country cottage. An elderly man lifted a varnish brush in greeting and a gray-haired woman smiled from a chair on the afterdeck.

"Friends?" Jim asked.

"Yes, a retired couple who never were afloat until after 50," I replied. "They bought a small outboard cruiser and learned to get around. When he retired three years ago they shopped until they found the right boat. Now they live aboard and go south every winter."

TALL SLOOPS *and gleaming power cruisers at boat shows across the nation lure thousands into fun afloat. Many start modestly in a tiny Sailfish (right).*

NATIONAL MOTOR BOAT SHOW, NEW YORK;
ROBERT F. SISSON, NATIONAL GEOGRAPHIC PHOTOGRAPHER

405

As we went by a small sloop farther along, a boy waved from a perch halfway up the mast. "Hi, Skeet," I called. "Going to win today?" "Hope so," he shouted. "Sure will be trying." I answered Jim's inquiring look. "Skeet is at

JAMES P. BLAIR, NATIONAL GEOGRAPHIC PHOTOGRAPHER

the other end of the boating scale. Been sailing ever since he could walk—got his nickname because he wasn't any bigger than a mosquito hauling on the end of a jib sheet. Now he's out for the junior championships. Got to go some to beat his sister, though."

Reaching *Finisterre,* we went below to put away the groceries. Jim's eyes widened as he took in the yawl's comfortable, well-equipped cabin. "Man's portable castle," I laughed.

While we removed the sail covers I pointed out other neighbors in the marina: the sporty runabout the Ames family uses for picnics and water-skiing, the bluff utility that takes Mr. Carey to his favorite fishing spots, the Sailfish —little more than a plank topped by a wedge of cloth—that Biff Jones sails around the harbor.

"I get the idea," Jim said as we got under way. "Boating has something for everybody."

OUTSIDE THE HARBOR a gentle southerly breeze was blowing, crinkling the water into a million sparkling points of sunshine. Gone were the heat of the land, the noise, the smells. Switching off *Finisterre's* auxiliary engine, we hoisted sail and stood toward the distant shore, happy with one of man's oldest wonders, the way of a ship with the sea.

A cluster of white triangles converged on an anchored power cruiser: the start of a One-Design race. Boats in these classes are built alike, so a race is strictly a contest of skill. Through binoculars we could see skippers jockeying sleek hulls in intricate patterns, topsides flashing in the sun—then driving for narrow openings, crews trimming sails to each shift. The boats were as finely tuned and taut as thoroughbred horses facing the gate, and we could feel tension flow across the water.

The excitement of competition is but one reason for the meteoric rise of boating in 20th century America. From only 15,000 pleasure craft recorded in 1904, the nation's recreation fleet has passed the seven million mark. As many as 35 million Americans are taking to the water—not just to the oceans and sounds, but to rivers, lakes, even the smallest ponds.

There are as many reasons for boating as there are sailors. Boating can mean companionship or solitude, violent exercise or complete indolence—a quiet cove, a frosted glass, a book in hand. Always it means direct contact with nature, with the primordial forces of wind and wave.

Jim began to enjoy the motion of the boat, the sight of sails like ivory against the blue sky. "Suppose I want to get into boating on my own. How should I start?"

I AM OFTEN asked this question and always find it a challenge. Choosing a boat is not like selecting an automobile, which differs from others basically only in horsepower and styling. Boats vary as much as people.

"First," I said, "never think about boats in landlubber terms. 'How big is the boat?' is not the main question. Size or elegance does not govern fun or skill. It's like fishing equipment: the boy with a cane pole and a bent pin often catches fish while the angler with the fancy gear goes home with an empty creel.

"Second, don't be like the sailing bug who asks, 'What kind of a boat do you have?' and harrumphs if it is a powerboat. There is no *best* type of boat, only the *right* boat for you, based on what you enjoy."

I told Jim that the would-be boater should visit marinas, boat shows, and dealers; read magazines and books devoted to the subject; talk to owners and seek to be invited aboard as crew. (An offer to help with spring fitting-out and other maintenance chores often brings an invitation.) In many areas you can rent a boat to get the feel of different types.

Very soon it will become apparent that there are two main channels ahead, dividing like the forks of a river—the choice between sail and power.

Generally speaking, less experience, less physical effort, and fewer skills are required to operate a boat driven by an engine than by the wind. Controls are similar to the family automobile. It doesn't take too long to master such maneuvers as leaving a mooring or coming alongside a dock. Press the starter button, engage the clutch ahead or astern, open the throttle, turn the steering wheel, and you're away. Park like a car and you are home.

Of course due respect must be given to the effect of tide and the tendency of a boat to pivot from amidships. But there are no complicated lines to tend, no sails to trim, and wind direction is not a major problem.

Powerboaters point out that their craft offer a greater variety of uses. You can't pull a water skier with a sailboat, and it is not very suitable for fishing. Powerboats give more living space per foot of length; absence of mast, rigging, and centerboard means more usable deck

MORRIS ROSENFELD. DIAGRAMS BY LISA BIGANZOLI, NATIONAL GEOGRAPHIC STAFF, AND (LEFT) MICHEL H. KFOURY

BEGINNERS *learn how sail and centerboard harness wind's power; put theory to practice afloat.*

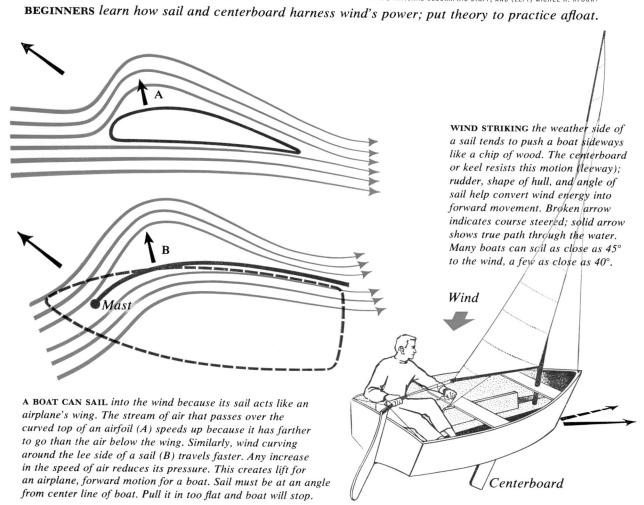

WIND STRIKING *the weather side of a sail tends to push a boat sideways like a chip of wood. The centerboard or keel resists this motion (leeway); rudder, shape of hull, and angle of sail help convert wind energy into forward movement. Broken arrow indicates course steered; solid arrow shows true path through the water. Many boats can sail as close as 45° to the wind, a few as close as 40°.*

Wind

Centerboard

A BOAT CAN SAIL *into the wind because its sail acts like an airplane's wing. The stream of air that passes over the curved top of an airfoil (A) speeds up because it has farther to go than the air below the wing. Similarly, wind curving around the lee side of a sail (B) travels faster. Any increase in the speed of air reduces its pressure. This creates lift for an airplane, forward motion for a boat. Sail must be at an angle from center line of boat. Pull it in too flat and boat will stop.*

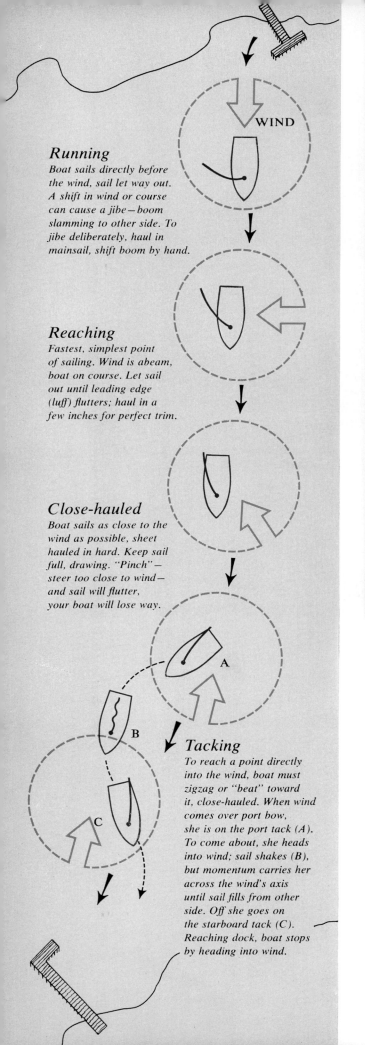

Running

Boat sails directly before the wind, sail let way out. A shift in wind or course can cause a jibe—boom slamming to other side. To jibe deliberately, haul in mainsail, shift boom by hand.

WIND

Reaching

Fastest, simplest point of sailing. Wind is abeam, boat on course. Let sail out until leading edge (luff) flutters; haul in a few inches for perfect trim.

Close-hauled

Boat sails as close to the wind as possible, sheet hauled in hard. Keep sail full, drawing. "Pinch"— steer too close to wind— and sail will flutter, your boat will lose way.

Tacking

To reach a point directly into the wind, boat must zigzag or "beat" toward it, close-hauled. When wind comes over port bow, she is on the port tack (A). To come about, she heads into wind; sail shakes (B), but momentum carries her across the wind's axis until sail fills from other side. Off she goes on the starboard tack (C). Reaching dock, boat stops by heading into wind.

LIFE-JACKETED JUNIORS *jockey 9' 8" Turnabouts,*

and cabin space. With no sails to trim, power-boaters have more leisure for conversation and sight-seeing. The constant power source enables them to travel faster and with greater predictability. They are never becalmed— unless the motor breaks down.

Sailing vessels, on the other hand, are a continuing challenge. "We learned something, many days many things, every time we went out and we went out at every opportunity," Harold Vanderbilt wrote of the *America*'s Cup defender *Enterprise*, after he had assembled the most experienced crew available.

Handling a vessel driven only by the wind presents as many problems as there are faces to nature. Work never ceases. Always there are sails to hoist, lines to handle, clouds to watch. It's "Flatten the main!" and "Slack

prove that same wind can drive boats on opposite courses: 339, close-hauled, passes 134 on a reach.

the jib!'' from the time the anchor is on deck until harbor is reached again—when an all-hands panic party may be the order of docking.

Yet sailing is pure joy of motion: the silent glide over a calm sea in a light breeze, the exhilarating hard thrash to windward, the pause and swoop of a downwind sleigh ride with the stern wave cresting over the counter.

Too, lessons learned under canvas are useful in any boat. The wind sailor can shift easily to a powerboat—the reverse is not so true.

THESE THINGS I explained to Jim as the haze of distance lifted from the far shore and we came close enough to see the green of trees. Occasionally *Finisterre* scooped the crest from a sea and sent it hissing aft along the deck while our wake stretched astern

as a white lane. Although civilization rimmed the shore, we had a feeling of being on our own, completely free from the cares of the world.

Already Jim had found the feel of the wheel and learned the delicate balance between heading, trim of sails, and direction of wind when going to windward. He kept his eye on the leading edge of the jib: it will flutter if you steer too close to the wind or if the wind shifts around to come at you from ahead.

Now he asked: "Suppose I choose sail. What boat would be best for me?"

"How much can you pay for purchase and upkeep?" I grinned. "How do you want to use this boat? How will it fit your interests, your physical abilities, your whims? How much time will you have for it? What distances do you want to go? And how seriously do you

409

Popular racing classes

ONE-DESIGN *or class boats like the Comet are designed for racing. They are built alike within each class, so skill of skipper and crew determines winner. The Lightning and many others are also comfortable day sailers; resale value is high. Check classes popular in your area; contact their associations.*

Restricted classes like the International 14 allow some variation in hull and rigging. Larger cruising auxiliaries like the Cutlass and Triton usually ocean-race with a variety of boats under a handicap system (page 374). Below: a cross section of the several hundred classes. Insignia is emblazoned on sail. Lengths given are overall.

PENGUIN *Centerboard catboat, 11' 5". Sail area 72 sq. ft. Simple rigging, light, fine for children. Racing crew: two.*

BLUE JAY *Centerboard sloop, 13' 6". Sail area 90 sq. ft. plus spinnaker. Popular with children. Kits available. Racing crew: two.*

INTERNATIONAL 14 *Centerboard sloop, 14'. Sail area 165 sq. ft. plus spinnaker. Tall, tricky, planing type. Racing crew: two.*

SNIPE *Centerboard sloop, 15' 6". Sail area 116 sq. ft. Small cockpit, easy to handle. Most popular class. Racing crew: two.*

COMET *Centerboard sloop, 16'. Sail area 130 sq. ft. Fast, widely popular. Larger cockpit than Snipe. Racing crew: two.*

THISTLE *Centerboard sloop, 17'. Sail area 175 sq. ft. plus spinnaker. Planes but handles easily. Roomy. Racing crew: three.*

LIGHTNING *Centerboard sloop, 19'. Sail area 177 sq. ft. plus spinnaker. Stable, roomy for family use. Racing crew: three.*

STAR *Fin keel sloop, 22' 8". Sail area 285 sq. ft. Sleek racing machine, oldest One-Design class. Small cockpit. Crew: two.*

CUTLASS *Fin keel or centerboard sloop, 23' 7". Sail area 242 sq. ft. plus genoa and spinnaker. Self-righting, safe for ocean racing. Galley, head, two to four berths.*

 AMPHIBI-CON *Combined keel and centerboard sloop, 25' 6". Sail area 266 sq. ft. plus genoa and spinnaker. Sleeps four. Can be trailered but requires a cradle.*

TRITON *Keel sloop or yawl, 28' 6". Sail area (yawl) 382.5 sq. ft. plus genoa and spinnaker. Galley, head, four to six berths.*

want to study seamanship and navigation?"

I told Jim that a good boat for a beginner who doesn't mind a bit of acrobatics or an occasional dunking is a light centerboard dinghy. The term originally applied to a yacht's tender but now includes most sailboats up to 12 feet.

Dinghies are cat-rigged—one sail on a single mast, with a minimum of lines to tend. Sensitive to every touch of the helm and trim of sheet, they teach "feel" as nothing else can. They shoot ahead with the gentlest puff, react immediately to each wind shift, and sometimes turn over to emphasize a mistake.

Many adults, particularly if they want to in-

SKILLED YACHTSMEN *hike out on bilgeboards to*

clude friends or family, may want to start farther up the ladder of sail with a boat between 14 and 20 feet. This will probably be sloop-rigged—two sails now, the smaller one before the mast called a jib.

In this range, One-Design racers are very popular. Able, responsive, thoroughly proven, they are fine for beginners yet provide plenty of action for the veteran.

More comfortable and less demanding are the day sailers. With their generous cockpits, they are perfect for afternoon spins and holiday picnics. Given a waterproof cover to spread over the boom like a tent, some basic camping gear, and a tolerance for accommodations less commodious than the Ritz, you can make extended passages in boats of this size.

I had two friends who cruised a Star from Miami to Nassau and back, stopping to visit many Bahama cays along the way. Sailor-campers are legion along the Baltic Sea, where families happily spend their vacations between a Folkboat and a tent ashore.

As we talked, a sloop crossed *Finisterre's* bow, running downwind. From the mast a nylon spinnaker blossomed like a flower against the sky. A woman steered while a man supervised two tiny crew members wearing orange

balance Class E scows on a beat to windward. These 28-footers can skim along at 20 miles an hour.

life jackets. All raised hands in greeting: the camaraderie of the sea extends to all afloat.

"What's she?" asked Jim.

"A cruiser that can go places," I answered.

A CABIN adds a new dimension to sailing. Not only does it provide more overnight comfort, but it is a blessing for day sailors who want to get out of the weather for a little rest.

Designers squeeze a gallon of livability into a pint pot of hull. Beginning with an overall length of around 25 feet, it is possible to sleep two people—some builders say four—in reasonable comfort, complete with galley, head (toilet), and storage. At 30 feet a bit of elbowroom begins to make a cruiser a floating home. Today 35-foot auxiliaries qualify as "ocean racers." Many never go beyond sight of land, but their seaworthiness is a bonus safety factor.

The auxiliary—a sailing cruiser fitted with an engine—is perfect for those who love sail yet acknowledge the advantage of power for getting home in a calm or maneuvering through crowded harbors. It has two disadvantages. The engine increases purchase and maintenance costs, and its weight and the drag of its propeller slow the vessel. I find the compromise worthwhile.

Cruisers are no longer the preserve of the wealthy. Assembly-line production splits the cost of a naval architect many ways. Standardized parts and molded hulls of plastic or metal eliminate expensive handwork in wood and simplify maintenance. Now they are popular family boats, and present no insurmountable handling problem even to a beginner.

The basic difference in sailboat design lies in the type of projection beneath the hull—keel or centerboard. This projection balances against the pressure of the wind aloft, resisting tipping, and grips the water so that the boat does not slide sideways like a chip of wood when going to windward.

A keelboat has a fixed fin or a wineglass-shaped underbody ballasted at the bottom with iron or lead. Properly designed, it will not capsize. If thrown flat on its side by a sea, it will right itself. Larger boats are usually keel types.

Centerboard boats use a plate of wood or metal which is raised and lowered through a slot in the hull. This allows you to sail shallows, to adjust centerboard depth to wind conditions, and to beach or trailer the boat. The smaller centerboarders are not ballasted and

HOME IS WHERE *the anchor falls when a yawl*

will turn over if mishandled. But unlike keelboats, they usually won't sink if filled with water—so are well suited for juniors. Larger centerboarders are ballasted and match keelboats in stability. To compensate for lack of draft, they are beamier, thus roomier.

Centerboard boats find their staunchest backers where the water is spread thin—from Chesapeake Bay to Florida, for example, and along the Gulf of Mexico. Keelboats are more general in New England, on the Great Lakes, and along the Pacific coast. Check to see which type is best for your area.

A final word about selecting your sailboat: People rarely keep their first one very long. Don't get a hard-to-dispose-of freak.

"SO I PICK MY BOAT, a 14-foot sloop," said Jim. "Now how do I learn to sail it?" I laughed: "Good question, but first we'll have to tack *this* boat!" I had caught sight of rocks off the approaching shore.

goes cruising. Aboard their magic carpet, yachtsmen savor sunset over a new horizon.

SAILING DONE *for the day, vacation hands gather in schooner's snug cabin for chanteys.*

STONY BROOK, LONG ISLAND; ROBERT F. SISSON, NATIONAL GEOGRAPHIC PHOTOGRAPHER. DRAWINGS (OPPOSITE) BY OSWALD BRETT

POWERBOATS *offer the thrill of speed. This inboard runabout can do 45 miles an hour.*

In a long arc *Finisterre* swept toward the eye of the wind. We released the jib when it began to flutter, and the mast eased back to the vertical as the wind was lost from the sails. There was a banging of blocks and slatting of canvas while she came about, then quietness as she heeled to the wind on the other side. I trimmed the jib and she gathered speed.

Even a simple maneuver in sail requires skill and timing. No galleries applaud; the rewards are personal and go deep. A lifetime is not long enough to learn all, and the pleasures never dim.

Settling back against a cockpit cushion, I tackled Jim's question. "You can learn to sail by reading a book, then taking a boat out to put the lessons to use. You may have a spill, but that can be part of the fun. It's best, though, to have an experienced hand along the first few times. You learn faster and get into the right habits."

Instruction is often available at marinas and the nation's 1,200 yacht clubs; from organizations like the Sea Scouts, Mariner Senior Scouts, the YMCA and YWCA; from local groups like Boston's Community Boating, Inc.; and from boat dealers.

The beginner learns to handle his boat when running, reaching, and sailing close-hauled. He masters the basic techniques of tacking and jibing—moving the tiller with one hand, trimming the sail with the other, and shifting his body weight as the boat comes about. When you feel at home in your boat, perhaps you will want to cruise.

If you would like the excitement of close quarters, the challenge of striving every second to make your boat sail its best—racing is for you. Few are the weekends when competition is not available, especially for boats that can be trailered behind an automobile. Even in winter Frostbite dinghies race among floating cakes of ice to console those who cannot go south to sail under the palms.

OVER FINISTERRE'S BOW appeared a narrow buoyed channel leading into a cove. The breeze began to ease as the sun settled lower, and disappearing from the open water astern were the small boats that go to bed at their home moorings – the racers, day sailers, and runabouts.

As we crept within the embrace of the land, we found other homes afloat. Swimmers splashed merrily off the ladder of a cruiser. From another boat two children ferried the family dog ashore in a dinghy not much larger than a pumpkin. An outboard cruiser, its twin motors tilted up, rested its bow on the beach, where its skipper bent over, lighting a charcoal grill. Nearby, a houseboat swung to her moorings with the proprietary air of being settled for the summer, complete to TV antenna and geraniums on the porch.

Anchor down, we relaxed in the cockpit. Shadows deepened under the trees and flowed out over the water. Overhead, clouds turned from gold to pink, were swallowed by the darkening sky. Lights winked on, became shimmering spears on the water. We felt separate and complete, as though our tranquil fleet lay in the harbor of some newly discovered land.

We moved below; a pot soon bubbled on the stove, a Bach concerto cascaded from the hi-fi. Nothing is so snug as the cabin of a small boat; nowhere does food taste so good, is sleep so sound. As we lay in our bunks, a drowsy voice asked, "Mitch, powerboating looks good too. Suppose—"

"Tomorrow, Jim!" I grunted and fell asleep to the faint lullaby from the treetops ashore.

MORNING is the best time on a boat. Always there is a feeling of anticipation as to what the hours will bring. As we stepped on deck, the cove's water seemed like a mirror, broken only by the spreading rings of fish rising to take insects. We swam, then sat blinking in the sunshine, sipping mugs of tea.

Jim returned to his questions about powerboats. "Would starting with a small outboard be comparable to beginning in sail with a dinghy?"

"In a way, yes," I answered. "You get the feel faster, and if you make a mistake it isn't so costly. If you come in to a dock too fast in a 14-footer, you can fend off with a hand or foot. Make the same mistake in a big cruiser and you may find yourself with a repair bill.

"But because an engine does the work, one person can handle a cruiser as well as a small runabout, although docking or mooring is easier with an extra hand. So more important than size is what you want to do with your boat, and where you plan to use it." You have a cot-

Which powerboat for you?

THERE *is a powerboat for every purpose, but only you can decide which will fill your needs. Many start with a small utility for fishing, trade up to a small outboard cruiser when they yearn to pile children and sleeping bags aboard for a weekend trip. Invited aboard a friend's inboard cruiser – with galley, head, berths, room for guests – they may step up again, like trading cars.*

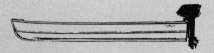

Utility
Sturdy, basic boat with maximum open space. Easy to trailer. Practical for water-skiing, fishing, skin diving, picnics. Windshield, decked bow, folding top, and other optionals. Choice of motor (outboard shown). 12'-27'.

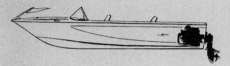

Runabout
Powerful sports car of the waterways. Ideal for speed rides, water-skiing. Offers luxury features like bucket seats, paneling, and sliding hardtops. Less open space. Choice of engines (inboard-outboard shown). 12'-32'.

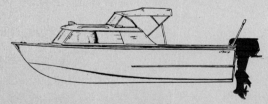

Outboard cruiser
Day cruiser with galley shelf and two short seats doubling as bunks; or weekender with galley, head, water tank, fold-out table. Minimum headroom. Most are express type (steering, controls outside). Usually 16'-24'.

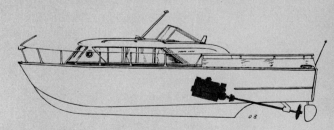

Inboard cruiser
Luxury liner of the fleet. Two or more berths. Galley with sink, stove, icebox. Perhaps enclosed head, shower. Generous headroom, locker space. Single or twin engines. Controls inside, outside, or both. Usually 25' and over.

tage on a lake, and would like to go out at daybreak to fish the lilypads. A light 14- to 16-foot utility with flat bottom and three- to 16-horsepower motor seems in order. You could have a demountable awning, backrest seats, built-in bait well and drink cooler.

If you yearn for the thrill and exercise that come with a pair of water skis, you'll want a boat between 14 and 20 feet. The motor should be powerful enough to push you along at a minimum of 20 miles an hour. Your boat should be equipped with a well-mounted towing ring and have ample stowage space for fuel tanks and skis. A rearview mirror is a good idea even if you follow the rule (a law in some states) of having a second person in the boat to watch the skier while you tend to the steering. A light ladder to put over the side takes the work out of climbing back aboard.

Pleasure cruising is a third major use for powerboats—pushing along the isolated reach of some river or bay, friends or family aboard, picnic basket at hand. Here the choice is wide: a streamlined runabout with cushioned seats; a spacious utility, or a cabin cruiser. With a cruiser 22 feet or longer, equipped with galley, head, and bunks, you are set for an overnight trip in comfort.

Some boats will perform several of these functions, but they will not do any one of them as well as a boat specially designed for it.

Consider the fisherman who forsakes his lake for offshore trolling. He needs a bigger boat to face rough water. He'll want considerable freeboard, a high bow, and a powerful motor to whisk him home if the weather turns bad. He'll know that a transom cut low to accommodate an outboard invites following seas to climb aboard—including the wave created by his propeller. He'll make sure there is a watertight well or bulkhead to seal off the stern. He can also select a high-transom boat with a bracket outside for mounting the motor.

Boats tend to follow patterns of size and type by areas, and it is wise to learn the reason. Check with people who know the local boating conditions.

Powerboats divide basically into two types: planing and displacement. The planing boat is designed for speed. When it reaches a certain speed it climbs out of the water and planes along, only its flat stern riding in the water. The racing hydroplane, skimming along at more than 100 miles an hour, is its ultimate development. Most small runabouts and util-

ities are of this type. A disadvantage: It feels every wave, bumps along in rough water.

Most larger cruisers are displacement craft: their hulls stay in the water, displacing an amount equal to the weight of boat and load. Being deeper, they provide more room, grip the water better, ride easier in heavy weather.

BEFORE BUYING a boat, try it out to make sure that the motor is a perfect match. If the planing hull leaps at each touch of the throttle, it is probably overpowered. If it doesn't lift up cleanly, it is underpowered.

The top efficient speed of a displacement vessel—her "hull speed"—is determined by length, not horsepower. First, establish the boat's cruising speed, the pace she can maintain under normal conditions hour after hour. This is usually ten to 20 percent below the maximum number of engine revolutions. There should be little vibration, a smooth and level ride, and no undue wake.

Now open the engine full. There should be little change in the way she rides. If the boat

Sky's the limit on materials

BOAT HULLS *come in three basic forms: flat bottom, round bottom, and V bottom. Each has its special advantages and disadvantages. The flat bottom, usually a scow or rowboat, is easy to build, stable in smooth water, and requires little power for its length. In rough water it may pound dangerously. The round bottom rides deeper and gives an easier motion in a seaway, but is more expensive to build. The V bottom is a compromise between the two; it grips the water better at high speed and slices through chop.*

You have a wide choice of materials. Wood—traditional and elegant—flexes repeatedly without fatigue, but

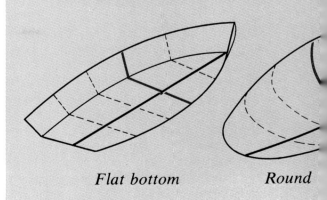

Flat bottom   Round

shakes, the bow rises high, and the stern squats deep, dragging along a heavy cresting stern wave, power is being wasted. Purchase cost and fuel bills will be pointlessly high.

Powerboats are also divided into three hull types: flat, round, and V bottom. Like everything else in boating, each has advantages and disadvantages to be weighed. Most larger craft are a compromise: the bow section may be a V for cutting through the waves without pounding, the midships rounded for easy motion, the stern flat for lift and stability.

In all but the largest boats, you have a choice of engines. The outboard enthusiast points out how easily his boat can be hauled on a trailer from the family garage to the launching ramp, even across the continent. Inboards have the advantage of permanent weatherproof installation. Mounted low in the hull, they add to stability.

The new inboard-outboard gives some of the benefits of both. Even more revolutionary is the jet. Developed for extremely shallow or weed-choked waters where a propeller would foul, it pumps a powerful stream of water through a nozzle in the stern. The stream is deflected from side to side to steer. Because the jet has no spinning blades, it is safest for water skiers. With a hose fitted to its nozzle, it turns the family runabout into a fireboat!

Since powerboats have become big business, they are now sold on styling, decor, and "magic" hull forms as well as new materials. Chrome plate and swept-back fins resembling the latest Detroit creations are not evil in themselves but are bad if they indicate a hull that ought to be on wheels. As a rule of thumb, take a second look at boats that put the emphasis on gimmicks and blatant eye appeal.

I'VE CROSSED the Atlantic a couple of times under sail, but the worst scare I ever had was aboard a friend's power cruiser in the North Channel of Lake Huron, well within sight of land. As the seas built before a fresh following wind, we had trouble with the steering gear. It was impossible to repair; the builder had provided no access. Then we noticed

for three basic hull forms

needs constant care against rot and borers. It swells in water, may shrink and open seams ashore. Popular fiber glass—glass fibers and hard, gluelike resin laid over a mold (right)—forms a seamless hull with many complex curves which add strength. Light, strong, it needs minimum care.

Rugged, flyweight aluminum can last a lifetime. Like fiber glass it needs built-in flotation—foam or balsa core, double hull or bottom, air tanks. Rinse off salt water to prevent tarnishing.

Other materials: steel, sheet and molded plywood, new plastics, and synthetic fibers like nylon.

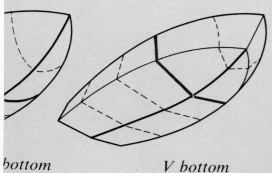

bottom   *V bottom*

LITTLE FALLS, MINNESOTA; DAVID S. BOYER, NATIONAL GEOGRAPHIC STAFF. DRAWINGS BY BILL THOMSON

PINT-SIZE WATER SKIERS *swish along behind a 14-foot outboard utility. Powerboats open doors to*

water sloshing in the hull not far below the level of the engines. The pump would not work. Peeling back a thick carpet, I found there was no way to get into the bilge. Finally I pried up a section of decking and groped below. The pump was clogged with matted lint from the rug. Tools could not be brought to bear. So I bailed with a bucket into the sink. Making harbor was a matter of luck—the leak being small, the distance short.

That day I learned to make sure a powerboat has access to vital areas, and to distrust equipment added purely for effect.

Other things to look for: Are the frames and knees sturdy, the engine securely mounted? There is no substitute for experience, so ask the advice of people who know—marina operators, men who build, rent, repair, and insure boats. Even an expert sometimes has difficulty judging soundness of construction. But keep in mind that a bargain-basement price may indicate that the builder skimped somewhere along the way.

It's different buying a large cruiser, particularly a used one. You tell a broker your needs, and he'll present you with a wide selection of makes. He'll feel obligated to see that you get the most suitable vessel. His commission remains about the same, and a happy customer is the bedrock of his business. Bringing in a professional marine surveyor will give you added protection.

Price to pay? That's up to you, but remember that boating is no fun when you don't know where the next payment is coming from. Purchase price isn't the last cost either: figure on insurance, mooring fees or dockage, fuel, extra equipment, parts replacement, painting, repairs, winter storage—perhaps membership in a yacht club, which provides not only an anchorage but opens new vistas of friendship and activity afloat.

Jim and I finished breakfast and put away the dishes. "Where shall we sail today?" I asked. He shook his head regretfully: "No wind, skipper."

"There will be later," I answered. "We'll start under power and hoist sail when it comes. As the sun heats the land, the air above it will rise. Then the cool air over the water will flow in to take its place. In fact, we may have more wind than we want before the day is over. It's just the kind of scorcher to breed squalls."

"Didn't know you had to be a meteorologist as well," said Jim in dismay.

"Look, Jim," I said. "Anyone buying a boat takes on a responsibility to himself and to

other family sports: skin diving, fishing, exploring.

others. Ownership confers command no matter how humble your vessel. Your decisions affect property—and lives. If a person doesn't want to learn the fundamentals of safe boating, he should stay ashore."

Each year trusting people drown because owners didn't trouble to phone the Weather Bureau or observe storm-warning flags fluttering above yacht anchorages and Coast Guard ships and stations. They hadn't learned to interpret the look of the sky, the action of the barometer:

When the glass falls low, prepare for a blow;
When it rises high, let all your kites fly.

They didn't know the rules of the road. Two boats meet: who has the right of way, what signals should be given, how do you warn a boat making a wrong maneuver?

Knowledge of piloting is another fundamental on all but the smallest ponds. Learn what the different shapes and colors of buoys signify, how to read a chart and lay down a course, to judge the strength of a current by the swirl around a buoy, to spot shoals by the agitated look of the water above them.

Most important safety factor of all is good seamanship. Know how to tie knots that won't slip, and keep your boat in top shape. Before

Which motor for you?

MATCHING *motor to boat is vital: the right choice can mean years of pleasure, the wrong choice continual frustration. Every hull is designed for a certain horsepower range; increasing power beyond this merely boosts costs with little or no gain in speed. Your motor should perform satisfactorily at less than full throttle; fuel costs will be reasonable, and reserve power is there for emergencies. Caution: Don't smoke while fueling, and keep hose nozzle in contact with fill opening to prevent a static spark. Wipe up spills; ventilate below-deck spaces. While light, powerful gas turbines are in development, and heavy-duty diesels are gaining new attention, these gasoline engines power most boats.*

OUTBOARD *Most popular. Light, portable, inexpensive, easy to trailer and store. Clamps on stern, pivots to steer. Most have neutral and reverse shifts to maneuver and dock. Larger models have automatic transmissions, remote controls, bailing pumps, electric starters. Simple, easy-to-get-to machinery; low repair costs. One to six cylinders (in-line or V); one to 100 horsepower.*

INBOARD *Permanent weatherproof installation makes it ideal for boats in water all season. Price is higher, operating costs are lower. Excels for heavy duty and as a power supply for lights and equipment. Low, midships mounting increases stability, allows high stern. V6's and V8's, many with automotive blocks, are supplanting long popular in-line units. Horsepower: 30 to over 300.*

INBOARD-OUTBOARD *Combines inboard's reliability with outboard's flexibility. Engine sits in stern. Detachable drive unit hooks up through transom, swings like an outboard for quick turns, tilts up to trailer and beach, rebounds if it hits an obstacle. Two or four cycle, six to eight cylinders. Horsepower: 35 to 200; usually 80 to 100.*

JET *Pump powered by inboard engine draws in water and blasts it out stern. Jet stream is deflected to side to steer, or forward under boat to reverse. Absence of rudder and propeller lets boat navigate shallow water and reduces drag but makes boat a bit slippery on turns. Less control at low speeds. Horsepower: usually 100 to 150.*

Pointers on motor care

1. *Clean spark plugs frequently. Measure gap with feeler gauge—if gap is too wide, motor will be hard to start; if too narrow, oil may clog gap.*
2. *Check battery often; add distilled water and recharge as needed. Clean terminals with wire brush.*
3. *Change, add, or mix oil according to manual. Watch dip stick and oil gauge on inboard; check lubricant in lower gear housing and moving parts of outboard.*
4. *Wash off salt water with fresh; flush cooling system or run outboard in tank of fresh water.*
5. *Check propeller for nicks, bent blades.*
6. *To store outboard, empty fuel and oil. Disconnect fuel line, run motor at half speed until carburetor empties. Stand upright to drain water. Take out plugs, inject rust and corrosion inhibitor in holes, replace plugs. Cover, ventilate. Keep in clean, dry place.*

you go out, check for leaks, gas vapor in the bilge, weakened motor mounts, and frayed lines. Test your engine to make sure that it is running properly.

In a small boat, caution passengers to step into the center and keep their weight low, arms free. Don't overload—distribute the weight evenly. Give a life preserver to each person.

START YOUR MOTOR, then cast off. Turn slowly away from the landing. Novices have a way of cutting the bow sharply and gunning the motor. They forget that the stern may swing into the dock.

Anchoring looks easy, but there's a trick even to that. Your cable should be five to ten times the depth of the water. This allows the anchor to lie flat and dig in. Head your boat into the wind or current—whichever is stronger—then shift into neutral so that you glide to a stop a bit beyond where you want to lie. Make sure the cable is clear to run, and that the bitter end is secured to the boat. Lower the anchor slowly, keeping your feet clear, until it touches bottom (you'll feel the line go slack). As the boat drifts backward, pay out a suitable amount of cable. Line up two prominent landmarks. Check this bearing from time to time to see if your anchor is dragging.

Approach a dock or mooring slowly against wind or current. Shift into neutral and let the boat's momentum carry you the last few feet. If necessary, reverse to check headway.

Learn to handle your boat in rough water, for even a lake or river can turn vicious in a thunderstorm. It's best to take waves head on, or at a slight angle, and slow. Don't run along in troughs; you may be swamped or tossed over. Running with a following sea can be dangerous too; stern and propeller are lifted out of the water, and control is lost.

If all else fails, cut your engine and drag a sea anchor—a cone-shaped canvas bag held open by an iron hoop—from the bow. It will keep the boat's head into wind and wave. You can improvise a sea anchor with a line and a bucket, spar, or plank.

Know what to do before an accident occurs. If a passenger falls overboard, swing the stern and its churning propeller away from him and throw a lifesaving ring, cushion, or jacket. Keep him constantly in view as you come around to approach from downwind. Cut your engine if seas permit, and take care when you help him aboard not to tip over the boat. Any

Equipment for safe boating

SAFETY *equipment required by law varies according to length and type of boat—but all must carry one Coast Guard-approved life jacket, buoyant vest (1), buoyant cushion (2), or ring buoy (3) for each person. All must show lights at night: usually a combination bow light (4), green on starboard, red on port; and a white stern light (5), visible from 360°. A fire extinguisher (6) is required on many powerboats.*

Wise skippers also carry mooring line (7), anchor and cable (8), oar or paddle (9), boathook (10) to pick up moorings and fend off piers, bucket (11) to bail and fight fire, whistle or horn (12), compass (13), tools, spare parts, spark plugs (14), flashlight (15), first-aid manual and kit (16), distress flares. Check Coast Guard booklets for your boat's needs.

Pointers on boat care

KEEP *your boat in top condition—it will pay off in safety, fewer repair bills, higher resale value, and pride of ownership. The golden rule: Correct little problems before they grow big. Usually it's best to leave major work to professionals, but here's what you should do.*

1. *Apply antifouling paint to bottom twice a year if boating in salt water, once in fresh. Make sure priming coat is suitable for hull material. Wax sides of fiber glass and aluminum to keep clean, shiny.*

2. *Scrub bottom frequently with stiff brush and detergent or boat cleaner. If you haul boat after each use, rub off scum with rough canvas.*

3. *Touch up abrasions and gouges as they occur. Fill dents with pigmented plastic wood, marine dough, or polyester patching compound.*

4. *Check seat braces, decking, and transom; strengthen if needed. Replace missing hardware screws. Repair loose wiring connections, frayed or cracked insulations.*

5. *Keep brightwork smooth, shiny; apply new varnish every two months. Cover hardware with polish or film of oil. Rinse salt water off deck and fittings.*

6. *Inspect anchor and mooring lines for chafing, breaks in strands. Reverse for even wear.*

7. *Lubricate blocks, winches on sailboat; steering gear, other mechanisms in powerboat.*

8. *Dry sails and canvas before stowing; wash before winter storage. Watch for weak spots, tears, frays; reinforce or mend at once. Replace missing fasteners.*

9. *Remove oil, grease from inboard's bilge by letting cleaner slosh about as boat runs; pump out. Pick debris from bilge pump. Wipe or sponge outboard's bilge.*

10. *Don't leave boat closed tight; it will sweat in sun. Cover should have air vents. If possible, leave doors, ports, or windshield ajar. Open lockers; lift floorboard occasionally to air bilge.*

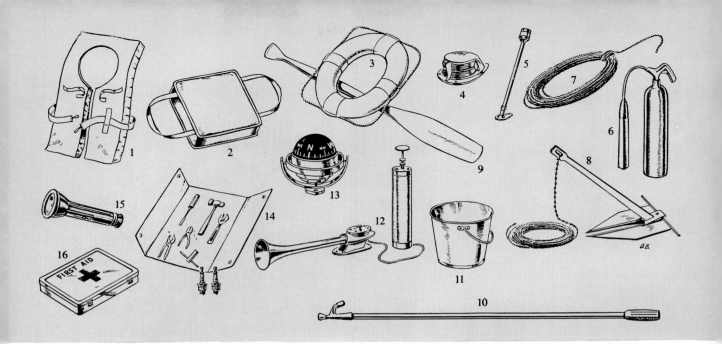

CLARENCE E. LOVEJOY, NEW YORK TIMES. DRAWINGS BY OSWALD BRETT

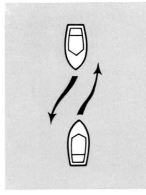

POWERBOATS meeting head on usually pass port to port; give one-second whistle blast. Pass to starboard: two blasts.

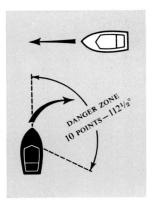

WHEN two powerboats approach at an angle, boat to port must stop or give way by turning to starboard.

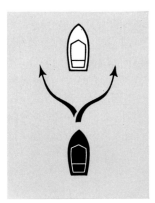

OVERTAKING boat must keep clear of overtaken vessel; one short blast passing to starboard, two passing to port.

SAILBOAT running free must keep clear of boat close-hauled or reaching. Sailboats give no signals.

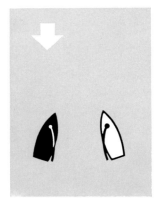

BOAT sailing close-hauled on the port tack must keep clear of a boat sailing on the starboard tack.

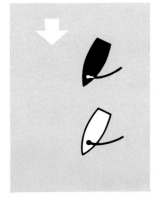

WHEN two boats are running free with wind on same side, boat to windward must keep clear of boat to leeward.

WHEN both are running free with wind on different sides, boat with wind on port side must keep clear of the other.

AN OVERTAKING sailboat must keep clear of the overtaken craft, even when the latter is a powerboat.

Rules of the road

TRAFFIC *laws of the waterways apply to all boats, large or small, power or sail. Their purpose is to prevent collision. Generally, powerboats must give way to sailboats. The basic rules: Keep to the right and practice safety first. Slow down in narrow waters and when passing docks, dredges, swimmers, or small open boats that might swamp—you are liable for damage caused by your wake. Give way to fishing boats with lines or nets out. Sound long blast on whistle or horn as you leave dock. When another powerboat's signal is confusing or its course dangerous, reverse engine and give four or more short blasts—the danger signal. Offer aid to a boat in difficulty, or following an accident. Do not anchor in channels or traffic lanes. Specific rules of the road are shown above. (Rules and signals vary on Great Lakes, Mississippi system.) Dark boat is burdened—must yield to others.*

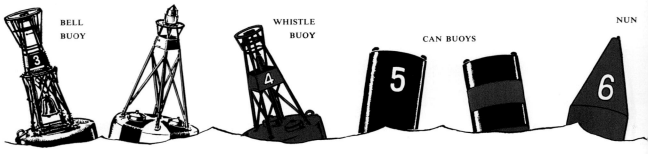

BELL BUOY   WHISTLE BUOY   CAN BUOYS   NUN

LIGHTED BUOY

DISTRESS SIGNALS *Repeatedly raise and lower arms; fire rockets, flares, gun, or explosives at intervals; sound foghorn or whistle continuously; display International Code letters NC or a square flag with a ball above or below it. Repeat "Mayday" on radiotelephone, usually on 2182 kc.*

FOG SIGNALS *Sailboats sound foghorn—one blast a minute on starboard tack, two blasts on port tack, three blasts with wind abaft beam. Powerboats sound whistle, air or electric horn—prolonged blast every minute. Boats at anchor ring bell rapidly five seconds every minute.*

LIGHTS *Under way: green on starboard, red on port, white visible all around. Rowboats, canoes show white light when approached. Anchored or moored: white visible all around unless in special anchorage recognized by Coast Guard.*

SKIN DIVING *Red flag, diagonal white stripe; keep clear by 50 yards.*

STORM WARNINGS *Flags by day, lights by night at Coast Guard and Weather Bureau stations, yacht clubs, marinas, and on patrol boats warn of high winds.*

SMALL CRAFT	GALE	WHOLE GALE	HURRICANE
To 33 knots	*To 47 knots*	*To 63 knots*	*Over 63 knots*

BUOYS *Proceeding to port or upstream, keep red, even-numbered buoys to starboard; black, odd-numbered ones to port. Numerals increase from seaward. Vertical black and white stripes indicate mid-channel buoy; pass close on either side. Horizontal black and red stripes mark a junction or obstruction: red top, keep buoy to starboard; black top, keep it to port. Buoys vary in shape; many are lighted. Entering harbor, keep red light to starboard, green light to port. White lights may appear on both sides.*

BUOYS

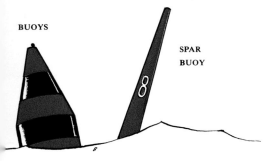

SPAR BUOY

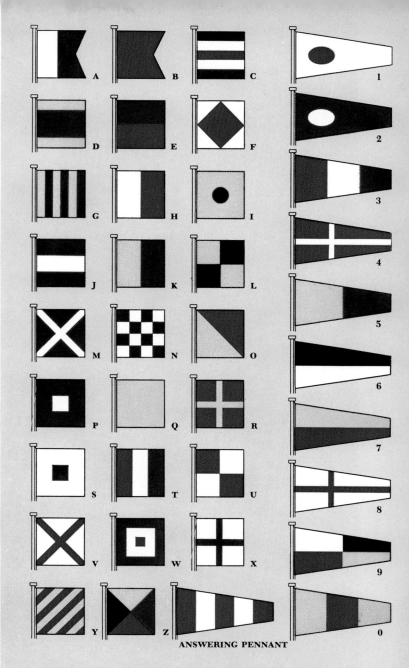

INTERNATIONAL CODE FLAGS *Each flag or combination of flags has a special meaning. Example: V indicates "I need assistance"; RV asks "Where are you bound?" Names are spelled out. Answering pennant is raised or lowered as signals are understood.*

U. S. YACHT ENSIGN	U. S. POWER SQUADRONS	U. S. COAST GUARD AUXILIARY	CRUISING CLUB OF AMERICA

FLAG ETIQUETTE *Powerboats may fly the United States flag, yacht ensign, or United States Power Squadrons ensign at the stern. A sailboat flies the United States flag or yacht ensign two-thirds up the leech of the aftermost sail under way; at the stern while anchored. The U. S. Coast Guard Auxiliary flag may be flown at the bow of powerboats or main truck of sailboats; the burgee of a yacht club like the Cruising Club of America at bow or foremost truck; private signals at signal mast or aftermost truck. Most colors are made (raised and lowered) at 8 A.M. and sunset. Never fly colors while racing. In foreign waters display host country's flag at bow, foretruck, or starboard shroud.*

PLUSH BAHIA-MAR YACHTING CENTER *welcomes boaters to Fort Lauderdale, Florida.*
Arrivals are directed to berth by radiotelephone; dock attendants rush on bicycles
to help with lines. Marina includes shopping center, restaurant, swimming pool, club.

DEEP-SEA TROPHY, *a white marlin, rewards family for a day's trolling. Cruisers can be chartered with skipper, bait boy, tackle.*

skipper worth his salt will know how to give artificial respiration, and how to swim.

If your small boat capsizes or swamps, stay with it. Many have built-in buoyancy, and a boat is easier to spot than a bobbing head. Slip into life preservers and signal for help with anything at hand. The shore always looks closer than it is, so don't try to swim for it.

When water-skiing, always cut your engine to let the skier climb aboard. He may slip and fall into the propeller.

Common sense should be part of your safety kit. I remember too well a Saturday morning not long ago when a flashy red and yellow runabout came speeding into a quiet cove crowded with boats. The man at the helm steered a zigzag course; swerving to avoid a dinghy, he almost ran through a swimming family. Shouts mingled with the staccato roar of the exhaust as his wake rocked anchored boats and dishes clattered from tables. Now thoroughly flustered, the man made a sweeping turn past a dock—causing a small catboat to snap her lines and pound her rudder on the shore—and zoomed out of the harbor, passing a buoy on the wrong side. He ran aground on a shoal and had to await rescue by the Coast Guard. His boating "fun" was ruined, but for a while the water was safe again.

Powerboat owners owe it to all concerned to sign up for courses offered by the Coast

425

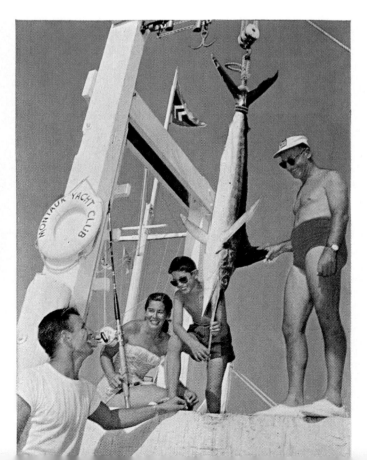

ADVENTURE'S CALL *brings a houseboat to the jungled Weekiwachee River in Florida. Upswept bow, runnerlike keels help boat over fallen trees.*

MIGRATING SOUTH *on the Atlantic Intracoastal Waterway, an auxiliary ketch cuts a herringbone wake in Virginia's Dismal Swamp Canal.*

BATES LITTLEHALES AND (OPPOSITE) J. BAYLOR ROBERTS, BOTH NATIONAL GEOGRAPHIC STAFF

Guard Auxiliary, the U. S. Power Squadrons, the Outboard Boating Club of America, and other organizations. Call your nearest Coast Guard office—in major cities throughout the nation—to find out where instruction is available. The Coast Guard also offers booklets on safety practices, equipment, legal requirements (most boats must be numbered and registered, and an accident causing $100 damage must be reported to state or federal offices).

Charts are available from the U. S. Coast and Geodetic Survey, Washington, 25, D. C.; from regional offices of the U. S. Corps of Engineers; and other agencies. Your boat dealer or marina can tell you where to get charts for the waters you sail.

The boating boom has brought conveniences scarcely dreamed of a few years back. Marinas provide not only a slip for your boat, but electric outlets, extension telephones, water connections, ice and grocery deliveries, and repair facilities. At new "dry land" marinas, forklift trucks stack outboards on racks like boxes in a shoe store. There are smaller yards too,

ANOTHER BEND, *another moment of discovery always lies ahead for the boater. Exploring the Inside*

friendly places with perhaps just a few planks strung between pilings. Like the incoming tide, the boatman will find his own level.

No other country in the world is blessed with waterways to compare with ours: magnificent seacoasts, the Great Lakes, the Mississippi system, countless other lakes, rivers, and canals. Only recently I flew over Arizona; miles and miles of sand, rock, and cactus. Suddenly a marina was under our wings, and little boats were nosing into coves where Indian campfires once burned. We were flying over Lake Mead, formed by Hoover Dam.

Adventure awaits on the sprawling, manmade lakes of the Tennessee Valley, where water skiers zip past grazing cattle and breathe the sweet smell of farmland. Cruisers push up the Hudson River, follow the canal route to the Great Lakes. The Intracoastal Waterway leads from below Boston's Beacon Hill past Carolina pine swamps and Florida's palm-dotted beaches and on around the Gulf coast. Among the Florida Keys lie colorful coral reefs to dazzle the boater turned skin diver. Steep,

Passage from Washington State to Alaska, a cruiser becomes a caravel, her skipper a Columbus.

forested mountains dip into blue water along the Inside Passage from Seattle to Alaska; red salmon lure boaters to many an anchorage.

A BREEZE had begun as Jim and I talked, cat's-paws barely riffling the surface. Now tiny wavelets marched across the water. We hoisted sail and glided toward the far shore, perfectly content.

The wonderful thing about boating is that although we happened to be on a vessel that had won races and voyaged across the ocean, we could have been equally content on a houseboat drifting down a river or in a runabout skimming across a bay. There would have been the same joy of motion, the same sense of freedom at the helm of a tiny One-Design.

Those of us who know boating feel about it like Water Rat in Kenneth Grahame's *The Wind in the Willows*, who said to landlubber Mole: "There is *nothing*—absolutely nothing—half so much worth doing as simply messing about in boats. Simply messing." Messing or cruising, cruising or racing—welcome to the fleet.

429

Index

Text references are indicated in roman type; illustrations and illustrated text in **boldface**.

HERRING GULL BY JAMES P. BLAIR, **NATIONAL GEOGRAPHIC** PHOTOGRAPHER

Maritime museums

LONDON'S *Science Museum, the Museum of the City of New York, Washington's Smithsonian Institution, and other general museums offer maritime treasures. The following specialize in chronicling man's life at sea.*

PEABODY MUSEUM, *Salem, Mass. Bowditch navigation collection; portraits; reproduction of cabin saloon of Cleopatra's Barge, America's first oceangoing yacht.*

WHALING MUSEUM, *New Bedford, Mass. Half-size model of whaler Lagoda. Whaleboat, scrimshaw. Museums also at Sag Harbor, N. Y.; Nantucket, Sharon, and Chatham, Mass.*

MYSTIC SEAPORT, *Conn. Re-created early 19th century port. Charles W. Morgan, last surviving wooden whaler; Villiers' square-rigger Joseph Conrad; MacMillan's Arctic schooner Bowdoin; War of 1812 schooner Australia.*

U. S. NAVAL ACADEMY MUSEUM, *Annapolis, Md. Trophies and other exhibits trace history of the U. S. Navy.*

MARINERS MUSEUM, *Newport News, Va. Blueprints, Crabtree collection of models record development of ship design. Figureheads, small craft, instruments.*

NATIONAL MARITIME MUSEUM, *Greenwich, England. Admiralty ship plans, 1700-1900; relics of Lord Nelson; Harrison's chronometers. Extensive paintings, prints.*

VIKING SHIP HALL, *Oslo, Norway. Restored ninth century Norse ships and the equipment buried with them.*

STATENS SJOHISTORISKA MUSEUM, *Stockholm, Sweden. Models, charts, instruments, weapons.*

HANDELS-OG SOFARTSMUSEET, *Elsinore, Denmark. Models and pictures trace development of ships, lighthouses.*

NEDERLANDSCH HISTORISCH SCHEEPVAART MUSEUM, *Amsterdam, The Netherlands. Maritime library, Van de Velde paintings, booty captured from English and Spanish.*

NATIONAAL SCHEEPVAARTMUSEUM (Steen), *Antwerp, Belgium. History of European navigation since the Vikings.*

MUSEE DE LA MARINE, *Paris, France. Centuries-old models include galleys. Yachting, undersea exploration.*

MUSEO NAVAL, *Madrid, Spain. Manuscripts of Spanish explorers, 16th century navigation books, weapons.*

MUSEO STORICO NAVALE, *Venice, Italy. Galley models.*

Famous ships you can see

Ticonderoga, side-wheeler, Shelburne, Vt.; U. S. frigate *Constitution,* Boston; *Mayflower II,* Plymouth, Mass.; U.S.S. *Olympia,* Dewey's flagship, Philadelphia; replicas of *Susan Constant, Godspeed, Discovery,* Jamestown Festival Park, Va.; U.S.S. *North Carolina,* World War II battleship, Wilmington, N. C.; *Sprague,* stern-wheeler, Vicksburg, Miss.; battleship *Texas,* veteran of two world wars, San Jacinto Battleground, Texas; *Gjöa,* conqueror of the Northwest Passage, and square-rigger *Balclutha,* San Francisco Maritime Museum; square-rigger *Star of India,* San Diego Maritime Museum; German submarine *U-505,* Chicago Museum of Science and Industry; replica of Gokstad Viking ship, Lincoln Park, Chicago; *St. Roch,* traversed Northwest Passage both ways, Vancouver, B. C.; H.M.S. *Victory,* Nelson's flagship, Portsmouth, England; *Cutty Sark,* tea clipper, Greenwich; H.M.S. *Discovery,* Scott's first Antarctic ship, London; *Turbinia,* first turbine vessel, Newcastle; 17th century warship *Vasa,* Stockholm, Sweden; school ship *Mercator,* Antwerp, Belgium; replica of Columbus's *Santa Maria,* Barcelona, Spain.

VESSELS IN FRENCH PORTS *were fair game for Antoine Roux's sketchbook in the early 19th century. Son of a hydrographer of Marseille, he used pencil and watercolors like a camera to record the come and go of ships—a Spanish felucca (upper left), a sprit-rigged fishing boat, brigs at anchor (lower left) and slipping out of Bordeaux.*

ACKNOWLEDGMENTS

THE EDITORS are grateful for the generous assistance of many scholars in the United States and abroad, only a few of whom can be listed here: Howard I. Chapelle, Curator of Transportation, U. S. National Museum; Kenneth M. Setton, Director of Libraries, University of Pennsylvania; Garrett Mattingly, Professor of European History, Columbia University; Lionel Casson, Professor of Classics, New York University; Ernest S. Dodge, Director, Peabody Museum of Salem; Edouard A. Stackpole, Curator, Marine Historical Association, Mystic; Capt. Wade DeWeese, U.S.N. (Ret.), Director, U. S. Naval Academy Museum; Gösta Franzen, Director, Scandinavian Studies, University of Chicago; Frank G. G. Carr, Director, National Maritime Museum, Greenwich; R. C. Anderson, past President, Society for Nautical Research; H. E. Pedro Theotonio Pereira, Ambassador of Portugal; Thorleif Sjøvold, Asst. Director, Universitetets Oldsaksamling, Oslo; Huibert V. Quispel, Mng. Director, Instituut voor Scheepvaart en Luchtvaart, Rotterdam; Fernand Benoît, Director, Musée d'Archéologie, Marseille; Prof. Jung-pang Lo, Far Eastern and Russian Institute, University of Washington; William J. Morgan, History Division, U. S. Navy; Capt. R. L. Mellen, Chief, Public Information Division, U. S. Coast Guard; Edwin H. Bryan, Jr., Bernice P. Bishop Museum, Honolulu; Charles McKew Parr; Capt. Frederick Way, Jr.; Frank O. Braynard; Victor Jorgensen; Miss Jane Lawson; Boies Penrose; David MacGregor.

"Sea Fever" by John Masefield (quoted in Chapter 42), © *The Macmillan Co., New York.*

FOR ADDITIONAL REFERENCE

The more than 800 issues of the *National Geographic Magazine* contain a wealth of information on men, ships, and the sea. Check the Cumulative Index. Also, these stimulating, colorful National Geographic books will add meaning to the story:

EVERYDAY LIFE IN ANCIENT TIMES—The splendors of Mesopotamia, Egypt, Greece, and Rome, cultures that gave rise to early mariners. 368 pages; 215 illustrations. $6.00

INDIANS OF THE AMERICAS—From Eskimo to Inca, the Indian as hunter, warrior, farmer, artist—and builder of many specialized boats. 432 pages; 394 illustrations. $7.50

AMERICA'S HISTORYLANDS—Our nation's epic told in its landmarks of liberty. Portrays explorers, sea captains, riverboatmen, naval heroes. 576 pages; 676 illustrations. $11.95

THE BOOK OF FISHES—Adventure-packed portrayal of how man harvests the sea for pleasure, profit, and knowledge. 340 pages; 377 illustrations; 236 species in color. $7.00

WILD ANIMALS OF NORTH AMERICA—Action photographs, vivid biographies of 138 species. Narratives of whaling, sealing, the sea otter trade. 400 pages; 409 illustrations. $7.75

Postpaid. Order from National Geographic Society, Washington 6, D.C. Brochure on request.

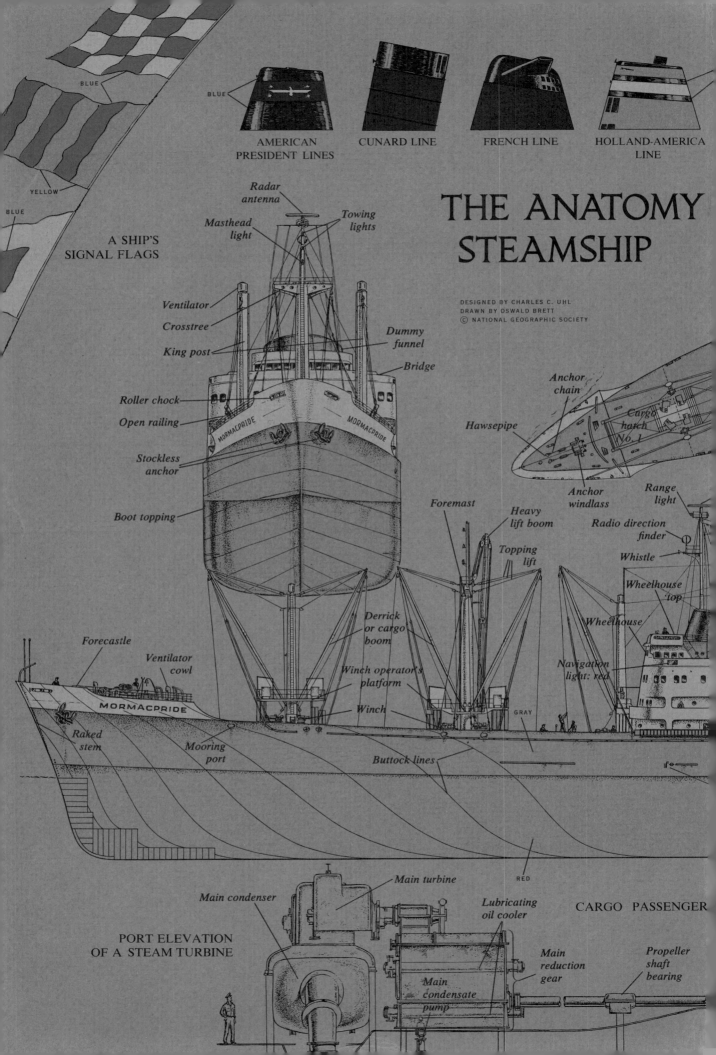

THE ANATOMY STEAMSHIP

AMERICAN PRESIDENT LINES

CUNARD LINE

FRENCH LINE

HOLLAND-AMERICA LINE

BLUE
YELLOW
BLUE
BLUE

A SHIP'S SIGNAL FLAGS

DESIGNED BY CHARLES C. UHL
DRAWN BY OSWALD BRETT
© NATIONAL GEOGRAPHIC SOCIETY

Radar antenna
Masthead light
Towing lights
Ventilator
Crosstree
Dummy funnel
King post
Bridge
Roller chock
Open railing
Stockless anchor
Boot topping
MORMACPRIDE
MORMACPRIDE

Anchor chain
Hawsepipe
Cargo hatch No. 1
Anchor windlass
Foremast
Heavy lift boom
Range light
Radio direction finder
Topping lift
Whistle
Wheelhouse top
Wheelhouse
Derrick or cargo boom
Navigation light: red
Winch operator's platform
Winch
Forecastle
Ventilator cowl
MORMACPRIDE
GRAY
Raked stem
Mooring port
Buttock lines
RED
Main turbine

CARGO PASSENGER

Main condenser
Lubricating oil cooler

PORT ELEVATION OF A STEAM TURBINE

Main reduction gear
Propeller shaft bearing
Main condensate pump